The New Musician

The New Musician
The Art of Entrepreneurship in Today's Music Business

Menzie Pittman

ROWMAN & LITTLEFIELD
Lanham • Boulder • New York • London

Published by Rowman & Littlefield
An imprint of The Rowman & Littlefield Publishing Group, Inc.
4501 Forbes Boulevard, Suite 200, Lanham, Maryland 20706
www.rowman.com

86-90 Paul Street, London EC2A 4NE

Copyright © 2024 by The Rowman & Littlefield Publishing Group, Inc.

All rights reserved. No part of this book may be reproduced in any form or by any electronic or mechanical means, including information storage and retrieval systems, without written permission from the publisher, except by a reviewer who may quote passages in a review.

British Library Cataloguing in Publication Information Available

Library of Congress Cataloging-in-Publication Data
Names: Pittman, Menzie, author.
Title: The new musician: the art of entrepreneurship in today's music business / Menzie Pittman.
Description: Lanham: Rowman & Littlefield, 2024. | Series: Music pro guides | Includes index.
Identifiers: LCCN 2024005850 (print) | LCCN 2024005851 (ebook) | ISBN 9781538194867 (cloth) | ISBN 9781538194874 (paperback) | ISBN 9781538194881 (ebook)
Subjects: LCSH: Music entrepreneurship. | Music trade—Vocational guidance.
Classification: LCC ML3795 .P57 2024 (print) | LCC ML3795 (ebook) | DDC 780.23—dc23/eng/20240207
LC record available at https://lccn.loc.gov/2024005850
LC ebook record available at https://lccn.loc.gov/2024005851

This book is dedicated to my father and brother for teaching me their love and passion of music, as well as for illuminating the way and clarifying the standard.

To my daughter, Summer, for teaching me the definition of a creative. I am in awe of your passion for the arts and the respect you garner from others by simply being yourself.

To every musician I have ever played music with, as well as to every music student I have had the privilege to teach.

Lastly, this book is dedicated to all the new musicians past and present, for sharing your wonderful gifts with the world. Let's turn it up!

Contents

Foreword ix
Preface xi
Acknowledgments xiii
Chapter 1: How to Read This Book 1
Chapter 2: Sound Check, The Opening 3
Chapter 3: Dave Cobb 6
Chapter 4: The Calling 27
Chapter 5: Scheila Gonzalez 30
Chapter 6: Welcome to the Jungle 44
Chapter 7: Chuck Rainey 48
Chapter 8: Vision 77
Chapter 9: Rick Barker 80
Chapter 10: Study the Greats 100
Chapter 11: Dr. Robert Fisher 102
Chapter 12: Entrepreneurship 110
Chapter 13: Ashley Campbell 116
Chapter 14: Imagination 129
Chapter 15: Craig Alvin 132
Chapter 16: The Power of Influence 155
Chapter 17: Dom Famularo 159

Contents

Chapter 18: Distractions 181
Chapter 19: Mike Curb 185
Chapter 20: Down to Business (DIY Plan) 208
Chapter 21: Secretary Riley 213
Chapter 22: Rejection 222
Chapter 23: Tommy Harden 225
Chapter 24: Procrastination 244
Chapter 25: Sierra Hull 248
Chapter 26: Tenacity 273
Chapter 27: Brent Mason 276
Chapter 28: Self-Mastery 294
Chapter 29: Jamie Tate 297
Chapter 30: WILDEYES 316
Chapter 31: Emily Kohavi 331
Chapter 32: The Outro 348
Chapter 33: Bernard Purdie 353
Chapter 34: The Idea 366

Index 367
About the Author 387

Foreword

Many of us who love music and have chosen to make it part of our professional lives find ourselves enamored of the creative expression of melodies, harmonies, and rhythms. However, we don't always think about the creative aspects of the business of music which has its own melodies, harmonies, and rhythms. In fact, the business of music is an art form in its own right. One of my favorite quotes from the book (page 46) notes that, "creativity is the lead vocal, business is the harmony, and there is an art to understanding both."

This groundbreaking work by my friend and colleague, Menzie Pittman, is a journey through the intersection of both of these creative expressions—the music itself and the music business. Through a series of thoughtful conversations with some of the leading musical luminaries of our time, Menzie guides us in how important it is that we embrace our creative spirits in both the music we make and the entrepreneurship required to create a sustainable enterprise as a musician.

This is not a conventional textbook or academic treatise on the music business. There are many good resources for that. Instead, as the direct result of Menzie's incredible success and reputation in the music industry we have the privilege of hearing from many of the best in the business. From the corridors of record labels to the legendary studios and stages, each conversation offers us a window into the minds of these incredibly successful people who have made music their life's work. But this book is more than just a collection of interviews. Menzie weaves a rich tapestry of storytelling, shared experiences, and collective wisdom. From the legendary producers to the artists who defy convention, we have a front row seat to the candid reflections and hard-earned lessons of industry titans, and we realize that the business of music is more than just a transactional endeavor; it is the place where passion meets pragmatism, and both require artistic creativity.

I have known Menzie for over ten years, and his passion for music, teaching, mentoring, and moving the business of music forward has been an inspiration to everyone who has had the privilege to know him. In addition to being a musician himself and running an extremely successful music business, he volunteers his time to advocate with government officials to help them understand just how important music education is to the development of the whole person.

As you journey through these pages, prepare to be inspired, challenged, and transformed. Within the anecdotes and revelations lie the keys to unlocking your own creative potential, to reimagining the music business as an incredible opportunity for artistic expression. We learn how the art of contracts, negotiations, and marketing are as important to long-term success to the musician as the music itself.

This book is a friend and companion for every musician, entrepreneur, and industry enthusiast who dares to chart their own course amidst the ever-shifting currents of the music industry. It is a testament to the resilience, ingenuity, and unwavering passion that defines our collective pursuit of musical excellence.

May these conversations ignite your imagination, fuel your ambition, and inspire you to redefine what it means to thrive in the ever-evolving landscape of the music industry.

Barbara Wight
CFO, Taylor Guitars

Preface

The term *successful* is defined by the person being observed, not the observer.

We are well served to remember this as we embark on our creative career. I have taught and played music for an eon, embracing business-leadership roles along the way. From basements to stages to high-profile board meetings, I have encountered every style of leadership (or lack thereof) one could possibly experience, including a cigar-smoking bar owner who once said, "Hell, I fired Molly Hatchet one time, so you ain't s—t to me."

Experience dons many coats, to say the least, and that is why this book matters to you. The most regretful words muttered are "If I had only known then what I know now." Our goal is avoiding those words, so I have made sure you have a good playbook to draw from, one that will give you dependable fodder to digest as you begin or maintain your creative journey.

The New Musician follows a simple formula. My goal was to pick the brains of great musicians, writers, techs, and legends of their crafts, getting them to spill their guts to someone they could trust—a fellow musician and businessperson, not an outsider. I wanted to celebrate the geniuses that they are while celebrating the gutsy decisions they make every day. My intent is to pull back the curtain to see what makes legends and unique creatives do it "that way," revealing the motives behind the mysteries of their genius.

As a teacher, performer, and businessperson, I have helped many navigate their careers and, just as importantly, their understandings of personal growth and business acumen. Helping young artists understand

Preface

how to achieve success in their careers is the single energy behind this work. My intent is to save you time and heartache by helping you navigate success.

If you look closely, you will find the answers you are looking for in every interview. What an honor it has been to conduct these interviews with these very gifted music masters. The essays were born out of professional feedback, influenced by listening to the concerns of the army of musicians that crossed my path as a fellow musician, educator, NAMM board member, business owner, and *Musical Merchandise Review* (*MMR Magazine*) columnist.

This book was written as a guidebook to serve the new musicians. It's your turn!

Acknowledgments

I want to personally thank every musician, creative contributor, business leader, and educator who was gracious enough to accept an in-depth interview with me. Thank you for sharing your valuable time and unique insights into the world of music, as well as for pulling back the curtain, allowing the readers to have a seat at the table.

Charlie Tompkey, thank you for supporting me early in my career and letting me know that the music business doesn't suffer fools gladly.

Summer Pittman, thank you for your editing work and rekindling my love for words and creativity. Your support on this project has been unwavering, and your creative contributions and vision are invaluable.

To Little Richard, for the gift of the book and the best story I could ever share with others.

To Walter and Christie Carter, along with everyone at Carter Vintage Guitars, thank you, you are family.

To Diane Stedman and Cassady Givens, for all your work with research and for transcribing.

To Fred Campbell, for your editing work and showing me what the word *clean* really means.

To Chris McKinney, for your editing work, patience, and guidance. I am a better writer because of you.

To Larry Morton, Doug Lady, and everyone at Hal Leonard for believing in this work from day one.

To Barbara Wight, for your contribution to this work and continued support of my creative endeavors.

To Contemporary Music Center, no matter your role—be it manager, supplier, educator, employee, customer, or friend—there are no words to

Acknowledgments

properly express my gratitude for your help in building one of the most unique, funky little music shops and for keeping it going.

To every drum student that has ever endured spending time with me in the box, you have helped me be a better musician, educator, and person.

To Mike Lawson and Christian Weissmuller, for the opportunity to write the Small Business Matters column for *MMR Magazine*.

To Joe Lamond and Zack Phillips, for illuminating the standard of great leadership.

To NAMM, for providing me the opportunity to serve on the board and serve the music industry.

To John Mlynczak, for having the courage and vision to take the wheel and guide the future of the NAMM organization.

To Shelly Sperry, for your editing guidance and eleventh-hour heroism.

To John Cerullo, Michael Tan, and Rowman & Littlefield, for believing in and supporting this work.

To all new musicians, both young and old—let the music show you the way.

Chapter 1

How to Read This Book

HAVE YOU EVER PLAYED A SONG FOR SOMEONE, AND BEFORE IT'S EVEN finished playing, that person is offering comparisons to other songs and speculating on what the writer's influences and motives might have been? Everyone wants to feel smart and informed. Everyone wants to say, "Yeah, I already get that."

To reap the benefits of this book, however, you, the reader, must let the artists speak. Do not assume anything. Don't assume that because you may know a little about certain interview subjects, you will know how the interviews are to unfold. The interviews are designed with a certain flow in mind.

Read this book like you would listen to a song for the first time.

Be in harmony with it.

Then wear it out!

Then go to work.

Look up every name and reference. Every person mentioned in this book has made important historical contributions to the music business. And if a style of music is mentioned, you need to know what it is.

If you read about an equipment brand, look it up, and consider why that artist uses that particular brand. If it's an idea or an opinion, consider it deeply; then if you can relate, embrace it. If you don't relate, reject it. But here is a word of caution: the musicians in this book are some of the best and most respected figures in the music business. Consider what they say as important and actionable information.

Chapter 1

Once you have read this book cover to cover, read it again. Take an idea that speaks to you, and repeat it often and out loud. Steal a line and memorize it. Make it your mantra.

Let this book empower you.

Let the conversations inspire you.

If you are proficient on an instrument, study the interviews pertaining to other instruments. Find the common threads buried in every conversation. See where everyone agrees, as a consensus is a powerful endorsement.

There are a few fun ways to engage with this book—for example, at the same time you read an interview, it's smart to also listen to the individual's music. But go even deeper, and listen to the music that influenced the interviewee. Look for offshoots; study the other players and producers involved in the music. Study the region the music comes from and other influences from that region.

Another fun way to work with the book is to open to any random page and just pick a paragraph or two and spend time with just that thought. Go deeply into a single random idea. Take a random idea and run it in reverse. If you relate and connect to an idea, write it on a three-by-five note card, and tape it to your bathroom mirror.

Invite a group of friends to study the book with you. Take it apart, debate it, because it's your job to create the next new musician. If you are in the music business, then it's your music business to steward. If you don't like an aspect of it, then be the agent of change. Be inventive. Be the creators. Be the protectors of the highest music standards by honoring the music that came before.

Bring us the changes we need to understand so that we can be a better industry.

Bring us the music of tomorrow because you are the new musician.

Chapter 2

Sound Check, The Opening

THIS BOOK IS DESIGNED TO BE A PLAYGROUND OF THOUGHTS AND IDEAS that stimulate and encourage the creative aspects of all developing artists while, at the same time, providing a window into understanding the art of business.

The mission is to help rising musicians manage the aspects of success while avoiding the pitfalls that invite failure. My hope is to stimulate your creative curiosity by shedding light on the topic of professional development.

All aspects of the music business are discussed in the interviews and essays woven throughout this book. Opinions on sustaining a successful career in the arts are bandied about and are here for the taking or the challenge.

Conversations and observations providing guidance for those who seek a career in the music industry are laid out and structured to everyone's advantage, and there are hidden gems on every page.

Throughout the book I inject the word *creatives*, referring to those who are developed in one or more aspects of the arts. In today's music business, the expectation for the rising artist is to be able to play, sing, write, and have unique performance skills (be it performing as a songwriter at a writers' round or as an artist dropping from the ceiling in a birdcage). There is also a benefit to having at least a working knowledge of all the visual arts, not to mention a working knowledge of marketing and sound business practices. The good old days of having others do it for you are long gone. But in truth, that might be the very reason you succeed: because you did it yourself.

As you read this book, you will find one central theme: providing the reader access to the time-tested beliefs that are embraced by masters of their crafts. The professionals interviewed here are a cross section of music legends, ascending stars, and leaders of unusual accomplishment. The interviews give you a unique seat at the table.

Most creatives are naturally more enthralled by the artistic aspects of music rather than the demanding details of business. But if you do not develop a strong understanding of how the music business (or business in general) works, you suffer the consequences of your naivety. That is exactly why the focus on the business strategies and discussions in this book are so important. A naive comprehension of business skills is the Achilles' heel of musicians, and letting your business matters be led by others is akin to trusting your destiny to a fool.

The key to sustaining success is finding a balanced proficiency between artistic expression, an understanding of business matters, and prioritizing your personal well-being! That's it!

Success is a marriage between the creative, the functional, and the purposeful.

When dealing with music, there is risk in the overly simple and tomfoolery in the unnecessarily complicated. That also holds true for business and personal matters. Balance is always the hat trick. This book is about understanding that balance.

For today's artists, connectivity takes only a click, so we have the chance to embrace business with a new vigor. We are agents of change, and that is the role of the new musician. But we should never forget or assume the amazing contributions and sacrifices that have come from the artists before us. We can learn both from their successes and their mistakes. Let the interviews in this book take you backstage, where you'll get to know how successful musicians think as they share their personal feelings, insights, joys, and ponderings. Take time to get to know how great musicians and savvy creative leaders think.

Today's new musicians and artists must once again think like pioneers. Let's consider the mind-set of the early rock 'n' rollers of the mid-1950s and how they graced us with groundbreaking, unique ways in presenting the new feel and new message from their music. Expression came first, regardless of the risk. It was the dawning of a new and exciting time for music. Rock 'n' roll was the message, and musicians were the messengers. Rock 'n' roll delivered a pathway to the big time. It was cool to be cool, and so they left nothing on the table. It was their ticket to the big show.

It happened again with the British Invasion, Motown, Woodstock, the electric 1970s, Laurel Canyon, the funk and disco eras, and punk music. It continued with the impact from behind-the-scenes influencers like the Brill Building, Mussel Shoals, the Wrecking Crew, and too many guitar heroes to name. Right, Mr. Van Halen? Of course, Americana, country, pop, jazz, bluegrass, and gospel music continued to weave their magic and influence through every era, inspiring many legends.

Today it's your turn! You are the new pioneers!

You have the advantage of massive amounts of information, but gross amounts of data should not make us lazy. You can't Google your way to creative genius, because creative genius takes soul. It's not static, it's dynamic!

To be great at your craft takes conviction. A successful career involves risk and demands perseverance. It's time for the next big thing. That's the point of this book. We need to get the debate louder. We need great writing and great craftsmanship to come back into vogue. It's time to rekindle passion. It's time to rekindle risk.

It's time to meet the new musicians. You're on in five!

Chapter 3

Dave Cobb

Ask anybody in music, and they will tell you there's magic in anything Dave Cobb produces. Cobb has an understanding that borrows from all the iconic producers that have preceded him. He is redefining the game by being himself and trusting the honesty of the music. Helming the producers chair of RCA Studio A in Nashville, Dave Cobb has become one of the music industry's most sought-after producers—and for good reason.

INTERVIEW

MENZIE: We'll start with optimism. You're completely optimistic about today's music scene, yet there's a lot of pull and tug from many who say the heydays of music are behind us. Your success doesn't reflect that, neither does your attitude. You've equated the Nashville music scene to the London music scene in the early sixties.

DAVE COBB: I think that building community is everything, and I have always tried to do that with artists I work with. I will sometimes set up a dinner and have another artist show up unannounced, and the next thing you know, they've become friends and they're collaborating, and you start to build a scene. I think that's why the hip-hop scene is so strong: because there is such a community to that. I think maybe in country (although there is definitely community in country) and with rock 'n' roll, there is such a competition—so much so that I feel it has halted the advance of the art form. Everyone is kind of just in it for themselves. I think community is everything.

MENZIE: During certain periods in music history (like the thirties, fifties, and seventies, for example), the theme of community seemed to be what everyone embraced. I'm not sure what made that go away, but it's interesting how you've turned that around.

DAVE COBB: Money! [He laughs.] Money for sure, but you talk about being optimistic, I got to where music was the only thing I cared about. Other people had other hobbies, but I was obsessed with playing instruments and record making, and I really had no other fallback plans. I would do it for free. I am just happy that I don't have to. But I think you should get into music because you can't do without it. I think it should be one of those obsessions that, no matter what, you're going to do it—no matter if it's not your day job; no matter if you're sidetracked. It's the only thing you're focused on. I'm optimistic because even if I won the lottery and won a million dollars, I'd still show up to work seven days a week because I love what I do.

MENZIE: That makes total sense. Let's move to Ringo for a second. You had this amazing moment. You got the chance to meet one of your heroes. I've pulled a quote of yours: "I always thought there was the Beatles and then everybody else. You can't compare anybody to the Beatles." So how did meeting Ringo happen? That must have been amazing for you.

DAVE COBB: I was really fortunate. This year I went on tour with Chris Stapleton, playing guitar with him, so I got to experience a lot of things I wouldn't get to see in a studio. I was in a band and toured for a lot of years, until the age of twenty-seven, and then I just decided to concentrate on being in the studio and kind of left being in a band behind. This year was my one exploratory revisit to that. So [Ringo] was playing a benefit for veterans that Joe Walsh puts on, and so we got to go and play and meet Ringo backstage, and then we actually got to perform onstage with him at the finale of the show with Joe Walsh. It was just one of those things that didn't feel real. [The Beatles] might as well be deities to me. I adore that band so much and spent so much time trying to understand those records, and then getting to see the real person right in front of me—it was a lot to handle. I don't think I've ever been that shell-shocked in my life.

MENZIE: Ringo's got an amazing feel, and he is absolutely the reason I play drums.

DAVE COBB: He is literally my favorite drummer because he is one of the few drummers in the world who's a lyrical drummer. I can sing you any drum fill he's ever done. Most drummers just play drum parts. They don't play to the vocalist the way Ringo does. You know, he is always interacting with the lyrics. That's why I love him so much.

MENZIE: You mentioned something—you've studied their stuff [the Beatles' repertoire]. What are some of the things about their music that have really gotten your attention and that you think are uniquely special?

DAVE COBB: I don't think there was ever a better team of writers in the history of music. I mean, you have Lennon, McCartney, and George Harrison. I don't think there's ever been two songwriters that went from writing pure sugary-sweet pop songs to writing "Helter Skelter," that went from writing "Happiness Is a Warm Gun" to "Revolution" to "The End." Not only did they change music compositionally, they pretty much invented anything I do in the studio or I like in the studio: reverse tape, tape feedback slap, phasing, flanging. All the stuff on those records—loops, extreme equalization and compression, putting mics close to drums. They really invented everything as far as modern recording goes. All of the above. They are kind of like the textbook for what's great about music.

MENZIE: So George Martin certainly must be one of your favorite producers. Who are some of the other producers and engineers who have touched you?

DAVE COBB: Glyn Johns. I adore Glyn Johns. I think his records just really sound 3-D, and they are never really overly compressed. They just sound like you're in the room with the band—the best version of the band. Drums sound like a drum set. Acoustic guitars sound like the dream acoustic sound you want. Just everything about him. He always has an edge to his records that I really dig. And Geoff Emerick, who did the Beatles' stuff as well—just, for all the reasons I stated before, all the experimentation and creation that he did and left behind for all of us.

Those are my big favorites. There's people like Eddie Kramer, [whom] I adore because of all the ethereal effects he kind of created and the way he set things, the way he thought about mixing and the erratic panning that goes around your head and the trippy tape stuff he was doing. I think he was one of those guys for me as well.

Brendan O'Brien too. When I was coming up in Georgia, he was such an inspiration. He was from my same state and making all these incredible-sounding rock records of the nineties. So I like him a lot as well.

MENZIE: That's a great segue into my next question, about growing up in the South. Obviously, you have a multitude of other musical influences besides the Beatles, and growing up in the South—people like Little Richard, James Brown, [and] Otis Redding all came out of there. All are from Georgia.

DAVE COBB: Yeah, all Georgia. Ray Charles as well. Everybody was in that area and [the South] is really the birthplace of American music in so many ways. I was in Berlin, making a record a couple of years ago, and I was walking in the city and seeing these beautiful orchestral halls and thinking [that] this was the capital of music for hundreds of years. And now America has become the capital of music for the last hundred-plus years—for popular music, at least. And there's the importance of where I grew up in the South, where all those things kind of meet. It's where you have bluegrass and you have rock 'n' roll, and you have soul music, and you have jazz, and you have southern gospel music, and it's all right there. Country music. It's all right there in your backyard. It's kind of fun, and I think the church is really the incubator for that stuff in a big way. Because people are religious. You've got to go show up for church on Sunday, and when you are a kid and you play music, you just have to get up there and do it. You don't really have a choice.

MENZIE: Right, I think Little Richard and James Brown are as completely relevant today as they ever were. Both [are] amazing artists to still go back and look at and listen to, and both were great visual artists as well.

DAVE COBB: Little Richard's the best rock 'n' roll singer that ever lived. I think the fire he had in his voice just is unparalleled. I mean, there is not a metal singer who can out-scare you with [his or her] voice like Little Richard could. "Keep on Knocking"—listen to the vocal on that. It will knock your face off.

MENZIE: It still does. That's what's amazing.

DAVE COBB: Oh yeah. Pure fire. Both my favorite singers come from Georgia. Otis Redding is my favorite soul singer, and Little Richard being my favorite rock 'n' roll singer.

MENZIE: I don't know if you ever saw the Rock and Roll Hall of Fame intro that Little Richard did for Otis Redding's [1989] induction, but it's Little Richard's first time back in thirty years, and he just stands at the podium and rips one tune after another—makes for fifteen minutes of classic Little Richard. And then add in Will Lee on bass. Wow!

DAVE COBB: I did. The thing about him that's so great, and you hear it in his music, is the struggle between good and evil. I think you can hear that. It's like you can hear his authority but also his vulnerability when he sings. That's what I think is so magical about him. I really like the stuff after the fifties and [the] early sixties' stuff. In the late sixties and seventies, he's got great records, too, that maybe people didn't dig into, but there's a song called "Green Power" that I love. He does soul stuff, too, you know. There's a song called "I Don't Know What You've Got, but It's

Got Me." It's just devastating—a great, great, great song. He's definitely one of my favorites.

MENZIE: There are moments in music that influence everybody, but what have been the major moments in music that have influenced you?

DAVE COBB: My earliest memories are of my grandmother, who was a Pentecostal minister. I had an uncle who played bass and pedal steel and acoustic guitar. My aunt played piano. Just watching him play that Fender bass—I was probably more intoxicated with the instrument—just looking at it, this vintage Fender bass. Those are the things that got me really early.

My parents were pretty strict with the music we'd listen to, but my uncle—he had Buddy Holly and Elvis, and he had a lot of fifties-kinda mixtape stuff. Just hearing the beautiful, simple fifties' songwriting—I thought it was great. Hearing Buddy Holly's song "Everyday" for the first time or Elvis—hearing "Love Me Tender" or songs like that—just the vulnerability in the singing. I think that those are subconscious things that I heard really young. It hit me later how important those really were to kinda what I love about music: that honesty and the vulnerability those records have—those records and then discovering the Beatles on my own, because my parents didn't listen to the Beatles. They didn't like them. That was my band. I think my aunt left a Beatles record at my house. But the first record I fell in love with was "New Kid in Town" by the Eagles. I had the 45 for it. And of course, that led me to find the Beatles. I realized where they were getting those harmonies from. I just loved all those really beautiful and also extremely complex harmonies that are in that song. They are a lesson in music.

MENZIE: From those beginnings, you've ended up at RCA Studio A in Nashville. To me there's no better place for a music history fanatic to be than in that studio. Can you talk a little bit about why Studio A is so unique and why it's important to you personally?

Chapter 3

Dave Cobb: Well, Studio A—I got to go there [for] the first time with Chris Stapleton. We recorded the *Traveller* album there. When we were there, we all thought it was getting torn down. It felt like a piece of history that was about to be lost, and it was sad to see it go. Fortunately, a lot of people got in there and put in their time, money, and energy, and the community also came together and saved the place. But if you're a musician and you're into music, it's like seeing the seventh wonder of the world. It was built at a time when the music business was thriving and healthy. It's a gigantic place. I have no idea how to tell you how big it is. Let's just say, "Big." But it was a time when Nashville had developed the Nashville sound. They realized that Sinatra and Dean Martin were selling all these records, and if they just popped out country a little bit and put a classical arrangement on it and some choir, then they could get in that kind of game that was going on in California. So they built that studio to capacitate full choir, orchestra, full band, singer, drums—everything in one room, and [no one has to] have headphones, which is pretty magical. I don't know any other place you can get away with doing that. It feels like they built a temple, and it was built by people who knew what they were doing, and it doesn't look like there was any expense spared while they did it. John Volkmann's the guy who built it, and it seems like there was such a high level of math going into that room to be able to capacitate that wish. I don't think it could be built now. I think it would be an impossibility, especially in a thriving city—not the square footage, not the acoustic treatments. I really appreciate everybody who came before me and all the heart, effort, soul, and love they put into that temple. When you walk into it, you can feel all the happiness that went into that place through the years. There's a lady who's researched the building and found all these incredible photos of sessions. But as many photos as there are of sessions, there were also photos of parties. I think RCA used it as a big party space. You can just tell people cut up and had a good time and also did that on record as well. We try to continue the tradition now.

Menzie: I think it's ironic that what you're doing and how you do it and where you [are] doing it have all come together not only with great people but the iconic RCA studio and the philosophy too. That's a rare combination to be able to attain. It's refreshing, and it's really making a lot of people rethink how the industry has been doing it. I think the industry grew complacent and sort of lulled to sleep with the ease of the tracking approach, auto tune, [and so forth] because it seemed quicker.

Dave Cobb: Well, I don't know if it is quicker, though, because when I started making records, I made them like everybody else did. I mean, you thought you had to have a click. You thought you had to do the drums first, then you do the bass, and it's—it was never fun. I don't enjoy that kind of record making. Then it becomes like a job, and I think most musicians, most artists, they got into music because it was a blast to do. Nothing is more fun than getting together with your friends in the garage or wherever and just [plugging] in and [making] noise. And I think that gets removed a lot of times in record making. All of a sudden, it becomes a business, and there's a lot of smarter businesses to get into than the music business, so if it's only about money, don't get into the music business. You should get into it because you can't do anything else and you love what you do. We try to create a space in the studio that just feels like we're fifteen in our garage, cutting up again.

Menzie: It's interesting because, for example, loops—there's no risk. There's nothing except what sound pressure levels you're going to get because they're consistent, but that's also something that's boring.

Dave Cobb: Well, I'm just really terrible with computers. That was never really an option for me, because I don't know how to work them, so it was a lot easier for me to play and put down a drum take by myself and then start putting stuff on top of it. I spent a lot more time playing instruments than I did playing on the computer, so it's a deficiency for me, the technology aspect, and I think that's probably what led me to doing it all live. I could never understand why—you go see a band live, and people go, "Oh my god, they're so amazing live, so much better than the record!" So why don't you make the record as if you're playing live? It makes sense to me. It seems like cutting out the middleman, just actually recording people in a room, cuts out some of the drama and the process and the cerebral aspects of playing with technology.

MENZIE: So I found a fun quote of yours that really hit me. In an interview you're talking about people's affinity for vinyl, and you say, "It's not really about chasing the quality of vinyl. It's about chasing humanity." I think that goes back to the idea of doing it all in one room. It's the great, honest record approach. Is that your reason for saying, "Let's just go back and do what we really came to do in the first place"? What pushed you into that approach?

DAVE COBB: Again, people say it's harder to record that way, but I don't think it is. I think it's a lot easier. Vinyl sounds great, and I'm happy people are buying vinyl because it's a great experience—to look at the album cover and have a tangible product that makes you pay attention. But if you look at anything that came out of LA—the Wrecking Crew or anything out of Muscle Shoals or anything out of Stax—you had the best players playing together in a room with the best engineers, producers, and arrangers, [as well as] the best songwriters and the best equipment that they could have in a lot of these instances, and that's why it sounds so great. I could give the best guitar player in the world the crappiest guitar, and it sounds amazing no matter what. And that's why those records sound great. It's not just an EQ [equalization] or even a microphone as much as it is the way somebody plays or holds the instrument and interacts with another professional. That's why those records sound good. You've got the best studios, . . . arrangers, and songwriters. It goes on and on.

MENZIE: In reference to the Sam Phillips's [Sun Records'] approach of "no plan" in the studio, you are quoted as saying, "I come to the studio for the danger of not knowing what we're going to get into that day." That's a great philosophy, but some people might find it too high risk.

DAVE COBB: I don't think it's high risk. I think as long as you think of music as an art—some days you don't feel like painting, and you come back the next day—what's the risk? You lose some hours? Usually, it's a benefit. I was always doing that, even before I heard Sam Phillips say that. I was doing it for years and scaring the crap out of people, and after I heard that he did it that way, it was validation for my lunacy. So I like that. I love that.

I love the fear of not knowing what's going on until you get in there. I never liked calculating things or preproduction too much, because you go through it all in a rehearsal room, you work out what the bass player's doing, what the drummer's doing, and this cool solo, but by the time you get in the studio, everyone's forgotten everything, and then you spend half your time going, "Listen to the rehearsal tape. Go back, go back. No, no, no. It's not that one. Go back. Find the part you were doing." And it's such a bummer. I think I got that idea from going back to the Beatles too. You hear all these anthologies come out now, and it's like take seventeen of whatever song; they just had tape rolling the entire time, and I think the moment they figured something out, they had it on tape, and they were done with it. That moment of discovery and invention—I always think that's the best time someone is ever going to play something. It's going to be the most exciting time when they think they've landed on "the thing." Going back after you've played six months of shows on this song—I think you're over it. As a writer myself, [I see how] you're always into the most recent thing you've done as a writer, and I think it's the same for any writer or artist, so I hate to lose that moment of invention. That's why I risk it all the time in the studio.

MENZIE: That speaks to the point that some people would look at the live-tracking approach as inefficient. But you look at it as efficient because you are capturing something honest and fresh, and if you were to track everything and then overdub until it's "perfect" to some, [then it] appears to be somewhat safer, but it's less spontaneously creative. I really appreciate your philosophy on that.

DAVE COBB: I'm going to say that, and hopefully people believe me because, again, I think it scares people so bad, but all the records that I love and that I've worked on and that have done well have all been done that way. They've all been done flying by the seat of their pants. I think, to me, it's just more efficient and more exciting.

MENZIE: All the artists that you're producing are very special, and you have a really diverse roster. Will you talk a little about the character of the artists you're producing and how each artist attracted you to partner with them?

DAVE COBB: The one common trait between everyone I work with, whether it's country, rock, or pop, [is] always authenticity and honesty. I love people that are not pretending. They're not trying to brag or pretending to be someone else. They're not trying to play music for a game. They're not in the hustle of music. They're in music for the same reason I'm in it—because they can't do anything else and can't think about anything else. I always pick those artists that are naturally born with a voice. They're naturally born with a gift for songwriting or musicianship. I'm never picking based off of "X band has had X number 1 hits" [and] "I should probably do that to make money." If I think about the music business for money, like I've said, I think there are better businesses to be in. I pick things I just really enjoy and . . . love. I try to find that. It's always fun to find a new artist that's never made a record and go in with them and see the excitement of the first time they hear something back that they created in the studio. I love that.

MENZIE: Interesting that you use the word *energy*—very apropos. What do you look for in a voice, and what characteristics do you think are consistent in great songs?

DAVE COBB: We were talking earlier about Otis Redding and Ray Charles and Little Richard. I love that raspy thing—people like Rod Stewart and Steve Marriott and Paul Rogers. I love that kind of singer. The first time I heard someone like Chris Stapleton—I love that kind of voice. He's got that power and rawness and just that raspy thing I think is just really, really great. And there are people I love, like Waylon Jennings. Waylon kind of lilts when he sings, and you hear the passion when he sings; you can feel his meaning in what he's talking about—like Merle Haggard or somebody like that. And there are other great artists [whom] I work with. Brandi Carlile—she has that amazing ability, like Freddy Mercury would have—just this crazy range.

MENZIE: Yeah. She's certainly got a crazy range.

DAVE COBB: Yeah, and [she has] a heartfelt kind of delivery when she sings, and I like her voice because of that. And she's a great songwriter. I love Jason Isbell's voice because you're hearing the raw emotion between his lyrics and his performance. It feels like he's never trying to pretend. He's just being [himself], and I love the way his voice sounds and the way he delivers his own lyrics. Another great writer.

MENZIE: I love his lyrics.

DAVE COBB: Oh man, yeah. Insanity.

MENZIE: The third ingredient in all this, especially in Nashville, is guitar tones. Will you share your passion about chasing great guitar tones and how you go about recording them? Are there any special tricks that you do to get some of these great sounds?

DAVE COBB: I just remember being a kid and starting to mess around with studio stuff and not understanding how to get tones I loved on records. I loved Led Zeppelin guitar sounds, and I loved Lynyrd Skynyrd guitar sounds, and I just didn't understand how to get that. Again, I think it goes back to a great guitar player. A great guitar player can make anything sound good. A friend of mine, producer Mark Neill, always told me you never get the sound in the control room. You get the sound at the source, in the live room. So I started collecting guitars. I have a Tele that makes X sound and a 335 that makes X other sound, and I have this amp, this little amp thing, that will do kind of a *Zeppelin 1* thing, and I have a Fender amp of this particular era that does the Waylon Jennings thing. I started cherry-picking eras and guitars and amplifiers to match what I'm chasing, and it doesn't necessarily sound anything like these people I'm talking about, but it definitely gets you in the ballpark. The player can kind of take it from there. Miking and recording is pretty simple when you've got a great source and a great player. But I would give the talent the credit for the guitar sounds, not me, because they are doing all the work.

MENZIE: Let's talk about *Southern Family*. With this amazing roster of artists that you've been producing, you did this compilation album. I have to tell you, the first time I heard "You Are My Sunshine" by Morgane and Chris Stapleton, I just had to stop for a second and recalculate humanity because it was—I was just not ready for that. Will you discuss the making of the *Southern Family* album?

DAVE COBB: Well, for "You Are My Sunshine," I have to give all the credit to Morgane and Chris Stapleton. They were already playing that song like that. I think maybe my role in that song was just being very comfortable with them, and after making an album and playing live with them, they're like family. That record is really about family and things that I thought represented growing up in the South and emotions about children and parents and grandparents and loss and birth. I was very comfortable with them, and I feel like they were pretty comfortable with me, so I feel like we got the raw emotion of them performing that song altogether. I couldn't take any credit for that except for being a safe place to record it and capture that emotion.

MENZIE: So how did the *Southern Family* project itself come together?

DAVE COBB: There's a record that I love called *White Mansions* that an English songwriter, Paul Kennerley, wrote. It's a concept record produced by Glyn Johns and had Waylon Jennings [and] Jessi Colter, along with Eric Clapton playing guitar and just an incredible cast of talent on it and players. It was a country record made in England at Olympic Studios, and it kind of married the two worlds I love, which is that sound of Rolling Stones' records with country music. I was always trying to think, what would be a good concept record to make? I moved to California when I was just twenty-seven and lived out there for about eleven years. Then I moved to Nashville, and I got really homesick. There were a lot of things I didn't like growing up. I didn't like greens or black-eyed peas or any of the typical southern food you'd eat. When I had pizza for the first time, I thought, "Man, I'm out of here. I'm going to New York." I had Thai or Indian food for the first time, and my first thought was "I can't wait to get out of here." I always said I was going to New York, but I wound up in LA. All those things—living in LA and being gone for so long—really made me homesick, and that record was kind of the realization of connecting with my childhood, connecting with the way I was brought up and celebrating that, as opposed to running away from it. I think that was a big part of it—and working with like-minded people who've had similar backgrounds.

MENZIE: An amazing record.

DAVE COBB: Glad you dig it.

MENZIE: Speaking of records, Low Country Sound is your label. Most people acknowledge that Sun Records and Stax had very unique cultures around their labels, and they had certain approaches they embraced that made them unique. Will you talk about your label and what you do with it? What is your vision for the label?

DAVE COBB: The label is a great, amazing opportunity. When I started, nobody was calling me to make records. It's not like I had any credits or precedent for anybody to work with me to begin with, and then when I finally did X record, I'd have to find a home for it. Sturgill is a great example. He was unsigned. When I worked with Jamie Johnson, he wasn't on Universal Records at the time. We always had to find a home for these albums for people to get to hear them, and I think having a label with Electra and Atlantic gave me the ability to just find talent and go straight to the source and get to put it out. But I wanted to have a culture. I wanted the same thing you refer to. I'm signing people because I believe in their talent and their songwriting and [in] them as human beings,

Chapter 3

and it is great having this label. I mean, it's beautiful to see artists like Anderson East, who's one of my closest friends and whose voice I love, hang out with Brandi Carlile, whom I adore—I was a big fan of hers way before I met her. And new artists like this girl Savannah Conley [whom] we signed—they all hang out with each other. They go on tour with each other. They write with each other, and it's really a magical thing. It's like a community. Anderson East had made everybody these Low Country Sound rings. It's almost like we have our secret-club rings, and everybody fights over getting one. It's really cool. I have always been about community with music, and that's just kind of an excuse to all get to hang out and continue making art with a great partner—with Electra being able to market these records and show up whenever they need to show up.

MENZIE: You talk about touring together. It almost sounds like the road shows of Motown in the sixties, like [in] the movie *That Thing You Do!* Right?

DAVE COBB: Absolutely. I love that.

MENZIE: There was an amazing moment during the 2015 CMA [Country Music Association] Awards when Chris Stapleton and Justin Timberlake played "Tennessee Whiskey" and Timberlake's "Drink You Away."

In my opinion, it's an indelible moment in music that I believe was powerful enough that it affected the way that some artists were looking at the industry formulas, and they began to reconsider what else you could do. You were part of that performance. Will you share how that moment came together and what happened behind the scenes?

DAVE COBB: I think we were feeling very lucky to be included in that community. To get to play at a country-music award show was huge for us. None of us had done it before, so it was very, very scary to do that the first time. But when we got out there, I remember we started to play "Tennessee Whiskey," and I was looking into the audience at these people's faces, and I didn't know any of these bigger country artists. I wasn't necessarily a big part of the scene or anything, but I remember looking at people and seeing their faces melt with happiness, just pure smiles. They were grinning and singing along. I thought, "I just can't believe what we're seeing right now." It felt like Chris had done a lot of groundwork. He'd done songs for these other artists, and he'd also been extremely sweet to everybody along the way, and you could just tell everybody was rooting for him. So it was fun to see that. It felt like the culmination of friends and peers embracing him, embracing what was going on that night. It was a pretty magical night. It definitely changed all our lives.

MENZIE: Fortunately, the camera did catch some of the faces you're talking about. People couldn't get their heads around how ridiculously wonderful the performance was. During "Drink You Away," the camera catches a great moment of Jerry Douglas just grinning from ear to ear, loving it. How much did the moment change reality for everybody? Did it change the way the phone rang?

DAVE COBB: Yeah, I got on a plane literally the next morning. I had to go cut a record in Berlin, and so I wasn't in town to experience the aftermath. To me, it felt like reading a comic strip. Wow, the record's number 1 on *Billboard*! It sold X amount this week. It felt like it was just kind of a dream and not real until I got back to the States, and there was all this talk about how this was going to change the way country music is perceived. This is an honest record, and now everyone's going to start making honest records. I don't think that [had] happened. I don't think any of that was really a thing. I think it just created a parallel lane for people to make these records and have an audience and have people show up to shows. I don't think it stopped what was going on, it just created a new lane for people who do want to do that, to have a new opportunity.

MENZIE: Whenever people ask, "How do you see things going forward?" one of the things I've always said is that there are moments along the way that have always given us dependable coordinates to consider. When I saw that moment, there it was—great performance, great voices, great backup band, unique writing, and a big audience reaction. So it's interesting that it has now created a parallel lane. I guess, ultimately, that's best because it still gives you something to compare to, but I had the thought when I watched it that this moment is completely sobering, no pun intended. It certainly gave clarity and perspective to the word *authentic*.

DAVE COBB: Like I said, I think it just created another lane. I think that was the biggest impact of it. Prior to that, I had definitely always felt more like an underdog or kind of left of center, and I feel, after that performance, that maybe I'm not so much an underdog. I got to meet a lot more people in the music business and feel like a true part of it in a good way—taken seriously. That was a good thing to come out of it as well.

MENZIE: You and Chris Stapleton are obviously just having an amazing year: CMA Song of the Year, Male Vocalist of the Year, Single of the Year, and a Grammy for Broken Halos. Chris is having an amazing run with you, and so is Brandi Carlile. She had three Grammy wins; that makes for quite a night. What does success do to the creative process? Does it distract as much as it helps?

DAVE COBB: I think if I stopped and thought about it too much, I would freak myself out. You may have success now, but who knows if it's going to last? I think it's a frightening thought to try to compete all the time. I went back to just making records. I don't think I've changed making records, I just keep doing what I'm doing. I never got into this stuff for a quick pop hit, and if I knew what a hit was, I think I'd have a few more of them. I just keep my head down and strive to keep making great records. They will probably go out of fashion again, and maybe they'll come back in fashion again at some other point. Who knows? It's a lot to take in, that's for sure. I think one of the benefits is that now you could have someone like Chris or Brandi and [then] immediately, people listen to the next record that comes out. That's a really big benefit. You're not having to do all the legwork to introduce somebody to the world.

MENZIE: Heightened visibility and credibility make it easier; that makes a lot of sense. Let me move into *A Star Is Born*. You were involved in this movie that just burned up the world. Everybody loves it. How did that all come about?

DAVE COBB: It all came about when Bradley Cooper reached out. He had heard records I'd done and wanted to get together. I flew out to LA, and we talked about the character and the vibe of the music. I played him some of Jason Isbell's music, and he freaked out. I also played him my cousin Brent Cobb and people that I just thought were honest because he really wanted an honest artistic character. My initial role was to help develop the music and the vibe of the character. I had Jason Isbell write a song, and that became "Maybe, It's Time" in the film. The original character was going to be a country artist, so I called some of my favorite writers in Nashville: Natalie Hemby, Hillary Lindsey, and Lori McKenna. And we all flew out together to LA to write and do tracks there, and the tracks wound up being a few of the songs in the film. "Always Remember Us This Way" [was] cut out there, the end title for the film, and several other ones. It wound up being a lot of songs in one week, and I think they were taken aback by how powerful the Nashville songwriters are.

MENZIE: It's a great presentation and interesting to see Lady Gaga embrace this type of role. She did a great job of singing, acting, and writing.

DAVE COBB: She did. It was incredible to see her sing—I'll just reference "Always Remember Us This Way." When she recorded it, she was so honest and really put herself out there; she became this character—pretty amazing to see. Like I said, she wrote a few of the songs from the film with those writers, and she really hit it off with them.

MENZIE: You have signed with CAA [Creative Artists Agency] to have representation as well as the opportunity to do more film work and perhaps television. Will you discuss that?

DAVE COBB: I've always been fascinated with that world. I started off as a session musician, and even though I make records and I get to play on records for other artists, I still like to compose stuff. That gives me an opportunity to score. Scoring is what I really want to do. I've always been fascinated with that and the people who do it, so really, my goal is to score for film and also assemble custom songs for films, kind of like *A Star Is Born*. I'd like to do it again.

MENZIE: Well, you certainly hit it out of the park with *A Star Is Born*.

You have LA, and you have Nashville. LA used to be such an amazing scene, and Nashville has certainly gone through its changes. A lot of younger musicians will ask, "Should I go to LA, or should I go to Nashville?" Where do you think the opportunities are? Do you see one place as stronger than the other?

DAVE COBB: Nashville's a no-brainer. In a lot of ways, with a shrinking music business, Nashville is the Alamo. It really is. I say that half-jokingly, but also I'm really serious. It's the only place where art really meets commerce and affordability. You can actually have a job just so you can get together and practice with your band. You can start touring. You can have a garage to practice in or a basement. You also have record labels that can sign you. You have studios to record in. You have the best songwriters in the world, the best musicians to capacitate all of your dreams with that. So it's really the only place.

LA is great for entertainment. TV and film are obviously amazing things. But it's really hard to support a local scene there. It's so expensive. You've got to work so hard to pay your rent. [It's] the same with New York. Nashville is really the only place you can marry all those things. That's why I also think the community is much more open here. I think living in LA—there's incredible talent and songwriters and the whole lot, but it's more of a competition. Here it's a community where the live scene is really healthy. People come out to shows. Friends from other bands will come out to support their friends' bands. They play on each other's records with no what-am-I-going-to-get-out-of-this attitude, and I think that's why it's such a great place. [It has] community and affordability, and you have labels and studios here, producers and writers—all of the above.

Menzie: The Alamo—that's great. Going forward, what do you have up your sleeve, and what are you hoping to do?

Dave Cobb: I'm hoping just to continue to be able to afford making my house payments in ten years. I don't know, to me, it feels like there's a lot of opportunity. Who knows where it will lead? I do want to do TV and film, and I definitely want to make records. I'd like to explore the executive side to the music business more. I think it's fun to watch an artist go from playing in coffee shops to selling out a tour. I love that experience.

Menzie: That almost sounds like the Chet Atkins philosophy. He never fell out of love with playing music, yet he accomplished so many bigger milestones. To me, he always remained about the music.

Dave Cobb: He's definitely one of my heroes. The guy was able to have a successful career on his own as an artist. He was also able to produce; he had such a successful career doing that. He was an executive. He got to do it all.

Menzie: A lot of artists have the tendency to look at executive responsibility like it's a disease, and I don't think that's the case. That's one of the reasons I am writing this book. I want musicians and artists to understand that you can marry art and executive together, but you have to think like an entrepreneur. You can embrace business as a craft, and while they have different responsibilities, both music and executive can be creative. I don't know if the executive appears as romantic as music performance, but you can make it an art form, and without it, you lose the ability to sustain ease in your career.

Dave Cobb: I think when Chet walked [into] the studio with Elvis, Chet knew what he was looking for. He knew how to communicate in music terms, and I think that's what's fun about exploring the executive side for me is being able to say it all. Not saying I'm wrong or right or whatever, but at least being able to speak the same language as an artist—I've been on that side, too. I was in bands that made records and dealt with a lot of executives through the years, so to me, being able to be an executive who's also able to communicate musically sounds exciting.

MENZIE: Yeah, Quincy Jones.

DAVE COBB: Absolutely. That's a great example. Huge example. There's so many incredible talents.

MENZIE: Chet, Quincy—it speaks to that same spirit, right?
I think you've got to try things that you think matter, you've got to be consistent, and you've got to take a couple of hits that you don't see coming.

DAVE COBB: Absolutely. I couldn't have said it better myself.

MENZIE: I'm sure the readers look forward to hearing all you do. There is no doubt in my mind it will be a treat.

Chapter 4

The Calling

Finding Your True Inner Voice

Be it music's magnetic allure, seeing a performance that moves your soul, or perhaps hearing a song for the first time that changes your state, no matter your gateway, if you're seeking music as a profession, your personal relationship with music is unquestionably a calling. Whether we completely understand it or not, we become restless, and something compels us to develop this creative relationship with an art form that introduces us to ourselves.

As burgeoning artists, we listen to music and find ourselves mesmerized by the performer's artistry. Soon we find ourselves drawn deeply into the sounds, relating to the artist's unique individualism; we find ourselves feeling the purity and soul in the music. It is through that connection that we begin to recognize the artist within.

In the hands of a capable songwriter, words marry melody, and art gives birth.

That art moves and entices us to become lifetime musicians. Through the gateway of listening, performing, writing, or composing, the music calls us into an artistic way of life and tasks us with expressing our decisive moments through sound.

Embarking on the professional path of music, we begin writing our personal storylines, unveiling our true voices, and as we begin to understand the art form, we mature into playing the spaces as well as the notes.

Chapter 4

Growing as artists, we begin to consistently marry expression into our way of life! As a tribe, we are different; we listen deeply to the patterns of random events. A squeaky screen door plays in our head, like in the opening to Michael Jackson's "Thriller" as we await Michael's footsteps. Involuntarily, we have become the song as our way of life. Thankfully, it is a calling, not a choice.

How do we really know when music is our calling? Here are a few simple clues that may help you answer the question:

You are working from instinct, not from logic.

You have an energetic and emotional response to good music because the music leaves you no other choice.

Art in any medium changes your state because you are affected by quality expression.

When something is funny, you laugh unapologetically.

You experience life through your heart and respond with a song.

Dealing with reality for you is like hearing, "The gallery is getting ready to close."

You lose yourself in any good read—you become the characters; often you bring a song with you when you return.

When you are in the creative zone, time doesn't exist. You don't report to a watch—you are on artist time.

You are sensitive to current events and happenings because you feel life fully.

Gifted musicians go "into the music" when they listen. While they are in the song, they visualize all the idiosyncrasies as they hear the instruments execute the arrangement. Great musicians can imagine parts before they are actualized. Actor Mark Ruffalo captures this idea beautifully in the movie *Begin Again* as Keira Knightley sings "A Step You Can't Take Back."

As you mature as a musician, you begin to understand intuitively that music is a gift and yours is the role of the messenger.

These are all traits of a creative. We do not choose music as a career. Music chooses us, and it does so for one simple reason: it wants to be expressed!

That is the calling, as well as the journey of the musician.

The Calling

We work for the song, we work for the music, and we work for the opportunity to play and communicate with others through our craft. We have been gifted with a calling, and because of that, we are charged with the task of sharing our gifts with others. We can lift others up, we can make people feel, and we can make people want to dance. The purpose of our gifts is to move others. Whether you are called as a writer, a player, a voice, or a sound engineer, you influence the listener.

To quote the Rolling Stones, "Can't You Hear Me Knocking"?

Chapter 5
Scheila Gonzalez

SCHEILA GONZALEZ IS THE PURE DEFINITION OF A GREAT MUSICIAN. She plays all of the types of saxophones and keyboards, as well as flute and percussion, and she sings. Scheila has played with Dweezil Zappa in Zappa Plays Zappa (ZPZ) since 2006, and when possible, she also tours with Colin Hay (Men at Work) and joins forces with the DIVA Jazz Orchestra. She is never afraid to accept a freelance opportunity or a recording session. Scheila is married to James Santiago (of Voodoo Labs fame), a remarkable guitarist. You can find videos of Scheila with ZPZ on YouTube, and there is a live Zappa Plays Zappa DVD. James Santiago is also on YouTube, and you can find his music on Spotify. His gear knowledge is legendary, and researching James will benefit anyone seeking to advance their guitar skills and knowledge.

INTERVIEW

MENZIE: At the time of this interview, you were in the process of recording and tracking some of Dweezil's original compositions. Tell us a little bit about that.

SCHEILA GONZALEZ: Yes, that's right. So many fans, when they come to the Zappa Plays Zappa concerts, have been asking him to release some of his own material, as well as perform the Zappa catalog that they appreciate.

MENZIE: Dweezil has a lot of unusual pressure on him: fans saying, "Dweezil, we need you to be you!" and also the Zappa Plays Zappa fans who remember Frank's music a certain way and want to hear it performed in that way.

SCHEILA GONZALEZ: I can't imagine what it's like to be Dweezil Zappa. There is a lot of pressure on all fronts, but he's done it all with such style and grace and technique and humility. He approaches all of it to serve the music. So it's fun watching him shine in his own light. It's a different kind of sound—interesting and, I think, surprising. It's a departure from Frank's music in that it's more eclectic rock and pop. It's kind of going back to Dweezil's initial influences, like Randy Rhoads and Eddie Van. But also, it's eclectic and interesting. There's some odd time stuff, some odd meter things, and some interesting orchestrated things, [as well as] cool arranging in the songs.

MENZIE: You worked with Geoff Emerick and Joe Barresi, two amazing folks involved with the record. Knowing that Geoff did so much iconic Beatles stuff, coming in on *Revolver* and continuing with [*Sgt. Pepper's Lonely Hearts Club Band*]—what was that like for you?

SCHEILA GONZALEZ: Because Geoff had been around quite a while, it was very exciting. In fact, I was driving home from a gig on a Sunday afternoon and listening to talk radio, and I heard his book *Here, There, and Everywhere* [*My Life Recording the Music of the Beatles*] referenced. And it was only a few weeks later that Dweezil mentioned that he ran into Geoff Emerick and said he's going to be engineering this session, so I knew I would be working with a very important piece of history, and it was just a beautiful day.

MENZIE: Knowing in advance that he was such a part of major history—was that distracting at all for you? Or were you able to settle in, realizing that although Geoff is iconic, more importantly, he's simply a wonderful engineer?

SCHEILA GONZALEZ: That's it. It's not about recognizing who is standing in front of you or what kind of opportunity this is. It's about always being as prepared and as professional as possible. Because, ultimately, you're there to serve the music regardless of who is or isn't standing in front of you or what equipment is or isn't around you. No matter what setting you may or may not be in, your job is to still serve the music. So although it was very exciting, my head would gently remind me, "I'm here to do this session, it's time to work." But humorously, I had to say that to myself a few extra times.

MENZIE: I read that Dweezil uses a guitar that has a different neck with some quarter-tone, different intervals in it. How does that affect your parts on sax, voice, [and so forth]?

SCHEILA GONZALEZ: On Monday we're going to be tracking background vocals on a song where he has used it. The guitar is a Fender Eric Jonson–model Strat, and the neck is made by Performance Guitar. That'll be interesting, I'm sure, if we're trying to sing microtonality since we come from a Western society. It usually happens by accident. So we'll see. I think it may be just a setting where there are some drone-type things that he might be playing over. It's Dweezil, so he's going to be creative and do as he likes.

MENZIE: What are the complexities you deal with when playing Frank Zappa's music?

SCHEILA GONZALEZ: It is some of the most challenging music I have ever played in my life—that anyone will ever play in his or her life. It's incredible and challenging to listen to at times. It really demands a lot of the listener, and there's so much going on. There's such a depth to the music. I like something that Dweezil said when asked what he thinks of music other than his father's music. The way he put it is "I grew up listening to my father's music. He was writing at home. When I finally started listening to stuff on the radio, I thought, 'Where's the rest?' The music was sparse in comparison." The complexities and the challenges are the things that I really thrive on.

I never thought there'd be a gig like this out there for me. It didn't exist between the time of Frank's last touring and [Dweezil's] embarking on this project in 2006. We finished the first run of six weeks at the Warfield in San Francisco. It was June 2006, and we played our last show and didn't know if this project would continue. Everything was thrown at it. We did three months of rehearsals five days a week, six hours a day, just to wrap our minds around the vernacular. Dweezil grew up with it, as did Joe Travers, the vault meister, a huge Zappa fan since he was ten years old and just an encyclopedia of all things Zappa.

MENZIE: Doesn't Joe Travers oversee the library?

SCHEILA GONZALEZ: Yes, Joe Travers is in charge of the vault, the audio and video archives, and working with pulling new releases out of the vault. He works with Gail Zappa on those releases and preserving old tapes.

And there's also the score meister, Kurt Morgan, who currently plays bass for Zappa Plays Zappa and also plays in Joe Travers and Friends—a great bass player, incredible musician. He is in charge of the written-note archives.

So I realized I'd found a musical place where everything I had worked so hard to learn could be used in Zappa's music. My entire skill set was able to be exploited and pushed as far as I could push it. Frank Zappa's music is a commitment: it's an investment, and you have to want to work that hard to be in a band like this. As we all walked off stage at the end of the initial six-week commitment and embraced and reflected on the special moments, there were a lot of tears of both joy and sadness. I hadn't begun to blubber and cry until I said to Steve Vai, "I never thought there was a gig like this out there for me," and Steve just put a hand on my shoulder, and I completely lost it. I thought it was over. We took months to put together this amazing band, and we got some great runs in, but I wanted to have this last. Then we started to gain interest and momentum, and here we are, still going strong.

MENZIE: It's important to preserve the music of the great pioneers, especially those that pushed boundaries, which Zappa clearly did. His catalog is immense.

SCHEILA GONZALEZ: Bach, Mozart, Debussy, or any of the great composers—he is among them, without a doubt. I'm glad that his work exists, and I'm glad to be a part of it.

MENZIE: How did you get to be considered for the Zappa gig?

SCHEILA GONZALEZ: Well, it's really a matter of networking—you have to network. And it's also important not to burn bridges. I can't stress those two points enough. I was told Dweezil was putting together a project to perform his father's music. I had done a few auditions for this agent, and they went well. Since he was familiar with my work when the Zappa opportunity surfaced, the agent reached out to me about auditioning. He was familiar with my skill sets, and he knew I was a good match.

MENZIE: So you and the agent had developed a rapport?

SCHEILA GONZALEZ: Yeah, I had previously done an audition for Kenny Loggins, and I got a callback, but a former member of Kenny's old band became available for the position. Since Kenny already had a good working relationship with him, that is who he went with.

So the agent knew I could handle hard auditions. You never know until you're in the audition what the artist may want. There's a whole gamut of skill sets and abilities, and it's not until audition time that it all comes to fruition. Agents who line up auditions pay close attention to how you fare with the whole professional process. They watch how you deal with everything.

MENZIE: As you said, Loggins asked for a callback, and he enjoyed your work, but he chose to go with somebody he was already comfortable with. You see that a lot in studio work. Professional rapport is everything.

SCHEILA GONZALEZ: You have got to be tough and resilient.

MENZIE: And you can't make it personal.

SCHEILA GONZALEZ: Decisions can be for any number of reasons, and it may have zero to do with anything you did or didn't do. And I think it's important to remember not to take something personally. If I don't get called to do a session, it's because they wanted "that sound" from "that person over there." If I do get called, it's because they want what I bring to the table.

MENZIE: Obviously, recording in the studio with Dweezil is a very different experience than playing live with ZPZ. How does your approach to the music change?

SCHEILA GONZALEZ: There's a different set of rules. The way you approach things might shift a little bit. The challenge is to bring life to the music—even though you're sitting between four walls with headphones on and hearing a click track in the background and trying to match this and that.

When you are preparing to perform live, you prepare by listening to the material, familiarizing yourself with the material, and then getting your hands and your mind around the material technically so that you can execute with spirit. Once that is together, that's when I love approaching music with reckless abandon. The rest is all heart and soul.

MENZIE: So when ZPZ plays live, the expectations are extraordinarily high because fans of Zappa's music are so ardent. How do you deal with the distraction of having to be everything that the listener expects you to be, when there were so many different incarnations of Zappa bands?

SCHEILA GONZALEZ: I know I keep going back to Dweezil, but truly, it's his name on the line, and I think that he knew going into this project that all the fans were going to be out there thinking, "Let's see what Frank's kid is going to do with this." Understandably, people are completely loyal fans, so passionate. I've never seen anything like it.

It's beautiful to see fans bring their kids to shows and just pass it on. But Dweezil knew that was going to happen, so in the initial incarnation of this band, his goal was to play exact versions—down to the most minute detail—and I think the moment we hit the stage and played it with such accuracy, people were just taken aback. They joined in with us on the fun and the love that we all have for Frank's music. I love that over the years, there's become a looseness within the band, as well as the audiences, that has come into play, and that reflects in the spirit of the band.

ZPZ is its own thing. Different musicians have come and gone with ZPZ, and like the Zappa bands, each incarnation has its own flavor and its own spirit. I think there's always been this sense that once Dweezil established the bar and set it as high as possible, then we were all going to meet that standard, even pass it if we could. It's always been what we have strived to do, just as that was the standard that Frank set with every musician that played with Frank Zappa. The musical integrity is through the roof, and everyone works very hard to make sure that everything's not only accurate but met with the true Zappa spirit. Over time it's also developed into its own thing, and the audience sees that and feels it and has learned to trust that.

MENZIE: Do you get the chance to do much LA studio work?

SCHEILA GONZALEZ: I do some LA studio work, but I would like to do more. It gets harder as the demand for "real musicians" gets smaller. It's tough when one person can track so many parts in their home studio. I was recently reading that a lot of orchestral musicians end up losing studio work because the work is farmed out overseas, where, depending on the circumstances, it might be tracked more economically.

Studio work in LA has always been a tough nut to crack! It has always been a very tight-knit group of session players. It's no secret that every opportunity to network matters.

Fortunately, while the Zappa Plays Zappa project is a lot of work, we're only really busy with touring around four months out of the year, so it allows me the time to be in town. I have a couple of projects where my place is held for me, so when I come off the road, I'm able to pick up where I left off. Many people that I work with know that with ZPZ, I will have to come and go. But I still have my connections firmly planted.

MENZIE: What are the different hats that you wear in the music business?

SCHEILA GONZALEZ: I'm a performer, a session musician, a teacher, an occasional arranger, and an occasional and unofficial musical director, [as well as] band leader. Those are the general headings as far as hats in the music industry. What really gets me fired up is having variety. That is definitely the spice of life for me.

Now I know that somebody that plays straight-ahead bebop jazz seven days a week is going to own that and sound more authentic than I ever could in a million years, spreading myself across different genres or different types of work or different instruments. But I endeavor to be able to switch hats depending on the setting to serve the music that I'm playing in that moment.

So I've played in small-group jazz settings as a saxophonist, I've played in big band settings, I play lead alto sometimes, and [I] sometimes lead tenor, sometimes second tenor, which is crazy because it's all the leftover harmonies in the section. Sometimes I play baritone, and that's a whole different role. I've also played baritone and tenor in R&B- and Motown-type settings. I've also played all the woodwinds in a musical-show type of setting.

MENZIE: And you play the flute as well?

SCHEILA GONZALEZ: Flute, clarinet, soprano, alto sax, tenor sax, baritone sax, and keys. I don't play any double reed, like oboe or bassoon. That's a very different kind of playing. I'm a church musician as well, and [I've] played the same spot in the church band for over twenty years. It's a great band full of session players and great musicians—really fun. Recently, the church got wind of the fact that I play keyboards, so now I've been playing sax and second keys. Of course, that's a familiar position that I love. It's a lot of fun to add those colors.

I've done cover bands, I've done corporate bands, [and] I'll fly out to wherever. We had a gig in Maui, so we flew out to Maui, and I played "Brick House" for the masses to shake a tail feather.

Chapter 5

Menzie: Let's talk about your teaching.

Scheila Gonzalez: I enjoy teaching, but I don't get to do it as much as I like, because my performance commitments don't always allow for that. There was a period of time when I taught an after-school program a couple of days a week when I was in town. I have also taught private students, but because I have always been a performer first, if and when I have the chance to teach, I've been fortunate enough to have students whose parents understand the flexibility I need. They know I can get a last-minute session call or a gig with very little notice.

When I did the after-school class for the students, it was extracurricular, so they were showing up because they wanted to be there, not for a grade. They attended because they wanted to learn. We covered some jazz history, and we covered improv. We covered small group arrangements and that sort of thing. I remember having groups made up of three flutes (but no bass player), two drummers, a baritone horn player, a bassoon, and a trombone. So I said, "Come on, let's improvise!" Sometimes I would jump on bass because I'm a closet bass player, and that was a lot of fun. Frank Zappa would have definitely enjoyed writing for this group.

The student, of course, is ultimately [his or her] own best teacher, but for those who do teach, the secret is finding an opportunity to show the student how to learn. I just loved watching the lightbulb go on for the student. So I understand why teachers teach, and I'm even more grateful for all the great teachers that I've had.

Menzie: What major changes are you seeing in the music business that encourage you?

Scheila Gonzalez: I think we can all agree that methods of delivering music to the audience have definitely changed. Streaming is now the new 45 RPM [revolutions per minute] record. That's certainly different, but I think that all of this could spawn another type of musical renaissance. In a lot of ways, you're seeing independent acts gaining strength and momentum. Everybody is doing fine, and even though elusive are the glory days of big record label deals for rising artists, we're still going to start grassroots projects and build from there. Musicians have always endured change, and we've always found a way to make things better even if we have to invent it.

MENZIE: The current spirit in the music industry seems somewhat reminiscent of the mid-1960s, early 1970s. During that period there was a unique synergy in the industry. There were the big traveling tours, where so many of the Motown artists were creating great music and a great culture—almost like an extended family. Now the new energy is streaming with Spotify, Apple Music, and other services. Control of the music is returning to the artists. Although it's a very different format, once again, more voices and fresh voices are being heard.

SCHEILA GONZALEZ: I think that's the gateway to the creative renaissance. There's an undercurrent of independent artists right now, [who] many listeners haven't even heard of yet. And they're incredible musicians doing incredibly creative things. At first its "small market" things, but little by little, by building and connecting, everything just slowly shifts in another direction. The one catch is that there's no set formula for making money directly, so that's why you have to send your feelers in all directions—because anything could come out of that. Always say yes, but don't compromise your worth. I love unique players [who] are true to themselves. And true players with unique ideas generally achieve success and make a good living.

MENZIE: Being LA based, do you try to basically stay on the West Coast, or do you travel to meet the demands of the gigs?

SCHEILA GONZALEZ: Call me, [and] I will get on a plane. I will accommodate and go wherever the gig is, and I love it because I enjoy traveling. I certainly prefer to record in the room with other players, but sometimes it doesn't work out that way for financial reasons. In the new reality, if someone needs a track done, the virtual or remote model can work. And because the industry has embraced that approach more over the past few years, new recording opportunities continue to open up, though you lose a touch of impromptu chemistry, which can be expensive.

There's an organic thing that happens when people are all together, and I think that creates a different feeling. When you think of the music that came from those iconic studios, you can't deny the chemistry factor. But I'm getting ready to record a couple songs for a vocalist in Austria, and since it's impractical to fly me out to Austria, I will get the digital tracks sent out to her. There are some advantages to the file-sharing approach.

MENZIE: Your techniques are very developed, so if we could just touch on a few of the practice disciplines in your routine. I'm sure you are no stranger to long practice sessions.

SCHEILA GONZALEZ: A lot of the intense multihour practice sessions were in the practice rooms at college. I would go until two or three in the morning when I was preparing for the end-of-semester juries. That musical foundation absolutely has to be there, and you do have to put in the hours over the years to get to a certain proficiency level. That's just part of the deal. What's the old saying? "Luck is where opportunity, skill, and preparation meet."

Taking something, slowing it down, transcribing it, and committing it to memory is a process. When you transcribe it, you begin to own it and internalize it. There's going to be passages that are very simple, but other passages are going to be finger twisters or tongue twisters. Sheer repetition at a slow tempo is going to get it done, and then I suggest practicing backing up a few more measures, that lead into the tough section, and then playing a few measures past it. That approach has always worked for me. Make it into an eight-bar phrase, connect the dots through the eight-bar phrase, then take sixteen bars; build it out to where it's a whole passage, and eventually, you get it up to tempo and play it along with the original recording.

If you're trying to emulate a specific artist, listen to the recording for all the different inflections and nuances because music is always more than the written notes. It's the articulations, it's the dynamics, it's the breath. How much of an accent is there? All of these things start to build this cluster of notes on a page into the music that you wish to express. And it just takes hours and hours. The first thing for me is to familiarize myself with the sound of the music. Gary Pratt, the great bassist and jazz professor at Cal State, used to say, "If you can sing it, you can play it."

And even some of those wacky Zappa lines—I know I was not singing them perfectly on pitch, because they're so angular and intervallic, and there's such leaps in them. But once I hear it, once I really hear it, then I say to myself, "Oh, here are the notes. That's what that jump sounds like. That's where I'm supposed to land."

If there is a recording, get the recording. If it's a jazz song and it has lyrics, learn the lyrics and what the song is about. Sometimes they're corny, cheesy old lyrics, and sometimes the lyrics came after the song, but if it's a standard, like an American songbook standard, then learn those lyrics and how they tell the story.

MENZIE: Let's talk about your husband, James Santiago, and his role with Voodoo Labs. James is a spectacular guitarist!

SCHEILA GONZALEZ: James started as a player but always had a fascination for gear and studying great tone. So he bridged the gap between playing music and going into the music-products industry. He had a trio in the Central Valley of Northern California, and people from *Guitar Player* magazine heard his playing and could tell he had an ear for tones. So around the time he was nineteen, they asked him to come in and review gear for them, and his name started to get out a little bit. This led to a career in product development and marketing, but most recently, he's the vice president at Voodoo Labs. It's product developing and such, and he continues to do sound design for other companies as a consultant. He's a guy that wears many hats. He also finds time to write for film and TV and commercials, and he has a voracious appetite for the recording process, so he just continues to research and play on the engineering side of things. He also still plays music with some other gifted musicians.

MENZIE: Do you get to work much with James?

Chapter 5

Scheila Gonzalez: I do, but I wish we had the opportunity to perform together more often. Like I said, his tone is ridiculous. I think he's an incredible musician, incredibly melodic in his soloing and [in] his compositions. We play together with Joe Travers and Friends, and we've also shared the stage with Zappa Plays Zappa. Dweezil invited him to sit in on quite a few shows while we were doing the Roxy tour.

Menzie: I have heard his compositions. The tune "Sleepies Lullaby," with Jimmy Johnson playing bass, Joe Travers on drums, and Derek Sherinian on keys, is four minutes of bliss for anyone who loves great tone.

Scheila Gonzalez: James is a very, very gifted person and a jack of so many trades. He's got a skill set that I don't think anyone else could match.

Menzie: Zappa Plays Zappa won a Grammy for their rendition of "Peaches en Regalia," and there is an amazing video of the band playing it, which features Steve Vai and Napoleon Murphy Brock. That video certainly shows how hard you work when the band plays live. Will you share a bit about the Grammy moment?

Scheila Gonzalez: I feel really grateful for that moment. On the business side of things, there's a lot of politics behind the Grammys, and they can be given or not given for many reasons. They can also be valued or not valued for many reasons, and you can have opinions about the state of music today and who received a Grammy and what a Grammy really means. On the logistical front, it's a wonderful resume piece. Just being able to put that on a resume may mean that a door opens that may not have otherwise, or maybe your resume floats to the top of the pile.

On the personal side of things, I will say that it meant a great deal in that Zappa Plays Zappa works so hard to achieve such a high level of accuracy and spirit in the performance of Frank's music, to recreate it, and [to] bring to life this music that needs to be heard again. So the idea that we received [the Grammy Award] for Best Rock Instrumental Performance and that we received the highest honor the industry could give us for our performance of an incredible Frank Zappa song is a huge deal. I'm very proud of that, just knowing that [I] and everybody else in that group worked so hard. I walk into our rehearsal studio space and see the statue there, and I'm still dumbfounded. It's just a beautiful recognition.

MENZIE: I would like to wrap with a discussion on the prominence of women instrumentalists in the music industry. How do you see the roles shifting in today's music industry? Are there more opportunities now?

SCHEILA GONZALEZ: There have always been lots of women vocalists, pianists, flute players, and string players in orchestras, and there have been certain areas where women have been more prevalent over the years, but now it has definitely started to shift. We are experiencing less resistance than in the past. The resistance today stems more from the question, How good [of] a musician are you?

Now you've got Beyoncé and her all-female band, and you've got Sherrie Maricle and the DIVA Jazz Orchestra. Both are examples of incredible bands full of incredible people—full of incredible musicians that happen to be female. I personally feel incredibly grateful that I haven't really encountered any glass ceilings, and I am keenly aware that I stand on the shoulders of women [who] have had to fight to be seen as equals, to be seen as capable, to not be dismissed or discounted as "just a girl" even before she's gotten her instrument out. Sherrie Maricle wanted to start on trumpet, but she was told women didn't play trumpet, so she switched to clarinet and then eventually to drums. I think her playing settles that argument. There is no shame in being beautiful, glamorous, or sexy—and that applies to both male and female musicians! Because if you want to dress or portray yourself a certain way, and you can bring the goods in with your musicianship, then bring it, and wear what you like. It's about being genuine.

Be who you are, and be your best. Let your craft speak for you.

Chapter 6

Welcome to the Jungle

If you are seeking to make music your livelihood, the best advice I could ever give you is to think of starting your career as if you are starting a small business—because that is exactly what you are doing.

At this point, you must no longer think only as a musician but also as a businessperson because, once you make the big decision, the game changes. From that moment forward, you are a professional, and it's down to business.

If you have done your homework, you understand going in that the process is arduous, and while it is possible to succeed, it is not for the faint of heart. There are many different paths. You are the difference in the equation.

Being successful on your instrument is one thing. Having a successful career is quite another. For now let's assume you have your art in check—because you already know your art is your superpower. So let's start with a few basic business questions:

How do I create and sustain an acceptable income so I have the funds to grow my career?

In the beginning is it better to have a dependable job outside of the arts, or is it best to try to create income with my music from the start?

As a young musician, it's a demanding task to generate enough income quickly. In the beginning you may have to work two or more jobs while making time for your practicing, your composing, learning music, booking gigs, and handling promotions, along with other distractions, like managing your social media and maintaining your professional presence.

Remember: in the beginning, it's just you. You are literally a "one-man band" with two hands, one mind, infinite tasks, and a big vision.

Some young musicians elect to take a job in a second career field to supplement their income, perhaps working in the restaurant industry or driving for Uber. Many prefer this route, while others make side money playing cover music or making themselves available for pick-up gigs. Some young artists find a lane quickly by helping others get their projects moving in the right direction, and before they know it, their networks spread like poison ivy.

The bottom line is that as you develop your career path, you need to eat, so a side hustle is usually a necessary reality.

Some rising artists feel that their legitimacy is compromised if they do anything other than make and play music for a living while they are working for their turn on the "big ride." In today's music industry, however, there are many more opportunities for side hustles, and multitasking has become more normalized. But you can't have this discussion without addressing time management and priorities. All side hustles and distractions eat up your most cherished asset—*time*.

If a side hustle enables you to eat and pay bills, taking that route is no crime. Often, it is a healthy decision, but there is just one catch: it means you have to be even better at time management. It's no secret that playing music every day is the key to performance excellence, and it also helps in expanding your relationship with creativity. Successful musicians perform, practice, and make time for writing. Consider whatever competes for your time, and make sure you manage your priorities productively. Find what works for you, and if you find a particular approach that keeps you relaxed and creative while also paying your bills, then so much the better. Just always remember the trick is to create content, improve your skill sets, widen your knowledge, and grow into the artist and musician you know yourself to be.

We are talking about embarking on a journey down an unpaved road with rock slides around every bend. I am one to believe the term *rock star* should be awarded to anyone brave enough to attempt the feat.

These next paragraphs include a few things to remember and strategies to embrace when entering the fast lane of a professional music career.

Embracing a Musician's Mindset

The creative and the organizational minds are very different in personality.

Being both a creative and having the additional responsibilities of running and maintaining a successful business model involves two completely different mind-sets. You need to feed both beasts. Simply put, there will be times where business matters dictate policy, and your sense of executive skills must lead the way. There are other times where solitude is necessary for your creativity to rise and express itself. Lastly, your artistic skill sets must never rust.

Creatives thrive when they are open to the moment. Your best creative tool is spontaneity. Creativity is the lead vocal, business is the harmony, and there is an art to understanding both.

The rules of business run on a separate track comprised of negotiations, deadlines, demands, and expectations. The stress from burdensome business matters chokes off creative flow. The goal for the creative, then, is fighting to remain open.

Embrace the work ethic of a champion, not a superstar.

Plan on getting your hands dirty. Plan on doing more creative "lifting" than others might be willing to offer. If they work as hard or harder than you, then you have met a member of your tribe! Keep them near you—fellow tribesmen are rare, so show them appreciation and respect. You will receive it in return. A simple civility can change the trajectory of your career.

Make the work ethic of a champion your standard! Make it your true-north marker. Maintain that work ethic your entire professional life.

Remember your standards. If you lead, others may follow. Business is, in a nutshell, leadership.

Turn down the outside opinions. Control your personal headspace.

Once you really start going for it, there will be advice gurus on every corner, and some of them might be close friends. They mean no harm; they truly believe they are helping. Because the advice is generally unsolicited, however, it tends to gunk up the works. Multiply that by everybody who thinks they know what you should do, and you have now arrived at white noise. My advice is to filter outside opinions, and become friends with your inner voice. Take your inner voice on a hike or to the country. Learn to trust your gut, but watch what you put into your head. Don't contribute to the distractions. Spend time focusing on your dream. In fact, spend a lot of time focusing on your dream.

Embrace the process of directing your destiny.

I believe that the best protection anyone has in the music business is owning the content. If you don't write and create original content, then you are left with fewer lanes as a performing musician. However, if you are not a writer, your next best lane is to develop an original voice on your instrument.

All mediums of expression are instruments. I consider a mixing console an instrument. I consider the art of visual performance an instrument. I don't care if you play the kitchen sink—be creative and find your voice.

If you're not a writer, then create style and content wherever you express your creativity. Who's the best in that particular lane? Set that as the standard to meet, then redefine and aim to surpass that standard, no matter how challenging a goal that is.

Navigating your career is like being on an interstate. There are multiple lanes, exits, destinations, good and bad drivers, and people driving at varying speeds with different agendas. Some people let you in their lane, and some cut you off. Your language and behavior change accordingly. The difference between driving in LA and Nashville is very similar to those regions' music scenes. Each is slightly crazy and unpredictable in their own way!

If you love the ride, put the top down, and enjoy every second of it. But if by chance there's an accident ahead and a long backup, make sure you know the side roads. Understand that you can always change lanes.

The quality of your music-business "driving" skills greatly affects the experience of your trip.

The quality of both your creative and business skills greatly affects the experience of your career.

Always remember Jimi's question: Are you experienced?

Chapter 7

Chuck Rainey

CHUCK RAINEY IS A NAME EVERY MUSICIAN NEEDS TO KNOW—NOT JUST every bass player but every musician. His bass work and contributions to the music business are legendary, and his discography is staggering. Chuck has contributed to more major artists' records than can possibly be listed here, but I suggest the reader look up his discography, as well as research every name and style of music mentioned in this interview. Chuck's work ranges from Marvin Gaye to Steely Dan and the Queen of Soul herself, Aretha Franklin. He is a true music legend, a world class musician, and one of the nicest people you could ever know.

INTERVIEW

MENZIE: I'm really excited about having this opportunity to catch up with you. I know musicians everywhere will gain great insights and get good takeaways from all the amazing work you've done and unique experiences that you've encountered in your career. So let's jump in and talk Chuck Rainey.

CHUCK RAINEY: It sounds like a wonderful plan.

MENZIE: You've enjoyed a tremendous career in the music business, and you are known among your peers as a legendary studio musician. The studio is an environment that requires patience and creativity, alertness, and the wisdom of knowing both what to play and what not to play. You and John Anthony Martinez have written a book called *The Tune of Success*.

Let's start with your book and your intention in helping young musicians understand the music business. My first question [is as follows]: What do you think of the current state of the music industry, both the good and the bad? What's your takeaway for young musicians regarding the state of the music business?

Chuck Rainey: Well, I don't focus on the bad parts, because there's a bad part in every decade of the industry. But the good part is it's a productive time in the music business. Electronics and technologies have created new categories and have made things a lot easier for people that aren't necessarily skilled as playing musicians. Technology can be a tool that brings out talent in people. I did a job for a friend of mine [whom] I've known since he was a young child. His dad and I were very close friends, and he knows a little bit about music because his dad was a great writer and a great musician. But at the same time, he has no specific playing talent as a musician per se. He did, however, have a talent with deejay equipment, and he was skilled at sampling. He had a keyboard, and he was able to put things together to where he was successful. It was a rap project that he asked me to play on, which was my first one, and he wanted a bass line played over a preprogrammed track. He had played certain parts on the keyboard, and some of those parts sounded like they could be bass lines or guitar parts. Basically, I was there to open up ideas for the bass lines. What I did was fool around and play the bass the way I felt best fit the music and tracks, and around that idea, he was able to put together a lot of different things that worked.

I would think that today, people who don't necessarily have the musical skills to be a playing musician may have talents in other areas, like with equipment and software that [is] available, and enable them to have a creative path to record tracks, cut, paste, copy, sample, and stuff like that.

But for a playing musician, the true challenge today is the same as it ever was, and it goes across the board and all the way back to before I started playing. You still have to deal with the industry—the social aspect of it, the political aspects of it. They still have to deal with the stresses and social environment that they're in, but they are successful. So success to me is someone who has a talent in the arts to do something and make it work. For example, back in the day when [I'd] started playing, we didn't have some of the gadgets or the electronics or social media to help us. We were focused more on being musicians. Now you don't have to be a great musician in order to do something successful.

MENZIE: Certainly, the mediums have changed. But you believe that the industry is still strong and inviting to young people who are willing to work hard and [that they will] perhaps even have some new advantages from technology and social media and the like?

CHUCK RAINEY: True, I think that today's musicians are doing very well. Of course, now—and I'm being honest with you—the music today is a little bit different. I came up in jazz, pop, and R&B, and nowadays, it's harder to name the styles of music. At one time, there were only eighteen categories for Grammys. Now there's 124, so there continues to be an evolving fusion of styles. Even I use a sound on a sound pedal every now and again because that's what's happening. You've got Michael Manring, [who] represents a large group of bassists [who] in particular do solo performances with loop pedals and electronics, and they're very successful, whereas I came up playing with a band. The guitar player, piano player, and drummer have a lot to do with how I think and how I play. Over the years those things have gotten established in my head, and very little is going to change with those seven notes that are flattened or sharpened. Through experience you learn to play from what you hear and from what your habit is, so I'm able to get by just being a bass player from memory and from experience. I'm still an old-fashioned player who wants to play with a band because they feed me, they feed my soul when I play.

MENZIE: Yes, it's chemistry.

CHUCK RAINEY: Although it's different, I have no problem with today's music or music business—none at all.

MENZIE: What would be your most important advice to those seeking the role of a professional musician today if they were to come up to you and ask how they can make it in the music industry?

CHUCK RAINEY: Well, number one [is] I would think that young people need to understand that experience is grounding and the best platform for musicians and artists and producers to become successful. You can't just wake up in the morning and want to be a producer or want to be a musician. You have to go and do what you think you want to do as a specialty in the environment in which it is done. Because, along the way, you also learn what not to do. You also learn how to be socially present and politically present and astute in both areas. I am talking specifically about the politics of business.

What I'm talking about are the experiences that come from watching the ego. Everybody has an ego. You have to have an ego in order to play, but sometimes the ego gets out of hand. With social media, everybody wants to be a star or to be known, and it doesn't happen that way even in today's music business.

Back in the day I loved to play, and it was that way with all the musicians I came up with. We just loved to play the instruments, and there was complete reverence for it. A lot of people today want to make immediate money, but that's not the way I came up. There were a lot of times when I didn't make any money, even when I was promised money. But the love of playing the bass kept me focused. And, of course, [with] loving to do anything, you do it well. And the more you do it, the more you love it. So I would advise musicians to seek every opportunity to gain as much hands-on experience as possible, and at the same time, appreciate and respect the experience. You can't ignore social media because it is very prevalent as a marketing tool in today's music scene. However, at the same time, you have to really understand that there is no substitute for real, hands-on experience.

Another helpful tip for musicians to realize is what worked on Monday may not be the right approach on Friday, because circumstances and people change. You may play a gig or a session on Monday, but come Friday, even though the same people are involved, you may have to change or adjust some things that you are doing in order to make the same things work. And that comes without a word; you just got to do what you gotta do. It's an instinct that you develop. The more you work around other top professionals, the more you recognize these things without having

Chapter 7

to describe a formula for what to do or what not to do. You simply begin to *feel* what to say and what not to say. It's like a conversation.

Great musicians understand it's really all about the art of listening. Today it seems like everybody wants to do the talking and hold the floor. There's a time to just lay back and listen. A lot of rising musicians do not listen well. They listen to respond verbally, as opposed to listening to find out something. Especially when someone else has the idea. You have to listen to the idea before you start wanting to respond with your opinion. The goal should be to satisfy the people [who] hire you or who may hire you or that you're working with.

Now, of course, if it's your project, you have to be responsible for who you hire and for what's going on, but I do find [there's] one thing about today's newer musicians: [that] they have the tendency to feel empowered and that they're really full of a lot of ego. Social media has everyone thinking that they can be a star, and that's not the case at all.

MENZIE: I have read that you practice yoga and teach meditation. So for those who want to make the music business their livelihood and who will need productive ways to ground and focus, will you delve into the importance of these centering practices and how they've helped you?

CHUCK RAINEY: I'm a Hatha yoga student, and I find it's a good way to maintain overall healthiness. I've had my ups and downs with my health, so I try and make health a priority. My wife is a yoga instructor, and she's one of my teachers. But I mainly work with and teach meditation.

I find that there are many people, younger and older, who are so caught up in thinking and praying and wishing and trying to achieve something that they don't give their mind or themselves time to be quiet for a second. Most people don't make time to practice stillness, and I believe it's important because in being still, you allow for insights that you might not discover otherwise.

I've spent the last twelve years of my life learning how to meditate and getting accredited to teach meditation. I find that morning is a good time for me to meditate, and I don't think about anything other than following my breath. And it quiets me; it quiets my body. Then when I finish and begin my day, I am starting the day peacefully, as opposed to being aggravated by thought or by trying to accomplish something before I am centered.

I am a believer in meditation, but musicians have to really work at it because, man, it's hard for a musician to be quiet—because our art is so involved in doing something and trying to create something.

People are into different disciplines, like Herbie Hancock and Wayne Shorter are into Buddhism, where they chant, which gives them a different kind of feel. There are a lot of disciplines available, and we try to find what works best for us. After spending a couple years involved in it, I chose to return to the disciplines that have worked best for me. Now I do enjoy Hatha yoga a lot, and I do meditate daily, and I try and get my students to be aware of the benefits that centering practices offer. I believe it helps you stay healthy, young, and vital, [as well as] able to be energetic. Of course, my first introduction into centering was as a student of the bass.

MENZIE: At what age did you start to explore the disciplines of meditation and yoga? Obviously, they've helped you; were you young when you found that out?

CHUCK RAINEY: I was around sixty when I began to listen to certain speakers. My teachers in meditation and yoga were from a Hindu and Buddhist faction. I came up in the Pentecostal Church, but as I got older, I began to hear and read about people like Paramahansa Yogananda (*Autobiography of a Yogi*) and those types of Hindu philosophers and speakers. I've always been interested in any religion, and I've been through a lot of them off and on, and I don't mind saying that coming out of a Christian background. So I developed a natural curiosity about religions like Hinduism and Buddhism.

MENZIE: How has all this helped you in music?

CHUCK RAINEY: Over time these practices taught me patience and to truly listen, and that really helped me because a lot of artists have difficulty expressing exactly what they mean or what they want you to do with the music. One way to become a good listener is to put yourself in a frame of mind where you strive to understand what the artist that you are working for needs from you, a skill I developed as I advanced in my career. You learn to accept the fact that a lot of famous people are not able to clearly explain to the band what they want, because they don't play your instrument, so they don't really know. But the ego has them acting like they think they know; however, the music has to be done and it has to be successful.

Walter Becker and Donald Fagen from Steely Dan were two of those people who were mainly introverts, not really social people. So [with] explaining something to a bass player or a guitar player, you have to know how and what to say or what not to say if you want something played a certain way—and not show ego when you're doing it.

Walter Becker never came to me with a bass in his hands, saying, "Try this," or "Can you do that?" but he always suggested something for me to play. Sometimes you would see both Becker and Fagen musing over whether they liked it or not. If they were dissatisfied, you knew that there's something they're looking for that they can't explain. But the more and more you listen to them and the more you go through the motions with them, you begin to see what they mean and what they want. Sometimes you come up with stuff that they don't think they want but... end up liking.

It always helped that I was someone they liked. They liked me, and I liked them because I loved the music, and when I love the music, I am very easy to get along with because I want to please. I did want to please; I still do want to please. So the key is just listening to someone. It's hard to be a good listener if your ego is not checked.

MENZIE: What are other awarenesses rising musicians should truly consider?

CHUCK RAINEY: Well, as hard as it may be to hear, it's also true that everyone can't always do what they think they want to do unless they understand the necessary preparation it takes. A lot of people want to choose this profession, or they want to choose that profession, but they don't always research the skill sets they may need, or they don't have the correct mind-set. Let's say they want to be a policeman or a teacher or a bass player. A lot of people just want to be who they see on social media or who they hear, but they don't realize the work that goes into that thought. A young bass player who's been playing for six months immediately wants to be a Stanley Clarke or a Chuck Rainey, Lee Sklar or Nate East, and they don't realize that we went through a good six, seven, eight, or ten years of experiencing what to do. There's a whole lot under the surface, and people only see the tip of the iceberg. For example, in my career, they don't always see what's beyond the water level, which is a mountain of disappointments and learning through experiences, along with successes and failures. But you become a better musician because of all of those experiences.

I came up in music at a time when producers said, "No, Chuck, don't do that—that's too much," or whatever the case may be. And the ego says, "Well I think that's cool," but the ego has nothing to do with the person who hired me and what they want me to do. In order to make a living, you have to play stuff that you don't think should go down. But who am I at twenty-three years old to tell someone like . . . Quincy Jones [that] this isn't going to work or [that] I want to do this? I have to treat him like I did my father and listen to what he's saying and do what the part is—even if I think it's dumb, or I don't think it works that well. But when it becomes a hit, I realize it isn't all about the bass, it's about the overall song. Musicians also have to realize that people hire people [whom] they like or they can work with.

MENZIE: Let's talk a bit about some music. I personally think you are the king of bridges. The way that you will treat a tune by just enhancing parts with a touch of excitement at the bridge or the chorus is so musical. So will you talk about how you approach bridges versus choruses?

CHUCK RAINEY: Growing up and listening to organized or pop music, [I found] every song has a verse, then it has a bridge or a chorus, whatever they want to call it. But the bridge of the song, or the chorus of a song, is just a little different. You're supposed to raise the level or draw the attention of the listener a little bit differently. With me, over time, it became a natural way of doing it. When you get to the bridge of a song, the lyric is usually different, or you play the hook a little differently than the verses—that way, the listener understands there is a different emphasis. I would just naturally enhance the energy. It's important to understand that it's not supposed to happen out of the range of what the feel of the song is, but I am always doing something different by adding nuances to what I'm already doing so that the bridge or the chorus of the song feels a little different because most bridges and choruses—that's the hook of the song. Over the years you hone in on your approach and refine your technique. I touch on different techniques, like slides or slurs, or play something just a little different, perhaps a different rhythm, or add a little something to what I'm already playing. That's what the listener remembers. This is an approach that I learned from coming up through the doo-wop era. They understood that the bridge of the song is usually where the hook is and that's where something is supposed to be a little bit different. So I've always tried to do that when I play, especially when I'm playing to a chord sheet.

Menzie: The Flamingos, The Platters, Little Anthony and the Imperials—the quality of music in the doo-wop era was completely unique, especially the voices.

Chuck Rainey: Yes, it was.

Menzie: So [with] drums being my instrument, I'm drawn to the subtle rhythm nuances that you do that lift the energy of the songs. Those subtleties make the songs more dimensional, more exciting.

Chuck Rainey: If I weren't a bass player, I would probably be a drummer. I play as much rhythm as I can over as few notes as I can so that my part doesn't get in the way of the guitar player, but I still create a good feel. And I do lean on the drummer. I've always stood on the shoulders of great drummers. I've had the pleasure to play with some of the best drummers in our business, and [they've given] me many ideas for rhythms. Of course, working with great players, you learn to watch out for the trap of overplaying. I've learned how not to overplay, and that came through experience. At least a third of my career work has been overdubbing bass parts; say, maybe a player just played too many notes, or their notes weren't clear enough, or the tone didn't work well. I would be hired to overdub the parts and fix the trouble spots. Another technique I use is to play with the very tip of my two fingers on my right hand; the very tip is where I get a little bit of nail so that the notes are clear. Recording engineers like that because it keeps parts from sounding muddy, and it makes their job easier.

MENZIE: Let's tackle one more rhythm-section topic that you don't often hear much about: pulsing. Bass players and drummers have a different role here than other instrumentalists do. Will you talk about how you approach timekeeping?

CHUCK RAINEY: I do focus on the energy of the part, but I don't push time, and I don't pull time. I've heard a lot about some rhythm sections—for example, Ray Brown and Grady Tate. Ray played ahead of the beat, and Grady played behind the beat, so together it sounded as one.

I try to play exactly in the center of the time, and then I strive to match the energy of whatever the drummer is doing. I really don't push or play back on anything; as a matter of fact, I follow. I have been sitting on the backs of some very good drummers most of my career, and the ones that have unique talent—for example, Steve Gadd, Bernard Purdie, James Gadson, or Harvey Mason—they all have their styles, but they know exactly where the time is and how to make the pocket feel right. Back in the day, there were no click tracks, but today in organized music, they have click tracks especially for overdubs, and they make sure everything is lined up. So I prefer to have a click track in my ear, too, and like I said, if I weren't a bass player, I'd be a drummer. Wherever the drummer feels the time, that's what I want to do as well. Coming up in New York in particular, [I found] the time had to be right on, so I learned to marry the drummer for the duration of the time I am working with them. I like to talk about Bernard Purdie because he's a genius at playing a specific drumbeat, but underneath are these nuances of rhythm. Steve Gadd does the same thing; he incorporates little, soft nuances that help support the groove, and I do hear them, and I act that way as a bass player. I sort of act as a drummer with a little tick here, a little clip to make it feel different. Again, it's just a matter of adding these nuances. It makes it groove.

MENZIE: You have worked with some of the most iconic artists and producers in the music industry. How about I give you a name, and you share thoughts with the readers? Let's start with Quincy Jones.

CHUCK RAINEY: Well, he's the master. There's no one else in the industry who has had so many hits in so many different music genres. He's always been smart in the way he and his team have hired musicians that work well together. One thing about this industry—sometimes people like Quincy (or anybody who has had tremendous success), they naturally become somewhat isolated, so they are not as exposed to the new talent developing outside the community that they're in. Surrounding yourself with a great team helps keep you in the know. Because as you get to be a higher-profile producer or artist, you don't get to hang the way you used to, and you don't know who is doing well or who's using new innovations.

Quincy is a genius, and he's been very successful. He's a great friend, who always tried to socialize a lot, but he understood the politics of the business. He always had a contractor hire the players, so he never personally hired or fired anyone. He may hear of someone and ask about them, but he would probably not contact them directly. Someone on his team would do that. If you made everyone's life easier, then they developed a relationship with you.

MENZIE: Gary Katz. I know you've said in another interview that you got along well with Gary because he understood the interworking dynamics of the musicians; will you expound on that?

CHUCK RAINEY: Gary Katz represents a special kind of producer. For example, say, as a producer, you find out halfway through a session that the session is not working; Gary would get rid of somebody, and over a period of time, [he'd] developed his own trusted roster of musicians. And he would stay with those musicians. So in a case where someone gets run over by an elephant or something, he would have contacts who were smart musicians [and] who would fit nicely within the rhythm section he had already set for the date.

Gary had a unique sense, [which was] very similar to Joel Dorn at Atlantic, who was also very smart and did not overproduce the rhythm section. What Joel did was let the rhythm section play the idea of the music, and he just mainly told the artist if the song was too long or if it wasn't long enough, things along those lines. Joel was an ex-disk jockey from Philadelphia, so he had a feel for what people wanted to listen to.

But getting back to Gary—he is very, very good to work with in that he understands music; he's had so much experience with what works and what does not work and who gets along with whom. Gary Katz and Quincy Jones always had complete control over the artist, which a lot of producers don't have today.

But I always realized when I got a call from Warner Brothers or a Warner Brothers artist [that] the number one thing is the artist is going to sell records—because everybody at Warner Brothers, from Russ Titelman to Gary Katz (any of those producers on the A&R [artists and repertoire] staff), they are there because they have been very, very successful.

When you're are asked to work on songs like "Eye to Eye" (Chaka Khan) or "Chuck E's in Love" (Rickie Lee Jones) or any Steely Dan material, you're hired for two weeks, and they're paying good money, and they're going to do the same thing when they start to market the record. Whenever someone established hires me, since they're already successful, I know that the record is going to be heard. That's why I always take the job seriously, and I do the best that I can because my job is adding to the success of that record. That, of course, leads to other musicians hiring me, and other producers then hire me for being on a successful record.

That's one thing, too, that young people don't realize. It's not wise to argue with people who are successful when you're not—unless they ask you for your opinion. Perhaps "argue" is too strong a word, but you don't disagree with things. If you disagree, then you better start producing your own records because you never know what the idea is between the artist and the producer, and you simply don't argue with an orchestrator, even if it's seems wrong.

Chapter 7

The producer cannot afford to have someone not understand why they have been hired as a producer. Quincy never told anybody what to play; he just had a contractor hire people who would work well together. Quincy never wrote anything for me to play, because the true idea of a studio player is someone you hire because they have the necessary skills and experience. Quincy's not a bass player, so he doesn't write bass parts; he's not a drummer, so he doesn't write drum parts, nor is he a guitar player or a piano player. He's an orchestrator.

When I receive a call from Quincy or his contractor or any producer, my job is to play a part that can be thought of as though they wrote it. Even if I make up or compose the part, it has to be an integral working part rather than just rambling bass notes. I always construct my parts with the understanding that the job of the bass line on a record has to be founded on the drumbeat that's consistent through the whole record. It's the same understanding with the bass line integrating with the guitar parts: you make it sound like it was written by the composer. And I noticed, over time, a lot of people recognized that I'm really good at that. I learned that during my career, so producers trusted that I could always make something work for the song and make their life easier. Donny Hathaway used to complain to me; he and I were good social friends, and I'd worked with him a whole lot, and he did not agree with me or other people sitting down and making up parts for Quincy, because he felt that should have been Quincy's job. The reason Donny took issue was [that] when Donny wrote, produced, or arranged a song, he wrote out the bass line. Not only did he write it out, he could also play it, whereas Quincy does not play these instruments, so he didn't do that. Quincy's whole approach was looked at differently.

Another perk from working well with Gary was that Gary basically used "his guys," and if you were one of his guys during his tenure in music, that also [made] you successful.

MENZIE: Let's delve deeper into Donny Hathaway.

CHUCK RAINEY: Wow! Donny—what a great artist to talk about. Donny had his ways because he suffered from depression, but he was an absolutely perfect musician. And being . . . [friends] of his, we all embraced Donny because he was such a good musician.

As a producer, writer, or musician, he never asked you to do something that did not work. Outside of music, he had his mind-set problems, which was a personal thing with him, but we put up with it because—this [was] Donny Hathaway. When he wrote a chart, it was going to work because he [could] play the instrument that he wrote for you to play. He [could] play it and play it very well. I valued my association with Donny immensely. He was a great musician, a great musician.

A unique gift Donny had was absolute pitch, as did the great pianist and studio musician Richard Tee (Richard Tee Committee and the Gadd Gang). There's a difference between absolute, perfect, and relative pitch. Nowadays, of course, we have tuners, and when you can't use a tuner, you do it the old-fashioned way and tune to a piano. Take an artist like James Taylor, for example. James has a unique approach on how he tunes, but my point is it can be very difficult for artists like Donny Hathaway or Richard Tee to work with musicians who have relative pitch because they have absolute pitch. I know a lot of very successful musicians [who], when they're told that they're flat or sharp, they disagree, but I am quick to realize when Richard Tee says [to] bring up the E string, I know that he's right and there is something he's hearing that I'm not hearing. So I will check my part and check my tuning, while at the same time, showing professional courtesy. I was social with Donny and Quincy and sometimes with Gary Katz. I always got along with them, and there were a lot of parties, a lot of fun and games, and that also helps too.

MENZIE: You did a lot of work with Gary, right?

CHUCK RAINEY: A lot of work. He was comfortable with me, and I was comfortable with him. Of course, I'm always comfortable with someone who is giving me a job.

MENZIE: What I find interesting about your Steely Dan experience is they were known to be very particular, whether they were always right or not or whether they always understood how to graciously express to others what they wanted. So the fact that you had as much work with them as you did [and] knowing that there were three folks at the helm—Katz, Becker, and Fagen—that speaks volumes to how well you work with people, because they were not known to be easy to work for.

CHUCK RAINEY: No, they weren't; as a matter of fact, it's sad that a lot of musicians did not care for them, because the musicians had to do things over and over again and they did not know why. Whereas to me, it was a new point for them to take. And the good news was that created plenty of opportunity for me to work, and because of that my wife is happy, the bank is happy, and the baby is happy.

Humorously, there was always the extra perk of respect among your peers, like when I . . . see fellow musicians, [and they] ask how I'm doing. I say, "I'm working with Katz and Steely Dan," and the reaction [is] always "Whoa!" It's always nice to be known for doing something that has been that successful.

With Steely Dan and Katz—it was a job, number one, and it's a job that [I've] liked because I do it very well. You're doing what people ask you to do, and they're paying you double scale and putting your name on the map. You know, I was just talking to Donald yesterday about the days with him and that it's so sad that Walter is not with us anymore.

MENZIE: I agree, [it is] a huge loss.

CHUCK RAINEY: Out of all the stuff I have been successful with in my career, playing with Steely Dan has put me in a place where I never would have been otherwise. Every time they come to Dallas, I get invited, and I go. The last time they were here, they brought me up onstage and thanked me for being involved. They had a lot of musicians play with them, but they were not often aired. [It is] like on *Aja*—every song on *Aja* represented an album for the players they hired; there's a different drummer on each track, but what a lot of people don't know is that each drummer played the whole album, and then they just chose what they felt was going to work best for the album.

MENZIE: Wow, that I did not know. You're killing me with that. I had no idea!

CHUCK RAINEY: There were seven drummers that did the whole album. It's my guess that they were also vetting musicians for the road band. I think Walter and Donald were aware that they were planning to go out on tour, so they were preparing and making sure that when they toured with a band, they had excellent musicians to choose from. They were probably right to do that because most of us were making really good money at home doing studio work, so why [would we] go out on the road? So, as it was, Steely Dan would have a road band that may be a different lineup of musicians than the studio musicians they used to cut their final tracks.

But getting along with the people who hire you is very important, especially if you love the music. Everything I played with Steely Dan I just loved. It was the same way with Rickie Lee Jones. She was not always easy to get along with either. As a matter of fact, there were times she was not cool at all.

MENZIE: I've heard that story. I wanted to talk about three drummers that are three of my very favorites, and you've worked with all three—Jeff Porcaro, Steve Gadd, and Bernard Purdie. Let's start with Jeff because he was a very different drummer, and of course, like Walter Becker, everybody misses him tremendously. What was it like working with Jeff?

CHUCK RAINEY: He was an excellent drummer. I had already been involved with his dad, Joe Porcaro, in a lot of films by Oliver Nelson, Quincy, and Pat Williams. His dad was an excellent drummer, and Jeff was also an excellent drummer.

MENZIE: Joe Porcaro has written several great drum books. My favorite is *Joe Porcaro's Drum Set Method*. In interviews Jeff often talked about the effect of that book on his playing. All the rhythms are handwritten. The book is a work of art.

CHUCK RAINEY: Well, Jeff was fun to get along with. Everybody loved him. What people may not know is that he was responsible for me slapping the bass on "Peg" on the bridge. We had done a lot of sessions together where I had done slap bass, but Donald did not like slapping. Donald didn't want me to slap, but Jeff insisted that I slap. By the way, Jeff was on a lot of those Dan recordings after the original band; he was the original drummer to do the demos or to do the first track.

Toto had been signed to Warner Brothers at the same time Steely Dan was, and Warner Brothers no longer wanted Jeff to be aired or associated with Steely Dan. They wanted him associated with Toto, but he was still friends with Walter and Donald, and he was always the first drummer to play just about everything, especially on the demos.

So Jeff was the one that suggested I slap on "Peg," but at first, I had to do it discreetly. I would kind of turn to the side, and I put a sound baffle in the way so they couldn't see my hands, because I knew Donald didn't want it. The style of recording at the time was to have the rhythm section play, and Jeff would lay down a drum track for a reference. That way, there was a guide for [whomever] the eventual drummer would be. We always did all our sessions from noon to six [in the evening], and we would lay down two songs. They would track a song and listen back and isolate drums first, then bass, [and so forth]. While they were just listening to the drums, I did the slap on the chorus of "Peg" because I agreed with Jeff and thought that it would work, and Jeff pushed me to do it.

I always trusted Jeff because we were very good friends, and we played a lot of sessions together outside of Steely Dan. I experimented with the slap, and when they finally got to isolate me for that take, I . . . played the bridge with my fingers. Donald said, "That sounds different." And Jeff said, "Because he was slapping it." So that's when Fagen said, "Let's hear the slap again." And that time, they really listened to it and kept it in.

Jeff was a really good friend, very well loved and respected by everyone. I loved him dearly. I've got quite a few stories about Jeff. Jeff was the first-call drummer in Hollywood, and he was the original drummer on Rickie Lee Jones's *Pirates* album. The problem was she had no idea who her rhythm section was. She would arrive from Chicago and had no idea or caring of who we were. And when Jeff started the session the very first day, Rickie was not really easygoing and had a tendency to be rude when you were talking with her, whether she meant it or not—definitely challenging to work with. Of course, she was an excellent songwriter. She reminded me of Laura Nyro. Laura was a very good friend, a very nice lady, great songwriter.

But in the session, Rickie's music would get faster, then it would slow down, and she kept referring to Jeff during that first session as "Drummer": "Drummer, you got to do this, and you got to do that." She kept talking down to him, and that was very unnecessary as well as unproductive. So, after the first session, he quit. That's how Steve Gadd got involved. She was not showing any respect to Jeff—a world-class, first-call drummer. So he didn't have to deal with it; therefore, he left because he didn't like her. You know, when you have enough money and enough clients, you have a tendency to walk away from situations that are unhealthy and that you don't care for.

MENZIE: That story is especially interesting because Gadd's work on "Chuck E's in Love" is masterful. He sits a signature lick in before the later verse that has been the topic of many a drum discussion. It's fun to know the backstory, because it almost never happened.

For me, as a drummer, when I look at Purdie or Gadd or Porcaro, they are all very different, but they are all extraordinary masters. So you played with Gadd on Steely Dan's *Aja,* but I'm assuming you also did a lot of other session work with him as well?

CHUCK RAINEY: Absolutely. Back in New York, I did a lot of sessions with Steve. As a matter of fact, Steve Gadd replaced Bernard Purdie at Atlantic Records. Bernard was the main drummer that Atlantic used, but at that time, Bernard was a bit hard for Atlantic to handle, so Steve Gadd ended up showing up rather than Bernard. Steve Gadd is one of the greatest drummers that ever lived. He can play any kind of music, he listens very well, and he plays very, very well. We called Steve "Junior"; I believe Gordon Edwards [bassist for Stuff] started that nickname because Gadd played for Stuff but wasn't a member of the band yet. Gadd is a world-class drummer and very easy to get along with—a really cool guy.

Chapter 7

Menzie: It sounds like your philosophies for the studio were the same as far as working for the song, as opposed to working for yourself. Am I right on that?

Chuck Rainey: You're absolutely right. You got to get the job done, especially if you're working for a company, like Atlantic or Warner Brothers, that's very successful with the records that they're putting out. And Steve was perfect in doing so. I really value my experiences with him.

Menzie: I'm a huge fan of Gadd's, and I'm also a huge fan of Bernard's. You and Bernard did a lot with Aretha Franklin together, right? You are both on her songs "Rock Steady" and "Until You Come Back to Me."

Chuck Rainey: Right. In a way Bernard and I came up together in New York. When we had both just arrived in New York, we did live club gigs together all the time. If I were a drummer, I would play just like him. Bernard is very much a part of my career. As a matter of fact, today I'm doing three overdubs for Bernard. He's doing a new record, and today I'm going into the studio to do an overdub for the songs. Bernard is very gifted and very special, and he is a very large part of my success. We have played together a million times.

Menzie: That's a hard combo to beat. You worked with Aretha; what was it like working with the Queen of Soul?

Chuck Rainey: Before I got to work for Aretha, I was a huge fan of Shirley Caesar, "the First Lady of Gospel Music," and so I was drawn to that style of singer. Aretha had a record called "Won't Be Long," and she was young and powerful and full of energy. When I first heard her voice on that record, it just stunned me. I just knew her name, but when I got to New York, the famous deejay Frankie Crocker played her song "I Ain't Never Loved a Man the Way I Loved You," and Frankie made that record into a hit in New York. He played it four or five times every morning on the air and, man, that feel was so special. I just fell in love with her voice immediately.

Later on, as I got embedded into the New York society, I had become close with King Curtis, and he was my introduction to Aretha.

I did a CBS recording with Aretha, too, because I was one of the first-call players in New York, and when she was signed to CBS, I was contracted to do an album with her. But it was when she signed with Atlantic that King Curtis made sure that I was involved. Jerry Wexler was the producer, and at that time, King Curtis was the head of the A&R staff for Atlantic, so I did a lot of recordings with Aretha.

Aretha was very sweet and quiet. She reminded me a lot of Mahalia Jackson, who was very quiet and ladylike. Aretha was always very good to me. It's funny, when I worked for her, we never really spoke that often. We spoke more in the last twenty years than [in] the three years I spent with her. Every time I hear any negative stuff about her, I will stand up for her because I never experienced anything negative about Aretha—nothing. She is truly the Queen of Soul.

Menzie: We were talking about King Curtis. You guys had a unique experience that few can claim. Tell me about opening for the 1965 Beatles tour.

Chuck Rainey: Well, King Curtis was also someone very special and another very smart musician. A lot of side musicians don't know how to go about getting work, and they may not understand the importance of visibility, but King Curtis did, and the promoters for the 1965 Beatles tour had heard of King Curtis. We had no idea who the Beatles were. In Manhattan there were billboards that said the Beatles were coming, and we all thought they were talking about some kind of insect. When King Curtis said that we were going to get away from New York for a couple weeks, . . . our pay would go up a bit, and it was going to be a quick tour with the Beatles, we didn't question it, because a gig is a gig. King Curtis was a good father; he never took us into situations that were negative, and it was all very exciting. Up to the point of our rehearsals at Shea Stadium with the acts supporting that tour, I had never been in front of more than two or three thousand people at one time. That was when I was playing in a band with Jackie Wilson, and he would do a large audience with two or three thousand people. Back in that day, that was a lot of people. But here the rehearsal was at Shea Stadium with at least fifty thousand people at the rehearsal and sound check. That was mind-boggling, for sure.

Then, of course, when we did the actual gig, it was something very special. They had over one hundred thousand people at Shea Stadium, mostly screaming girls. And still we were not aware [of] who the Beatles were, other than they were at these very huge venues in eleven or twelve cities across the United States. And we had never been in front of that many people at all, ever.

We opened the show and then played behind the first six acts before the Beatles came on. We still had never really been able to listen to them. We found out over time that they were immensely popular and obviously famous, but because we were a working part of the show, we didn't get the chance to listen to them until we got to the Cow Palace in San Francisco. At the Cow Palace, there were so many people that we couldn't get to our dressing room after we'd finished. So we had the chance to stand offstage and listen to them. I found them to be exceptionally talented. They were perfectly in harmony, and the crowd was enjoying them so much. In fact, the crowd was berserk—screaming unbelievably.

They were doing a lot of songs by American artists, like the Isley Brothers. And a lot of people today think that the Beatles had the first recording of "Twist and Shout"; they don't realize the Isley Brothers had a hit with it years before. That tour was great, magical. Even as I describe it now, the hair on the back of my neck is standing up because it was such a completely incredible experience. They flew all the musicians by private plane into every city, and in every city that we went to, when the plane landed, there were thousands of people waiting. So we had police escorts to the hotel and back.

That was their second tour of the states. They had done a tour the year before, so this was at the height of Beatlemania. Other than Elvis, I don't think anything like that has ever happened or will happen again. Incredible!

MENZIE: I agree. I don't know if it's possible that we will ever see an event like that again. Let's talk about Roberta Flack. Donny Hathaway was also involved with that project, correct?

CHUCK RAINEY: Oh, bless her heart. Yeah, I think that first record was Roberta Flack and Donny Hathaway. Donny didn't think too kindly of that, but that was the heyday of male/female duos, like Brook Benton and Dinah Washington, duos like that. I think the duo was Jerry Wexler's suggestion. Donny Hathaway wrote and arranged that whole record. Roberta was Donny's choral instructor at Howard University, which seemed to create a sort of tension, and I felt that they didn't get along extremely well. Roberta could sometimes come across as kind of pushy and, of course, the same for Donny. With Donny, you never knew exactly what he was thinking outside of the music. But the music that came out of those sessions was certainly great.

MENZIE: The tune "Gone Away" is incredible.

CHUCK RAINEY: Oh, beautiful! [Chuck sings the bass line.] He's a master. That song is in E flat, and he wrote the bass part in E. So I tuned my bass down to E flat, and that way all my strings would ring—because Donny wanted to hear the E-flat ring like an open E string when I played it. As a matter of fact, there were sections of that song that were difficult to play, and I remember him coming behind me and putting his arms around me and putting his hands on my bass and saying, "Chuck, look at it like this." Donny was showing me how to finger what he had written. Master musician. Master.

MENZIE: Well, speaking of master musicians, you are very knowledgeable on the style and work of James Jamerson. Let's talk a bit about that.

CHUCK RAINEY: Absolutely. Jamerson was the hallmark of Motown. I don't care what the song was, the bass line is what identified every record that he played on—every record. But Jamerson had his demons, alcohol mostly, and so he was also a different kind of person outside of the music. A lot of people have very negative things to say about him, which I do understand. But Jamerson's background was upright bass, and upright bass players weren't known to play a lot of notes unless it was jazz. When I came to New York, I really began to study Motown because there were a lot of opportunities to work if you played and knew the Motown music. So in order to live and pay my rent, I learned all the Motown songs, and I became really involved with the style of the bass lines. Of course, I would always add my stuff to it and make it my own.

Jamerson played very simply yet with a lot of rhythm. He was very inspirational to all of us who played the electric bass in pop music. He claimed he was the father of the electric bass. Of course, he was wrong [laughs], but when it comes to pop music, he was and will always remain the founding father of the electric bass.

Berry Gordy was so successful with all those magnificent artists, and Jamerson played 90 percent of the bass lines on all those Motown songs. So as a working musician, if you wanted to eat, you had to learn those songs, and when learning those songs, you kind of learned how Jamerson played. Even today, when I hear his isolated parts, the bass parts are specifically clear, and they are very sound and very musical!

Jamerson was definitely the father of electric bass in pop music, and anytime somebody has something negative to say about his outside life, I stop them because he was always very kind to me. I first met him before I left Cleveland, Ohio, for New York, and although he never truly admitted he knew who I was, he was always very kind to me. He was known to be aloof, and it's no secret that he was the kind of guy who only liked to read his own press. He never talked much. As a matter of fact, all the stuff that's been said about Jamerson or that's been written about him was mostly said by someone else.

No one ever really got too much chance to ask him anything, because he never talked to anybody. That's the kind of person that he was. He did not like to do interviews. He was just a bit different. You know alcohol does not help us. It doesn't help anybody socially.

MENZIE: I always tell rising musicians to be aware of the pitfalls of distractions, and I define distractions as anything that interferes with personal well-being or that stifles success.

CHUCK RAINEY: Yeah, I call it baggage—because, like with Jamerson, once he got to LA, nobody hired him, not even Motown, because his reputation outside of the music preceded him.

When Motown was in Detroit, there were fewer bassists available to hire, other than perhaps Bob Babbitt and Michael Henderson, so Jamerson was king in Detroit. But when Motown moved to LA, there was more than one good bass player. There were hundreds of them. So he did not work much in Hollywood at all. People still hired him here and there, of course, but he was no longer a regular bass player for Motown. People like me, Carol Kaye, or the great Wilton Felder—a lot of people in LA wanted to work for Motown.

MENZIE: Motown seemed to be a very different beast once they moved from Detroit to LA.

CHUCK RAINEY: Things did change a bit, especially with bass players and guitar players and some other musicians. One big change was [that] the crew Motown used in Detroit did not move to LA, so the new crew was not a part of the old Motown staff. Things were handled differently with the musicians, and the vibe just had a different feel.

MENZIE: Do you think that had something to do with Motown's popularity fading? I mean Motown in Detroit was almost unstoppable, but in LA, things seemed to shift, and it seems then that Motown began to fade a little bit.

CHUCK RAINEY: I don't think they faded at first. Motown added a lot of new and different artists to their roster. Both studios were always working, and the studios operated twenty-four hours a day. They were still very well-known, an iconic brand, and a lot of us were making good money when we did work for Motown.

So I don't think moving to LA hurt Motown at all. But Berry Gordy began to get into other things, movies and such, and began to move away from what had been the roots of Motown. That's always risky. Motown started to lose its identity, and I think that's when the decline began. Eventually, Berry sold the company.

Chapter 7

MENZIE: So talk to me for a second about LA back in the day and LA now. I have young musicians come to me and ask, "Where do you go for work?" You have LA, New York, Nashville, New Orleans, Austin, etcetera, and I noticed you work a lot in Japan. Do you want to talk about those different markets and what you think makes them special?

CHUCK RAINEY: It's just a different time, and all the music scenes have the same thing happening to them. It's both good and bad. When I left LA in 1982, things were beginning to truly change because everybody had the ability to have their own studio. Warner Brothers studios closed, Atlantic studios closed, and artists and musicians were not going to the major studios—especially for demo work—because they had their own studios in their houses with their own technology. But when I left New York, I didn't leave for the same reason [I'd] left LA. I left New York because Quincy Jones took me to LA.

When I left LA, the work—especially at the major studios—was not happening as much. So Nashville was the place where everyone was going. They were making mostly country music there, and my background was pop, R&B, and jazz. Although Nashville is a place known as the Country Music Capital of the World, it's much more than that.

MENZIE: Much more, especially today. But I don't know if musicians realize how much R&B and other styles have seeped into Nashville's music scene. Certainly, Americana has a huge presence in Nashville. And it is absolutely the songwriters' town.

CHUCK RAINEY: I think the music scenes changed because now you [can] have your own studio. In Japan they still embrace the old, traditional way of having recording studios. Tokyo is a city a lot like New York, very congested and all the flats are small. The recording studios are small. So putting a studio in your flat in Tokyo is like trying to do it in New York. Everybody lives in a box in New York. There's no place for a studio except for [in the homes of] some people who have places with more than one or two rooms. There were some people who did have their own studios in New York, but music was still traditional, and just as it is today, in Tokyo, there were a lot of sessions available. Again, it depends on who you are.

There is a benefit to name recognition. I always told everybody that I have been on many recordings because my name was a habit, not because I am the best. I think I'm a good bass player, but I got a lot of jobs because my name was a habit. When people would say, "Who should we get on bass?" they [were] thinking of people you see all the time or hear about all the time. It's the same way in Tokyo because they go for name value. They hire the people who are going to draw attention to their product or to the album. So I love working there because you get paid, and I'm treated very well because of the value of my name. In the United States, people also want me because they may not be attracted to the way I play, but they are attracted to my name's value on the record.

MENZIE: You do a lot now with education, and you give back so graciously. Your book *The Tune of Success* [*Unmask Your Genius*] is out now, and it's a great book. You and John Anthony Martinez are doing some fun clinics, and I know you've also been a guest speaker on some of Dom Famularo's *The Sessions* panels. Will you discuss what you're doing with music education?

CHUCK RAINEY: John and I started a company a few years ago, and we got a little patron support. As you know, John is an excellent drummer—smart and well educated. He's originally from New York, so John and I get along very well, and what we're trying to do is add a different type of contribution to what we're already doing in the music business. Over the last three years, we've done a lot of clinics at magnet art schools and also worked with *The Sessions* panels. I've been invited to be a panelist for Dom and *The Sessions* panels three or four times. Dom always has amazing panelists. John and I did one or two together.

MENZIE: *The Sessions* interviews are great, and I was lucky to catch one with Vinnie Colaiuta, Steve Vai, and Paul Matthew Quin at winter NAMM. [It was] great stuff.

Chapter 7

Chuck Rainey: John and I host the same kind of sessions about twice a year, and we have a panel where we discuss certain earmarks [of] the industry. We just add that to what we are doing outside [of] being working players. I especially enjoy talking to young people and catching them before they get set in their ways. We do it because it is of value to a younger player [who] doesn't have the years of experience but . . . still needs the inside scoop. I've done a lot of clinics and seminars all through Europe. I've spoken at Berklee several times and held clinics there. I just left the University of Arkansas at Little Rock last week, where I did a two-day music seminar.

Basically, what John and I do is we talk to forums, and we have all types of people there—engineers, producers, singers, guitar players, horn players, bassists, and drummers—although my favorite format is [the] smaller, specific groups. These universities and high schools, they have an idea of what they would like us to do, so the format is adjusted to their specific needs. But it's all about the education. John is trying to finish his MBA at Oxford. He's a hard worker and burning the candle at both ends because Oxford is on the other side of the world, but it's a noted school. John attended Colgate first and then Berklee. So he does have a lot to say when it comes to playing and preparing for a career. He is passionate and wants to help young people to get a proper grasp of the way things have changed. We want to help younger players prepare and be ready for the challenges of a career in music. We don't want them to fall into the trap of thinking they are prepared when they are not.

Menzie: Many times young musicians don't realize they're not completely prepared for the extraordinary demands of a music career. That's the true purpose of this book—to be an aide to those who want to learn, and not everyone can afford the expensive music schools.

Chuck Rainey: It's important [that] if someone wants to be a producer, . . . they know every aspect of producing. They need to understand the role of the engineer, they need to know sound and how it works, they need good people skills, and they should be a good musician. They should also study music history. This is not an industry for the naive. Not enough people truly study sound and its properties.

MENZIE: I see a lot of sound people lately [who] are mixing with their eyes, and I find that very strange. They love dials, faders, and lights, but they mix from graphs, not their ears. They don't anticipate the music or observe the stage for what is really going on musically. I grew up with sound people who, if you got in their way, . . . didn't hesitate to tell you what you needed to adjust or understand. They were great at their craft and expected you to be the same. They taught me how to respect the principles of sound and performance.

CHUCK RAINEY: You just used one of my favorite phrases—people are listening with their eyes. I was a guest at Gerald Veasley's Bass Bootcamp, and I noticed that more than half of the participants were dressed in the way you would see a rock act dress on TV. Image plays a big role in the arts, and it's important, but you never want to put the cart before the horse. We were there to focus on the music. People are listening with their eyes and looking with their ears. That's about the only negative thing I would say about today's musicians.

MENZIE: The most encouraging thing I've seen recently was at the Pilgrimage Music Festival in Franklin, Tennessee. I was absolutely knocked out by how good the musicians were. Everybody was playing and with very minimal gadgetry—just honest, heartfelt music, [with] lots of ears and lots of sensitivity. Nashville is a town where that's their heritage, so they take it seriously. That's one trend I am excited to see stay in vogue, and I believe the fad of great ears may be returning.

CHUCK RAINEY: Oh yeah. You are absolutely right. Bernard Ighner wrote a song about it: "Everything Must Change." I believe somewhere around one hundred artists have recorded that song to date, including Quincy, George Benson, and the great James Ingram.

MENZIE: I can only guess how many of those sessions had Chuck Rainey on bass. You are a gift, sir.

CHAPTER 7

NOTE
According to a speech by Salesforce CEO Mark Benioff, the last gift Steve Jobs gave to his family and friends came in a brown box, and it was Yogananda's *Autobiography of a Yogi* with a note that read, "Actualize Yourself!"

Chapter 8

Vision

Vision—the one idea that's uniquely yours.

As the music world continually changes, you are well served to remember one important constant—the word *vision*. Vision is the unique differentiator.

Most developing musicians, entrepreneurs, and artists have some understanding of visualization and its power. The greats seem to come by it naturally, but it is a tool for all to use. Elvis Presley believed strongly in the power of will and vision, and he honored them.

Let's start by looking at the difference between the words *vision* and *visualization*. By definition, vision is the ability to clearly see an idea in your mind. It seems easy in description, but in truth, getting strong enough clarity and belief behind an idea is what begins to separate the successful from the struggling musicians and entrepreneurs.

We never want to admit that there is any doubt in what we believe, but creatives are always riddled with doubt. Anxiety is a natural by-product of high-level creative output. Step one is getting truly clear on what you intend your journey to be. Most young participants entering the music business don't truly comprehend what that means; it means you have to be willing to risk everything for the success of your idea. When everything is coming down around you, you must be able to remain unflappable. It means living with no safety net and still being comfortable. It is no different for those in business.

It means never giving away your dignity, even when you can't make rent. You understand that your vision is your capital. This clarity allows you to walk with a straight back and a head held high—no arrogance, you simply walk with dignity.

It means you need to strive to see with the same quality of vision as someone like John Lennon, Yo-Yo Ma, Duke Ellington, Bob Dylan, or Joni Mitchell, to name a very few. It makes no difference what specialty you pursue, because vision pertains to all disciplines. It is the power to see your path clearly and with conviction, ahead of its physical manifestation—the path of expression, the path of who *you* are. That is your vision.

You must understand your purpose first, and you must be crystal clear on who *you* are. Then develop the necessary mechanics and, of course, your specialized knowledge. If it is a quality vision you seek for your future, it will manifest because it is undeniable. You just have to clearly set your intention to make it so.

Let's not kid ourselves: if you envision less, you manifest less. And if you have a quality vision for a magnificent future but a lousy work ethic, you've got nothing. Successful musicians have a great work ethic; mediocre musicians have a typical work ethic. There is nothing typical about success, and there is certainly nothing typical about any form of mastery.

Let's now examine the word *visualization*: visualization is a practice.

It is the act of energizing and focusing thought to aid manifestation of a belief. Practicing visualization techniques helps musicians, artists, and entrepreneurs gain clarity and understand what they want their future to look like.

It is believing to see instead of seeing to believe.

The practice of visualization raises your energy levels and helps align and focus purpose, thereby breathing life into your vision. It is a practice that adds intention to your inner beliefs.

The practice is simple: in your mind, you clearly see the future you want to experience. The quality of your future comes down to the quality of your vision and the level of conviction you have in it, and practicing that future through consistent visualization techniques gives you better clarity on the outcome you seek. The rest is just executing the details consistently.

Vision

In business, before you can bring a successful model to life, you must understand the purpose behind your vision and then maintain the quality that you wish to express.

Vision is the one idea that is uniquely yours! Market conditions will vary, but successful entrepreneurs, musicians, and performing artists protect their visions and strive continually to find productive ways to express them. Your vision simply becomes a way of life.

CHAPTER 9

Rick Barker

RICK BARKER IS PRESIDENT AND CEO OF THE *MUSIC INDUSTRY BLUEprint* in Nashville, Tennessee. He is a manager, entrepreneur, author, and consultant focusing on recent changes in the music business. Barker has seen and done more than most, and he has had the unique experience of being an early personal manager of Taylor Swift, from 2006 to 2008. He has worked for Big Machine Records and continues as a consultant. Rick's podcast, the *Music Industry Blueprint*, is a gold mine for anyone wanting to learn about social media trends and effective strategies for growing a fan base. To quote Scott Borchetta, "He knows how to identify opportunity."

INTERVIEW

MENZIE: When it comes to getting things done, you appear to be a no-nonsense guy. You believe that artists are responsible for the successes and failures of their careers. What's the most common success "problem" you encounter?

RICK BARKER: The most common problem is that people are unrealistic in their expectations. Just the other day, I was in a conversation with a guy, and I asked, "Why are we the only industry that thinks that everyone can just go straight to the pros?" Why should some kid, just because he's been told that he's great and thinks that he should be on the radio, expect a record deal? He has never even built a business model, much less achieved a functioning level of success. So where is the evidence, and why should a label or a manager be expected to take a risk?

MENZIE: It's not only about knowing your musical craft but also about knowing the craft of professionalism. Most musicians figure out their craft from whatever influences they have access to, but they don't always study the business aspects of the music industry or how it works.

Let's bring the reader up to speed on your background and experience so they can understand your voice.

RICK BARKER: My whole goal in life was to be a radio disk jockey. I never had any plans to work for a record company or manage an artist, because radio was what I wanted to do. I have always loved music, but I wasn't disciplined enough to master playing it. So I ended up getting on the radio in 1989 in Los Angeles, as an intern at KISS FM.

Two years later, I got the opportunity to be a deejay in Santa Barbara. At that time Santa Barbara had this really cool music scene that was developing. I was on the local rock station, and we had something like nine bands from the region signed to major label deals—bands like Dishwalla, Toad the Wet Sprocket, and Ugly Kid Joe. All those bands were coming out of the Santa Barbara scene, and I was asked to be the executive producer on a CD compilation called *Santa Barbara Unsigned Heroes*.

At the time, I knew very little about the music industry, but as the executive producer, I immediately learned that my most important job was to get the thing paid for. I was in charge of all the business decisions that got the project completed. After you raise the money, you earn this cool little executive producer credit on the record. And that was really my first time promoting bands.

In 2001 I was asked to build a country radio station. I grew up in Alabama and knew who Johnny Cash was, so I figured I was as qualified as anybody else, but that was right after 9/11. The world was in a different place, and the music reflected that change. Prior to 9/11 I was the guy who used to make fun of country music—you know, play a country song backwards, and you get your wife back, your truck back, your dog back. I was that guy until 9/11 changed things. I started honestly hearing the stories

Chapter 9

behind these songs, and the lyrics were very powerful. People were truly listening [to] songs like Alan Jackson's "Where Were You?"; Darryl Worley's "Have You Forgotten?"; Toby Keith's "My List"; and Jo Dee Messina's "Bring on the Rain." I began to understand the gut and grit behind modern country music. We built the radio station, and it was awesome.

Record companies started introducing me to artists, and I started asking a lot of questions. I came to find out that the music industry wasn't as smart as I thought it was. I would ask questions like "When are you guys bringing these artists by?" and "Why don't we ever get to hear them or see them play? Why don't they ever do an in-studio radio show or a small venue show to promote [themselves]?" And the answers were odd to me: "They don't have enough material." You've signed a band to a record deal who can't play thirty minutes? That's not a great business model. There's no business investment in the artist. It's just kind of rolling the dice on this one song.

Then the next comment they would make was "Well, no one will show up, because no one knows who they are." I said, "No, that's wrong, because if I play their music and I tell my audiences how excited I am about this band and that they're going to play a local show, people will show up!"

My thought was "Let me make the station or a local venue a destination point where musicians and artists would be encouraged to just drop in." And that's what put me on the radar of some of these record companies—because it worked.

MENZIE: Your radio concept sounds sort of like . . . *Tiny Desk [Concerts]* or what Howard Stern is doing now.

RICK BARKER: I thought that if a band promoting their new record was going to be out here anyway, they might as well play. And it wasn't full-band shows. It was more intimate. This was just an artist and a guitar or a guitar player—unplugged and very low cost. At the same time, I was also getting a chance to know the artist and develop a rapport. And they had a chance to get personal with the listeners and build up their following.

We started launching bands like Sugarland and Little Big Town, who went on to win multiple Grammys. That's when Scott Borchetta approached me and said, "I'm starting this record company right now with this fifteen-year-old girl no one's ever heard of named Taylor Swift and also this regional artist out of Texas named Jack Ingram. I would love for you to come work for me at Big Machine Records." And that's how I ended up getting into the record side of things.

MENZIE: How did you meet Scott?

RICK BARKER: Scott found out there was this kid in Santa Barbara [who] would play new music. He knew I didn't care if [he or she] was a superstar or just an average Joe. We also had this weird little connection—we both went to Sylmar High School, and I ran into him and reintroduced myself at the ACM [Academy of Country Music] Awards at the Universal Amphitheater. He looked like Prince, wearing this purple suit and this big, tight, permed curly hair. He always loved the fact that I was different, and a lot of his acts started coming through on my tour. That's how we got to know each other.

MENZIE: It's funny how the seeds of casual beginnings turn out to be so fruitful.

RICK BARKER: Agreed. It speaks to another thing I try to tell people: you never know who's watching or what they can do for you. You don't have to have a PhD in music business to help people. People will seek you out if you can solve their problems.

In the music industry, we get paid "per done," not for "almost." There're so many great starters out there, but not a lot of great finishers. And that's what our superstars are—finishers. Our superstars understand the business better. They put together a team that keeps them accountable, and simply put, they finish.

MENZIE: In your videos you focus a lot on work ethic, and I believe that work ethic is the 1 percent factor that, when added to talent, makes the difference in success.

Chapter 9

Rick Barker: Today talent is expected, and quality is expected. Most rising artists today simply turn on the internet, and they're off to the races. Hello YouTube!

And here's the current model: you create it, and no matter the medium, if you put it out in the world, the market decides. If it's good, the world says it's good, not a manager, not a label president. It's always the fans.

So if you become a business-minded musician (or as I humorously call it, a capitalist musician), you put it out into the world, and if it's working, they're buying it. If it's not working, they're not buying it. There should be no more asking for permission. People ask me every day if I will listen to this or that song and tell [them] what I think about it. But in truth, I'm not your audience, and to succeed, you must know who your target audience really is.

Menzie: Your take on the importance of an artist's fan base is spot on. I've heard for years that [the] fan base determines whether or not a label will look at you. I believe your quote was "Your fan-base trumps radio; the radio is not your savior—fans are your savior." It's knowing the value of marketing that gets this done.

Rick Barker: I did a great interview with a buddy of mine, J. R. Schumann, who's the program director at Sirius XM's *The Highway*.

I said, "All these people come to you wanting to be the Highway Find artist because they know exactly what it means for their career. We all know the music has to get your attention, but if it does, what's the next thing?" And J. R. says, "I want to see your business. It's called the music business!" That's what artists forget about.

For instance, let's say your song gets some radio attention, and we all say congratulations. People are loving your song, but when they put it on the radio, there's no deejay who tells them who you are. Your song was just passively played as a spin.

You've spent all this money to get on the radio, but nobody knows exactly who you are. Why? Because, generally, the first time somebody hears something passively, it just blends in. It takes about ten or twenty spins for someone to think, "That's the song! I've been hearing this song a lot! I've got to go find out who this is."

It's not instant, even if the radio station says your name. Maybe the listener goes to your website, and it's subpar—or worse, you don't have a website, or they Google you and get to your social media, and all you're doing to promote yourself is posting inappropriate pictures or showing what a ridiculous human being you are. None of that works, even if your music is good. That's what I want rising artists to focus on.

Unless you get your business set up properly, all the exposure in the world is not going to help you maintain a solid following. Record labels respond to that. Record companies, radio stations, [and] managers are all looking to invest in well-run small businesses. They are not looking to start small businesses.

Menzie: I find that many musicians are trying to develop their careers from an art-only perspective. While that's the most important aspect, there's much more to achieving success. A lot of artists still hold the old-school belief that overseeing the business aspect is an outside responsibility of a businessperson, not their responsibility.

Rick Barker: I tell people all the time that if all they want to do is make music, then make music! That's why you got into music in the first place. But if you want to start putting your music out into the world and you intend to start generating income and striving for a livelihood, then it's a business. And of course, there are different expectations that come with it being a business. First, you have to identify what success means to you.

You can put one of your songs up on Spotify or other platforms, but that's only a first step. Say [that] I want people to come to my shows. How do we find those people? Because now you have to go put your product in front of a consumer and get them to exchange with the product. Once you start to treat your music and performing like a business, it has a different set of rules, a different set of expectations. And trust me, in business, nobody cares about excuses, so you can save them. Because business success equals functionality.

Chapter 9

Menzie: Once you have succeeded at step one, [your] craft, then the next step happens, business. That has additional responsibilities. You now have to understand accounting, additional organization, dedication to details when you may not feel like being dedicated—because creativity lives in one house, and business matters live in another.

Once you have achieved some level of success, you may choose to have two or three people that take care of all of that, but in today's market, it isn't as easy as it was. And when you hand it off to someone else, you lose control.

Rick Barker: What's hard for rising artists and musicians to understand is that you are your first booking agent, you are your first manager, you are your first publisher, [and] you are your first record label.

I have this course called Record Label Ready. It's not [about] getting them ready for a record label but teaching them how to get their own record label ready. We review how you register your music and how you set up an LLC. Here [are] the places you need to get your music registered in order to be paid, and I explain the difference between an attorney and an entertainment attorney, etcetera. I help rising artists understand the difference between a manager and a business manager. We're really teaching them the business side of things.

The problem is that there is terrestrial radio and there's internet radio. Performance rights organizations are going to collect your performance royalties from radio, YouTube, and things like that. What they don't collect on is internet radio, which is Pandora [and] SiriusXM, so there is all this money [that's been] out there because people didn't check the box to collect on royalties. So you've got three years to come back in and get it, but it's crazy that people just don't know.

It changes all the time. We're trying to function in a nonfunctional business. The audience can consume your product for free, and your rewards are not proportional to the work that you put in. That is the truth the musician must understand—that what the people invest in is the relationship, not just the music. But the music opens the door to the relationship. That is what the consumer invests in, so that's what we're really focusing on right now.

Menzie: Most musicians are aware that the music industry is in a constant state of change, but they are not always aware of how that affects their individual role in the management and advancement of their careers. Musicians should look at business and marketing as part of the requirements of the new art form and integrate those aspects into their formulas, along with the mastering of music, so they can build themselves as a business commodity and sustain a lifetime career.

Rick Barker: Obviously, there are still superstars, but whether they are superstars or not, I believe it is the best time to be in the music business because, in today's music business, the artist is in charge.

Menzie: In your current work, *The Music Industry Blueprint Podcast*, you are offering powerful information and making tools accessible for rising artists.

Rick Barker: If you're good, you should never need to play the role of the starving artist. Because if you're a starving artist, there's no place for you in today's music business. The music industry has its own rules, mostly driven by radio, and it can be expensive for an artist to get their music that far. But it's possible because now the expense is less than it was, due to the DIY aspect. In today's music business, you can wake up in the morning, come up with a great idea for a song, create it, and then capture it digitally, and you can easily go a step further and put it into a DAW [Digital Audio Workstation], like Pro Tools, and tweak from there.

Menzie: But that's only part of getting your music out into the world. This is where the labels used to step in, but now so much more is on the shoulders of the artists.

Rick Barker: That's why the fan base discussion is so important. After the creative side has begun, you have to find ways to monetize your product in order to sustain any type of career in the arts. There is no room in this business for a "you owe me" attitude. No one subscribes to that kind of thinking, because talent is everywhere and very accessible. There is no room for a sense of entitlement. You also have to be creative in the business side of music.

As professionals, we should be building equity between us, and so every time I open my mouth, I'm building professional trust, and therefore, I'm selling. If I'm not asking for professional considerations right now, I'm earning the right to ask later. This is also good for the industry as a whole. It shouldn't offend you if I let you know I have a product, and I shouldn't be offended when you do the same. Music is a very symbiotic business.

MENZIE: Where did your path take you once you parted with Taylor?

RICK BARKER: I left Taylor in 2008, and that's when I started working with Sony as a consultant. It wasn't long before I started seeing a lot of stuff that made zero sense to me from the label's standpoint. It struck me as odd when the bazillionth dad showed up with [his] daughter in cowboy boots and [a] sundress, thinking that was the magic formula simply because [he] had a blank check for you to make [his] daughter the next Taylor Swift.

MENZIE: Taylor made everything look effortless, and that's never the case. Taylor has mad skills and is brilliantly creative.

RICK BARKER: Agreed. So I started doing some research online, typing things into YouTube like "How to get a record deal," "How to get a publishing deal," and even "How to find a manager." Although this was around 2011–2012, everything showing up was at least ten years old. No one was talking about the digital age; no one was talking about the internet.

I started doing more research, and since I had access, I tried learning from some of the best digital marketers in business. I researched names for my project, and *blueprint* was a very popular industry term. Everybody wants "the blueprint," so I typed in "Music Industry Blueprint." It was available, so I snagged it. Then I went on a URL-buying spree.

I realized that I had some good answers for many of the questions that people [were asking], but most people just didn't know what questions they should be asking.

MENZIE: Musicians spend so much time learning their craft that they inadvertently put off learning the business side of music. And while it takes a different mindset, you should at least learn the basic principles of generating an income without being dependent on someone else.

RICK BARKER: I was constantly asked, "What does it take to get a record deal?" And I would reply, "Let's not start at the record deal. Let's begin by developing a workable business model."

I was fortunate to have access to a lot of amazing people in the music industry, so I decided to put together a showcase that gave the artists unique visibility to music industry leaders and gave the industry bigwigs a chance to have an early look at qualified rising artists.

I covered all the costs of the music industry folks, and in return, I was given permission to film the event. Out of that idea, I began to catalog smaller segments, and I began to create courses. One thing led to another, and because of the response, I continued to develop my online courses. The plan began to reveal itself to me through [my] vetting the process of connecting both sides of the success discussion. I continued to create reliable content and began selling more online courses.

People asked, "How do I improve my social media accounts to be more effective, and how do I gain better visibility?" So I created a program called Social Media for Music. My intention was to keep the cost low so more musicians and artists could have access. And I kept creating multiple courses. Many people now had access to solid, dependable, and time-tested information.

The new model also gives me more personal independence. I am free to be more creative. Success no longer comes down to just getting the record deal or breaking a song and having it picked up by radio. Success is now many events braided together and benefiting many.

The most important thing for me was I didn't have to put my family's livelihood on the back of any one artist. If I do the job right, the success or failure falls directly on me. I began getting invitations to speak at events, and on average, there were probably two dozen people in the audiences who had already purchased my courses. Suddenly, I was able to meet and interact with clients personally.

I was also asked if I would consider managing again. I began to consider it, but this time, I wanted my approach to be based more on a per-case basis because I felt this model worked better for me. I took on roughly twelve artists, [whom] I would meet with a couple hours a week. I intentionally limited my client load to no more than twelve artists. That worked well, and things were good. But before I knew it, I found myself back into managing artists at labels and working at television shows, and I had unintentionally recreated the same format that [I'd] wanted to get away from before.

The odd thing was the demand for my digital business products was continuing to grow nicely. So last year, I decided to make that my first priority. I decided to scale back my personal management clients, and my new goal was to keep developing my digital materials first and foremost.

It turns out [that] cutting back the other demands on my time was the best decision. Now I am completely focused on the one format, and I've got a couple hundred people from all over the world [whom] I do weekly management sessions with. They can ask me their most important questions or the questions that are currently perplexing them about their career development.

They have direct access to me by email, or they can shoot me a text if they have a question that needs immediate attention. Because of the new format, the pricing is now something a developing artist can afford to justify as an expense.

MENZIE: That's really good news for rising artists.

RICK BARKER: This approach allows me the opportunity to help more people.

MENZIE: Yeah, it's a completely different model, but [it's] a model with great accessibility that serves many.

Rick Barker: There are different education paths for all of us. Attending a qualified music university has its own unique rewards, and the physical experience is part of that. But at the same time, the expense of a good music university is putting that opportunity out of most musicians' reach.

I feel it's time to offer alternatives that still bring viable and accessible education solutions, along with dependable professional information, to the working musicians. I am all about education, and I'm really about hard work. I also want to help DIY musicians stay current and stay relevant. I want people to get the right education for what's going on right now—and one that fits their budget.

Menzie: The cost of a great music school is becoming prohibitive. But that's also the goal of this book: providing exposure to trustworthy and dependable information to everyone.

Rick Barker: This book will absolutely help musicians, and I agree that the cost of a college education is becoming prohibitive, and I also think that's wrong. However, there is one thing to remember: a good university offers a wide berth of specialized degrees and, just as importantly, a chance to grow into who you are as a young adult. But it's also important that musicians understand that nothing replaces hard work, ingenuity, hustle, and networking, and that isn't cost prohibitive.

You go to college for the experience and the opportunities. Taylor was lucky in that she found that opportunity at a very young age. My daughter wants to be in the field of nursing, so she has to go to college because she needs additional education for that trade. Taylor was getting that experience from touring and doing shows. My son, on the other hand, he's going [to school] for a completely different reason. He needs to go learn how to be a young adult. That's a great and necessary opportunity.

If I wanted to be in the music business and live in Nashville and learn publishing or songwriting, Belmont would be at the top of my list. If I'm in a band, . . . I'm a rocker, or I dig jazz, then I'm going to Berklee. If I'm a classical musician, I'm going to go to Juilliard, USC [University of Southern California], or maybe the New England Conservatory. Every good university has its niche, and they all provide a great opportunity to grow and learn, but it ain't cheap.

MENZIE: Reputable universities are the right path for many, but it's also important to note there are other approaches. Hard work opens doors too.

RICK BARKER: Absolutely. You can buy industry people's time, you can seek internships—you can find any number of ways to start working in the industry. That's the part I try to have people understand, people who want a career in music but don't have the ability to attend a music college. I want them to understand there is always a way. You just have to want it badly enough.

In Nashville on Music Row, it's much harder to get an internship without being associated with one of the music universities. So a degree from MTSU [Middle Tennessee State University], Belmont, or Berklee will open doors for you, but if you want to be a manager, then go manage a band. If you want to be a booking agent, go book bands. If someone wants to spend four years at a music school, they should go there for the right reasons, like networking. But never let anyone tell you that you have to have a degree in order to be successful in the music business, because you don't.

That's what my book, *The $150,000 Music Degree*, is all about. It's gotten great reviews, and the information I write about on the music industry is very helpful and valuable.

MENZIE: I think the readers would really appreciate knowing what the experience of managing Taylor Swift was like for you. Will you share a bit about what it was like behind-the-scenes?

RICK BARKER: The Taylor situation was super simple. From twelve to sixteen years of age, all Taylor did was write music. She wasn't out playing, she wasn't out trying to win contests, [and] she wasn't old enough to go on *American Idol*. All she was doing was focusing on her music. So before we were to take her out on a big radio tour and release her single, Scott Borchetta suggested we take her out on the tour that [I'd] created, the National View Radio Tour. He thought it was a good way to teach her the business side of the music business. We thought it would help her develop as a performer. So she went on this radio tour, and we spent thirty days together, and it kind of changed both our lives! I wanted to teach; she wanted to learn. Taylor didn't have a manager at the time, so her family, being new to this type of crazy, was calling me every night, wanting to solve the world's problems.

Finally, I went to the record label, and I said they needed to get Taylor a dedicated manager because [her family was] wearing me out. I lived in California, and they were in Nashville, and there is a two-hour time difference. I had a brand-new baby at the time; this was my daddy time. I was bathing kids, and they wanted to fix anything they perceived as problems.

So they went out and met with all the management companies in Nashville, but the majority of those companies turned them down.

Some of the management companies didn't quite understand what was happening, and most were naive to the growing impact of the internet. So the next thing you know, I get a call from her dad saying, "Hey, Taylor has decided she wants you to be her manager."

I told him I didn't feel that I was qualified, and he said to me, "Look, for one—Taylor believes in you, and I know that you believe in her. She trusts you. You're not afraid to ask for help. If you don't know something, you're going to figure it out. Taylor and I believe you are the right choice."

Along the way I had made a lot of great relationships through the Nashville to You Radio Tour, and I was used to helping out other managers with their artists. Through developing that network, I had access to several great mentors [whom] I could go to and ask questions. So that's the story of how I got the management position with Taylor. When she said to me, "Rick, I want a gold record," I said, "Great! Let's go meet five hundred thousand people."

Managing Taylor quickly became an even greater whirlwind than I had anticipated because we focused so intensely on her meet and greets. Every time someone met Taylor, her fan base grew, so we knew it was a good strategy. I had never been a manager on the road, but we got on these tours, and it was go, go, go.

My book was called *The $150,000 Music Degree* because that's what my salary was. It's important to understand that most managers don't work off a salary; they work off a commission structure. But the salary structure ended up being a blessing because the label wanted my complete attention focused on Taylor and the building of her fan base. So the meet and greets were almost as important as her performing. They wanted to be able to build her the right way. I wish every manager was given that opportunity—we would have much better artists because of it.

All this stuff was going on, I was trying to keep up with Taylor's meteoric rise, and I realized, "I can't do it. I'm going to end up divorced. The kids aren't going to know their dad." I worked five more months with her, and by then, her ship was going in a definite direction with a powerful trajectory. I knew if I stayed on that ship, it would destroy me.

MENZIE: You're talking about the years 2007 and 2008. What's the difference in the industry then [versus] now? Would the model work today?

RICK BARKER: I think the industry still relies on touring and radio, but touring got wiped out in 2020, so the industry is in big trouble right now. The 360 deals that the labels were participating in were based on touring and merchandise sales.

MENZIE: For clarity, a 360 deal is a music industry contract that allows a record label to receive a percentage from all the earnings of a performer's or a band's activities.

RICK BARKER: Yes, the record labels went from splitting dollars to splitting pennies, so the recording industry itself is in a very different place. But the music business is also in a great place right now. According to *Forbes*, this is one of the first times that the independent musicians are making more money than those signed to labels. There's this transfer of power, and everything is based on the artist's relationships, period!

That's what I did with Taylor. I told her, "Go meet people, go spend time talking to fans, tell them how much you appreciate them. Invest in getting to know them."

Right now, with the ability to run Instagram and Facebook ads to target people anywhere in the world—this is such an amazing time for developing artists.

Menzie: I find that unique and great original music is a bit harder to find. The current trend is production seems to outrank songwriting, and style sometimes overrides content.

Rick Barker: Good won't cut it anymore, though. It's gotta be great, and you have to have the ability to show how great you are. One important key to success is [you] don't wait for people to find you. One of my mentors said to me, "If you have something that could change people's lives, it's your responsibility to find them. It's not their responsibility to find you."

That's why I have a podcast and put out weekly YouTube videos and post on social media multiple times a day. The goal is to have conversations.

Trust me, there are many different styles of people seeking professional resources. There is the "do it yourself" type and the "done with you, as a co-contributor" type. But it seems that everyone loves the "done for you" model. I believe the "done for you" model is the most dangerous.

I spend as much effort repelling the wrong person out of my world as I do attracting the right person into my world. I don't want people who think there's a magic pill, that just having access to me is going to change their lives. I wish I had that much power.

Menzie: I want to mention your podcast. It's done really well, and it's very informative. You cover a wealth of topics, touching on important information that all musicians, songwriters, and artists need to know. So let's touch on publishing and then discuss your formula for an artist's success.

You have a podcast interview with session player Rod Castro on episode 243 [MusicIndustryBlueprint.com]. You guys cover some important topics like publishing, cowriting credits, and the value of professional relationships.

Rick Barker: You have to get publishing right because if you don't get your music registered properly, you don't get paid. That's the bottom line. I send everybody to Songtrust.com. They have the most easily understood publishing guide. They also hold multiple webinars that help musicians grasp all that's involved with publishing. Folks should look them up and maybe start there and compare their services to the other big names.

Chapter 9

Menzie: It's important for new writers to understand the differences between the performing rights organizations (PROs) and where songwriters are protected and by whom. Services and fees vary, so writers definitely have to do their homework. There are a ton of good articles online and books that deep dive into the details. But you have to get that right and protect your creative property.

Rick Barker: Agreed. You also asked about my personal formula for success. It's pretty simple. It starts with the music. Without that, there's nothing to talk about. Then you gotta have the people—the fans—and they have to have a reason to want to engage with you. You have to give them opportunities to grow with you and spend money and support you. That's the simple version of "the formula." But here's the catch that most artists don't understand: you can't start by giving them opportunities to spend money on you before the relationship is built. That's what most artists do, and I think that's somewhat backwards. I'm all about building relationships. Fans are not just buying a song or record. They want an experience, and they want a good one.

And too often we're trying to "feed" or attract the wrong people. If you open up your hamburger stand in a town of vegetarians, it doesn't matter how good your burger is. I think a better idea is to identify who "your" people are. Then let's go figure out where they're hanging out, and let's get involved in the conversation together.

To touch back on publishing, I would always recommend you deeply do your homework because I'm not a publisher. I'm the management guy, the artist development guy, [and] the social media guy. So for the readers looking for solid advice on publishing, they are well served to look into a specialist that focuses specifically in that field.

Menzie: How would you describe the service that you offer?

Rick Barker: I'm a coach and a consultant. The work I do is based on personal consulting and mentorship, which is tailored specifically to each artist. I don't handle any day-to-day management, but I am coaching artists to understand what constitutes proactive management strategies.

One really important thing I do is help rising artists and musicians understand how the business aspects of the music business actually work.

I have clients [whom] I teach on a weekly basis, and they have direct access to me. I review effective practices, goal setting, accountability—all the big picture stuff. Musicians and folks from every aspect of the business hailing from thirty different countries engage, and we cover every genius you can think of.

We set a two-hour Zoom call, and my clients send me questions in advance as well as in real time. Issues that clients raise are addressed, and everyone hears the answers that resolve those issues. Then if clients have additional questions, I address those as they come up. We're having a one-on-one conversation in front of many people. Everyone is learning.

Menzie: It's a good format and certainly a fresh approach. I have no doubt you help a lot of folks avoid big pitfalls.

Rick Barker: Here's one reason why what I do is so important: the real problem that many rising artists face is that there's not a lot of money made at the beginning stages of a career, because everything is being set up. So affording management is a difficult challenge. Even if you are offered some kind of record deal, typically they offer you a back-end deal, and there's no guaranteed back end. It takes a ton of work to get an artist or band recognized and generate a strong following, a good fan base, and a reasonable source of income. All that's all done on the front end.

I let clients know that if and when they get signed to a record label, they're, for all intents and purposes, cash-strapped. Or worse, they are in debt. It takes at least a year to get the act set up and touring. That's why people can't easily find management: the money factor is so tight that they can't afford it. It's not like potential managers don't think the artists are talented. They do. It's just that there's little or no money to pay for a manager's services.

So in my presentation, I explain that once the music groundwork is completely done, now they can go pay someone. But in the meantime, here are the skills they need to have, and this is what they need to know how to do.

For me, it's about exchanging productive ideas. In the beginning phases, everyone needs to be able to manage themselves. You have to know how to protect yourself. And in the beginning, most acts don't have anything too taxing to manage. There's no label that they're having to deal with, there are no major contracts that they're having to look at. So half the time, they may wonder, Why [do] they need a manager? Why do they need someone to help give them more gigs? But that's a misunderstanding because that's the role of a booking agent. In California you can't be the agent and the manager. It's illegal, and when people learn things like that, they're surprised. You need to learn the business that you're trying to go into.

That's why the courses that I offer and teach are varied. One of the videos that I have talks about music-business lingo. In the video I explain all of the different terminologies that a rising artist will encounter and what they all mean. I walk people through every level of business development, depending on where someone is in their project's development.

I show them how to get their website functioning, [how to] incorporate videos, . . . how it needs to be understood that their website is their store, and how to build an email list. We teach them all these things.

And if you want to be a manager, the best thing you can do is go find a band that you believe in and that needs help. But you need to bring something to the table. Sometimes it's the awareness of what they don't know and what they need to know to succeed.

MENZIE: I want to weigh in here and let the readers know that your podcasts are very informative and designed to introduce musicians and artists to new approaches that should be considered. You also shed light on breaking trends that could be tomorrow's new thing. And it is very apparent on your podcast that you know how to look for developing trends. You are well trained in recognizing potential business opportunities, as well as truly understanding an artist's needs.

RICK BARKER: I appreciate that. My programs are varied because they are designed to help many different artists with differing needs. Generally speaking, I have four buckets of people that seek me out. Of course, because of my history, the first potential clients I attract are the parents of talented teens and young musicians, and in Nashville, that's a large group.

The second [group of] clients I attract are the talented artists under thirty whose ultimate target is landing a record deal. They're very entrepreneurial, and they understand the importance of knowing their stuff and how everything works. This is a resourceful group of artists, and, to say the least, they are very motivated.

I'm also approached by the artist [who is] over thirty who has a long history in music. They understand their prime has probably passed them by, but they have a big catalog of music and may still write. They want to know how to get their music into film and television or in front of other performers.

And the fourth bucket are the folks who love the music business but . . . choose not to take the artist route. They want to be the person behind-the-scenes [who] makes things happen. Obviously, because of my history in the music business, I am well equipped to help this group and guide them productively.

Menzie: People [who] work behind the scenes in music need as much guidance as the artists do. That role is tremendously important because they bring sanity and stability to the performers. The audiences genuinely have no idea how much work goes into making a show or performance come to life.

Rick Barker: We're in the business of "next." No matter what role you play in the industry, you have got to learn the business and how it works. And though it's a hard truth, you have to realize that nobody owes you anything and that nobody cares—until they do.

That's why it is so important to utilize your relationships with the loyal fans you already have.

Chapter 10

Study the Greats

WHEN YOU TACKLE A CAREER AS DEMANDING AS BEING A PROFESSIONAL musician, you need every possible advantage. Earning a living as a musician is more of a challenge than simply playing music—they are two entirely different realities.

If you are reading this book, you are striving to be a successful working musician or music professional. The smartest thing you can do, then, is *not* reinvent the wheel. In our case, we want to steal the wheels from the best and brightest musicians who have preceded us.

Most inquisitive musicians study some of the great artists who have preceded them. Extremely successful musicians, however, understand the benefits of studying every aspect of music history. This includes all of the great artists who have paved paths of unique success, not just the ones who play their instruments. A smart musician will intensely observe artists they admire; study great writers, great leaders, and great thinkers; and become totally immersed in the comprehension of success. I have included interviews with Secretary Riley and Belmont's Dr. Fisher for that very reason.

Another trick is to study the causes of failure. Without studying failure, you are overlooking the yin and yang of success. Think about it: name ten historically great musicians. Were any of their careers interrupted by destructive choices? In some cases the answer is yes, but not in every case. Those artists who succumbed to destructive lifestyles have left behind a road map for the rest of us to observe. These maps give us insight into the temptations encountered by working musicians and provide clues as to how we can avoid their devastating tolls.

When you study the great minds of the music business, you should make sure to include every aspect of the music business, not just performance. By doing so, you will discover many intriguing creative intersections between artists, producers, and the like.

When you investigate great pioneers, the gift you receive from a name like Elvis Presley is a thread to the great Sam Phillips. Sam Phillips leads you to names like Jerry Lee Lewis, Carl Perkins, Roy Orbison, Howlin' Wolf, and so forth. Studying great minds in any profession is a positive practice, but the music field has unique peculiarities, one of them being rule breaking. You will discover renegades like Johnny Cash, innovators like Les Paul, and trendsetters like David Bowie—all of these artists were rule breakers.

Avoid staying in only one lane. Embrace all the best our industry's history has to offer. You don't have to be a great horn player to appreciate Charlie "Bird" Parker or Michael Brecker. Study everyone, with the understanding that studying Count Basie's music is just as important as studying Jimi Hendrix's music. Passion runs deep in both, and both artists were world-class and unique.

There are so many incredible moments in history from which new musicians can benefit. You should never stop learning, and the best tool you have at your disposal is to surrender yourself to the humble understanding that the great artists who have come before us deserve our respect. They have left us treasure troves of experiences, and the best way to show this respect is to honor and study their works.

To borrow a quote from Chick Corea, "Good musicians borrow, great musicians steal." My advice is to study, consider, mimic, and then ultimately find your own voice. When seeking something as elusive as success in the arts, you are well served to take the superhighway because, as the greats all know, it's a long journey.

Chapter 11
Dr. Robert Fisher

Though Dr. Fisher has retired as president of Belmont University since the time of this interview, his words of wisdom remain relevant because his vision is timeless. From the second people step onto the campus at Belmont, they can feel that the university is a unique place, and if they attended a Belmont preview day when Dr. Fisher was president, they had the opportunity to hear him speak. While most university presidents are motivating when they speak, I noticed one unusual and very impacting quality Dr. Fisher possessed when I had this opportunity: he was inspirational. One memorable phrase for me was from a university speech: "Students, I am here for you, and I want to help you realize your true potential." He went on to say, "If you establish your goals based on service to others, the rewards you will receive will be too great to measure." Dr. Fisher embraces human possibility, and that is a characteristic of a genuine leader and visionary.

Interview

Menzie: I would like to start this interview by talking about what qualities you believe the musical leaders of tomorrow must understand and possess to be successful.

Dr. Fisher: I think musical leaders of the future will have to be much more entrepreneurial than in the past. The structure of the industry has changed so radically that the leaders are going to be the ones with vision and who embrace change. They will also have to be more patient and take a long-term view of the industry.

MENZIE: What do you believe the current state of the music industry is for new [artists] trying to establish themselves and make a living from music?

DR. FISHER: The current state of the music industry is basically chaos as performers, songwriters, producers, music companies, and others scramble to find a viable economic model. This chaos, which has largely been brought on by the digital revolution, has created an opportunity for more artists to have direct access to the market through various online methods. I think more artists will make a living from their music, but the room at the huge-star level is getting smaller and smaller, and we will see fewer super rich superstars.

MENZIE: In this book I want to provide the reader with insights and tools for success. I am hoping musicians gain a better grasp of business, leadership, and the mind-set that will help them execute a successful career. When students leave Belmont, besides academics, what knowledge do you hope they have attained?

DR. FISHER: When students leave Belmont, we hope that they will have gained knowledge about how the "real world" works and how to survive and ultimately thrive in that world. We also hope they've acquired a set of skills—people skills, problem solving skills, [and so forth]—along with a set of values that include hard work, persistence, and respect for all people.

MENZIE: What are the business skills you feel a young musician needs to develop to survive in today's competitive music field?

DR. FISHER: Young musicians today, more than ever, need a basic understanding of how the corporate/business world works. That includes finance, legal, and especially marketing skills.

Chapter 11

Menzie: To what extent would you agree that the sooner a musician understands and determines their brand and begins to think like an entrepreneur, the more likely they are to experience a successful career?

Dr. Fisher: I think it's essential for musicians to think as entrepreneurs and to constantly be open to new methods of creating and delivering their art. At the same time, I think they need to figure out what . . . their specific gift and style is and then work and work and work to deliver themselves as themselves. I think that's what you may mean by "branding"—they just don't need to try to be someone else!

Menzie: Will you elaborate on ways musicians can follow a social entrepreneurial path?

Dr. Fisher: Musicians have a lot of choices about how to use their gifts. Some choose a path that may not have as much commercial potential, but [it may have] great potential in helping the individual fulfill their purpose. And of course, music has long been a tool for social change.

Menzie: In my opinion, pursuing a career in the music business is a very daunting undertaking. Unlike [in] sports, there is no developed scouting system. You can be a very developed musician but not a natural performer, or you can be very talented but lacking the competitive edge necessary to make it in the music business.

I would like to address a few questions with you regarding music performance and other careers in the music industry. When a young music student first arrives at Belmont, what is the process to help that student grasp where his or her talent could be best utilized? Does Belmont help them comprehend purpose, passion, and tying service into their career?

Dr. Fisher: At Belmont we believe that every student was created by God for a purpose. We also believe that each individual has been provided a unique set of gifts—talents, skills, and passions of the heart—that are uniquely theirs. While we certainly aren't able to tell every student what their purpose is, we can tell them what it's not about—it's not about them. It's about who can you serve: "You're gonna have to serve somebody / Well, it may be the devil, or it may be the Lord / But you're gonna have to serve somebody" (Bob Dylan). So from all this, we conclude that if you can figure out your purpose, develop your gifts through hard work, and then discover who you were created to serve, then you will have the most incredible career. When asked what the song "Do Wah Diddy Diddy" means, Manfred Mann said, "I don't know what it means to you, but to me it meant that I would never have to work another day in my life—it meant that I got to do my music!"

MENZIE: Do you believe it takes more specialized knowledge in multiple areas to succeed in today's music business than, say, ten years ago?

DR. FISHER: More than ever, I think it's essential for musicians to be well versed and as knowledgeable as possible in all areas pertaining to their career.

MENZIE: When reading through the graduate catalog of the Mike Curb College of Entertainment and Music Business, under goals, it states, "To provide a personalized, career-oriented, and practical education that emphasizes leadership, innovation, private enterprise and entrepreneurship." Compared to their predecessors, do you find today's musicians better equipped at handling the business side of the music business?

DR. FISHER: In regard to the Curb College information, I think today's Belmont graduates are much better prepared to deal with the business side of the business. They have management, accounting, finance, marketing, statistical, and general business knowledge that helps them to find their place in the industry.

MENZIE: I recently read a study that shows that the top 1 percent of recording artists accounts for 77 percent of all artist-recorded music income. How does Belmont approach aligning students who strive to be successful recording artists with the reality of such statistics?

Dr. Fisher: While 1 percent of the recording artists do receive a huge share of recorded-music income, we're finding that our students understand that and are finding other ways to make their way in the music world—especially in live performance. They post their music online, try to build a small but loyal fan base, and then use that to create income opportunities through live performance.

Menzie: How does Belmont teach a student to accomplish the balance of artistry while embracing the responsibilities of entrepreneurship?

Dr. Fisher: I really don't think artists have to give up their art in order to embrace strong business skills and become entrepreneurs. I think the line of thinking that suggests that these are incompatible is more a reflection of the typical artist [who is] lacking those skills and/or their unwillingness to work to acquire those skills.

Menzie: Nashville provides the perfect setting for Belmont's music-business focus; in the mission statement from the Curb College, the words *real world applications* are used.

How is Belmont able to use the alumni relationships of huge stars such as Brad Paisley and Trisha Yearwood to benefit current students entering the music business?

Dr. Fisher: Belmont is the beneficiary of the success of several of our graduates. Star graduates such as Brad Paisley, Trisha Yearwood, Lee Ann Womack, Josh Turner, Florida Georgia Line, and others create a certain wow factor and awareness of Belmont. These graduates also support the university in a variety of ways, from creating scholarships for today's students to just [adding to] the PR value. As noted earlier, there is another much longer and broader list of Belmont graduates who may not be known as stars today but who have built a significant national base. This list includes Moon Taxi, Apache Relay, Kopecky Family Band, Diarrhea Planet, and current students the Lonely Biscuits and Jackson Wells. As these groups move all around the country and the world, they create an awareness of the range of opportunities that exist at Belmont and in Nashville. But importantly, our alumni stay connected with us, and some alumni go on to forge unique relationships with Belmont that our students can learn from, and that also helps them develop their sense of service. For example, Brad Paisley and Kimberly Williams-Paisley have partnered with Belmont University to spearhead The Store, a year-round free grocery store, allowing people to shop with dignity for their basic needs. The vision is to work closely together to serve the broader community. This also serves Belmont's mission, which is to challenge students with an education that empowers them to use their talents and skills to engage and transform the world. I am very grateful that Belmont University has been invited to partner with them. This joint venture brings so much to so many.

MENZIE: You don't have to look very far to see the qualities of all involved. Will you address the internship opportunities Belmont offers?

DR. FISHER: Internship opportunities are huge for Belmont students. These exist not only in Nashville but at Belmont West in LA and Belmont East in New York. These work-like experiences may make a significant contribution in helping our students to determine their direction and in helping them find employment.

MENZIE: Belmont has expanded its campus with a new law college, and this is surely good news for a natural extension into entertainment and music-business law. No doubt any musician reading this book would love for you to elaborate on the benefits and new opportunities this new law college brings.

DR. FISHER: [Belmont] College of Law has a full array of normally expected specialties plus a pretty unique track in entertainment law. This area of emphasis prepares an attorney for work helping individual artists and companies in the entertainment field.

MENZIE: Music therapy is also a new degree for Belmont. Will you elaborate on the special nature of this degree and its place in the professional field?

Dr. Fisher: Music therapy is a program that is designed to use music to help people recover from physical, emotional, or psychological issues. Music can speak to people in ways that regular words can't. We're finding a great interest in this program at Belmont. It is clear that this program is perfect for Nashville as a health care and music center and Belmont as a university with outstanding musical talent and a strong allied health sciences program.

Menzie: Belmont is one of a few universities with a songwriting major, and of course, with Nashville being the perfect location for a songwriter, it's the perfect fit for Belmont to offer students this concentration. How do you gauge the success of the songwriting program?

Dr. Fisher: Nashville and Belmont are naturals for a songwriting major. The demand for this program is very strong, with our biggest challenge being finding a way to include as many qualified students as possible. Nashville is certainly a musical performing center, but it is even [more so] a songwriting center. Our students benefit from the teaching of our outstanding full-time faculty along with the amazing talent from our part-time faculty. It is not unusual for a student to coauthor a song with a Grammy Award winner!

Menzie: Do you see demand growing for the songwriting program?

Dr. Fisher: I only expect the demand for this songwriting program to grow. It is a degree that you have to audition for, but that is another reason it attracts such strong candidates. I think most people would agree that Nashville is the city for songwriters. James Elliott, chair of Belmont's songwriting department, makes reference to three key points he believes are important and differentiating and that make the program successful: the high caliber of our award-winning songwriting staff, the challenging and innovative curriculum, and our music-industry partners in Nashville, who are helping us develop tomorrow's successful writers—something Nashville is known for.

Menzie: In terms of expansion, Belmont seems to be a natural place to have a radio station to debut up-and-coming artists. I am curious why Belmont doesn't have a radio station. It's my understanding that early on they did.

Dr. Fisher: Belmont doesn't currently have a radio station, mainly because of the financial challenges. But there is a historical marker on our campus that points out that the first radio station in Nashville was established on the site of our campus.

Menzie: I thought it would be a nice way to close for you to talk about Belmont's new performing arts center.

Dr. Fisher: Belmont is committed to performance and providing students with access to stages that rival some of the world's finest, so we committed to building a state-of-the-art performing arts center. After all, Nashville has some of the finest music engineers in the world, so who better than these gifted engineers to bring this vision to life?

The Belmont University Performing Arts Center will house a 1,700-seat multipurpose theater, a grand lobby, and two contiguous event spaces that can hold more than 900 guests. Our goal was to build the finest music performance hall on any college campus in the world. I have dreamed of the creation of this facility since I first came to Belmont in 2000. When you combine the Massey Performing Arts Center, Troutt Theater, and McAfee Concert Hall, the addition of this venue completes our campus performance facilities, creating the most extensive suite of venues of any other institution of higher education. That's exciting, right?

Menzie: That is absolutely exciting and will benefit many.

CHAPTER 12

Entrepreneurship

THE PATHWAY TO SUCCESS IN THE ARTS IS A CURIOUS ONE. Advancing in most other career paths usually consists of traveling a well-worn road walked by many, checking off boxes, and/or simply continuing on the corporate conveyor belt.

But in the arts, you are dealing with a very different beast: from day one, you are an entrepreneur.

Being a successful entrepreneur means embracing the etheric factions of business and morphing them into an art form. That is the difference between being just a businessperson and being an entrepreneur. Do not make the mistake of thinking that you are not accountable for business responsibilities. In truth an entrepreneur generally has more responsibilities and accountability than the standard business executive, and this is certainly true when dealing with the creative aspects of business.

When entering the world of an entrepreneur, you grow to understand that everyone and everything bring potential value and opportunity. So instead of seeing business through the limited lens of the corporate competition model, entrepreneurs approach business from a redistribution and recycling model. They see all connectivity as positive.

I find that a helpful way to visualize this idea is to imagine yourself walking on a path. Since everything on the path is connected, it is your job to figure out what advantages stem from knowing those connections. Each moment can lead to another step forward in your career, and every moment should be recycled. You will advance only by acting on that knowledge.

The next step is incorporation.

Now that you have a grasp of your role, the plan should be to advance your brand. You will find that if you remain curious, your journey will not be mundane.

Understanding this helps you see the path differently than others will. You will find opportunity where others may not see it, and so your small successes become bigger.

If you are seeking a big result, start by connecting the many small moments; see how everything connects, and be aware that the smallest kindness is never forgotten—nor is any inconsiderate gesture. Successful entrepreneurs and musicians seek fulfillment of expression, and that means you must move forward. Your curiosity must remain insatiable.

All too often, good musicians become distracted by acceptance of the mundane. But look no further than the minds of great artists the likes of David Bowie or Prince or of fresh and impacting artists like Molly Tuttle or Jason Isbell, and you will see they are always moving forward on the path.

Yes, there are overlooks on the path, moments for investigation and distractions, but history proves the greatest artists and musicians have always found a way to keep a sober vision and move forward, reinventing themselves whenever necessary.

A career in music is a way of life, and good artists make it last a lifetime. Your health must be maintained, your sense of spirit continually refreshed. It is a journey that should be inspiring at every junction. It is a path that takes a lifetime to walk.

There is a misconception that if you are creative, there is little chance of you having a natural sense for business. That erroneous thought is incredibly inaccurate. Take the example of Paul Reed Smith: Paul is an extraordinary guitarist with a genius understanding of the craft of building beautiful instruments, but he also has tremendous acumen for business. He took his idea from West Street in Annapolis, Maryland, where he was building one guitar at a time, to becoming the third-largest guitar manufacturer in music history. He has continually expanded his product lines and has involvement in other businesses as well, some music related and some not. Another endeavor he founded is Digital Harmonic, a defense contracting company founded by Smith in 2015. The fundamental technology of the company was developed by Paul and his father, Jack Smith.

This kind of career depth has also been accomplished by the great guitarist Skunk Baxter. Baxter is also successfully entrenched in the defense industry as a consultant and is a chair of the Congressional Advisory Board on Missile Defense.

So the idea that musicians can't be great entrepreneurs is nonsense. How about the example of Gene Simmons? How about action figures, anyone? Consider Jimmy Buffett and his many Margaritavilles. Consider Bob Weir, Smokey Robinson, Dolly Parton, Quincy Jones, or Taylor Swift. And, of course, the granddaddy of them all is Paul McCartney. All of these individuals have skills in the arts and in business, as well as the understanding that music is a business and that it also has a strong entrepreneurial aspect.

Your success in this aspect is directly up to you. If you are disturbed by that realization, you only need to ask yourself a few important questions to feel better, then begin embracing solution-based thinking. The first one is the most important.

Am I able to embrace business as an art form?

You may balk at that concept at first, but I promise you, the artists that understand it function from this premise every day. Those artists are the ones you are hearing about, as well as the ones with the most successful and long-lasting careers.

How do you embrace business as an art form?

The answer is simple: treat it like one. Implement the same disciplines as you do your music, just with different data. Study the mind-sets and productive habits of the extraordinarily successful. Learn the organizational habits of entrepreneurial leaders. Study the hard business choices they had to make to protect the integrity of their brand and ensure long careers.

To study a world-class entrepreneur in the arts, look no further than the film career of Ron Howard. He was a successful child actor on *The Andy Griffith Show*, then continued his success with *Happy Days*. From there, he moved into writing and directing movies, such as *A Beautiful Mind* and *Cocoon*.

Read the classic books written by authorities on the subject, such as *Think and Grow Rich* by Napoleon Hill. Want a more current author? Read the works of Malcolm Gladwell or Daniel Pink. Seek out the materials of today's business leaders. Guy Kawasaki is an extremely influential entrepreneur who, in his book *The Art of the Start*, discusses the understanding that "The essence of entrepreneurship is about making meaning" and that if you set out to make meaning, you are very likely to make money. He also believes, however, that if your goal is to make money, there is little chance you will make meaning.

Don't limit yourself to only music-business materials. It's good to think of business as an additional skill set—a necessary weapon in your arsenal. Take the successful principles of business, vision, discipline, consistency, unique application, style, professional efficiency, ethics, language, artful and timely communication, and so forth, and incorporate them into your music career.

Do I have the discipline to be a successful music-business entrepreneur?

The skill sets necessary to be a successful music entrepreneur have changed, and the need to embrace "the new musician" mentality stems from that understanding. Rapid change is the current reality, and tomorrow's winners will have to embrace today's truths. While the models and styles of success have changed and will continue to do so, the fundamentals of success haven't.

There was a time when big money would get behind any music project with even the slightest potential. That is no longer the case. In today's market, you, as the artist, are expected to prove that you have a dependable following and strong marketing already established, both artistically and organizationally. The industry wants a well-developed, original product.

The top echelon in the music business will still appear if you are a stellar, undeniable, and bankable product. No one walks away from a hot product or an obvious winner, but you must be developed enough before you can even be considered as a viable candidate.

Chapter 12

Today in music, the bar is higher, and more expectations are put on the musicians than ever before. Developing entrepreneurial skills is more important than ever. If your goal is to succeed, it's as important as craft development.

There is a hidden gem in all of this. Because more business acumen is expected from the musicians, they are now better prepared to enter into contractual agreements and have a voice in other music business dealings as well.

How important is it to know the business side of the music business?

I am slightly intolerant of musicians who don't believe that the understanding of business is their responsibility. Some don't see the need to be as good at business as they are at their artistic offerings, but the industry has its own unique way of purging the unprepared. It's called a one-hit wonder.

Entrepreneurship isn't a new way at all. It's been around forever, and for the risk takers, it's always been a successful and lucrative approach. Look up the backstory of James Brown's first *Live at the Apollo* record. When Brown pitched the idea, King Records said no. So James put up his own money and did it anyway, capturing one of the more iconic live records of all time.

In prior days big labels would front big money in hopes of gaining control of the artist's work. The approach was lucrative for the labels, but like in many other industries, decadence, greed, and complacency rotted the apple on both sides of the equation. Label support is still available, but the game is very different.

The new model is harder yet potentially better for musicians—but only for those willing to do the heavy lifting. Artists like Michael League of Snarky Puppy understand and embrace the benefits of entrepreneurial thinking to the highest level.

It is a new time in business for all industries; the game is changing as you read this. Even for the top brass, corporate job security has lost its luminosity, and no position is guaranteed in any field. After artistic vision, mastering the understanding and interworking principles of entrepreneurship becomes the second most important tool in the toolbox.

What does it take to be a great entrepreneur?

In the end the answer is somewhat obvious: it's a matter of courage and the ability to act with confidence when the outcome is uncertain. You act because you have worked hard enough on your craft and you are confident enough in your vision.

The new entrepreneurial leadership comes to the table prepared. There are so many bands doing unique work and finding new ways to gain a stronger following and better visibility. Look no further than bands like Walk Off the Earth and Snarky Puppy or an artist like Charlie Puth. While they are still developing bigger and bigger followings, they maintain sustainability. You must break a few rules to win. The art of entrepreneurship is simply managing the business side of your art with the same passion and creative confidence that you manage your musical expression.

> *"When you trust your television, what you get is what you got, 'Cause when they own the information, they can bend it all they want."*
> —JOHN MAYER, "WAITING ON THE WORLD TO CHANGE"

Chapter 13

Ashley Campbell

IN THE MUSIC BUSINESS, IF YOUR LAST NAME IS CAMPBELL AND YOUR dad's name is Glen, people will automatically have high expectations of you and expect great results. The reason is simple: you are the child of one of the most respected musicians and entertainers to have ever graced the stage, who was also a member of the Wrecking Crew and a TV host with his own show.

Ashley is a highly respected musician and performing artist in her own right. She and her brother Cal advance the Campbell tradition of being great musicians, as they bring their unique touch to their personal careers. In this interview Ashley shares many great backstories and gives the reader insight into her world as a rising success story in the music business.

Interview

MENZIE: Ashley, there are just so many things we can talk about, but I thought the best place to start would be with your record, *The Lonely One*. You coproduced this work.

ASHLEY CAMPBELL: Yeah, I coproduced the record with my brother Cal. He had a studio in Los Angeles in his house in Angora Hills, California. I had been with Big Machine Records for about two years, and it just wasn't the right fit for me. They were great, but it wasn't who I am as an artist. So when we parted ways I thought, "Man, it's been four years that I've been in Nashville, and I haven't put out a record yet." I'd been doing shows, but I didn't have any music to give people. I had grown tired of waiting for someone to say I could make a record, so I recorded it with Cal. I really wanted Cal to produce it because he's not country or Americana, so he has this edge that he brought to what I do, which is more acoustic and old-school country. It was really fun working with him. It was the process of making a record that I'm used to: it was woodshedding and being in the studio and trying different things out. In Nashville there was a lot of "Time's a wasting, money's a wasting." You would go into the studio, and you would not have a lot of time to truly be creative or experimental, so that was the great thing about using Cal's studio. We could work through all hours of the night and not worry that the studio is costing so-and-so much an hour.

MENZIE: Was Big Machine looking for the rural country stuff, or did you find that they wanted more mainstream, radio-style country?

ASHLEY CAMPBELL: I don't consider myself mainstream. I definitely have commercial qualities, but I feel like with most any record label, the emphasis is on trying to get on the radio, and that's where it went wrong with me. It made me miserable. Because of these expectations, I was trying to write songs that I thought would get on the radio or that I thought the label would like, as opposed to writing songs that I love and that mean something to me. And I think everyone understands that sometimes you can write something meaningful to you and radio will like it, but if radio is the starting and motivating goal, then I feel that's going about it wrong. My gut let me know that that was definitely wrong for me.

MENZIE: So the first single you put out, "A New Year," has a really infectious feel, and it leans on the pop side more than [the] traditional. What made you choose that direction for the tune?

ASHLEY CAMPBELL: When you're making a record, you have to listen to what a song feels like, and that song always had more of a pop feel and a pop influence. I don't think people should let genre get in the way of what a song needs to sound like or what you want a song to sound like. You shouldn't have to worry about things like [asking,] "Is this country enough?"

MENZIE: Sometimes the music industry seems stuck, favoring current trends instead of allowing for fresh innovation. When labels attempt to dictate artistic direction, they are flying from the passenger's seat. With your diverse background, how do you decide your target audience?

ASHLEY CAMPBELL: I definitely started with a bit of a following from my dad's band, but I guess I wanted people in my personal camp. I believe that people [who] like the kind of music that I like will probably like and enjoy my album. So I honestly tried to make something I like.

MENZIE: Just honest music, right?

ASHLEY CAMPBELL: Yeah, I wasn't really going for any certain demographic. I consider myself more of a country-style Americana artist, but obviously, I love banjo and bluegrass. I definitely plan to do a full bluegrass album someday.

When an artist is first establishing themselves, I feel like it's easier to start off in a more mainstream format. If you start off in a unique format like bluegrass and then try to do something else, people will ask, "What's she doing there?" But when Dierks Bentley decided to also release a bluegrass record because he loves bluegrass, that approach seemed to work well for him. So I think it's very possible to do that without losing the loyalty of your fans. I'm not saying bluegrass is more of a side project, but right now, for me, it might be. It's part of who I am, and it's part of what I love, and on my record, I have one bluegrass banjo song. But I don't think pure bluegrass tunes would mix with my current direction and what I'm doing on my album.

So if I'm going to do multiple bluegrass songs, I would want the chance to do a whole album committed to that idea and do it really bluegrass and really right—but still in my writing style. I would want to do it justice. I don't want to just have a nod to bluegrass. If you are going to do it, you have to do it right!

MENZIE: There are so many details involved when rolling out a project like your record. It's decision after decision after decision. How have you gone about this process?

ASHLEY CAMPBELL: Not having a record label has its ups and downs. I have to pay for everything myself. Everything costs money! Making CDs costs money, making vinyls costs money, touring costs money, [and] merchandise costs money. So we're kind of flying by the seat of our pants because I've never put out a record before. I've got my artist management [TKO] helping me and . . . my agent helping book shows, and advice comes from everywhere. I have a label in the United Kingdom now, but it's not the same type of involvement you would get from a major label here.

MENZIE: Is that more for distribution?

ASHLEY CAMPBELL: It's more of a distribution label in the United Kingdom, and they're awesome and very helpful. But it's tough when you have to do everything yourself. When I was with Big Machine and my single came out, they did everything for me, and it was really nice. But I'd rather have artistic control with a lot more work to do. So if I ever did go with another label, it would have to be more of a partnership.

MENZIE: [With] doing it yourself, how are you going about selecting venues and dates? How do you put the tour part of it together?

ASHLEY CAMPBELL: Well, since we're just starting out, we really can't be too picky. We have to choose venues based on what's beneficial and financially sound. Everyone knows it's very expensive to tour. So when we set the dates and details, we make sure we get good exposure and coordinate it so that we don't lose money when we do it.

Chapter 13

Menzie: Do you try and set a handful of dates [and] assess what's happening, then add to that? Or is the goal more along the lines of the touring you did with Glen?

Ashley Campbell: For the last couple of years, it's been a lot of one-offs with days in between. I'm looking forward to the day when we can play show after show, but that's a lot more financially doable when your record is out and you're with the same touring musicians. It's much easier to add nearby locations and additional venues to an established tour. We can't be choosey right now, and there are some shows where we do lose money. But we have to decide if the exposure is worth it. I always try to make sure my musicians get paid. There are a lot of shows I don't personally make money on, but I make sure everyone working gets paid.

Menzie: Since we're discussing touring, will you reflect on the impact that participating in the farewell tour with Glen had on you? You played quite a role, and I have no doubt that was not only an amazing experience but [also] challenging on many fronts as well. Performing over 150 shows on a grand scale, you were able to gain a lot of knowledge and insight on how touring works.

Ashley Campbell: Getting to back up my dad in his band was like a master class. Getting to spend so much time with him on a personal level was so amazing for me; just being able to watch him onstage and learn from what he did was also incredible. He could handle anything onstage.

Menzie: You also played with your dad at the Grammys Lifetime Achievement [Award] evening; will you share a little bit about that experience? Obviously, it was quite an event.

Ashley Campbell: That was really cool. It was at the peak of the tour, I think, right in the middle. I had never attended the Grammys before, so it was exciting for me, and to be performing at my first Grammys made it incredibly special. I got the chance to see all the backstage workings and how the show all comes together. Backstage, McCartney was walking around, and [so were] other artists like Taylor Swift, Coldplay, and Katy

Perry. It's really cool to see so many different people from all different walks of life and music just all hanging out and celebrating music. But it was an extra special evening, seeing my dad get honored while he was still able to enjoy it. It meant so much to our family.

MENZIE: It looked like an amazing evening. On a personal note, I have to ask, What is it like meeting a Beatle?

ASHLEY CAMPBELL: Oh my gosh, it was the best thing ever. My first sighting of Paul was during our run-through with the cameras. The whole Staples Center was empty, and they have the chairs with the names of the people who are going to sit there. So . . . we were running through the medley, my dad was singing "Rhinestone Cowboy," and I look out and [see that] Paul McCartney is sitting in his chair with his fist pumping in the air and singing along. What was mind-blowing was that he came because he wanted to relax and watch the rehearsal. Afterwards, I ran into him backstage and got a picture with him and said how much I admired him, and then I brought him back to meet my dad. Paul was wearing an all-white suit. It was really cool to see their mutual love and respect for each other—such a cool moment.

MENZIE: The gravity of that moment really comes across on film. Not too many people can say, "I've met a Beatle," and when you hear McCartney say to your dad, "I just had to come and tell ya, I love ya—that's all!" that's an amazing moment in music history, very genuine.

In an interview you were asked about your dad's influence on your music. Your answer was succinct and immensely powerful: "He is the influence." I'm sure his influence seeps into the daily decisions you make about your own career.

ASHLEY CAMPBELL: Yeah, definitely. For example, he always told me, "Do what you love, make something you love—because when you do, the chances are that someone else is going to love it too. Never do music or art for any reason other than that you love it. Don't do it because you think someone else will like it."

Chapter 13

A great example of that that I take a lot of strength from is when my dad wanted to record "Highwayman" back in the day, when he was with Capitol Records, and they wanted him to record "My Sharona." He said, "I'm not a bubblegum pop artist," and he walked away from the record label and did what he believed in. It takes a lot of guts to walk away from a situation like that.

I was honestly surprised to get any advice at this point because of the advancement of his Alzheimer's. Most of the time, he didn't have a lot of new things to say, but later on in the tour, he asked me how my music was going, and then he specifically asked how my songwriting was going. I said, "It's going great," and I jokingly added, "I'm going to be a superstar." He got really serious, and he looked me straight in the eye and said, "Be a super person, and the superstar will follow." It was a true mic drop moment. My dad was very aware of what was important and what it took for someone to be successful in their pursuit of a music career.

MENZIE: You and Carl Jackson performed your song "Remembering" on the *Country Road* [*TV*] show, and Larry Gatlin was sitting across from you. Your song and performance struck an emotional chord with Gatlin, and as you continued, the camera captured these emotions felt not only by Gatlin but by everyone in the room. That kind of reaction from a fellow performer reflects great songwriting, performance, and artistry.

ASHLEY CAMPBELL: Gatlin is the sweetest guy, and he's such a hoot.

MENZIE: He's also an amazing performer and singer, and he was obviously touched by your song. I know he performed with Glen many times, and that moment was truly powerful!

Continuing with songwriting, you have enjoyed exposure to one of the greatest writers of all time, Jimmy Webb. Most everyone agrees [that] Webb is in a class with very few members, so how does that affect you as a writer, knowing that he's part of your family's music history?

ASHLEY CAMPBELL: It definitely makes me want to step up, and it encourages me to write more and write to the highest standard that I am capable. I never want to take it for granted that I'm able to be a writer and that I'm able to make a living as a songwriter and performer. We are privileged to be given that opportunity.

MENZIE: Being the daughter of Glen Campbell, do you find that people hold you to a different standard?

ASHLEY CAMPBELL: When you grow up around the music business, you meet the professionals [whom] your family knows because they are family friends. So I am aware that I don't have quite the struggle with connecting professionally as [do] others who are doing the same thing as me. But I do my best to never take that for granted. And although it's a fact that my dad's a music legend, I never take that for granted either. Sometimes that can open doors for you, and sometimes it makes little difference or even causes people to raise their expectations.

MENZIE: To whom much is given, much is expected.

ASHLEY CAMPBELL: Overall, I try not to think about it too much. I just try and do what I think is good. Being an instrumentalist, I try and just be me, and that's what my dad always did. I don't think comparisons are very productive. The question shouldn't be "Do you do things better or worse than other people?" The better question is "As an artist, what perspective are you bringing to the table?" My intent is to be the best version of myself and let the rest just be.

MENZIE: Besides Jimmy Webb, do you have other favorite writers?

ASHLEY CAMPBELL: I love Roger Miller's writing because my dad grew up telling Roger Miller jokes and singing Roger Miller songs, so I've just recently, in the last couple years, fallen in love with Roger Miller's stuff. And then Dolly Parton, of course, [is] one of my favorites. I just love her voice and her voice as a songwriter too. She's very vulnerable.

MENZIE: I put Dolly in the Beatles category. I've never heard her say one thing that wasn't phrased exactly like it should be,

Chapter 13

and although beautifully feisty, she always puts everybody at ease.

Some songwriters have lyrics just pop into their heads; other writers have a routine for developing songs. When you write, do you have any rituals, or are you from the school of "When it hits, I write it down"?

Ashley Campbell: I find writing a song differs every time. There are definitely certain ways that work most of the time, like starting with a melody, maybe a banjo riff, and it will go from there. I ask myself how it feels or what subject matter it sounds like and go from there. Sometimes I'll start with a title, or I'll think of a cool line, something meaningful, and I'll build the song around that. It might end up being only one line in the song, but it led me to the song. It's a process, and it's just about working an idea any which way you can. I try to let the process be as natural as possible.

Menzie: I saw in an interview that you said you wanted to be an actress when you were younger. How do you feel like that art form [and/or] any other art forms impact the way you write songs?

Ashley Campbell: Well, when I was in college, I was taking improv classes, and I was really interested in sketch-comedy writing. When you're a comedian in LA, you have to write all of your own material. Otherwise, you're not going to make it. The people who are hired for shows like *Saturday Night Live* are all very talented sketch writers, scriptwriters, and screenwriters. I was taking writing classes and learning about storytelling, and I definitely have put that to use in my songwriting.

I remember there was one exercise in an improv storytelling class where we stood in a circle and started telling a story. The teacher would say stop and then say one of two words: either "expand" or "emotion." We would then embellish that moment in the story with whichever word she called out. It's a cool exercise to do because songwriting is really a form of storytelling, whether you're writing love songs or breakup stories.

Menzie: You have been fortunate to know and work with amazing musicians, and you have maintained a close relationship with Carl Jackson, who is such an icon. Will you shed some light on Carl's relationship with both you and your family?

ASHLEY CAMPBELL: Well, to start, Carl introduced my mom and dad, so he's the reason I'm alive. Carl was dating my mom's best friend, Lynn; both Mom and Lynn danced for Radio City Music Hall, and one weekend, Carl and Lynn were attending a James Taylor [JT] concert—my mom loves James Taylor—so Mom asked Carl and Lynn if they would set her up with someone in the band because she wanted to go with them to see James Taylor. And they were like, "Hahaha, let's set her up with Glen Campbell." So the JT concert was Mom and Dad's first date. Mom didn't really know who my dad was, but obviously it worked out.

So because Carl was playing in my dad's band, my relationship/mentorship with Carl really took off when we started coming to Nashville on my dad's tours. By then I was already in my twenties, and [we'd] started getting together to play. We would play together at the Station Inn every time I was in town, and he would teach me banjo licks. I have so much more to learn from him. He's the sweetest man in the world and wants nothing but to share his vast knowledge of music, which I'm so thankful for. He's like a second father, pretty much.

MENZIE: It's a nice synergy because he has such a unique knowledge of music history, and you add a fresh energy to what he's doing.

ASHLEY CAMPBELL: I definitely pull him out of his comfort zone quite often. Yesterday he was like, "I don't exactly understand the rhythm you want me to do." I was like, "Just do you, it's fine."

MENZIE: People may not know this, but you play a great role in the Rascal Flatts video *Banjo*. How much of an impact do you think that had on your visibility as an artist?

ASHLEY CAMPBELL: It had a really big impact because that's while I was still touring with my dad, and I hadn't really released any of my own music yet. It was kind of a nice way to break out and for people to see me and know that I'm a "chick who plays banjo." I didn't actually play on the recording of it, because it was done way before the music video; I heard it was several banjo players who put together the track. It's a really cool part. They asked me to play it at the CMT [Country Music Television] awards, so I learned it and played with them. That was really special.

MENZIE: What advice would you give young rising musicians who are pursuing a career in music? What are some dos and don'ts?

ASHLEY CAMPBELL: I would probably give the same advice that my dad gave me, which is just make music that inspires you and that you love—music that means something to you! I believe that if you do that, you can't go wrong. Also, kindness will take you all the way because no one wants to work with someone who is difficult or mean or entitled. Luckily, you don't run into too many people who are like that, especially in Nashville. So just be you, don't let the haters get you down. Do something that's meaningful to you!

I think to be successful as a musician, you need to constantly be "doing" music. You should be playing with other people, making new friends, always writing, [and] always jamming with people. I think a winning approach is [putting] fundamentals first and defining your artistic vibe after. One thing that is certain [is] you can't sit around and expect success to find you. Because if you sit around, waiting for club dates to show up, by the time [they do] come, you're going to be a rusty bucket of bolts. More importantly, the music industry expects you to hustle. You can't just sit around and say, "I wish people would write with me." You have to go out there and make new writing friends and go to writers' rounds and events like that.

MENZIE: How important is networking from your point of view?

ASHLEY CAMPBELL: Unless you already have some kind of amazing allstar team that's going to do everything for you, success in the industry is all about networking and relationships. You can be the most talented person in the world, but if you don't go out there and show people, no one is going to see you. There is no way they can know what you have to offer.

Oddly, you also have to know when not to oversell yourself. It's the most cliché thing, but timing is everything. If you meet someone in the industry, your understanding of the art of subtlety is to your advantage. You have to know how to read professional situations. Too much is just as bad as too little.

MENZIE: There's an art to timing.

ASHLEY CAMPBELL: Most of the time, if you hand someone a demo, they're going to throw it in the trash. When I signed at Warner Chapell, they actually told me, "Do not accept demos from anyone, because it could come back to bite you legally." So they just said, "Don't accept anything" just to be safe.

MENZIE: You now live in Nashville, but you're originally from the West Coast. Are there advantages to living in Nashville?

ASHLEY CAMPBELL: LA is definitely a shark tank, and it's not such a big spot for country music. I do think there's country music and bluegrass out there, but Nashville is really the place, especially for songwriting. I wasn't really that involved in the songwriting community when I was living in LA, because of being on tour with my dad. I've since gone back and done some writing with people there. Like every city, LA has a totally different feel, but I think Nashville is where the city and the scene are a little more focused.

MENZIE: When I'm talking to new musicians, I try to explain the difference of the music feel from one city to another—LA, New York, New Orleans, and Nashville are all different. It's also tougher to break into some scenes because they're locked tight by a select few, like [with] film work in LA.

ASHLEY CAMPBELL: It's really tough here in Nashville for those trying to be accepted as studio musicians. It's hard to break into that scene because everyone in Nashville already has their accepted core group of musicians

[whom] they call for every demo and every session, so that makes it even tougher if you want to be a studio musician.

MENZIE: As Tommy Harden and Brent Mason discuss in this book, in the studio, you've only got a few seconds to make a good decision, and it has to be good 80 percent of the time, or your phone does this weird thing . . . it stops ringing.

I'd like to wrap with my favorite Ashley Campbell quotation: "Leave everything a little better than you found it."

ASHLEY CAMPBELL: Awe, that's a Steve Ozark quote. He was a close friend of my dad's. Steve was living here, helping us take care of my dad, and he was our closest family friend. He was another big father figure for me. He put that quote on the refrigerator on a cardboard heart: "Leave everything a little better than you found it." He meant it for the kitchen, but I thought, "No, this is a life philosophy."

Chapter 14

Imagination

ALIGNING WITH YOUR IMAGINATION IS PARTNERING WITH YOUR MOST powerful creative tool.

Imagination is the foundation on which all possibilities stand.

Creatives understand this maxim intuitively; they intentionally fan the flames of imagination, fully embracing it and understanding that it is the secret code that opens the doors to unique expression.

Imagination is one of the more important words in this book. It unlocks unlimited opportunities, and it is your creative vehicle to anywhere. Like a fingerprint, your imagination is singularly unique to you.

We are all well served to understand that, like any creative muscle, the imagination can be enhanced and strengthened through constant use. Making the commitment to allow your imagination freedom may be the most important creative practice you undertake. Imagination reflects back to you exactly what you feed it. It is influenced tremendously by what you personally seek, experience, perceive, feel, and consider.

There are many opportunities to expand and strengthen your imagination. Some artists combine meditation with visualization techniques. Others read more or listen to new musical styles, adding these new utterances and different art forms to their palette. Many musicians involve themselves with other disciplines, such as tai chi, yoga, the visual arts, or other forms of expression and reflection. Simply being outdoors can put you in a more creative state, encouraging the development of imagination. All environments leave their fingerprints on your imagination without prejudice.

CHAPTER 14

The imagination works exactly like an amplifier; connect it properly and productively, and you invite high volumes of clarity and creative thoughts. Connect it carelessly, and you get static and interference.

Think of imagination as a still pond; all activity is influential, and any disturbance creates a ripple effect. Imagination also works in harmony with the subconscious mind; therefore, intended or not, you influence your imagination simply through the environments you expose yourself to. When you listen to certain music or discover new creative environments, you are influencing your imagination. The more creative your environments are, the greater the influence on your imagination. The same is true in reverse—junk in equals junk out. Matty Healy of the 1975 is quoted as saying, "We create in the way we consume."

The imagination is a no-restriction zone. There are no rules, just pure potential. The more vivid your daydreams and visualizations are, the better. Ideas that people outside of the arts would define as risky become fair game. Unconventional, daring, and far-fetched become working terms.

One of my favorite examples of this freedom is the song "Tomorrow Never Knows" by the Beatles. They recorded the song in 1966, and they broke every previous rule of rock 'n' roll recording in the process. The timing of the recording, the way they created those sounds, and why they created those sounds—all of these elements and more add up to imagination and creative genius on full display. Now that's imagination! Do yourself a favor and find the backstory on the song and how it came to be what it is—you will be inspired!

There are so many artistic other examples of full-force imagination for us to explore. Here are just a few great names that pushed the boundaries through imagination: J. S. Bach, Jimi Hendrix, Jeff Beck, Queen, Joni Mitchell, Stevie Wonder, Miles Davis, Oscar Peterson, Charlie Parker, Duke Ellington, Yo-Yo Ma, David Bowie, Finneas, Michael Brecker, Quincy Jones, Sam Phillips, Rick Hall, Berry Gordy, Bob Moog, and Les Paul—the father of multitracking.

All of these creatives changed the way others looked at creating music and expressing ideas. Imagination was their first and most important tool.

Imagination

Imagination has no boundaries, and everyone has access to the multitude of creative and musical genius that's available. When it comes to imagination, the rule breakers always pave the way, and we can elect to follow and learn. Better yet, we can trust our imaginations and choose to lead.

What do you envision as your future? To experience that vision as tomorrow's reality, you must first know your tomorrow through your imagination and vision today.

As within, so without.

Chapter 15

Craig Alvin

IN THE MUSIC BUSINESS, EARS ARE EVERYTHING, AND THAT IS CRAIG Alvin's gift. But ears without heart don't hear the same as ears with it, and that is the special unsaid something Craig brings to his work when he engineers. The ability to earn the respect and trust of an artist like Kacey Musgraves is a direct reflection of Craig's unique talents. He brings soul to the sessions and his mixes beginning at the first phone call.

INTERVIEW

MENZIE: Craig, I am ecstatic you are contributing to the book. Let's jump right in and start with *Golden Hour*. Obviously, [it is] an amazing record and a huge success, so the first question that popped into my mind was "How does an engineer get on the radar for a gig of that magnitude?" Were you approached by Ian Fitchuk? Did you already have a relationship?

CRAIG ALVIN: Yes, Ian and I have been friends for at least ten years—the same with Daniel Tashian, the other producer on the record. I had met them shortly after I moved to Nashville back in 2007. I just knew them from around town. I had done a couple of things with Ian; he works as a session drummer as well. I was a fan of Daniel's band the Silver Seas, so I had gone to see them several times, and it was more like we were acquaintances [who] knew each other and saw each other around the neighborhood. When the Kacey record came up, I think it was a couple of things that put me on the radar. One, Todd Lombardo, who played acoustic guitar, banjo, and mandolin on the record, as well as other things—he and I were sharing a studio at the time, so when they were debating who to call to engineer, Todd brought my name up, and I think that was one of the things that helped the most. And the other is that I live in Nashville but I'm not a typical Nashville engineer. I'm not doing three sessions a day on Music Row or in Berry Hill. I think they were just looking for someone who takes a different approach to things, who wouldn't give them the standard Nashville treatment—whatever that is, I'm not exactly sure—but they were just looking for someone who would take a little bit more of a creative approach, a little more stylized.

MENZIE: Stylized—that's a great word. I stumbled across some of the work you did with Renn, and I know that's not a mainstream album—although it should be—but the word *stylized* really applies to that record too.

CRAIG ALVIN: I was so shocked that nobody paid attention to that record because I was sure we had found the next new thing.

MENZIE: I'm not sure that you didn't.

[Both laugh.]

CRAIG ALVIN: Well, what's funny is a lot of what I did on that record, because obviously my thumbprint is on both Renn's album *Heartache and a Song* and on Kacey's *Golden Hour*, but that's not the only style I do. I've done a lot of big rock records and a lot of country records and lots of red dirt records—all different styles. But that was kind of a sound that I've always loved since I was a kid because those were the kinds of sounds that were on the radio back in the [1970s], and they always resonated with me.

MENZIE: I see a lot of people really trying to recapture that particular kind of essence and feel from the 1970s, but unless you have had a lot of exposure to that music, it's really hard to capture that sound authentically, because a plug-in can't create feel. And even though there were many different factions, the 1970s music has a definite, different feel to it. The tools were different, the social causes were different, and the passion for live performance was different. But when you hear the way you capture music and see the way you approach things, it's very obvious that you understand the heart of the 1970s music. It shows in the respect—no pun intended.

CRAIG ALVIN: Yeah, and that's something that does take time to learn. Some days everything just goes great, and then other days, it doesn't, and the thing you have to do is trust. As long as you keep applying yourself to the process, you'll find it. Or maybe it'll be with another artist; I found that when I insert myself too much in those situations, it doesn't usually go well. I like to assist the musicians in finding their best voice, and that does take time.

MENZIE: Yes, and it also takes a certain sensitivity. So you have become an artist yourself by not getting in the way of the recording artist. That's one of the secrets to your formula, one that I don't know that every major mainstream producer cares about, because they're in the fast-production frame of mind, or they're in a "we gotta do it this way" / "it has to have that sound" frame of mind. [They're thinking,] "It has to be played at this tempo," or "The backing vocals need to be mixed at this level." In the process you become inefficient, and although you might be technically sound (no pun intended), you don't necessarily honor the song or the artist or the art form.

But I think on *Golden Hour*, you guys realized that you could do both; that's certainly the way the album comes across.

CRAIG ALVIN: Well, that makes me really happy to hear because that is definitely the mind-set we had. That record sounds deceptively easy to make because there's not much going on, but the hardest part of that was that we recorded so much other stuff, so many additional parts that just didn't make the record. Lots of tracks were recorded and then scrapped for one reason or another. Probably 90 percent of the parts we laid down didn't make the record, and not because they weren't sound musical parts but because we were searching for perfectly efficient sounds—you know, parts that did only what they were supposed to do and did that very well and got out of the way.

MENZIE: Who made the final decisions as to what was kept?

CRAIG ALVIN: It was Kacey. Absolutely, it was Kacey. There was a bit of a joke between Kacey and [me]—we kept trying to lay down conga parts because, if you listen to [1970s] music, there's always conga and bongos, and Ian is an incredible percussionist, so I kept trying to get him to lay down these parts, and they were so great, especially on "High Horse." We had one part that I thought made the song, but when it came down to it, Kacey just didn't like it. She didn't have the history with that style of music, and she wasn't trying to make a record of that style of music.

She had a vision in her head—and it was really important that we make that record. So we threw away so many conga parts, and she would laugh at me every time we had to throw one away because I would be so disappointed.

MENZIE: As an artist, one thing that really jumps out at me about Kacey is the simplicity and respect she has for space; it's really impressive. Those were the first things to get my attention when I first listened to Kacey—both the tonality of her voice and her honor of space. Those are pretty tricky characteristics to capture.

CRAIG ALVIN: Yeah, it's hard to figure out how to make a moment that can be simple and yet compelling and then just to have the courage to leave it there, especially when you have musicians like we have in Nashville, [who] can always do something interesting. I think, for her, it really does come down to the voice and the song and then the atmosphere you put those things in.

MENZIE: Yeah, that's a great descriptor—atmosphere.

CRAIG ALVIN: One of the things I love about Kacey is that she's just not following anyone, she's not trying to be anything other than herself.

Chapter 15

MENZIE: To me, that's the difference between the top-tier artists and those [who] are just one notch below. The best artists take the risks because they know in their heart that's the right expression for them, and though that's a bold position more often than not, it's the right one.

CRAIG ALVIN: Yeah, I agree.

MENZIE: So what were your specific roles in making *Golden Hour*? I know you did all the tracking; will you weigh in on that a little bit?

CRAIG ALVIN: I did all of the tracking except for the strings; that was done elsewhere. Then there were a few tracks on some of the songs that were done while they were writing the songs, so we incorporated those as well. I did mix the two piano/vocal songs, "Mother" and "Rainbow." I have mixes on the rest of the album, too, that I like, but I really love what Shawn Everett and Serban Ghenea did with the other songs. Then I was mainly just doing what I normally do, which is engineering. One of the things I do that's a little different than most engineers is I tend to tune the drums to the key of the song.

I also like to get involved with cymbal choices because cymbals all have different qualities to them—they're shiny or darker or have longer decay or a little more attack, and so I like to choose those with the drummer so that we get the right sound with whatever part of the song we're working on.

MENZIE: Do you do that by song?

CRAIG ALVIN: Yeah, and I have been collecting vintage cymbals for probably twenty-five years now, so I have a pretty good collection that I keep around. And we had some of those there, and we also had Ian's cymbals. I pay a lot of attention to those things, and I also believe one of the things that gets overlooked by tracking engineers is snare drum tuning. I find that when the snare is sitting perfectly at the right pitch with the right amount of decay, it just pays off, it feels like it's supporting the song, and there are so many things you can do with snare tuning that really help a record sound good.

MENZIE: That brings up an interesting discussion. So you're a 1970s guy and a fan of the mid-1960s music, like me. One of the reoccurring discussions that gets debated is [as follows]: Nashville has a ton of records with what I call the "gushy" snare sound. And when trying to capture the authentic drum sounds of the late 1960s and early 1970s, engineers run into a funny problem because the drummers of that period tweaked up their snares to drive the backbeat. They didn't have some of the miking capabilities available today, and when you go back and listen to the live recordings of James Brown, Otis Redding, Sam and Dave, or any of the hip soul stuff, the snare sounds have a different intensity because they were using rimshots and a tight tuning to drive that nice backbeat.

CRAIG ALVIN: Yeah, and I find it's even harder trying to capture the emotional essence we had in the 1970s because [they] had wizards like Russ Kunkel. Those guys were just masters, and they had such tremendous touch.

MENZIE: I am a card-carrying member of the Russ fan club, and the touch of these players was simply masterful.

CRAIG ALVIN: I got to work with him on a record once, and it was a real privilege.

MENZIE: Russ's work is legendary; his approach on "Fire and Rain" was trendsetting. [There were] Russ, Jim Keltner, and . . . another great drummer from the same scene: Andy Newmark, who was Carly Simon's drummer on "Anticipation." He also played on many great records.
But to get back to your approach, how was it for you when you knew you were going to be part of this new team to bring *Golden Hour* to life? If I'm not mistaken, they changed creative teams entirely, right?

CRAIG ALVIN: They did. It's funny how that happened. Kacey had been friends with Daniel and Ian for a while, and they had been writing together. I'm not 100 percent sure how it all came together, but I do know that we kind of just went in and started recording without officially announcing it to anyone that we were starting.

Chapter 15

The idea was just to see how the music would go, and if we liked it, then we were going to show it to her management, and then if they liked it, we were going to take it and show it to the label. And that's exactly what happened.

Sometimes you just have to go for it and try. I mean, it could've been a disaster, but we actually recorded four or five songs before we showed anyone what we had done, and even then, we knew we were taking a chance. They could've hated it, but [then] we showed them the first few songs, and they went, "Oh okay, well, carry on," and they let us finish the record.

MENZIE: So the chemistry with the new team of people was obviously natural and working well?

CRAIG ALVIN: Yeah, it was there from the very first note, but we were all friends anyway. Actually, Kacey was the only person I had never met on the session.

MENZIE: So when you were working with her, how did she communicate the direction she sought for her vision? Did she just come in and say, "I've been working on these tunes"? How did that all come together?

CRAIG ALVIN: Well, really all that happened was that I had set up before she got there; I hadn't really heard the songs, and she came in and just played the songs. I don't remember which song was first, but she started playing it, and I instantly thought in my head, "I know what to do with this." It took me back to so many great records like Fleetwood Mac and the Eagles, and [it took me] kind of back to a time when it was okay to have that seventies pop sound. Because at one time, that sound was part of country. A lot of those records, especially with artists like Ronnie Milsap and such, have a lot of those sounds, and it just clicked. So I instinctively knew what I thought would work.

We didn't really discuss what we were gonna make the record sound like. The record just presented itself that way—partially because of what the songs were and the way she was singing them and partially because of the people who were in the room. We all naturally went that way together, but there was no discussion or strategy for how to make the record sound, we just did it. It was a really natural process.

MENZIE: So how do you think the industry has gotten to a place where they overlook so many qualified artists? You have all of this rich history, and yet the industry has gotten into this baseball-cap mentality; as someone who is on the creative end, you have to be frustrated by that.

CRAIG ALVIN: I am totally frustrated by it, but I will never pretend to understand the music business, especially not the country music business. I love country music, and I love pop music, but I've never sat in an office at a record label and had to make the hard decisions about other people's careers, so it's really hard for me to judge. We have to remember the record business isn't always about music.

MENZIE: How do you think Kacey has pierced that moment? She's one of the few artists that has managed to break through all of those invisible barriers. Of course, I gotta give her the credit she deserves as an ambassador of vibe. Her presence as an artist is up there with the best. I'll go back to Bowie, Jagger, or Dolly—Kacey has that mysterious kind of thing where she seems like she's accessible and then she's not, and you wonder what she's thinking. She's kind of got that mystery about her.

CRAIG ALVIN: Well, that's how you do it—you break all the rules. So many artists don't understand what makes them special, because they can't see it. They don't understand it. It's like when you hear your voice recorded for the first time and it sounds so strange, and it's almost embarrassing because [you're] like, "Well that's not what I sound like!" but it is what you sound like.

Other people don't hear you as sounding strange because they are used to you and they like you, but I think most artists suffer from a version of that sometimes, where they are not aware of the perception they create.

MENZIE: Yeah, but Kacey is, that's for sure.

CRAIG ALVIN: Oh, she definitely is.

Chapter 15

MENZIE: So when you approached your role in capturing the sounds on *Golden Hour*, you obviously had to start from the songwriting. Did you have any demos before you tracked, or did you hear the material for the first time in the studio?

CRAIG ALVIN: Usually on that record, there would be some kind of songwriter demo where I could at least hear the song before we started. There were usually a few tracks or loops or something we would bring in that would bring us the basic structure of the song, and then from that, I could kind of figure out which way we needed to go. I always try not to think about it too much; I just try to trust my gut and go do it.

MENZIE: When you were doing the session with Kacey and you were putting the tunes together, did you have any favorite songs or special moments where you were really aware of how well the music was working?

CRAIG ALVIN: I really loved the song "Love Is a Wild Thing"—partially because it did remind me of that seventies vibe, almost like a Linda Ronstadt feel or something along those lines. I just felt like that was a good midtempo song that kind of moves along and [feels] and sounds great, and she moves so effortlessly on it. "Oh, What a World" was another one of my favorites. The funny thing is the song I didn't immediately like on the record is now my favorite, which was "Slow Burn." When we were doing it, I thought it had some great lines, but I was not connecting with it, and now it's my favorite. The way it came together is perfect. How funny is that?

MENZIE: The approach to the bridge is so subtle, with such a nice lift. Two bars, three words—magical!

CRAIG ALVIN: [He laughs.] Yeah, there's lots of little moments like that, and again, that's coming back to just letting the atmosphere be right and not having to adorn it too much with fancy things. Because if you choose the [exactly] right simple thing, it's perfectly satisfying.

MENZIE: How did the vision for the record unfold and progress during tracking?

CRAIG ALVIN: For the most part, the basic tracking of songs went pretty quickly, with the exception of "Space Cowboy"—that one was a bit of a puzzle, but tracking the rest of the music was pretty simple. The hardest part was figuring out how [to] capture these songs without overembellishing them and detracting from Kacey's vocal and the feeling she creates with her writing. There were many times we had to go back and either edit a section or recut a section on the drums because she didn't like the sound of the ride cymbal, and she didn't want it there. And I think that's one of the reasons why her voice sounds so great—because there's really nothing competing with it, you can really hear it.

MENZIE: That's really an interesting thought, and I agree with you 100 percent.

CRAIG ALVIN: Kacey knows what sounds good, and she knows what she likes and, more than that, what she dislikes.

MENZIE: Well, one thing we know for sure [is] it worked. So obviously, Kacey had already written a lot of tunes, but did they write together in the studio?

CRAIG ALVIN: The songs were finished, so it was mainly the arrangements we worked on, and she was definitely open to ideas. That's just part of the job: you have to be open. But for the most part, Kacey, Daniel, and Ian had done their homework, and they were ready when they walked into the studio. They knew what they wanted, and the basic structures of the songs were already there. It was more about [asking], What do we add? What's the exact right background vocal treatment, or do we need a shaker on this? Do we want congas on this? Do we want to try to add a synthesizer part?

We tried so many things on so many songs that were fine but not exactly right, and it was about having the courage to throw things away, even though someone in the room might be really excited about it, and to go ahead and say, "Nope, that's not it, throw it away."

Chapter 15

MENZIE: Something you just said I believe separates the leading artists—they have the courage to make the hard calls, like knowing when something either doesn't work at all or, in the case of something like *Golden Hour*, knowing you have one of the best products to come out in the last five years. So that goes back to what we were talking about earlier—the artistic integrity to say, "I don't care if anybody else likes it, we like it, and Kacey likes it." So you stand by it, or even bolder, as you said, you toss it.

CRAIG ALVIN: It is absolutely the difference, and that may seem subtle, but it's not.

MENZIE: Kacey has always pushed a lot of traditional boundaries, but one of the things I truly appreciated about *Golden Hour* was that she and the team played with a lot of sonic boundaries, took liberties with textures, and blended unusual sound combinations together, and by doing that, they crafted fresh sounds for her listeners—a very different approach from the baseball-cap trend we were talking about earlier. So are there particular boundaries you would like to see go away? Do you think we're due for a creative renaissance?

CRAIG ALVIN: Well, I think there is a creative renaissance going on. With the decline of radio, people aren't buying music. They're listening to it on streaming services and such.

There's so many records coming out now that it's hard to keep up with all of them, but there's a tremendous amount of creative energy and people creating fantastic work. It takes time to seek it out and find it, but as far as things like what's happening with country radio and all that—gosh, this has been something we have been discussing for as long as there has been a country music business. And I don't know if we'll ever get around that. Some people will naturally be a little more creatively inclined, and other people will be more likely to try and come up with a formula that always works or follow what worked last week. It's one of the interesting things, trying to follow what's happening now. By the time the record comes out, it's two years old, so you're never going to be thought of as interesting if you follow what's happening right now.

MENZIE: But . . . as true as that is, it happens every day.

CRAIG ALVIN: Oh, we all fall for it—I do too. I'll hear a record and think, "Oh wow, that knocks me out!" And I'll go searching for those sounds, which is always a good exercise, but really, in the end, you don't want to make that record again; it's already been done. You already have that record, [so] you want to try to find something that feels new or at least fresh.

MENZIE: Originality—the great differentiator! You talked a little bit about the tunes you mixed for *Golden Hour* with just piano and voice. Tell us more about that.

CRAIG ALVIN: When you have only a piano and voice or only an acoustic guitar and voice, every nuance is heard. In the case of "Rainbow," we didn't really record it in a soundproof studio. We were at Sheryl Crow's studio, which is actually the upper floor of her horse barn, and it's so far away from everything, there [has been] no need to soundproof it. The piano was right next to a window. Kacey was standing next to the window, and there was a thunderstorm going on, and after we tracked, we all really liked the vocal take, but I had to spend a lot of time using noise-reduction software and automation to make it not sound like we recorded it in a thunderstorm, which sounds like it would be cool, but it wasn't.

MENZIE: That story immediately made me think about Ann Peebles's "I Can't Stand the Rain."

CRAIG ALVIN: Yeah, we like those rain songs, but this rain was hitting the window really hard, and any time you tried to do anything to EQ it or compress it or make it sound like a good recording, it got completely overwhelmed by the storm. I think there's a few moments where you can hear it if you listen closely with headphones. I hope it's "Rainbow"; it might have been "Mother." I can't remember which one it was, but I spent so much time trying to make that work because Kacey's performance was so good.

Chapter 15

Menzie: That's a great story.

Craig Alvin: Yeah, we just had to use that vocal, it was so spot on.

Menzie: So that brings up an interesting studio discussion—you were in a few different studios for the record, right? How does that work?

Craig Alvin: Well, we recorded it mostly at Sheryl Crow's, and we were also at House of Blues for a little bit of time. We were also at my studio for some of the overdubs and things like background vocals, and then we were at Sound Emporium for a good portion of it as well. The way it works is we just bring the hard drive along and plug it in and pull things up and start getting to work; these days it's not as hard. I remember, back in the days, we had to carry around two-inch tape reels and make slave reels and all that—that was a lot more difficult, but nowadays it's not that bad, especially in Nashville, where everybody has kind of standardized things. They tend to all have Pro Tools, and it tends to be up-to-date and working properly, so it's not that big a hassle.

Menzie: So it's easier now than it was. That makes sense.

Craig Alvin: The hardest part was that the microphone we used on Kacey was Sheryl's Telefunken 251, and then, when we went to other studios, we couldn't go and grab it, because it's a $25,000 microphone, so Sheryl's not going to just let that out of her house. So we went over to Blackbird, and we rented one and got it to the studio, and it didn't sound at all like the one we had been using. [It was] still a good microphone, but it didn't sound anything like it. So we had them send over all the 251s they had, and we went through them one by one and eventually found one that was a perfect match so that we could continue working with it. And they know which one it is, because we've done sessions with Kacey since then, and I call up and say, "Hey, I want the Kacey microphone," and they rent it out.

Menzie: Ah, you renamed it.

CRAIG ALVIN: I'm sure a lot of other amazing people have sung into that microphone—that's usually par for the course—but that's how I identify it. Anyone can do that, though, if you want to rent a microphone. Blackbird rents microphones; just call and ask for the Kacey microphone.

MENZIE: Going back to how big events can affect careers—four Grammys for *Golden Hour* is just crazy. And I think what's really crazy about that is you were up against some tough competition, like Brandi Carlile, and Brandi also had a big run that night. Between [her] and Kacey, the two of them took over the whole evening. So what does working on an album like *Golden Hour* do for your personal reputation? Obviously, when you're associated with an album that has had that kind of impact and success, there's got to be some positive fallout.

CRAIG ALVIN: Yeah, there has been. The nice thing is [that] now people I have met four or five times [who] have never remembered my name before suddenly remember my name. [He laughs.]

It's really nice, and a lot of my colleagues and peers have been so happy for me because they know me and have known my work for many years because I've been doing this for twenty-six, twenty-seven years, and I've worked on projects that have been nominated for Grammys several times but had never won a Grammy. So going into it, I was hopeful, but I had gotten my hopes up before, and it didn't happen. I was just thinking, "This will be a great time if nothing else." I was gonna go with my friends to Los Angeles, and we were gonna go to some parties, eat some great food, meet a lot of friendly people, and get to enjoy a really great show. That's kind of how I was looking at it.

But it's nice, the recognition. The funny thing about it is that I have had a lot of producers in Nashville call me and ask things like how I got the acoustic guitar sound or the reverb or the snare drum sound. It's oddly funny, though, because I'm not getting all the calls to track all the records in Nashville. I'm working a lot, and my rates went up, but Nashville is a funny town, and it works the way it works.

Chapter 15

MENZIE: It's funny how tight-knit factions work. It's that way in every town and business to some degree. People stick with what's comfortable. But you would think [that] occasionally, when you hit something that square in the middle, it would change things. And it's good to see that it has, and I'm sure as you go along, you'll have more and more opportunities to be part of that winning discussion, and that's the way it should be.

I loved discovering that you like having a conversation with the songs when you're mixing. I thought to myself, "If people knew how much creatives did that, they might be disturbed, right?" [Both laugh.] I thought it was great when you said, "Yeah, doesn't everybody do this?"

CRAIG ALVIN: I do talk to the song a lot; talking might be too mild of a word—I spend a lot of time yelling at the song, going, "Why won't you do what I want you to do?" The problem is songs are going to do whatever the heck they want to do, and I do have conversations with the music—and that's [speaking] literally—but also I feel that if the song isn't speaking to me, then it's not going to speak to anyone. I have to find a way to connect to that emotion. So, especially when I'm by myself working and mixing, I spend a lot of time talking to the music.

MENZIE: Well, if you think about it, forensic science works that way. Good surgeons work that way. They both work in reverse; they go in and assess problems and then recommend theories, solutions, or a diagnosis.

That's why it struck me: "Okay, I'm going to interact with this song and give it some human characteristics, so I can talk with it, as well as listen to it, so I can get it to its best place." I thought that was an awesome approach.

CRAIG ALVIN: It's so funny—I work with an artist, and we've been friends for a long time. Her name is Marie Hines, and she was talking to me about mixes that I was doing for her, and she said that she liked the fact that one of the things that happens when I'm mixing is the parts become more like characters, and she sees them as characters, almost like they're animated characters that come in and out of the song and perform acts and talk to one another. I thought that was interesting because I actually do think of it that way. I was so happy that someone had picked up on that.

MENZIE: That's a fun and creative way to look at it. You're saying, "Hey, look—have fun with the creative process." Every single person who reads this would benefit from considering how you're looking at the songs as living, breathing entities.

CRAIG ALVIN: Yeah, so true. It's a special process to get the song to breathe, and that's really the job.

MENZIE: So in today's competitive market, how does an engineer or a sound person differentiate [him- or herself] as the one you want to pick? A lot of engineers, like musicians, really get caught up in the idea of gear and end up mixing with their heads and their eyes as opposed to their ears.

CRAIG ALVIN: It sounds like a cheesy Disney movie, but be yourself, and listen with your heart, not just your head. That took me a long time—to match up my ears and my heart because I am like a lot of engineers. I do like the equipment; the gear is fun. I like so much about it, and I've learned so much about it, but there came a point in my career that I had to realize that nobody was listening to my console and nobody was listening to my compressors, they were listening to a song. Even though my knowledge of those things is tremendously helpful, I had to really take myself back to being a pure listener and stop thinking about that stuff. I think the good and the bad news is the way you do it is the same way you become a great artist—[that is,] to have a good solid identity of who you are and what makes you special and [to] go do those things and practice.

Having passion and talent is good, but you have to practice. I could go buy the nicest drum kit in the world, and no one would let me play sessions next week in Nashville, because I don't know how to play drums. I haven't practiced. I know how to tune drums really well, but I don't know how to play. I think a lot of young engineers get frustrated because they get out of school and they have all this heady knowledge, and they don't realize that

Chapter 15

you have to put in a ton of time before you're worth anything to anyone.

You've got to put in ten years of practicing for hours every day before you start to really develop the sensitivity and the skill set you need to be able to get through sessions with any kind of grace or speed and with the persistence to make it that long. I'll tell you—I spent a lot of years wondering how I was going to pay the rent and going and working on records I knew were good, with no one really acting like they cared [and] being talked down to. This isn't a fun job most days, it's really not. There's a lot of hours of sitting around, waiting for people, and you still have to be vigilant the whole time and ready to go and anticipating people's needs. There's a lot of tension in the studio that you have to be okay with; you have to be able to sit through it with people and not be part of the problem. I don't know how to tell people how to succeed at this, because it took me a lot of years of trying and failing, doing some things well and other things not so well, and I'm still learning. I'm still trying to figure out how to be successful at this.

MENZIE: You said something in an interview—you talk about mixing from the second you get the phone call forward. So when you first walk into the studio, you're mixing by observing the room, and it goes from there. Will you weigh in on that a little bit? I thought that was brilliant.

CRAIG ALVIN: Yeah, that's a concept I learned from Joe Chiccarelli. It was the very first day we were working on a record—I was green as could be—and we were setting up and working on a twenty-four track at the time. And we were bussing—the overheads, high hat, and toms—to two tracks. I thought that was crazy. My thought was "Why don't we save those for mix?" So I asked, and Joe turned to me and said, "We're mixing right now. We're mixing all the time. Mixing is our job."

And the truth is he was right—if you don't have the courage to mix from the first moment, then you probably shouldn't be doing this, because mixing is the job. You're constantly having to adjust mixes, make headphone mixes, make rough mixes—just making sure that, as musicians are getting up from their chairs and coming into the room to listen, you're pulling up the best possible mix for them to listen back to so that they can know what needs to be done next. They need a good mix to figure out where they are in the recording process. It's a constant game of mixing, which is why I tell people that the most important skill is learning to mix, even more than tracking.

I think it's odd that we think of people as tracking engineers or mixing engineers; if you're not a good mixing engineer, I don't want you tracking anything, because how do you know what sounds good together if you don't know how to mix or if you don't have a plan or the know-how to approach a mix? There's no way you know how to get sounds. Especially with drums, you'll have anywhere from four to fifteen mics up. So what are those mics doing? What is their purpose? How are they intended to be used? And then [it's important to know] how much and what type of EQ or compression to put on, how to check for phase, how to listen for phase, how to find what's causing the sounds to do what they're doing.

MENZIE: And to think good engineers make it look easy—kinda like fighter pilots, right?

CRAIG ALVIN: Yeah. The thing is that you've got to be mixing all the time, and part of that happens very early on in the process. Because when people call you and tell you that you're gonna make a record together, they start to tell you right away about the songs and who they are and what they like and what they dislike. So, you have to make all kinds of mixing decisions before you even get to the studio. For example, you have to decide what equipment needs to be there and what studio you're going to work at and how many hours you think it's going to take for setup to achieve the types of sound that they want. And this is all mixing—at least, in my mind, it is. Maybe other people try to compartmentalize it, but I can't. It's all one thing.

MENZIE: I don't think you can compartmentalize it and get the results you get. That's where it becomes an art form. Now you're into a conceptual understanding that is far beyond the technical side of engineering, and that's where the magic is. The technical is incredibly important, that's

Chapter 15

a given, but what you took from Joe Chiccarelli is on a different level of creativity—it's best of the best kind of thinking. I thought that was important to share.

CRAIG ALVIN: You have to study the masters.

MENZIE: You were just down in Muscle Shoals at FAME [Florence Alabama Music Enterprises], what was going on there? Tell me about the impact that style of music has had on you.

CRAIG ALVIN: Man, Muscle Shoals is an interesting place. It's a small town in northern Alabama that is known for having made a lot of hit records. So many amazing albums and artists have come out of there, and [with] FAME, you had the Allman Brothers Band who were formed there, Aretha Franklin recorded there, [plus] Bobbie Gentry, Wilson Pickett—all these classic albums. Even the Rolling Stones recorded at Muscle Shoals Sound on Jackson Highway. They recorded "Wild Horses" and "Brown Sugar" there. Paul Simon, Rod Stewart, everyone. Especially back in the seventies and eighties, they were all going to Muscle Shoals, not Nashville.

MENZIE: I have seen clips where Rick Hall says he couldn't break into Nashville, so he just went to the best place he could to make things happen.

So, as I said, there's a studio there called FAME, which was kind of the original place to do a record, started by Rick Hall. Rick was a famous producer and a tremendous hit maker, and he just built this beautiful place. The musicians down there are called Swampers. That's what that line in "Sweet Home Alabama" is—"Muscle Shoals, they've got the Swampers"—that's what they're talking about, the session musicians in Muscle Shoals. They have a very special, kind of greasy, swampy sound. Some of these guys who were playing on Aretha Franklin records were White guys from Alabama.

There is a video clip of the FAME session band talking about the time Rod Stewart booked the studio, and when he saw the band setting up, he thought he was having a fast one pulled on him because he expected a Black band, and he started to get pissed.

CRAIG ALVIN: Yeah, it's funny what we associate with that music. We don't think of White country boys from Alabama making that music, but they were. I find it interesting how places have a sound regardless of who the musician is. In Memphis there's a Memphis sound, and when you go to Memphis and work in the studios there, that sound gets into the recording. It's that way in Los Angeles, it's that way in Nashville, and it's definitely that way in Muscle Shoals. Even [in] places like Tulsa, you think about J. J. Cale, Dwight Twilley, [and] Leon Russell.

MENZIE: I'm humored when you make references to artists like Bobbie Gentry and Leon Russell. If you're in the music business and you don't know who Leon Russell is, that's your own private hell, but when you toss out a name like Bobbie Gentry, that's also some uniquely cool stuff. "Ode to Billy Joe"—that song simply smolders. It's a very sultry tune.

The takeaway is [that] they're important references, and you can study the modern stuff all day long, but there's a lot of rich character that you can benefit from when revisiting the great moments that have come before, and of course, that goes back to Kacey's secret. You go back and listen.

One point I keep drilling down in this book—I'm really trying to get the reader to understand that if somebody mentions a name, you should look them up. Look up Rick Hall; you'll benefit like crazy. Look up Sam Phillips; look up Bobbie Gentry. While you're at it, look up Berry Gordy—and all of the artists that influenced these people.

CRAIG ALVIN: Oh my gosh, there's a tremendous documentary that was recently made about Muscle Shoals, and if you want to know about Muscle Shoals, you should go watch that documentary. They interview Rick Hall, and you find out so much about that guy and what a hard life he lived. He was a genius but also a really kind of tortured man, and you understand so much more about why someone who was in nowhere Alabama could force the music business to come to him and set up shop in his town. He was special, no doubt about that.

Chapter 15

Menzie: In that way Rick Hall and Sam Phillips strike me the same. I know Sam was a huge influence on Rick Hall.

Craig Alvin: Well there ya go—because Sam Phillips was originally from Muscle Shoals.

Menzie: Their impact on the music business is almost indescribable; [it] makes ya think of folks like Berry Gordy.

Craig Alvin: Everybody thinks of Sam Phillips as a Memphis guy, but he actually grew up in Shoals, so it's interesting to me because there's something about these places and the characters that come from these places that is essential in understanding the music that they have generated and this great body of work that we have now—just the history of the people and the places that they built, . . . all the incredible music they made, and [the] barriers they were able to break through.

Menzie: You're hitting on a key word when you say "essential." It's so important for today's musicians to see where the risks were taken by the likes of a Rick Hall, . . . how driven and determined he was, and how many hurdles he overcame—plus, the whole backstory around the betrayal from the Swampers and his tumultuous relationship with Jerry Wexler. And of course, the Aretha story is one of those iconic stories that people should look up. There was an amazing recording session that changed Aretha's career yet ended up disastrously with a fistfight. All of that is the truth. The industry has a million personalities, and not all of them are great. It's kind of like a family—not everybody in it is how they appear on Sunday at church.

So Hall's history perfectly clarifies [that] if you choose music, a career is a lifetime, and that means you've got to be able to do a lot of different things. Because it's competitive, and sometimes it's also thankless, but most importantly, sometimes it's flat-out amazing.

Craig Alvin: Well, it's to the point now where I love the people who are easy, but I look for the people [who] are crazy because, man, they get things done.

MENZIE: Man, that's a great quote. What trends do you see currently in the industry? Where do you see things going with recording and in the business in general?

CRAIG ALVIN: Pertaining to the music, I don't think about that stuff too much, although I do like to stay on top of what's happening. But it's hard to predict because it's changing all the time, and it's better to set the trend than to follow it.

As far as the actual industry goes, we all see a trend happening with our main music cities—it happened in New York and Los Angeles, and now it's happening in Nashville—where the music industry, especially the musicians, are being pushed out because things are just so expensive. You have beautiful places like RCA Studio A that, if it wasn't for a billionaire philanthropist, would've been torn down and made into condos, and this is the studio where the first song recorded there was "Jolene"!

That was Chet Atkins's palace. He built that place, and they were just going to tear it down and put in condos—what a horrifying thought to think that was considered okay. I've had the privilege of working in that studio a few times, and it's such a magical, wonderful room to be in. The idea that there are rooms that are magical and wonderful all over, especially in places like New York and Los Angeles and Nashville, that are being lost and turned mainly into luxury condos . . . We have to wonder what we are going to do when it's too expensive for any of us to exist in a place like Nashville. I hate to think about it because Nashville is such a wonderful city, and it's been so good to me. And I love the people here, but at some point, it's going to be too expensive for someone who's a tremendous young guitar player who's roughly twenty-three years old and has a ton of student loan debt to just rent an apartment.

I honestly think that we are going to see things decentralize a little bit, so maybe a place like Muscle Shoals will come back into vogue because it's still relatively inexpensive to live there, and they have all the infrastructure needed to sustain the music industry.

Chapter 15

Menzie: So obviously, that's something that we don't know how it will play out, but with record companies, do you see their role improving or retracting more?

Craig Alvin: I hope there's always good labels around, but I see a lot of people like Hanson, which I think is a good example. They were dropped from a major label deal, and it didn't hurt them at all. It's actually the best thing that ever happened to them—they went on to form 3CG Records.

Menzie: So they had the vision to take on their own label and embraced the idea of entrepreneurship. Maybe without problems, that idea doesn't get developed. So maybe that's the good side of the problem.

Craig Alvin: I think a lot of people are starting to figure out that maybe you don't need a major label to make money.

Menzie: There are certainly some different avenues that are available today that weren't available even ten years ago. But that also puts more responsibilities on the artist, and they will have to develop yet another skill set—entrepreneurship! Maybe that's a good thing. It makes it harder, but maybe that ends up being productive and gives the artists more control.

Craig Alvin: It definitely means we'll have different kinds of artists succeeding.

Menzie: That's a creative thought—different kinds of artists succeeding. Let's leave it there.

Chapter 16

The Power of Influence

If you asked me to choose between a large sum of money and the *power of influence*, I would always choose the latter. The reason is simple: the power of influence is an unlimited and renewable capital. However, attaining the power of influence has its tests.

The first step to understanding the components of the power of influence is understanding the "what" factor—the unique something that you bring to the table. More specifically, the "what" is whatever talents or skills you have mastered and are willing to exploit. Without the "what," your career in the arts does not happen, and the better the "what" is, the better the ride.

The "why" factor is your purpose and passion; it is completely defined by you. It is your motivation to stay constantly evolving as your professional and personal circumstances continually go through changes. The good news is that these two components are directly under your personal control, and that is a big deal!

Then there's the "who" factor, where the power of influence is an immeasurable capital.

In the worlds of music and business, the "who" matter is as follows: you definitely want to know as many "who" as possible and become a card-carrying "who" member. If there is any label worth having in a business of personas, it is the label of "who." There is one catch, though: the "who" badge is only given to vetted influencers, and it can be revoked or downgraded at the drop of a hat. So the one trick you want to have up your sleeve in a fickle business like the music industry is consistency.

Chapter 16

What, then, defines the power of influence? It is the currency of your personal impact on professional situations and the ability to sway a professional environment in one direction or another, either for yourself or for others. In short it's the respect that other professionals have for your abilities, feelings, and opinions on any professional topic in any professional situation. The power of influence is the master key that opens all the doors to the world of networking and bares the offspring we call opportunity.

How do we build our power of influence? Let's go back and look at what we can control: the "what" in our "soul stew."

What have you done to make *you* the one to choose? What is the quality of your personal product? What makes your contributions unique? What is special about your vision? What is the quality of your professional preparation? What various styles of music are you competent with? What does your professional involvement do to help a music project move forward? Lastly, what qualities about you make you enjoyable to work with?

The "what" is the foundation of all of the above. That box has to be checked, and it should be checked as definitively as humanly possible, as well as upgraded consistently. The more dimension you can bring to your "what" factor, the better, and in today's music business, this has only gotten harder.

This is where the "why" comes in handy.

Let us consider the example of two or more musicians competing for the same role in a professional audition or performing group. Everyone trying for the position has highly developed professional skills, or the "what" factor. In that moment, everyone can play. Because of these abilities, the "why" becomes a larger-than-life perspective.

Why do you play the way you do in the audition? Why are you attracted to the tones you have chosen? Why do you carry yourself with such personal confidence while also bringing a healthy dose of humility with you? Why do you have a slightly better ear than the others who are vying for the spot? Why did you elect to prepare more diligently than the other candidates trying out? Why is your energy, concentration, and quickness at a higher level than the others auditioning? Most importantly, why are you coming up with better suggestions to advance the music and the moment?

As I said earlier, control over the "what" and the "why" is in everyone's arsenal, but how you employ these tools is completely at your discretion and generally affects the outcome. The following is a quick side note: the "why" is very cryptic, and the more you study the greats, the more value your "why" amasses.

To borrow a quote from the great Buddy Rich, "This is where the hatchin' starts."

Oddly enough, many of your opportunities for success come down to the "who." What a great name for a band, right? The "who" are everywhere. You simply never know which "who" is who. Most who are a "who" have influence to one degree or another. For instance, imagine someone offers you a quick pick-up gig for fast cash, and maybe you feel the opportunity is slightly less appealing than what you are truly striving for in your professional career, but you take the gig simply because you can use the extra cash. No harm, no foul!

Fortunately, you have integrity, and musically speaking, you bring everything you can to the performance. After the first show, during the break, you start talking with the keyboard player, and you bond with him because your musical approaches match. You discover that he is also a sub on the gig. The keyboard player compliments you on your playing and begins telling you about his "real" project. He invites you to come hear his band when he comes back through the area, and fortunately, you are motivated enough to do so.

Here's the unexpected "pin action" of this story. It turns out that his "real" project comprises five monster musicians, and the music they play is phenomenal. Over time, all of them go on to become national touring players with several major acts. By connecting the "who" factor and taking the keyboard player up on his offer to see his "real" project, you develop relationships with several members of the band, which leads to national connections. By understanding the "who" factor, you have now pushed into the potential of the moment. Welcome to the power of influence. The most important aspect of the story is you have widened your network, which will now continue to grow, and in a musician's career, those moments are the secret to future opportunities, which often lead to success.

There are only a few rules to all of this. First, you must maintain the quality of your "what" factor, though that is not quite as easy as it sounds. You must remain relevant to sustain your magnetism, as trends change by the hour. Originality is king, followed closely by heartfelt passion and commitment.

The "why" is always your driving force. Again, I caution musicians to base their "why" on internal motivation, not on external circumstances. Great art is created, not manufactured. Excellence fuels longevity.

Here are a few final thoughts on the power of influence.

Genuine influence is garnered from respect. It sounds so simple, but genuine respect is the slowest-growing tree in the forest and the most deeply rooted.

Research music legend Chet Atkins. Atkins is one of many who understood and aligned with the power of influence, and because of that, his work in the music industry was legendary. The deeper you look into this idea, the sooner you will discover that every great in the industry understands it well.

Most importantly, they honor it!

Chapter 17

Dom Famularo

DOM FAMULARO'S MARK ON THE MUSIC INDUSTRY IS INDELIBLE. Respected worldwide as one of the finest music educators ever to grace the music industry, Dom was as entertaining as he was insightful.

Whether as an educator, performer, or author, his quest and passion for excellence earned him the nickname Mr. Motivational. View his Session Panel videos on YouTube because they are all treasures.

INTERVIEW

MENZIE: You understand an aspect of the music business that not enough people talk about: *success*. You constantly share the wisdom that you've gained over the years to help others succeed. All musicians can use solid guidance when discovering ways to augment their career, and you have written a book, *The Cycle of Self-Empowerment*, that addresses ways to embrace success. Let's begin by talking a little bit about the benefits of understanding the power of intention.

DOM FAMULARO: The industry is in a different mind-set now. The old mind-set was you just waited for the phone to ring because there were tons of jobs out there. So you picked it up and booked it, or you said, "No, I don't like that job," and you didn't take it, because there was such an overwhelming amount of work that was constantly available. You could be choosy.

In today's industry, because of the amount of competition, a lot of that has changed. Not only has the mentality of music retail changed with online sales [and so forth], but the entire

Chapter 17

music business has changed, including the performance aspect.

Growing up, I felt I had a lot of different things that I wanted to do in my life. I love performing. I started performing professionally at the age of twelve, and I kept doing it. Then I went to St. John's University, where I studied in communication arts, business, and philosophy, and it was those three things that inspired me. I was studying privately with some of the top musicians in the world—Joe Morello, Jim Chapin, Louie Bellson, Max Roach—these were great legends [whom] I had the fortune and opportunity to study with because of living on Long Island, a short drive to New York City, where they were located. These guys were really filled with such great wisdom. Since I was studying with them privately, I decided that when [I] got to school, I wanted to study communications and arts and develop the ability to speak clearly and be understood. If life is about the message, I needed to be sure I knew how to deliver that message.

The second thing was the business skills. I felt that the better player I became, since I was the product, the easier the product would be to sell. So I had to understand the business of how to sell the product of Dom Famularo. The third part, the philosophy part, was more about the study of the human mind. If I could study just a little bit about how people think and what their intentions are and be able to read into them, that would give me an edge.

That really did give me the scope of who I am now. I began to realize that I had to have the clarity of who I wanted to be and what I wanted to achieve. Those are two very important things because who I want to be is a person I can live with, and I want to be able to meet people and empower people and have relationships that are positive for the rest of my life. Money is really not my motivator, and I am really a firm believer that if you live your passion and go for what you believe in, the money will follow. And it has. I have made way more money than I could have ever imagined in my life, but I don't focus on that. I focus on staying true to my mission statement: the importance of me being the person I want to be, working toward the kind of artist I want to be, and then being the businessperson I want to be.

So I started with the mentality that I am a businessman, but I understand that my product is Dom Famularo, and Dom Famularo, the performer, has many different aspects. He likes to perform, but he also likes to teach, so I have a private teaching practice that I built up over many years. I built a studio on the back of my property where I live on Long Island, and I have over 1,600 students that travel to me from over thirty countries.

MENZIE: There is a video tour of your studio on YouTube, so, readers, check it out.

DOM FAMULARO: The tour is available for anyone to go watch. Thirty percent of the lessons are online, using Skype or FaceTime or Zoom, and in the process, I'm able to deliver this information to anywhere around the world. I put high-end internet service in my house and studio, [as well as] a flat-screen TV and a huge computer. I'm able to reach the world and help these drummers everywhere without them having to leave the confines of their home or studio. By embracing twenty-first-century technology, I opened up my reach, and my communication got better.

And when they come to the studio, they're able to learn. I've got these one-on-one lessons; students come in for an hour or two hours—many of them even book a solid week. I do about fifteen or twenty of these a year with students who come in and book four to six days of eight hours each. They are committed musicians and educators. They have a passion, and they are driven to learn the skills that can unleash and free them, so the teaching end of it is very exciting.

And now with my current teaching studio, I'm able to teach individual lessons as well as conduct master classes. I am fortunate to have teachers from around the world who are organizing anywhere from twenty to thirty students in a room, wherever they are, while I'm broadcasting from my studio. And in master classes, I usually present for an hour.

So my teaching approach evolved as different technologies became available. The magic of a room full of musicians hungry for advice is pretty unbeatable, but I also still conduct live-performance stuff because I still love to perform live with other musicians.

There's a lot of traveling to different cities around the world to host clinics because of my relationships with different manufacturers, like Sabian

Chapter 17

Cymbals, Mapex Drums, Vic Firth Drumsticks, and Evans Drumheads.

While traveling, I found interest and questions about applications in drumming, so I realized there was also a need for specific books to be written. I began to write drum books, and there are instances where I will cowrite with longtime advanced students.

I cowrite because I want their careers to grow, too, so I tell them I want to be involved in the process. I say, "I want you to know the process, and we'll do it together. We'll split the royalties." Or if they do most of the work, I give them three quarters or even all of the royalties. It's my publishing company that I have with Joe Bergamini. We publish these books, and Alfred distributes them worldwide.

So the hats that I've learned to wear when I get to my desk at 6:00 a.m. every morning are [of] Dom Famularo the artist, the teacher, the author, the clinician, and the education consultant to these companies that help build education programs globally, which affects other companies I'm involved with.

MENZIE: Which is the model that, through necessity, is now becoming the standard.

DOM FAMULARO: Everyone's starting to do this.

MENZIE: Right, you're only about twenty years ahead, not bad. [He laughs.]

DOM FAMULARO: Absolutely, I could visualize the idea years ago because I understood the educational part of it. When they asked Warren Buffett in several different interviews what could be done to help the economy grow, he said, "Invest in education." That really is the secret, and I kind of understood that. I also realized that if I kept on doing this, it would grow into something impactful.

MENZIE: The ripple effect is huge.

DOM FAMULARO: It's powerful. All the different companies that I am working with are migrating to that model, which I think is wonderful because when companies improve their level of education, it brings in more people to play music. It makes the industry bigger. As we raise the standard of knowledge in the art form, our music industry gets stronger because of it.

MENZIE: A strong music industry is a good thing!

DOM FAMULARO: Yes! The twenty-first-century musician has to be more savvy in business. Musicians should map out a good strategy for developing the necessary business side of things and learn to be comfortable wearing the different hats they need to wear in order to build their brand and their reach.

MENZIE: There is definitely a new model in the making, and the old model of record labels [having done] the lifting for you—or feeling that, because you were a musician, you didn't need business skills—is dead and gone.

DOM FAMULARO: At one time that model worked great, but now, because of the internet and online accessibility, there are different options available to us. I sell a lot of my products through my online store; consumers buy from me directly. So with that, an artist [who] has a product can develop platforms and sell through their own efforts.

Additionally, they can incorporate streaming to get their music heard or use whatever new mediums are currently available. Given enough time, you build up your catalog and a strong following, and along with your music, you create merchandise, like shirts and hats. And as you, the artist, build and sell more products, a record label sees what you've built and that you have started to make good sales and have an established following. They come in and say they want to be involved with you. So because of the approach you have taken, you walk into that negotiation with greater leverage.

MENZIE: I believe rising artists are beginning to understand that what motivates any buyer of their product is the advantage the artist brings to them. So the responsibility falls on the artist because buyers expect an established fan base. Your intentions dictate your reality. If you're at all unclear on your intentions, then your outcome is directly affected and muted by that uncertainty.

DOM FAMULARO: Absolutely. I once had the chance to speak with Wayne Dyer, who wrote the wonderful book *The Power of Intention*. His book reinforced and helped me understand what I was taught by my mom: visualize what you are trying to achieve, and when you can clearly see that idea in your mind, put your focused energy behind that vision, and you will eventually enjoy it. And although I didn't understand it completely in my early stages, I trusted it and always repeated it. Finally, I understood that she was talking about intention, and I firmly believe in that positive energy.

I don't allow negative energy into my life—even when I have been powerfully challenged. I've realized that there is going to be an eventual point of defeating any negativity by always being positive. So if I answer a phone, I'm happy, and if my frame of mind is not what it needs to be, I don't answer the phone. But if I answer that phone, I am ready, prepared, and reporting for duty. It's a matter of maintaining that committed level of intensity. So intention to me is an important part of the clarity of what you're trying to achieve.

One thing I did was write down my different goals, the important ideas that I wanted to accomplish. The plans I wrote were anywhere from one- to five- to ten-year plans. I kept on writing down different ideas for drum books, even when I knew I wasn't anywhere near ready to write that book; I just wrote down the book's concept under "Ideas for books." Over time I've gotten twelve drum books written. So intention matters.

MENZIE: And they're great books, by the way.

DOM FAMULARO: Thank you! Each of them is written as a part of a larger curriculum. Each book I put out feeds off of the prior book and leads to the next book. The drum books became a major part of my journey of intention. Musicians need to understand that big ideas take time and discipline; I had book ideas written down as goals that took me literally twenty-plus years to write, but those books are published now. I was excited to see them come to fruition.

Success is not only about your plan but also your determination. To a master, determination is nonnegotiable.

MENZIE: A musician's career is an ongoing endeavor, and determination can get you through a rough patch.

DOM FAMULARO: When I was traveling around the world doing hundreds of clinics a year, I began to notice a pattern of questions from musicians, questioning their self-worth. So that's how I began to write the book *The Cycle of Self-Empowerment*.

Empowerment means to give power, but before I can give power, I must first possess that power. If I have that level of empowerment, then I can empower you. If I'm a happy person, then I can . . . make you happy. If I love myself, then I can love you. You need to understand that process.

So the power of intention comes from that realization and understanding. I really need to understand myself first. Ask yourself the [following] questions: Am I at a place where I'm happy with myself, and can I clarify the plan or the intention that I have? I focus on intention every day, so it shouldn't surprise you that I've got my next five- [and] ten-year plans already laid out. I just turned sixty-one, and at a time of my life where most artist's careers are stabilizing or slowing down, last year was my busiest year.

MENZIE: With the music industry changing to a self-empowered format, what is your advice to today's musicians regarding the important things they should do to empower their position as artists?

DOM FAMULARO: I really do believe it's up to artists now to fully take charge and not wait for someone to do it for them or wait for an opportunity to possibly come their way. In today's music business, you create your own opportunities. Today's musicians need to really be in go mode. Business has always been and always will be about networking. Business is really about meeting people, inspiring people, and sharing your vision.

Chapter 17

If your ideas are wonderful and you're energized, connecting with others creates new opportunities.

MENZIE: Artists in the past had the privilege of being able to be withdrawn and a bit to themselves because the record companies did the lifting. Now with social media, fans expect you to stay engaged twenty-four seven, and of course, that creates yet another task for musicians.

DOM FAMULARO: In today's music business, it is important that every musician takes an active role in [his or her] business dealings because you, the artist, are the product. If you have success, that makes it all the more important to have good people skills. I went so far as to take communication classes to help me gain comfort when speaking in front of large crowds.

At the very least, today's musicians must have a solid foundation in the general aspects of how business works—computing, social media, communications, [and] even things as basic as being a good scheduler. The more hats you wear, the more scheduling becomes a critical responsibility. I also think having a good handle on marketing and visual promotion matters too. You almost have to be a photojournalist to boot—kind of like Annie Leibovitz meets Jack Antonoff meets Steve Jobs.

In my case, I do have a secret weapon: my wife. She is a scheduling machine, and we work well together. Family equals sanity, so I don't miss family events if possible. When a call comes in for a performance, they might say, "Dom, we want you to leave Thursday evening and get here Friday morning so we can map out some rehearsal plans for the performance Friday night." But if I look at my calendar and see there's a family concert on Thursday night, I'll respond that I'm not available Thursday night but I can fly out early Friday morning. How I map that out really allows me to balance the family and the business sides of my life. Scheduling is an important skill to develop.

Now, there are times when I get a call for a performance that is really high paying, and my wife will be the first to say, "Your bags are packed, nice talking to you! Taxi is out front; they're waiting for you." She understands the balance too. If you have a real working relationship, you have to make sure it's in balance. And your business is in balance, and your purpose is in balance. Purpose is what really inspires me, which brings us full circle back to intention, and it continues.

MENZIE: You have the vitality and energy of a thirty-year-old. Other than drumming, what do you do to maintain such great physical health?

DOM FAMULARO: I really don't do anything like work out, except I drum all the time. That's a workout of a different nature. I've always been active with my three boys, like by going to their games and being involved with what they're doing. But it's really been a matter of respecting and being mindful of what I eat. I'm not a real drinker, and I respect the fact that I want to be around as long as I can for my children. I learned years ago that it's really not about me; I am the low man on the totem pole in my house. My children are the focus, along with my wife.

I strive to maintain the highest level of humility in what I do, and I think when you experience humility, that also gives you energy. Humility teaches you that no matter what you think you're doing well, there are ways to improve and be better.

MENZIE: And you can also help the next person, who might not have quite the understanding that you do. It's definitely a ladder.

DOM FAMULARO: Absolutely. When you share your knowledge, you begin to see the growth in others, and when you empower others with teaching, parenting, or performing—that really is the energy cycle. I'm up early every morning, inspired by the opportunities I see every day. There is energy in that too.

MENZIE: And, therefore, you treat it with respect.

DOM FAMULARO: Absolute respect—because I don't know what tomorrow brings. In my first book, *The Cycle of Self-Empowerment*, I discuss how my passion helped me clarify my vision, and I examine core words like morals, virtues, ethics, perseverance, and accountability.

MENZIE: [You were] going with old-school terms.

Dom Famularo: Yes, but we both know those old-school terms are fundamental foundations that still work today. That awareness empowers me.

My second book, which I'm currently working on, is called *Owning Now*. It's about understanding and owning the present moment because all we really own is now. We only own this moment. Yesterday is gone, and we don't own tomorrow. So trying to squeeze the most out of each moment really is what life is about—stealing time inside the moment of now.

Menzie: Who have been your favorite motivational figures in your life?

Dom Famularo: My parents. They were both extremely avid learners. That was a very important part of their journey, and they passed that love of learning onto me. My dad passed away at the young age of eighty-nine, and believe it or not, he was the most decorated volunteer fireman in America. He gave sixty-five years of active service as a volunteer fireman, so I didn't need to look too far for heroes.

Menzie: I know you have also had great mentor relationships in the industry as well.

Dom Famularo: Absolutely. [There's] Bob Zildjian, who I had the chance to work with at Sabian Cymbals for over twenty-five years. I still work with Andy Zildjian and that great company. Bob was vibrant about learning and discussing new ways of being able to manufacture and market cymbals. He was absolutely vibrant. And, of course, another mentor was Vic Firth. I still work with the Vic Firth company too. I learned a ton from Vic about his passion for quality and love for innovation. Being in the music industry has provided me a unique seat at the table. You never run out of things to learn, and inspirational relationships are everywhere.

Menzie: I know you encourage all people to play and enjoy discovering the creative processes, but for those who are considering music as a career, give [them] your list of essential traits.

Dom Famularo: The first is you have to understand passion. Passion is a strong desire to do anything, so you have to understand passion, and you have to keep on refueling it because you will be tested.

I would probably say the second trait is perseverance. Perseverance basically means you never give up. With every obstacle I have ever encountered, perseverance has made the difference, and [it] still does because you will always hit resistance—*always*!

When you hit a wall, you need to break through it. Or you go around it or jump over it or dig under it. There has to be a way, and I'm going to figure it out. It might take me months or years to figure that one out. But I will do it!

Menzie: People mistakenly put a time line on finding solutions, so another good word is patience. As you said, you keep digging, which also means you have an understanding of sacrifice.

Dom Famularo: It takes an understanding of personal evolution. If I'm hitting that wall, I have not evolved enough to discover how to overcome the challenge in front of me. I have to keep on learning, which allows me the opportunity to evolve to the level of a solution. If you don't work to evolve, the problem will just keep repeating itself.

Menzie: Einstein is credited with saying, "We cannot solve our problems with the same level of thinking that created them," which mirrors what you are saying now.

Dom Famularo: Another trait would be accountability, especially in teaching. If a problem is ever encountered in a lesson, it's never the fault of the student. It is always me. If that student is not learning, I have to go back and find out what I'm doing that's not connecting and find the key for that student.

Menzie: It's a teacher's responsibility to understand how a student learns. Great teachers listen and observe from the student's point of comprehension, not theirs.

Chapter 17

Dom Famularo: I have to accept that responsibility and strive to discover how to reach that student. I've got to find out what other techniques are available that I can use for that student. Every student is a completely different venture. I think another important trait is enthusiasm. Enthusiasm is based on the Greek word *enthousiasmos*, which means "filled with God." [Being] enthusiastic about the quality of what's out there in this great life—that enthusiasm is an extremely important motivating force.

Lastly, I would say [that] you have to have an insatiable desire to learn. If I were to use the same curriculum over and over with students I've maintained for years without growing the catalog, then I would be losing the opportunity to extract the highest-quality results that I can from them. I would be just giving them information, and that's information they can get from the internet.

Menzie: How important do you believe it is for drummers who seek professional status to also play a melodic instrument, sing, or understand production?

Dom Famularo: Oh, [it is] absolutely required. I play piano, and I'll throw one more in there: it's important for them to dance.

Menzie: Two of our favorite drummers both studied tap dance—Buddy Rich and Steve Gadd.

Dom Famularo: [They are] two great tap dancers. Sammy Davis Jr. played great drums. Gene Kelly played drums. Fred Astaire played drums. Think of all the great tap dancers [who] played drums—and there are also a lot of notable drummers who danced: Jack DeJohnette, Roy Haynes, Papa Joe Jones, and Ed Thigpen.

My sister was a dancer, and I danced when I was younger. I really believe tap dance specifically opened me up to a better understanding of rhythm, movement, and balance.

Playing piano helps a drummer with the understanding of melody and the theory behind what they're doing. Then when you perform with other musicians, you hear changes better. It helps you understand song form better, so you complement the music better. I've got a saying [that goes] "Rehearsal is for cowards." It really is a matter of going out onstage, calling the tune, and playing.

Impromptu performance opens your ears up. I'm playing with John Hammond this week, and it's kind of an open format. Rather than being over-rehearsed, I prefer to hit it live so the audience experiences the intensity of the moment at the same time the artists experience it. There's a certain magic in that. We have to listen, and we have to speak to each other musically.

MENZIE: How important is it for melodic players to play drums?

DOM FAMULARO: I think it's really important. In today's industry more musicians are playing multiple instruments. Chick Corea is a phenomenal drummer, and there are many other keyboard players [who] I've worked with who are also very good drummers. When you step into that world, it opens your mind, and an open mind is one of the most important things to have.

MENZIE: It makes you hear differently, and that's so important.

DOM FAMULARO: And to feel it. When I play the piano, I'm feeling it. When the piano player plays the drums, they feel it. They are then feeling what I'm feeling. That's really what music is about: compassion.

We exchange back and forth and try to get to the extremely exciting place where two or more musicians go somewhere together. You're experiencing this ecstasy of communication, and that takes you to a high that no alcohol or drug can get you to. It's the purity of what it's about.

MENZIE: How about knowledge of production?

DOM FAMULARO: It's very important. Years ago, you just walked out and did your thing, and the other guy did the job for you. Now the technology has evolved so quickly and plays such an important role in music that, just like with business, you have to have at least a good working knowledge of tech. It gives you more control of your career. It really is important to have a basic understanding of production and technology just to enhance whatever your professional intention is.

MENZIE: How do you drive home to drummers and all musicians that the critical understanding of "the pocket" and playing for the music is what gets them hired and paid? To quote Steve Gadd, "Space is just as important as the notes."

DOM FAMULARO: The question about technique and expression is always interesting. When great musicians are performing, they are never thinking or caring about technique or big chops. They're thinking about expression and the musicality of the song. That's what makes them great players.

Practiced diligently, technique becomes ingrained and is recalled automatically, just like language. It's not how many words you know, it's the quality of what you say that matters.

MENZIE: So how do you get someone to understand when not to "speak"?

DOM FAMULARO: One responsibility we have as qualified educators is to teach the concept of serving the song. That's very important. I'm a servant to the music. It's not about me or any single musician. It's always about the music. The works of the great drummers like Steve Gadd, J. R. Robinson, Jeff Porcaro, and Bernard Purdie express that philosophy. These are great players [who] have unbelievable technique, but they also know exactly what grooves and how to play the role of the minimalist in order to get the maximum out of any song.

Bernard's drumming on Steely Dan's "Babylon Sisters" is the perfect example of an unrelenting groove that is simply hypnotic. And what Gadd played on Steely Dan's "Aja" is a great example of a song that required a more featured expression, and it demonstrated both subtlety and ferocity. It's evident that technique was displayed loud and clear on both songs, but both musicians famously served the song.

And "Aja" was a one take, so these are musicians who really understand the language of drumming. I believe Bernard's book is even called *Let the Drums Speak!* The more we study technique, the easier it is to express ourselves musically, but it's important to take ego out of it, and [it's more important to] put the music first than it is to try to impress people with displaced overkill.

It really is about being as articulate and precise as possible in order to get the message across, which is exactly what groove is. The groove is a feeling, and we're trying to transmit that feeling through a song to the audience for them to feel it so that it lifts them up. That's where self-discipline and self-control come in.

MENZIE: Let's change lanes and talk a little bit about *The Sessions* panel and elaborate on the work you are doing with Jules Follet on music-business education.

DOM FAMULARO: Jules Follet is the energy behind the project, and *The Sessions* mission statement is "assist musical artists in the understanding of business, so they can pursue the excellence of their talents and their gifts." Jules is a photographer who, for years, took pictures of bands, and she always found it challenging to get good shots of the drummer because drummers are always in the back and never really lit very well. After finding ways to capture unique photos, she decided to compile a book just about drummers. She put together this large coffee-table book and called it *Sticks 'n' Skins*.

In it are five hundred world-famous drummers and their biographies, along with photos from Jules and noted photographer Lissa Wales. Jules shares unique backstories, and the book pays homage to this large family of renowned drummers. But as she put this book together, it became evident that a lot of these drummers, though they were in very famous bands or on very famous recordings, weren't as financially set as she felt they should be. So we began brainstorming around the idea, focusing on ways to educate and give back, and that was the birth of *The Sessions*.

We put together a panel of top industry professionals that rotates from session to session with world-class musicians and music-business professionals, and the expenses are funded by her nonprofit foundation so that we can take the program to universities at no cost. We coordinate with ten to twelve universities a year.

Chapter 17

In each session we review an extensive PowerPoint presentation that we put together, discussing all the aspects of the music industry and what you need to prepare: how to handle marketing yourself, what artist relation skills you will need, what production skills, [and] what technology skills, and we help clarify the understanding that you are the product.

Paul Quin, who is an entertainment lawyer, really gives terrific insight on how the music industry works now from a legal aspect—copyrights, recordings, [and] how all that works from a contractual standpoint.

Liberty DeVitto, who drummed with Billy Joel for thirty years, brings the experience he has from playing around the world and performing on all the Billy Joel records. We've had Rick Drumm on our panel; [he] was president of Vic Firth Sticks for ten years and then president of D'Addario for eight years and now has his own consulting company.

When the first part of our presentation is done, which takes four or five hours, I usually take one person from the panel and interview them. I ask them questions around their field of expertise, and the audience has a chance to interact and be involved, which gives them a one-on-one opportunity to ask questions they may have. We video that interview for the Legends series we have on *The Sessions* website. It's just great stuff.

Afterwards, we have a live jam session, and the students can sign up and perform with us or in their own groups. It's a unique experience that is receiving extremely positive feedback, and it really helps music students because they are getting expertise directly from the horse's mouth, and that opens up their minds.

I hear people say the music industry has changed and that it's much harder now, but it was difficult when I was twenty years old. It's a different difficult now, so we have to understand how different this new difficult is. Musicians need to ask themselves harder questions, like "Am I really committed to my passion?" Then they need to commit and declare that they will learn the necessary skills needed for today's music-business climate and incorporate those skills to attain the growth they're still looking for in their career.

MENZIE: Say you're a gifted musician, but you can't afford a college education, as is the case for a lot of people, yet you have all the passion and the natural instincts for music. What is your advice to young men and women in that scenario? What path would you put them on?

DOM FAMULARO: I am impressed with so many community colleges throughout the nation because they offer really great music programs at an extremely affordable price. On Long Island I know many of the music teachers, and they are great players and extremely dedicated teachers. Another suggestion is private education. An inspiring private teacher can take someone to unique heights because it's a one-on-one setting, the most ideal setting you will ever have. And last but not least, if someone wants it badly enough, nothing will get in their way. Determination is everything!

MENZIE: You are known as the Global Ambassador of Drumming. Let's talk about your globe-trotting fun all over the world.

DOM FAMULARO: That title was given to me by Ron Spagnardi, the creator of *Modern Drummer Magazine*. He was referring to a trip I took to Germany where I came across a teacher, Claus Hessler, who is a great player. I helped Claus connect to Sabian Cymbals and Vic Firth Sticks, and they brought him into the fold. And now he's one of the hottest guys in Germany.

As I've traveled, I've discovered many wonderful musicians from around the world and tried to aid their cause and widen the exposure we have to their talents. I gladly embrace the role of ambassador to help the bigger picture grow. The global part of it is that I'm in China, Germany, Canada, United States, Mexico, South America, [and] Central America. I go back down to Brazil again, then I'm off to South Africa, [then] Indonesia, and I'll go back to Australia this year.

MENZIE: I assume you study the drumming of these countries while you're there and listen to the native influences?

DOM FAMULARO: Yes, I submerge myself in the world music these musicians play. What a unique resource to be exposed to. In truth I'm just stealing a page from many of the jazz greats [who] have been influenced by world music for years, both melodic and percussion players. And

Chapter 17

when I take certain rhythms that these world players are using and find ways to incorporate that into my own drumming, it really creates great depth in what I'm playing. Some great examples of drummers blending world rhythms into their feels are Horacio Hernandez, Trilok Gurtu, Steve Gadd, and the unique New Orleans drummer Johnny Vidacovich. When Steve played "Late in the Evening," he incorporated the Mozambique. He wanted to sound like more than one drummer, so he played with four sticks. All of these people bring many unique world influences and flavors to what they play. I learn from the best, and I steal from the best.

Menzie: You are a master at networking. Will you share some insights on building a network?

Dom Famularo: First, I believe networking is the great differentiator. As I mentioned, I studied with many of the greats, so I was advantaged by that. But another word for networking is hustle, and as I began to teach and play locally on Long Island, I also started to go into the school systems, offering my services as a clinician.

I continued this over the course of maybe a decade. Over the ten-year period, I probably conducted five hundred clinics in schools. The idea here is that when something is done in an effective manner, it multiplies. If you are a good teacher, you pick up lots of students, which also gets noticed by other influencers, and before you know it, not only directors but manufacturers begin to know your name. Every opportunity brings us additional opportunities, and if you seek success, we must do everything we can to amplify those successes.

Through the years I expanded my network in every manner possible. It is important to understand visibility and just as important to act on every opportunity. Obviously, you need to develop your craft, but networking is also a craft—and one that is extremely important to sustaining a successful music career. What is successful for one helps all, and that grows the entire industry. Musicians win. Educators win. Students win. Manufacturers win. That's networking.

MENZIE: Serving others, whether that's fellow musicians or through the music, is the great inside secret.

DOM FAMULARO: Absolutely, because it's the right of the cause. I'm a firm believer that I give nothing away for free. Every time I paid for a lesson with Joe Morello, after every lesson for the eight years I studied with him, he would say, "The reason why I'm taking your money is because I want you to earn this and really appreciate the knowledge." After the first year, I said, "Joe, it's not about the money. You're earning it, every lesson." It really was important that I paid for it, knowing that I was earning that. It gave me a sense of pride that allowed me to own that knowledge and put it into effect.

MENZIE: Will you describe to the reader why the Moeller technique, taught to you by Jim Chapin, is so important in drumming?

DOM FAMULARO: The Moeller technique is a whipping movement that you evolve to naturally because it evolves directly from the nature of drumming. When you want to achieve speed and power, you definitely want to use it. If I try to achieve the volume sometimes required in today's music without that, it creates pain. I'm generally not a fan of pain, so to avoid that, I want to learn the right movements. The Moeller technique is one of three important aspects of movement techniques.

There are also George Lawrence Stone's technique and Billy Gladstone's technique. Gladstone really understood finger movement, which drummers need when playing, but George Lawrence Stone was about wrist movement and the understanding of the rebound stroke. Moeller was about this whip movement. Those three guys really had it down and understood that when you play the drums, you're going to use one of those movement techniques whether you're aware of it or not, so you might as well learn it knowingly.

MENZIE: You have written several great drum books, but if you could only have five drum books on your shelf, what would they be?

DOM FAMULARO: Book number one would be *Stick Control*, written by George Lawrence Stone in 1935. It's just brilliant. Book number two would be *Accents and Rebounds*, which was his follow-up book, written in 1961. It took what you learned in *Stick Control* and put it into movement with accents.

Book number three would be *Advanced Techniques for the Modern Drummer*, written by Jim Chapin in 1948. When that book came out, it was way ahead of its time as an independence book. Jim Chapin is often referred to as the Father of Independence because he focused on the independence of hands and feet movement.

Book number four would be Gary Chester's *The New Breed* because Gary Chester saw the potential of looking at movement around the drum set in a different way, or, as he puts it, "territorial rights." He didn't see the drum set in the traditional way. Having a bigger vision, he developed systems and wrote this drum method.

Book number five would probably be *Master Studies* by Joe Morello. He took *Stick Control* and *Accents and Rebounds* and, using that format, wrote a follow-up series. But it's kind of a tie in my mind between *Master Studies* and John Pratt's *Fourteen Modern Contest Solos*. That's a killer rudimental book that opens up your mind to how all of these patterns are put into movement.

MENZIE: One thing Pratt does in his book is take standard rudiments and continually phrase over the bar line. He kind of tosses the bar line out.

DOM FAMULARO: Truly brilliant. Back in the 1950s, when this over-the-bar type of phrasing was so unusual, all the guys with that approach were considered very cutting-edge, just like Gary Chester was with his "territorial rights" on the drum set.

MENZIE: The books you suggest as your top five are all iconic. Who are your top influences in music?

DOM FAMULARO: This might be an unusual answer for a drummer, but I love Mozart and Beethoven. Classical music constantly inspires me. Because there is no drum set playing, I can imagine drum parts in my head, which is no different than what any good studio musician does.

Of course, I love the big band era and all of the great jazz artists—Gene Krupa with "Sing, Sing, Sing," the Buddy Rich Big Band, Count Basie, Duke Ellington, [and] Artie Shaw. The big band era was magical. Some consider *Sinatra at the Sands* with the Basie Band one of the best live-music recordings. Of course, that's also produced by Quincy Jones. Any one of those songs on that recording just gives me a chill—that these guys together created that sound and brought an audience to their feet from note one. That's powerful.

Then all the great music from the bop jazz world: Dizzy, Miles Davis, Charlie Parker, John Coltrane, Johnny Hodges, [and] Ella Fitzgerald. [I appreciate] that exciting jazz world and all the great drummers that played with them, like Chick Webb, Max Roach, Art Blakey, Elvin Jones, and Tony Williams.

And that brings us into fusion, with Chick Corea, Jon McLaughlin with Billy Cobham and the Mahavishnu Orchestra, Weather Report, [and] Steps Ahead, just to mention a few. Those guys really opened up a whole other world. And where would we be without the legendary music from Earth, Wind & Fire, Stevie Wonder, the Beatles, and the music of Motown? There are simply too many great artists to mention them all. I can step into any one of those worlds and just crank up some music and be lost forever.

MENZIE: You've had the opportunity to develop relationships with the world's greatest drummers and other musicians, and there is so much honor and respect among you. Will you speak to the importance of those relationships?

DOM FAMULARO: I'm very aware of the honor, and I believe we all respect that. When I first started meeting these unique drummers and artists, they could feel my passion for music, and as I began to get know Buddy Rich, Louie Bellson, Max Roach, Papa Joe Jones, Philly Joe Jones, Ed Thigpen, and Ed Shaughnessy, I was honestly engaged and deeply involved with every conversation I had with them.

To this day it remains the same. When I speak with Steve Gadd

Chapter 17

or Vinnie Colaiuta, every conversation is always so well absorbed in the now. We all share a common passion, and I want to learn from them. I want to share stories with them about what I'm experiencing, and I want to hear what they're experiencing. We all work to expand the deep value of the relationships. The true sense of respect that I have for these people is so inspiring because they are always continuing to push themselves. Steve Gadd is playing better than ever. David Garibaldi is absolutely on fire, playing on the road with Tower of Power for over forty years. I always thought [that] if you're at a Tower of Power concert and you're not moving, you're dead and you just don't know it.

I just Skyped with Billy Cobham two days ago. He's living in Panama now and has a house in Switzerland, and we're communicating about educational ideas and working on things. Billy is such a legend in the industry. All of these great players are—and were—like family to me. I stole a little bit of magic from all of them, and they taught me to add my own little touch of magic. As friends, we share, and that's kind of what I do when I tell all these stories and share some of the history of these great players. I'm just sharing their magic. They've empowered me and shown me ways to discover my own magic, so now I can share it too.

MENZIE: As I said earlier in this book, Chick Corea says, "Good musicians borrow, great musicians steal." Hopefully lots of players will steal from this unique moment. You have given us lots of good history. Thank you!

Chapter 18
Distractions

As much as I would rather not talk about distractions, it may be the most important discussion in this book. If we strive to understand the impact distractions can have on a career, then we are armed and empowered with information and reason, and that's a great place to start.

Let's start by defining the term: a distraction is anything that pulls your attention away from your stated, specific purpose—anything! If it takes your time or your focus away from your intended purpose, it is absolutely a distraction. Some people only think of substance as a distraction, but that's just one of many. Other people think of distractions as unpleasant, but that's not always true either.

Relationships—one of the biggest distractions is maintaining interpersonal relationships.

Don't shoot the messenger, but relationships do require massive attention, so they must be handled productively, or they become a distraction. When I speak of relationships, I am not referring only to romantic relationships but to all relationships: business, family, bandmates, writing partners, and so forth. A relationship is when and wherever two or more people are involved in a joint venture or mutual understanding, so it's easy to see that the music industry is nothing but relationships.

When a relationship is handled in a productive manner, it's usually a rewarding and supportive experience, but relationships have the potential to either propel or snare you because they are charged with emotion, and emotion often overpowers logic.

Chapter 18

If a relationship starts to spin out of control, it can be very hard to interrupt, and it becomes a distraction from your career. However, if you work from this understanding, you will set boundaries, which allows for fewer distractions, and your relationships can be the most productive tool you have. I suggest studying the great partnerships in music, both productive and nonproductive.

Ego—another distraction, and it is certainly one of the biggest career killers.

Ego is seductive, and it can be so subtle that you never sense it growing. It builds slowly, one day after another, and augments as you get a little better at your craft or better known in your career, or you are making better money and playing to bigger crowds. Ego grows as you start to gain respect, and then—*bam*—you're a world-class jerk, just like that.

Ego is a fool's game; it weakens you. Ego takes very good artists and quietly destroys them. Ego ensnares an artist, enticing them, and they slowly become more self-centered and less creative. Ego is elusive, and you won't always see it beginning to take over.

Ego also attracts other egos to you. As you puff up with pride, other puffers notice you because ego is contagious. And so the flock builds. Look no further than professional sports or anywhere the attention is generated by individual achievement; all the while, ego is busy dismantling careers right and left.

From the music business to sports to politics to the tech industry, ego is ever present and the number one career killer. When you are intoxicated with ego, reason and consideration become inconvenient and disposable. Ego is a natural by-product of achievement, but it is not your friend. It is always present, but it is never justified and never productive.

Substance—anything consumed that alters your normal state of being.

Substance abuse has always been a problem in the world of performers. It causes too many artists to lose their way just as big things are starting to happen.

The reality of multiple demands and the need to always be "on" takes its toll on a musician. If you are a great writer, you are expected to always write songs as good as your best songs. If you are a great singer, you are expected to be great 100 percent of the time, even though your instrument is human.

Instrumentalists are not only expected to play at superhuman levels, but they are also expected to sing while doing it and be visually engaging onstage in the process. They must look the part, write the part, play the part, and sing the part. At the same time, they are expected to know all about the changing world of gear and technologies.

A new performer is expected to be on the road at all hours of the day and night while usually unable to afford a bus, much less a bus driver. These types of pressures often cause many musicians to turn to the distraction of multiple substances to aide them—and that choice is a huge mistake.

Social pressures result in substance abuse as well. There is certainly strong peer pressure to partake in it. It's a fool's notion to think that substance makes a musician more creative. Any artist who believes that for an instant needs to go back and watch any of the numerous movies about dead superstars. There is no substance that makes you play better, no matter who may say otherwise. Everyone starts with thinking, "I can handle this." They're wrong.

The ugly truth, then, is that all substance abuse is a distraction, and we have lost so many greats to this problem. It is a destructive behavior that ends careers and lives.

Fear—possibly the most destructive distraction, and it is a waste of good adrenaline.

Fear is usually what drives artists to doubt themselves and lose their mojo. Where fear is embraced, we lose confidence in our inner guidance system and begin to second-guess our true selves. Fear is a practice of reduction, not expansion, and in a business based in artistic contributions, there is simply no room for it.

Fear is a reactionary state, and fortunately, that state can be regulated. Think of the word *FEAR* as an acronym: false evidence appearing real. Fear is a perception, not a truth, and that's why artists have to rebuff fear when they feel its presence. It represents something that simply isn't true. Lose the fear, and look for the truth.

Chapter 18

These are just a few of the obvious distractions musicians face. A good career lasts a lifetime, but it will ebb and flow. You will have many ups and downs, many successes, and multiple setbacks. The only constant is you, so begin your journey with the end in mind. Your best friends on the journey are trust and faith; their cousin goes by the name of hard work.

He always pays off.

Chapter 19

Mike Curb

Few people have had the impact on the music industry that Mike Curb has enjoyed, whether it's through his record label, Curb Records, the oldest independent record label in existence; his philanthropy through the Mike Curb Foundation; or his involvement with top universities like California State, Vanderbilt, and Belmont.

Mike was active in saving Nashville's RCA Studio A and is an ardent advocate for saving the historic buildings on Nashville's Music Row. Mike has served in the role of lieutenant governor of California, as well as played an extended role in motor sports. Named Nashvillian of the Year in 2007, Mike Curb seems to be just getting started.

Interview

Menzie: Musicians always know a lot about their individual craft, but they rarely know very much about the business side of music, the unique nuances of live performance, or the many organizational responsibilities that will greet them when they become a professional. So I felt those concepts needed to be addressed in a reliable musician's manual, capturing ideas from successful industry leaders.

Mike Curb: If they don't understand the business side of it, they're going to get hurt along the way.

Menzie: Musicians are historically naive to better business practices because they focus so much on their craft. Brent Mason, who's a very successful studio musician, reveals that the skills needed for the music business are different from the skills he needs for playing guitar and composing unique guitar hooks for the songs he's recorded.

MIKE CURB: Right. Another great example is Chet Atkins. He was a world-class guitar player, but he also understood the need for a studio, how to produce a record, and how to bring all the elements of a great record together. And when I say record, what I mean is a fluid, complete work, not just a song. There is a world of difference between a cohesive record and a single song.

The songs, the studio musicians, the producers, the arrangers, the mixing, the mastering—they all have to be congruent. So many things go into making a successful record and trying to put the odds in your favor to win wide recognition and critical acclaim.

It's an honor to be the oldest record company that's still owned by the original owner. This is my fifty-fifth year now. I started this when I was in college at Cal State, out in California, and when I moved to Nashville twenty-eight years ago, we got involved in the Curb Center at Vanderbilt and the Curb College for Music Business at Belmont. We've been rocking along ever since, keeping our company going, and trying to get enough hits to keep everybody moving forward.

MENZIE: The Curb College is an amazing program concept for young musicians to experience. Originally, you are from California, having moved to Nashville in 1992, but there were a lot of steps along the way. You wrote a song that Honda picked up, right? Was it "Little Honda"?

MIKE CURB: The original song was "You Meet the Nicest People on a Honda," which I wrote in one of the music rooms out of Cal State in Los Angeles. That song was picked up by the Honda Motor Company for their commercial, and they made the title their slogan. They played the song in their commercial, and my group performed on it.

I tried to get a record deal, and I was able to connect with someone at Mercury Records. They decided to change the name of my group. We were called the Arrows at the time, and then one of the people at Mercury said, "Why don't you put together a whole bunch of motorcycle songs?" So we put together an album of Honda songs.

"Little Honda," believe it or not, was written by Mike Love and Brian Wilson. I wish I had written that one. I recorded it originally with my group, but then the people at Mercury Records didn't like the lead voice. That was my voice, so I thought I'd better fix it. We found a fellow named Chuck Girard, who was in another group, to sing lead on it. Mercury liked it, so they gave me a job; I guess I earned around one hundred dollars a week as an associate producer, but I hate to say that I got my first job by taking my voice off a record and replacing it. Nick Venet at Mercury said that when I took my voice off and mixed the record, he saw potential in me as a producer, not as a singer. So I learned early on that maybe I should concentrate on the business side of things.

By the way, Nick also signed the Beach Boys to Capitol Records—some trivia fun. Anyway, I always had my own groups, like the Mike Curb Congregation and the Buddies and the Arrows, but I really feel that learning how to produce a record was the most important thing I decided to do.

MENZIE: It's interesting how we all start out in one role and sometimes morph into others. My background is in performance as a drummer, and I was fortunate to have success playing on the road for a long time. Then I [started] working on an original project, so I started teaching to facilitate staying local. By the time the project had finished, I had seventy-five students. I looked at the reality of that and thought maybe that's where I was supposed to be.

MIKE CURB: And when you're teaching with that many students, you're probably learning at the same time, aren't you? Because their minds are going off in new directions, and you benefit by trying to find a way to blend what you're teaching them with what you're learning from them. You're trying to find that sweet spot where you can help them fill in the blanks so they don't have to go through so many unnecessary steps and continually reinvent the wheel.

When I started, I actually dropped out of college after two years. I thought I could afford an office, so I had to drag out a little bit of money from the Honda commercial. But shortly thereafter, I had to give up my apartment and move into the janitor section of the building, where I then had my office, which was not good. You know, I think we can save our students a lot of that misery. If these students can learn enough of this business, they don't end up losing it all like I did. Because when you lose it all like I did, a lot of people give up, but then they're not ready to do anything else.

The great thing about Cal State and Belmont and the other colleges that we're involved in is that these students also learn other things. They get a well-rounded college education, so if, for some reason, the music business doesn't work out for them, there's something else they can do. They have a diploma so they can get into so many different areas of the music business. They may want to be a musician, they may want to be an artist, [and] they may want to be a songwriter, but they can also be an accountant in the music business, or they can be an entertainment lawyer or an art director. Not everybody has the talent to be a musician or to write a song, but a lot of people have a sense of a song, and they can move into the areas of A&R or publishing, where their enthusiasm for a song makes a difference.

MENZIE: For the readers' sake, let's clarify how many programs and colleges you're involved with. There's the Curb College of Music Business at Belmont, and you also have a presence at Vanderbilt and the college at Cal State. But you have more than that. How many schools do you have?

MIKE CURB: There are about ten colleges, and they're all not as big as Cal State, which has over five thousand students. Belmont has about two thousand students. Our program at Vanderbilt is not aimed directly at [the] music business. It's involved in culture and all kinds of other cultural aspects: music as it relates to government [and] music as it relates to the other values that Vanderbilt embraces. It's not directly a music business college like Belmont is. We also have a great music business college at Daytona State, and we sponsor the Fisk Jubilee Singers program at Fisk University in Nashville. We have a program at Baylor University in Texas as part of their business college. We have a partnership with the

University of Hawaii and Honolulu Community College, where Belmont provided the curriculum.

MENZIE: Your education mission is to help rising musicians and songwriters and artists in every facet of the music industry [to] gain access to the best tools available, like specialized knowledge and unique insights from top industry pros.

NAMM's former president, Joe Lamond, is also a strong supporter of the philosophy that there are many different aspects to the music business besides performance, whether that's product development, accounting, law, education, design, or artistry. Something must have driven you to take on the idea of promoting higher education in the arts. What made you go in that direction?

MIKE CURB: Well, [it was] my own experience—or lack of it. The fact that after two years of college, I thought I was better off dropping out. It's not good to drop out, because if your dreams don't come true, then you don't have anything to fall back on. I have often thought [that] if there had been a music business program back when I attended Cal State like there is now with the Curb College, it might have encouraged me to stay.

I think [that] if I could have learned more about the overall music business, I might not have had to live in a janitor section and lose my apartment. So it's always been interesting to me to say, "Let's have a program here, and let's teach them."

Belmont's program was already going on when I moved to Nashville. It was very small at the time. Bill Troutt moved it forward for years, and then Bob Fisher came in and turned it into a complete college. I think it gives musicians a real chance.

About twenty years ago, my wife and I began saving a number of the old buildings on Music Row, mainly because we were afraid they were going to tear them down and build apartments or whatever. Now there's about twelve of them on Music Row, and one of them is RCA Studio B, which has turned into a tremendous historical music landmark for Nashville. Over a hundred thousand people visited last year, and with that project, we have a partnership with the Country Music Hall of Fame.

Chapter 19

We also completely restored the Quonset Hut, and then Belmont worked with us to restore Columbia Studio A—those are the two studios used in the songwriting program. [They are] incredible studios, where some of the greatest records were recorded. When I started out in the record business, one out of every two records—not just country records but one out of every two records that were hitting—were made in . . . studios like RCA Studio B, the Quonset Hut, and, a little later on, RCA Studio A and Columbia Studio A. We've restored those studios and other buildings that are historic on Music Row, including our own buildings, where Curb Records is located.

Then about three years ago, we bought Word Records, which is the oldest gospel record company in America. We've done our best to bring Curb and Word together and have both labels use the same legal, accounting, and marketing teams for improved efficiency.

By bringing Curb and Word together as much as possible, we've blended two long-established and well-respected record companies on Music Row. So we're doing everything we can to find a pathway for the future and try to restore the past through our big catalogs and through the buildings on Music Row that we've restored, where so much of the history of Music City was created.

MENZIE: You've hit on two points that strike me as important: the idea of artistry versus business and then the idea of history and the future being complementary, as well as extremely necessary.

You have been quoted as saying, "Let us start at the beginning, because we are more than just a moment in time. We all stand on the shoulders of those who have gone before us—both personally and professionally—and we owe a great debt to them for paving the highway on which we now travel." I thought that quote was powerful.

So you had a lot to do with saving RCA Studio A, correct?

MIKE CURB: Well, Studio A—most of the credit there I would give to Aubrey Preston, but I was his partner. Aubrey had a vision for how to restore it and, at the same time, make it a very competitive studio for the future. I think they won six Grammys at that studio last year.

MENZIE: Dave Cobb is another wonderful mind with a special vision for the music industry. That's a great combination: you take an important historic studio [and] the unique talents of someone like Dave Cobb, and [you] blend them with the great artists he has produced there. It's old meets new meets creative.

MIKE CURB: Dave Cobb kept the original layout of RCA Studio A. You walk into that whole building, and you see RCA Records as it was during all the incredible early years, back when Chet Atkins was there. Of course, it started in RCA Studio B, but then Chet Atkins' office was over at Studio A.

Through the years you see all the great people who worked there, all of the great artists who recorded there, and now you see Dave Cobb at the helm, with his unique approaches to equipment and recording. And [you see] the extraordinary talent that he has to work with, producing these incredible records by Brandi Carlile, Chris Stapleton, and Jason Isbell, just to mention a few. I think the secret there is that Dave and Aubrey understand and respect the history, and the history lives in that studio.

The artists he's recording have sounds that go beyond the present. You hear the influences of the great artists of the past when you hear Stapleton. And Carlile, the way she sings—you hear a little bit of Orbison-type stylizing and certainly influences from Joni in there. She's doing things that make you hear the history of the great artists who have influenced her. You hear her great talent added to it, then you have Dave Cobb producing, and then they're in a facility where some of the greatest records were made. There's something magical there.

MENZIE: There are some who might assume that the style of what they are hearing is completely new, but that's actually not the case, because Dave Cobb and the great artists he records embrace and honor the traditional ways that music was captured when it was done live. In his interview for this book, Dave and I talk a little bit about Chet Atkins, and we agree—he's one of the best studies for anyone who wants to be an artist but, at the same time, wants a broader career path.

So the Chet Atkins model and your thinking and Dave's thinking

CHAPTER 19

actually make for what I believe to be the healthiest model for today's music industry professionals.

MIKE CURB: And in my case, I had a chance to be an artist for a while, and I also had a chance to be a record producer for a while, and I've had a chance to be a songwriter for a while. And I did have success to some degree in all three areas, but I realized when I moved to Nashville that just about everybody I met was better than me. Yes, I had some BMI [Broadcast Music, Inc.] Awards in Country and Pop, but when I got to Nashville, I realized [that] there's so many people with so much more talent at those skills, and maybe I could be more effective focusing on the business side and creating an area—you know, a company—where a lot of people could use their different talents to succeed and be artists and writers and learn all aspects of the business and have colleges where we're training people for all the labels.

At RCA Studio A, I have nothing to do with making those records, but being a partner in the studio, I still feel a part of it. Even though I'm not involved at all in the creative process, I get to see what they're doing and admire it.

When all is said and done, just being a part of this industry is important. None of us are going to be able to do it all; we're all going to have moments when things are clicking, and we're all going to have moments when they're not. The key is to have a model that works whether things are up or down. It's the same way with the economy: you've got to structure whatever business you're in, whether it's the music business or any other business, to function under all conditions. You have to structure your life and your business so it works whether there is a recession or whether or not there's a bull market, because you just don't know. One of the key aspects of any business, including the music business, is making sure that your model works when things aren't hitting; that way, when things do hit, you can enjoy the success.

MENZIE: Will you talk a little bit about Curb Records—what got you into it, what your vision was, and what it's morphed into?

MIKE CURB: I told you how it started with the Honda commercial and how things didn't work out well initially. So I ended up having to move out of my apartment, and then I was basically willing to do anything, whether it was to write a song on spec for a commercial or write a song for a film. There were a lot of West Coast–surf, rock 'n' roll–beach-party-type movies being made back then, and I was able to provide music very inexpensively. Finally, we had some of that music hit with the film called *The Wild Angels*. It became a huge hit.

MENZIE: I read that you were involved with that movie. That's a Peter Fonda cult classic.

MIKE CURB: In that particular instance, I actually wrote all the music and produced it. I didn't always do that. A lot of times, I brought in others, certain members of my band and such.

But *The Wild Angels* was something where I did write the music, although Davie Allan, my bandmate in the Arrows, contributed a lot to that record with his sounds. All the fuzz tone guitars—that was all Davie Allan's work.

That was probably the turning point that got the ball rolling because there was an outlet available to me, and it brought in income. At that time, the singles were selling for ninety-nine cents, but *The Wild Angels* soundtrack was pivotal. Not too long after that, we signed the Stone Poneys, which of course had Linda Ronstadt as the lead singer, so we also got some credibility from that. Then my band had a couple of additional hits from *The Wild Angels* soundtrack—"Blues Theme" became a top 40 hit, [and] *The Wild Angels* theme was also picked up and covered by the Ventures, who are now in the Rock and Roll Hall of Fame, and that all eventually led to doing a lot of other soundtracks. I think, all in all, I probably recorded about fifty of them. By that time, of course, I didn't do all of the music myself. I developed a team, and it started feeling like I had a legitimately successful business going.

MENZIE: So when you were doing all this, had you formed Curb Records?

Chapter 19

MIKE CURB: Yes. At the very beginning, we couldn't call it Curb, because there was another label called Cub, spelled c-u-b, which was very close to c-u-r-b, so we called it Sidewalk Records just to get the label going.

We used that name for a number of years, and then I merged with MGM [Metro-Goldwyn-Mayer] Records. We put together a five-year plan, which is something I would recommend to any student—come up with a five-year plan. If you're ever going to get a loan from a bank, the bank is going to first want to see a five-year plan, particularly if it's a start-up company. If the company has been going for a while, they may not require it, but if you're just starting out, they're going to ask for your plan and how you are going to repay the loan.

Humorously, I was never able to get any investors and really didn't get much of a loan. I think, originally, I got about $300 from the bank, but I still had to do a five-year plan. I've done one ever since.

We got started in 1964, and it was after around five years that we had a chance to merge with MGM Records. They were having a lot of difficulties in New York, and our company was doing pretty well. We had very low overhead, and they had very high overhead, so they moved their company out to the West Coast and merged with us. That helped for the next five years, then we were able to get Warner to be our distributor.

At the very start, we were able to get Capitol Records to give us a five-year distribution deal. There was a man by the name of Eddie Ray. His book is called *Against All Odds*. This is a name I would hope all young musicians would take time to research and know. Eddie was the first African American vice president of a major label. He was also the man that was smart enough to sign Pink Floyd. He believed in our company, and he gave us a five-year distribution agreement, which gave us a little credibility with the banks. That gave us a nice start, but it takes a long time to build your catalog. One of the big things today, now that we have streaming and all that, is your catalog. So much of the income comes from the catalog that we've built over fifty-five years.

MENZIE: So you moved to Nashville. When? And why?

MIKE CURB: Well, we moved operations here in 1992. I had my first major hit as a publisher with Buck Owens on a song called "Big in Vegas," which I did not write. The next year, I wrote a song with Harley Hatcher called "All for the Love of Sunshine" that Hank Williams Jr. recorded, and it became his first number 1 record. We got BMI Awards for both of those.

Then the movies like *The Wild Angels* and *Devil's Angels* and the *Billy Jack* films—I had a lot of writing there, and then I wrote the theme song for *Kelly's Heroes*, "Burning Bridges," which I recorded with my group, the Mike Curb Congregation. It became a pretty big hit on the pop charts, and when it hit the hot 100, we won a BMI Award as well.

Then came the Osmonds. I signed the Osmond family, the Osmond brothers, and Donnie and Marie, and they all did very well. I have always had a love affair with R&B and gospel music, so I was excited to sign artists like Solomon Burke, Lou Rawls, and Mel Carter. We even had Brook Benton for a while, [as well as] the amazing Sammy Davis Jr. I produced "Candy Man" for him, with my group, the Mike Curb Congregation, doing the backups. That was a number 1 record. And great things continued to happen. We signed Lou Rawls and had one of his big hits, "The Natural Man." Then I was honored to win the *Billboard* Producer of the Year Award in 1972. And so, between the records, I was producing, and with all these great artists, things just started clicking.

We signed Eric Burdon and War, and we really had quite a run with African American music back in the 1970s. Then in the 1980s, we got more involved in co-ventures. Dick Whitehouse, who was the CEO of my company, and I worked together, and the two of us got very involved with joint ventures while we were still in California. We signed the Judds, but we had a co-venture with RCA where they did the promotional marketing and we owned the masters. We did the same with Hank Williams Jr.

And we had our Curb-Warner relationship. We owned the records and the masters, but we had a marketing relationship with them because they had the people in Nashville. So pretty soon, you had Curb Warner with Hank Williams Jr. and Curb RCA with the Judds, [as well as] Curb Capitol with Sawyer Brown and Curb MCA with Lyle Lovett, the Desert Rose Band, and the Bellamy Brothers. And then the Curb Warner hits—we had the Four Seasons with "Oh, What a Night" and "Let Your

Chapter 19

Love Flow" by the Bellamys, both of which crossed over and went number 1 on the pop charts. And then [we had] "You Light Up My Life" by Debby Boone. Shaun Cassidy had number 1 records, the Osmonds were having number 1 records, and we had a group called Exile who had "Kiss You All Over," which was a number 1 record.

MENZIE: Was there a trigger point that made you relocate to Nashville?

MIKE CURB: We had all those joint ventures with the Judds and Hank Williams Jr. and Sawyer Brown and Lyle Lovett going on. And being based in California, [we found] it was logically hard because the artists became closer with the labels that were doing the promotion and marketing. We had to either do it ourselves completely and be a complete record company or just be a production company, and we didn't want to do that. Since we owned the masters, we had an opportunity about thirty years ago.

In 1989 the president of Capitol Records, Joe Smith, who's known for signing legendary artists like Bonnie Raitt, said to me, "If you would bring all your records under one banner and let Capitol's distribution company handle it, we would work with you." He gave us access to distributors to repackage a lot of the Capitol albums. We entered into an agreement with Capitol at the end of 1989, [when] we brought all our artists and our catalog together under just the Curb label, and we stopped doing the Curb RCA and the Curb Warner. Then things just really took off, and we started realizing we better be in Music City.

I love California, but the business climate in California was becoming difficult and seemed to be falling apart. Nashville seemed the right city for us. Nashville is unique and has always had a lot going for it, and Tennessee has a lot going for it, especially when it comes to the economy and business. I think Tennessee needed us, and I think we needed Tennessee. And so we moved operations here in 1992, and we decided we were not going to rely on anyone else. We were going to have our own promotion department, our own marketing, [and] our own sales, and it really worked.

In the 1990s our company just soared. Tim McGraw, for twenty-three years, had monster hits on our label, probably thirty number 1 records. LeAnn Rimes started with "Blue" on our label and had so many big hits, as did Jo Dee Messina and a lot of the artists who came out of our joint ventures. They all prospered on Curb. We had fifty chart records with Sawyer Brown, as well as success with Hank Williams Jr. and Wynonna.

All these records came back over to our label, so now we have the Judds catalog and the Hank Williams Jr. catalog and [the] Sawyer Brown catalog and the Tim McGraw catalog and the Jo Dee Messina catalog and [the] LeAnn Rimes catalog, [as well as] all these hits by Exile, the Four Seasons, and the Righteous Brothers. Then we got into the gospel business very early on, which easily led us into contemporary Christian music. It all kind of started out of California. We were in it early on, but I'm not sure we knew what we were doing back then. They didn't even call it contemporary Christian music.

MENZIE: No, they didn't, but that turned out to be quite a market.

MIKE CURB: We had great success with my own group, the Mike Curb Congregation, and then [with] Debby Boone with "You Light Up My Life." It was one of the first major hits in Christian music, and I was able to build on that over the years. Of course, Natalie Grant signed with us twenty years ago. She's had an incredible career. Then when we bought Word Records about three years ago, that gave us their catalog as well as the wonderful Word artists—For King and Country, for example. They are just huge on Curb Word, and I was lucky to be a part of that when we first signed them, which was back when we just had a minority interest in Word Records. As time went on, we watched For King and Country grow. We just went to a concert of theirs with six thousand people at Ascend Amphitheater, and they just soared.

Francesca Battistelli and Big Daddy Weave are some of the artists we've been working with, along with the artists we've been building over the years, like Natalie Grant, We Are Messengers, Dan Bremnes, Love & the Outcome, and Stars Go Dim.

So between our country music catalog, our Christian music catalog, and the pop records, we've had hits over the years. We're one of a kind, though we've been a little disappointed that a lot of our competitors have sold. Big Machine just sold out of Nashville, and Broken Bow and Rounder sold a few years ago.

MENZIE: That I didn't know.

MIKE CURB: Yeah, and most of them have been sold to international companies. Broken Bow sold to Bertelsmann in Germany, and over the years, Sony bought RCA, Columbia, and Arista. Warner is operated by an international company, and then Universal is owned in France. Universal has a lot of those companies, like Chess Records, Imperial Records, Mercury Records. They own A&M, they own Motown, [and] they own Decca, Dot, Dunhill, [and] Geffen Records, [as well as] Interscope, Island, MCA, [and MGM Records, plus] the MGM label masters, Polydor. They own the greatest labels from the past. There are some companies that have started up, like Big Loud and Thirty Tigers, who are building new artists, and hopefully, they will sustain and build and grow their catalog. But I can tell you it takes a long time to do that. It's taken us fifty-five years to get where we are. I remember Kellen—who was one of my close friends when he sold his very successful Tree Music—he said he got a lot of money for it, but he lost his seat at the table. If I sold Curb, I would probably be fired.

MENZIE: That's what you get for having vision.

MIKE CURB: Well, we both know vision can be a risky proposition, right? And I like having my job, so I understand that I have to redefine it every year. Because I've got people who are one and two generations down, and pretty soon, it'll have three.

MENZIE: I believe one of the most important aspects of your success has been your eclectic vision. You embrace R&B as genuinely as you embrace country and pop, and you temper that with a healthy respect for songwriting, production, and music history.

One item I came across in my research on you is the fact that you're a Flamingos fan, and you mentioned Brook Benton. In Craig Alvin's interview for this book, he talks about mixing the song "Rainbow" for

Kacey Musgraves's record *Golden Hour*. He recalled encountering a problem with rain hitting on a window of Sheryl Crow's barn studio while tracking the song. Jokingly, I referenced . . . Ann Peebles's song "I Can't Stand the Rain" and Brook Benton's "Rainy Night in Georgia." Ironically, you are connected to Brook Benton.

MIKE: I didn't have "Rainy Night in Georgia," but I think Brook Benton also recorded "I Only Have Eyes for You," which was a tremendous hit record for the Flamingos. I was a huge fan of the Flamingos. George Goldner produced them, as well as Little Anthony and the Imperials, and the Chantels.

MENZIE: I was inspired by Billie Eilish and Finneas performing "Sunny" by Bobby Hebb on a TV special, which shows they won't be boxed in. I know it's a different time and place, but this music is timeless. Great is great, no matter what the decade.

MIKE CURB: I tried bringing a lot of that music back because, as you say, great never goes out of style. George Goldner was quite a talent, and he didn't get enough credit for all he did. They have yet to put him in the Rock and Roll Hall of Fame. He made some really great records back in 1958 and 1959 and later on with the Dixie Cups—you know, "Chapel of Love," "The Leader of the Pack"—those kinds of records. He founded Roulette Records and a few other labels. Indeed, [he was] quite a talent, but the Flamingos—my goodness, those records! They were marvelous—and the way he used the echo. As a producer, I learned so much from those records because, back in those days, we recorded live, so we had to get it right in the studio. We didn't have all the technical stuff that they have today where we could go back and revisit and pull something up, remix it, and have everything on sixty different tracks. If we didn't get the feel right in the studio, we were toast.

MENZIE: It's interesting that now people are trying to recapture that sound and that feel. But you have to take the risk, and you have to know your craft. Pro Tools is an amazing tool and a

Chapter 19

great way to fix things, but there's something special about the talent and craft development of being able to do something live.

I was happy when I saw you were a Flamingos fan. Though many of their songs have the same flavor, "I Only Have Eyes for You" is certainly iconic doo-wop.

MIKE CURB: It was a really well-produced record. Someone else who knew what he was doing at that time was Buck Ram, who produced the Platters. I'm talking about "The Great Pretender" or "Smoke Gets in Your Eyes." Those records were so well produced. "Twilight Time" is just great, one of the best-produced records ever, and he did it over and over and over because he was a great producer. A really good record producer, like Dave Cobb today or Buck Ram or George Goldner back in the late 1950s—those guys knew what they were doing.

Dave Bartholomew is another one. He produced Fats Domino. He would get hit after hit with those records, producing songs like "Blueberry Hill." He knew how to put it all together and make a great record. That's the big challenge—it's not enough without all the parts coming together. The song and all the other elements are so important, and if you don't pull them together effectively in a record, then you have missed the mark.

The fathers of Music Row, like Chet Atkins or Owen Bradley, all had a sense of how to make a really great record. And fortunately, the Ken Burns project has recaptured so many important, pivotal moments in the history of the great pioneers of country music and bluegrass.

It was interesting to me that Ken was coming from outside country music, from California. That's where I came from—outside. We didn't even have a country music station where I grew up in Los Angeles, so I only heard the records that crossed over—artists like Johnny Cash, Sonny James, Conway Twitty, Marty Robbins, and Elvis. Some of them actually were pop artists. Elvis started [in] country but became pop. Orbison started out [in] pop, and later on, he had some country success.

I remember when the CMA was formed in 1958, the whole concept was to cleanse country music and create a format that was really country in order to save the careers of Ernest Tubb, Tex Ritter, and all those great artists from the 1950s. So they purged the country music stations of the Sun artists like Johnny Cash, Elvis Presley, Jerry Lee Lewis, Carl Perkins, Conway Twitty, and Roy Orbison.

But I think they realized that you couldn't tell country radio not to play Johnny Cash. Johnny Cash came roaring in there with record after record, so he became undeniable, even though "I Walk the Line" was a pop record. Jack Clement—now there's another great producer, right up there with Atkins and Bradley, [as well as] Shelby Singleton at Mercury and Sun Records. Jack Clement did all those records with Johnny Cash after "I Walk the Line"—you know, songs like "Ballad of a Teenage Queen," "The Ways of a Woman in Love," "Guess Things Happen That Way," all those records. They were cut in Memphis, and when Johnny moved over to Columbia in the early 1960s, Jack was able to do "Ring of Fire," which was written by June Carter and Merle Kilgore.

Any time you make a great documentary you're always going to have people second-guess your decisions and say, "Where was Conway Twitty?" or "Where was Sonny James?" but that's not what it was about. It was Ken Burns's vision of country music from the outside, though he got a lot of interviews from the inside as well. My wife and I loved it; we watched every episode. Volume one ended with Garth Brooks right at the end of the 1980s / beginning of the 1990s, and that's about the time we moved to Nashville. I think it takes twenty-five to thirty years for someone to be historic. Now people are seeing Garth for the historic figure he is, and I think they'll do the same with Tim McGraw, Hank Williams Jr., Alan Jackson, and so many other great artists that came along in the 1990s.

And you can look at how Garth understood the art of making great records. All extremely successful artists understand certain unsaid, important things. For example, Tim McGraw understood how to use his voice, and he also had a great sense for choosing the right song and the right producer (by choosing Byron Gallimore). Having a great producer is so pivotal.

MENZIE: There is such a sense of reverence around this great music, both when you speak of today's artists and of the unique moments that came before. Because you've been in the music business for a lifetime and

Chapter 19

you've seen the same changes that I have, let's talk about what you see ahead for today's artists and what you see going forward as a label owner.

MIKE CURB: You've gotta make it work. You've got to make it work live, you've got to get the record right, you've got to make sure you get it out there and promote it effectively and market it. That's something successful artists really understand, and [it is] certainly something that Garth Brooks understood.

Different artists have different gifts. Eddy Arnold understood the art of the song. He could find a song, understand it, and turn that understanding into the biggest career in terms of chart success. If memory serves me correctly, he sold more than eighty-five million records. I think he's still number 1 of all time on *Billboard*.

Another artist who truly understood the art of the record was Sonny James. He had success as a pop artist with "Young Love" in the late 1950s, but then when he started making records in Nashville at the Quonset Hut in the 1960s and 1970s, he had like twenty-five number 1 records because he understood radio. He still holds the record for the most consecutive number 1s by any solo recording artist in any music genre. How's that for a statistic?

On the other side of the discussion, one of the things that really struck me in Ken Burns's documentary was the incredible issues these artists had with drugs and alcohol and other distractions. I've seen artists lose everything to drugs and substance abuse . . . you see how many of the great artists were impacted by that and what great artists like Johnny Cash had to go through.

I think the industry can benefit from their stories. Maybe we focus on the individuals who were so talented they were able to overcome their issues, like Haggard and Willie, and those who talked about it honestly, like Johnny Cash. It's because they've talked about it openly, and how they were able to overcome it . . . maybe helps others.

But for every one artist who overcame it, there's many who are gone, who've lost their lives or wrecked their family life. You never want to lose yourself and certainly not your family—nothing is worth that. It's important to remember that our job is being creative, and our mission is making sure that we have great careers and successful records and fun while we do it.

We just had a monster number 1 record with Lee Brice, called "Rumor," and we've had big hits with a new artist named Dylan Scott and artists like Rodney Atkins, who has so many number 1s with our company and has come back with big hits just this year. And then what's happening with contemporary Christian artists, like For King and Country, Francesca, Natalie Grant, and We Are Messengers, is very exciting. So what we're doing is making sure we put out the best records we can and being positive and having fun at the same time.

It helps that we have an entrepreneurial spirit at Curb. We've got sixty employees, and they're all doing different things. Many of them have come from the Curb College, and they love what they're doing. They all have different areas of expertise. Jeff Edmondson was an entrepreneur who set up a financial department with twelve of the best people you can imagine. In the A&R department, we have Brian Stewart, who takes a very entrepreneurial approach with our other producers. You don't have to start your own company to be an entrepreneur. You can be an entrepreneur in another company. Just grab a hold of something, believe in it, and stick with it. Hold it together through the tough times, and you might enjoy the good times.

MENZIE: Let's turn to songwriting for just a second. Historically, we have had great individual writers, like Bob Dylan and Joni Mitchell, and also great songwriting teams, like John Lennon and Paul McCartney or Felice and Boudleaux Bryant, [as well as] famous teams at the Brill Building and famous teams at Motown with Holland, Dozier, and Holland. But today, you have lots of songs by multiple writers and seemingly bigger teams on most songs. With songwriting, what do you look for at Curb when you're interviewing artists, and what's your take as a songwriter yourself?

MIKE CURB: You talked about connecting that younger generation. You and I are able to make assumptions about each other. You said, "Flamingos," and we know exactly what we're talking about. We know exactly what the guitar intro and piano sound like or the brushes on the snare. We know the echo on the lead singer's voice. We know exactly what the doo-wop shoo-bop on their record sounds like and how it keeps the record moving.

Similarly, when you say, "Brill Building," you and I know exactly what that means. It means Carole King. It means Barry Mann and Gerry Goffin. But how many of our students understand the real meaning of the Brill Building?

It was a factory for songs, and it certainly spawned the 1960s and the 1970s. They were able to turn that experience into incredible artistic careers all based around the great songs they wrote. You don't have to be a record producer or a songwriter to feel the music of Motown or Stax or the Brill Building. If you do, you have a head start, because it does start with a song. So I think the songwriting is everything!

When I was having my success as a songwriter, I was writing songs all the time—four and five songs a day. Writing for any movie, any soundtrack, any commercial, any record—anybody who needed a song, I was ready to write it. I think the key to being a good songwriter is being in it all the time. If I woke up in the middle of the night and thought up a new title for a song, I was writing it down on a piece of paper, anxious to get with my writing partners as soon as possible and get their input and their ideas.

It's the same with producing, like with Dave Cobb today. They are on it all day long, every day, [coming] up with the greatest sounds, working with the right musicians, knowing which musician can give them what they need for each artist.

The good students are the ones who can study and interface with other students and learn and absorb. It's the same with making a record. When you're a producer, that's what you're doing all day and, in my case, sometimes well into the night.

MENZIE: It's my belief that when you morph that concept of passion and excellence into the idea of the necessary responsibilities of business, you have today's entrepreneurial environment. The music business has changed so much with streaming and mediums like that. Do you see streaming as helpful? How do you feel about it?

MIKE CURB: I think it's great. I think you have to stream a lot to make what you did when you had a CD, but it's what I use, and so do most listeners. I turn on my phone and I stream. I think probably about 70 percent of the people in the music industry are streaming now, not as much in country and Christian music as they are in pop music, but it's getting there. Streaming is huge. It's right on demand. You don't have to worry about downloading or finding your CD somewhere in the closet and figuring out if it will still play on your player. You just turn it on and there it is.

We're doing great with streaming. We simply look at it as a new and different delivery system. The normal delivery system today is streaming; ten years ago, it was downloading. Ten years before that, it was the CD. Ten years before that, it was the cassette, and before that, it was the 33s [and] 45s. Ten years before that, it was the 78s, so it is what it is.

We call it, in a legal term, the normal distribution. The good contracts that were written when you signed a record deal said the formats now are after known [are subject to change]. That's what we used to do back then, and who would've dreamed that we would be downloading or even purchasing CDs back when we had the little 45s? And I guarantee you [that] ten years from now, there will be something else.

I can't help but notice you have a diverse understanding of music history, and you reference multiple musical genres. So what is your back ground that enables you to have those tools?

MENZIE: My dad played sax and was a lover of the big band music of the early 1940s, and he surrounded us with all the great music of that era. That obviously influenced me. I also had an older brother and older sister who were avid music lovers, so I got bombarded with Kingston Trio, James Brown, Flamingos, Count Basie, Ella Fitzgerald, the [King] Cole Trio, Motown, Stax, and, of course, all rock formats. That gives me a deeply varied and valuable historical vocabulary and a unique perspective on modern music.

In my work I'm surrounded by extremely talented rising music students, and they expose me to their favorite artists of today, as does my daughter. So I try to give to get.

Chapter 19

MIKE CURB: You have the Kingston Trio, who were folk; Count Basie, a renowned big band leader; [and] the Flamingos, a doo-wop quintet—you mentioned five or six different formats. Ella Fitzgerald had great success as a pop artist, but she was fundamentally a jazz singer. It was different back then because they would all be played on radio in a mixed format, and you could enjoy them all. Now it's isolated—country is on country stations, pop is on pop stations, R&B is on R&B stations, and oldies are on oldies stations. You don't really get that unique mix anymore. That's why streaming is so popular. The listener controls the mix, and I see that as a good thing.

MENZIE: I would like to talk about your philanthropy and the Mike Curb Foundation because I believe the work you do is truly important.

MIKE CURB: Regarding the foundation, we touched on the various colleges and programs in the universities. That's one giant aspect of it, and the second part of it would be the historic preservation on Music Row, where we have twelve buildings, like Columbia Studio A, RCA Studio A, the Quonset Hut, RCA Studio B, and various others. There's a lot of history there.

MENZIE: While music has been the engine of your vision, your history in the music business, as successful as it's been, is only one of your many chapters of success. Your foundation clearly illuminates your philosophy.

MIKE CURB: Well, we're always trying. An important aspect, as I mentioned, is supporting education. We are completely committed to that.

Another cause my wife and I are very passionate about has to do with a lot of programs for the homeless, [like] with the Nashville Rescue Mission and Safe Haven, [as well as] with new women's shelters, like Room at the Inn, which is a joint project with Belmont. We recently helped put together the new veterans' shelter that is being built now in Nashville: Victory Hall. That is a very exciting project that will help many veterans. So we are really involved.

People keep trying to come up with all the different answers and suggestions on the homeless, but you have to have a place for them to go. We can analyze it and say some have different types of issues, but a lot of them are people who are being priced out of their homes or [are] mothers with five kids who lose their homes. We can spend time debating the reasons for it, but in the meantime, they have to have a place to go. If anybody has a question about that, I recommend they go to Los Angeles and walk up and down the streets and see the fifty-five thousand homeless people camping on the sidewalks. Is that what we want? That's something we're working on now, and it's a great thing for college students to be involved in. We had a program the Christmas before last where the Belmont students worked with one of the shelters and did wonderful things, helping them clean their clothes and get fed, fixing things up, understanding their programs, and offering a little bit of mentoring.

We really do need to figure that out. We can't succeed and leave all that behind. I think a good foundation needs to have a good educational component and a sense of the region's history. At the same time, it's paramount that we work with understanding the underserved, whether it's [working with] the homeless—what Second Harvest is doing in making sure people are fed—or making sure people have health care. Different states have different issues, but there's a whole lot of people who are uninsured, and a whole lot of them are children. We've gotta figure out something.

MENZIE: In the words of the Frankie Beverly song, "We are one!"

CHAPTER 20

Down to Business (DIY Plan)

STRIKING THE RIGHT BALANCE BETWEEN THE CREATIVE AND THE EXECutive roles is imperative.

Most professionals in the music business agree that the music-business model continues to evolve at a very rapid pace, and as it evolves, the need for musicians to embrace the new changes and understand the current inner workings of the music business lies at the feet of the artists. The early years in a musician's career are a DIY business model.

Advancements in technology have affected and enhanced the fundamental business model in every industry; however, the music industry is an outlier because it is a blend of three unique components: artistry, technology, and business.

Most musicians who have considered a career in music are surprisingly good at artistry and technology, but oddly, most artists struggle with business. Those who have experienced success know that to succeed to your highest potential, you must create a plan that conquers all three aspects of our industry.

Every day, more business and communication tools become available to the DIY musician. Technology continues to evolve at a torrid pace, and every medium of communicating and delivering the musician's core product to market involves some form of technology. So while the learning curve is ongoing, today's youths own the technology game outright, lowering the bar for intimidation.

Another plot twist is that the listening audience continues to change the way they consume music because the delivery systems for music products continue to advance rapidly. Automation has its fingerprints on just about every aspect of the music industry. Production, performance, marketing, and listening platforms are all continuing to change in real time while a healthy debate continues around topics like music royalties.

One oddity is that the overuse of technological advancements has rekindled a shadow romance for retro products, which have now enjoyed a healthy resurgence and a renewed popularity. No matter the instrument of choice—be it a sax, the drums, a guitar, a Wurlitzer piano, or even a vintage recording console—today's savvy musicians dedicate as much or more time and energy to studying the history of music and iconic instruments as they do learning the latest technologies.

In today's DIY model, quality business information is available to anyone who seeks it. You just have to be motivated to find what you are searching for. Easy access to a plethora of digital business tools has paved the way for the entrepreneur to thrive. While it was once hard to get quality inside information, it's now just a click away. We want to own the information, as it is undisputedly a DIY business world, and one truth remains consistent: the determining factor of your success in the music industry comes down to you.

There are still record companies and big management, but in today's music business, the artist shoulders the responsibility of his or her initial success. That means you have to extend your skill sets even further because the music industry, with only a few exceptions, has morphed completely into the DIY entrepreneurial business model.

If you are a developing artist in today's music business and not an established artist who is able to delegate and outsource business responsibilities to others, then your knowledge of business matters and executive skills can no longer be handed off to someone who oversees your development and takes care of it for you.

Though that may happen later, in order to get there, you have to pave your own path. Strangely, this is a good thing—because the artist keeps control of the power. The one caveat is that if you want success in today's music business, you no longer have the luxury of exclusively working on just your artistic craft. Today business executive skills are an integral part of success, and it is imperative to include them as part of your working plan.

The good news is that all rising musicians, no matter their background, can easily access today's best organizational tools. If you want to study leadership skills, they are at your fingertips. Business strategies are also easily researched, and the philosophy of good business practices from all industries as well as success stories are abundant in multiple formats. Be pledged to doing the research, and keep the same integrity that you pledged to your craft.

Audiobooks are easily accessible and cover every business model and business topic imaginable. The same is true of a plethora of exceptional promotional tools that were not even an option just a few years ago. Today they can be easily found and utilized to help you construct your marketing strategy. There are even business books that specifically focus on telling you how to develop and build your music-business plan—you just need a healthy determination and a burning desire to learn. The more you know about productive business practices, the greater is the opportunity for your sustained success in the music industry.

The musicians who embrace the DIY model understand the evolving opportunities and can carve out a surprisingly good living. Understanding and embracing the entrepreneurial model puts them in the driver's seat.

There is, however, one quirky problem that occasionally arises. Most creative thinkers are bored by executive skill sets because executive skill sets are often highly structured and inflexible. While it's true that everyone has the potential to develop their executive skills, unfortunately, many musicians have invested so much time and energy into developing their musical disciplines that they don't have the interest or patience for developing good business skills.

Creatives are more than happy to delegate executive tasks that require additional skills to someone else, but as you begin your career ascension, that is not often a viable choice simply because farming out executive responsibilities is cost prohibitive. However, the surprise in the Cracker Jack box is you may find that after you've forged your own path and learned productive business skills, you are no longer willing to give away the control of your business. Once you have mastered and balanced craft, vision, and business acumen, you have better control of your destiny.

When you decide on music as a career, you create a reality much different from when you play music for enjoyment. Because of that decision, you have now introduced the executive aspect into the equation.

The next step is striking the right balance between the creative and the executive roles. Most good musicians have no trouble with the creative aspects of their career, but balancing them with executive responsibilities is another matter entirely. So we start with that understanding and work from there, treating it like we would if we were learning another instrument.

After you have gained clarity on your vision, putting your organized plan together requires the executive personality to take the lead. However, as I have mentioned, the mind-sets are different, so it takes some training. Just like with learning music, you have to be dedicated to developing business practices. It is also important to develop the skill of solution-based thinking.

Successful is not a synonym for effortless, nor is the music business without challenges and negotiations. Life is one big negotiation, and for those with an entrepreneurial spirit, negotiations are literally their daily bread. This is one of the few head-over-heart truths of the music business. If the heart and soul are blood and breath, then the head is the army that protects them. Negotiation skills and professional relationships are our weapons of defense.

Whether you are a new working musician or a young artist, it is imperative that you understand the necessity for quality professional relationships, both inside and outside of the music profession. These are the relationships that aid and support you personally. The list is long and includes accountants, lawyers, bankers, and so forth, and it goes hand in hand with your personal list of other industry professionals.

Let's also look into the benefits of developing relationships outside of the industry.

No matter what job you have in the music business, if you are smart, you find a good accountant. It's no secret that tax laws are always changing, and the rules are very different when you are a self-employed musician. Tax laws also differ from state to state.

Not too long ago, I had a conversation with Alan Friedman, an accountant for multiple high-profile music-industry clients. It became clear that my attempt to capture all the important details of tax law for self-employed musicians would entail writing a separate book on that topic alone. But one point from our conversation was very clear: tax law is ever changing. The best way we can learn the rules is to have a good accountant working with us, explaining how the tax laws work best in our specific case. A qualified accountant can clearly explain how tax laws affect us differently year after year. It's important to know the workings of withholdings, quarterly payments, and any allowable deductions. Dealing with all of these burdensome details alone, without a professional specialist, can take us away from focusing on our true job: being creative artists.

Understanding planning, communication skills, tax laws, contracts, time management, scheduling, professional relationship management, financial comprehension, and the setting of realistic business goals is all part of writing your personal DIY business plan. The better you understand this truth, the greater your chances are of sustaining a lucrative, productive, and enjoyable career in the music industry.

Chapter 21

Secretary Riley

IN THIS BOOK I AM TRYING TO REVEAL THE CONSISTENT BELIEFS THAT envelop successful leaders, entrepreneurs, and creative thinkers. I hope to shed light on the predominant internal code that's always present within successful people—the code that allows those individuals to materialize their creativity with an almost reverent simplicity, as well as effortless execution. So to introduce the reader to Secretary Riley, I would like to begin with one of my favorite stories about respect. Hopefully, he doesn't mind if I tell it.

The story goes like this . . . Secretary Riley and I were attending a dinner and working together with NAMM in support of music education. I was seated at the table across from his, and at both tables, there were very successful music-industry leaders—people who are tremendously admired by their peers.

As the evening began to wind down, many corporate presidents began to bid good night to one another, but what occurred when Secretary Riley stood to leave is something not easily forgotten. When he did so, the entire room of people rose to their feet in a show of respect. It was absolutely genuine, and it made an indelible impression on me that will last a lifetime.

INTERVIEW

MENZIE: What are your thoughts about leadership and respect in our world today?

Chapter 21

SECRETARY RILEY: On the subject of leadership, I think the first thing that needs to be said is that the role of a leader in today's world has changed. We are moving so much faster, so there is much less time to consider or discuss an event before it becomes a public discussion; therefore, today's leader has more information to contend with in real time. It used to take weeks before a major story circulated through the news cycle; now it's done in a day. We used to double-check our resources and facts to make sure the facts were right; now we seem to accept that we can substitute an apology if we are wrong in place of the responsibility of accuracy. It is harder to be a leader today because our world and the events surrounding us are much faster. The understanding of respect is usually handed down from parents, but with more pressure on the families, that also has its cost.

MENZIE: In your opinion, is leadership waning? Or have we just come to a time when leadership is being redefined?

SECRETARY RILEY: I would say the latter, that leadership is being redefined. Social issues are changing, and in every aspect, the needs of the country are also changing and growing, so therefore, the role of a leader is changing as well. We are becoming aware that conversations regarding all of our diverse cultures, with consideration for everyone, is the best path.

MENZIE: It would be interesting to know what qualities you believe make up a good leader.

SECRETARY RILEY: Well, you can start with the obvious ones: honesty, compassion, the ability to listen, [and] the ability to hear and understand someone's feelings and point of view. The ability to teach and communicate. The ability to make a tough choice and then having the conviction to see it through, even when it's an unpopular decision. Real leaders have to be tough because people aren't always going to agree with you. Passion and conviction, as well as vision, are all parts of being a good leader.

MENZIE: Will you share your insight on the leadership you witnessed growing up and discuss how it affected your beliefs?

SECRETARY RILEY: Well, if you don't mind me telling a story, I remember, as a boy, being at an event where they were recognizing the achievements of my father [Ted Riley]—he was an attorney—and as the speaker introduced him and went down his list of achievements, qualities, and respected character traits that he admired in my father, the last accolade is the one I'll never forget. The last thing he mentioned about my father was that Ted [Riley] was simply a good citizen. That really struck me, and that day has stayed with me because I have always felt that was important. As simple as that is, it's really everyone's daily responsibility, and I have always tried to live by that understanding.

MENZIE: How much do you think style plays into the effectiveness of a leader?

SECRETARY RILEY: I think leadership style is always changing, and wise leaders adapt to that understanding. To lead doesn't just mean to be right; it means that you also have to be effective as well as understood by several cultures. So your style of leadership has to be flexible and also be open to growth, not only in understanding but in your ability to communicate and be understanding of the style of leadership in other leaders as well.

MENZIE: You have a reputation for surrounding yourself with strong leaders—people who can make effective compromises but who are not afraid to push back—yet you are also reputable for being tough. What leadership traits do you look for in people with whom you would want to surround yourself?

SECRETARY RILEY: Well I have a great story about tough . . . I like tough, and I like conviction, as well as the other traits we just touched on. Leadership deals with solutions, and solutions happen when people can have healthy discussions. It's the only way things get done, but if your heart tells you [that] what you believe is the right thing to do, and you are alone in the discussion, then you must act from your passion to make others understand what you believe the best solution is and why. I was always lucky to have great and inspirational people around me, and I tried to surround myself with the best people I could. At every major meeting, I would always strive to have a great teacher in the room and people from several backgrounds as well. That's why we got such good work done.

So back to the reputation of being tough . . . years ago, when I first ran for governor of South Carolina, I had been invited to a square dance in Greenville when I was first campaigning. I love events like country square dances and county fairs, and [with] this particular evening being a bit higher profile because of the campaign, many folks were asking me to join them in a dance. In particular was one young lady whose dad owned the farm. She was quite a stepper and very outgoing and outspoken. Well, after we finished the dance, as we walked to the side, she said, "Hey, aren't you Dick Riley?" And I said, "Yes, ma'am, I am." She looked right at me and said, "You sure are a little dude." I looked at her and said, "Yup, I'm little, but I'm tough." I think that's where my reputation for tough began.

MENZIE: What a great story! Over the course of your lifetime, how has the definition of a leader changed?

SECRETARY RILEY: Touching on what we said earlier, it's a different time and place. Technology has changed the speed of everything, so today's leaders now have to take new considerations into accord. But I believe the core values of a good leader are basically still the same. There are new challenges, so therefore, today's leaders need to keep up new skill sets—for example, certainly communication skills are one of them—and with expanded media, leaders have to know more about a broader array of global topics. But the definition of a good leader is someone who can lead, no matter . . . the circumstances, and that hasn't changed.

MENZIE: Do you believe we are leaving behind any timeless wisdom from yesterday?

SECRETARY RILEY: Well, I don't know that we are. I believe young people may be looking at it differently and communicating about it differently, but eventually, I believe that we return to traditional values with the intention of making things better, and therefore, we develop curiosity, and that leads us to seek out timeless wisdom. That's not to say we will do things in the same way, but we'll do them with new considerations because we are in a different time. There are new things to consider and new applications for timeless wisdom. Ultimately, that's probably a good thing.

MENZIE: How have core values changed in today's society?

SECRETARY RILEY: In my life there have been multiple times when I just instinctively knew it was time to take an action, and most of those times, the risk far outweighed the logical choice. I have always known to trust my instincts. Great leaders also know when a choice, although very alluring, is not ultimately the best one.

MENZIE: Will you talk about your decision to decline a Supreme Court nomination . . . twice!

SECRETARY RILEY: After his election as president, Bill Clinton asked me to chair his transition team that helped him select all sub-cabinet appointees. It was an enormous job because there were 1,500 positions that needed to be filled in just ten weeks or so. During that process President Clinton asked me to be his secretary of education. [Riley was confirmed unanimously by the Senate on January 21, 1993.] In the spring of 1993, I received a call from President Clinton, [where] he said, "Dick, 'Whizzer' White [Justice Byron] has submitted his resignation. I want to nominate you to serve on the United States Supreme Court."

I was shocked at this, especially since I had never been a judge. I had decided long ago that my public service could best be filled as a leader in the legislative and executive branches of government, where I could help the people move forward on issues that were important to them and the nation. Shortly after the president's call, White House Counsel Bernard W. Nussbaum and other White House officials met with me for about two hours in my office at the Department of Education in an effort to convince me to sincerely consider the nomination. So I asked President Clinton for a day to consider.

Chapter 21

I discussed the matter with my father because he was a lifelong attorney, and he thought such an appointment would be the epitome of any lawyer's career. He urged me to accept. Being one who likes to get opinions from trusted friends, I also discussed the matter with my dear friend and law partner Claude Scarborough, who concurred wholeheartedly with Mr. Ted, as my father was affectionately known. But my most trusted adviser was my wife, and she urged me to serve where I thought I could do the most good. So after grappling with it, I decided the best decision was to turn down the nomination. I reasoned that I could best serve President Clinton and the American people by remaining as secretary of education. Ruth Ginsburg accepted the appointment.

I had worked hard to get the Department of Education organized and mobilized, and I had been successful at getting highly respected leaders in education from all across the country to come to the department to serve with me. I was so pleased at how the department was shaping up, both in terms of the appointed leadership and the career staff. Education policy was my first love, and I felt I could make a greater contribution to the nation by leading efforts to improve teaching and learning than I could [make] on the Supreme Court.

In the spring of 1994, President Clinton accepted the resignation of Justice Harry Blackmun. White House Chief of Staff Mack MacLarty was putting together a list of potential nominees for the president to consider. He called me to ask if I had changed my position from the year before. I said that my thinking remained the same. I always believed that education was where I served the nation best.

MENZIE: Few people [whom] I know can reflect on a record as incredible as yours. So in discussing success, I would be thrilled to have the reader benefit from your core beliefs.

Dr. Bob Fisher, retired president of Belmont University, speaks about success and entrepreneurship through service. His point of view is reflected in his statement "If you establish your goals based on service to others, the rewards you will receive will be too great to measure."

I know you also hold this belief. Will you share your feelings on this understanding?

SECRETARY RILEY: In my opinion, Dr. Fisher would be quite correct, and it brings to mind one of my favorite Winston Churchill quotes: "We make a living by what we get, but we make a life by what we give." Service is the ultimate opportunity to fulfill the purpose behind the idea of success. There are some people who confuse success with money and things, but things can never truly fulfill purpose, and therefore, they don't really bring a sustainable feeling of ultimate success, reward, or fulfillment.

MENZIE: Will you share what traits you feel are imperative to lifelong success?

SECRETARY RILEY: Well, a few come to mind. I know you had the pleasure of knowing Butler Derrick [congressman from South Carolina]. Butler had quite an outgoing personality when it came to communicating with people. He had a likability about him that was undeniable. What always got my attention was how he used that skill to get so much done.

Butler was able to attain great success simply through his likability, and he not only found ways of achieving success but, because his likability was so effective, he could serve his purpose in helping other people. Once he had won over the trust of his opponent, he would focus on the issues that he felt were important, and to me, that is a [really] good characteristic of success.

MENZIE: It's interesting because that's my point about the intertwining aspects of leadership and purpose and success: they all tie together. How much do you believe a person's thoughts affect the result of their success?

SECRETARY RILEY: Well, I strongly believe that. I have a very positive attitude about things, and I am attracted to leaders who do. I had a CEO, who was on the board of Furman University with me, send me a little book a couple months ago called *The Positive Dog*. I don't know if you have seen it, but it almost looks like a children's book. It's by Jon Gordon. It's two dogs talking and living together. One is positive, and one is negative. And obviously, the positive dog wins out on everything. He's better liked. He enjoys food better. All the people taking care of the dogs like him best. It sounds like a very simple statement, and it is. But at the end, he asserts that all these characteristics of being positive are true for human beings and dogs as well. He then recites research-driven results, and he goes into all these facts like we live longer, we are more successful in our jobs, there's less divorce, we're happier and more effective parents—everything about life that is good is improved by being a positive person. I think that's very powerful. And I think the simplicity of this book and the fact that it comes out with research-driven characteristics of being positive is [rightly] impressive. So they tell me a lot of Fortune 500 CEOs are having their top people read this little book. That's my view of it, and I love that because it appeals to me. Again, I am a positive dog. They say that everyone has in them a positive dog and a negative dog. The way that you come out and have the positive dog win is you feed him the most. You can control that. That's another thing about the book. It says you are in control of whether you are a positive or negative person.

MENZIE: I am a big fan of the James Allen book *As a Man Thinketh*. It's a pretty simple book, and it was written a long time ago, but it's about controlling your thoughts and trying to make sure that you understand the power and impact of positive thought. It's certainly had a pretty big impact on my life, and I think anyone who's been successful would agree with its sentiment.

If you had one secret to share with someone about becoming the most successful person they could become, what would that secret be?

SECRETARY RILEY: Well, I don't think that I have any secrets. But I do think that if you are a positive person, you can handle success very well. One of the important things to me is to believe in something and then decide that this is something that I am going to be serious about and then [to not] bend on it. Passion is a characteristic of that, and it will reflect in your beliefs.

MENZIE: Will you share your views on passion and purpose and what role you believe they play in success?

SECRETARY RILEY: To me, passion is more or less believing in what you're saying. You don't have to shout. You don't have to scream. People can tell when you believe, and there is nothing more effective than [people] who are deliberative and thoughtful and believe in what they are saying. Then, when they get tested, you see clearly that they are not going to back up an inch. That's a critical definition to me of how passion works. Success always follows purpose and passion. It's a natural progression.

Chapter 22

Rejection

MOST PEOPLE LOOK AT REJECTION AS A BAD THING, BUT IN TRUTH, IT can be a very powerful tool. Ultimately, when you look at rejection from a different vantage point, it can be the single reason you succeed going forward, and any setback or failure can fall into this category.

A few famous rejections in the music business are as follows.

The Beatles' rejection from Decca Records—Dick Rowe and his team will always be known for rejecting the Beatles. It is said that he believed there were too many guitar groups and that the trend was shifting away from that type of music. After the rejection, the Beatles did make a few adjustments: Ringo joined the band, and they developed their relationship with George Martin, but the point is simple—Decca couldn't see the potential.

U2 was rejected by Alexander Sinclair of RSO Records, who stated that he did not feel they were suitable for RSO at present.

Madonna was passed on by Jimmy Ienner, president of Millennium Records, because he felt her material was weak.

Matty Healy of the 1975 has shared that they were rejected repeatedly by several record labels before eventually being signed to Polydor. The record labels did not understand or embrace the style of their music.

Ed Sheeran was constantly rejected by record labels because of his style, looks, and material. He explains in an interview that he was told he was "slightly chubby and ginger" and not marketable because of it. Of course, we all know the rest of that story.

Elvis Presley bombed at the Grand Ole Opry. He was told he had no place there and that he should return to being a truck driver. Last time I checked, the King of Rock 'n' Roll had a pretty good run.

J. K. Rowling, although not a musician, had her manuscripts rejected multiple times. At present her Harry Potter franchise has made her a billionaire.

Does that mean everybody who experiences rejection succeeds at some future point down the road? No. There is no guarantee of that success. The only guarantee is the control you have over your reaction to the rejection. This is where you can have an effect on the future outcomes you will face in your career.

Successful people have a few things in common when dealing with rejection.

First, they have developed a strong sense of self-worth. They don't let a decision made by someone else dictate their reality.

Second, but just as important, they consider the outcome. Even though it's different than they expected, they reevaluate their performance to see what they can improve on. Most successful pros have had moments where they realize how they'd now approach auditions from a much-different perspective. I have little doubt their preparation rituals have improved.

The other truth about rejection is that you simply can't know what the rejecter's perspective is. The natural tendency is to think everyone sees and feels what we see and feel. That is never the case. The observer sees only from their point of view. That truth remains constant.

Maybe they are right to reject you. Maybe you need to change a few things. But the number one rule in business is to never give anyone your dignity.

Once you realize that rejection in the music business is unavoidable, you can prepare for it with that idea in mind. It takes experiencing rejection to understand the motivational sting of rejection fully.

You must look at rejection no differently than an athlete would look at a gym. It is the resistance to rejection that enables you to embrace and strengthen your determination.

Rejection breeds one of two offspring. The first is the quitter.

This person reacts by finding fault in the process but not themselves. This is quick and easy, and you are off the hook. The thinking is "It's them, not me." The problem with this approach is that you don't learn, and the only way to advance in any undertaking is to learn and grow from the event of rejection. Thus, the expression "No pain, no gain" applies here.

The second offspring is the fighter.

It is better to react to rejection as a fighter. However, embracing this philosophy takes guts, consideration, will, and the admission that maybe there is room to improve. Thus, as the saying goes, "Music is not a career for the faint of heart."

If you muster the courage to show your work or audition for a gig or pitch yourself or your songs or submit a resume, the chances are always only fifty-fifty that your idea is accepted. The only protections you have in an arts-based career are preparation and honest personal review. Your friends will always say they like what you are doing, and often, they are right. But your friends aren't on the other side of your auditions or submissions. When you take on the arts as a career, you are putting yourself in front of someone who most likely doesn't know you, so automatic support will no longer be the case. Whether right or wrong, the critic is now objective.

That is the special gift rejection brings us, as far as I'm concerned. It's one of the best gifts you will ever receive in your career. It's the quarterback's interception, the ice-skater's fall, the audience that doesn't relate to your music, the record company's "No," and the submission that is declined.

From this moment forward, you are introduced to the fighter in you. You must get punched to understand pain, and nothing will ever motivate you to improve more than the pain of rejection. It is the gift that keeps on giving.

CHAPTER 23

Tommy Harden

FEW DRUMMERS ARE IN AS HIGH DEMAND AS TOMMY HARDEN, WHO has lived and worked in Nashville since 1991. Whether it be a call from a top recording artist to track drums for their new album, a call from a session leader to record tracks, or an invitation to perform with a top artist, Tommy Harden is always a first consideration. Harden is a master studio musician, drummer, vocalist, multi-instrumentalist, songwriter, and producer. His depth of knowledge, as well as overall industry respect, puts him in a very elite group. His sense of scope and vision while working in the studio is legendary, and in Nashville, to earn the reputation of a first-call studio musician is reserved for a very few.

INTERVIEW

MENZIE: For someone to know you and understand your workload, they have to understand that you are the father of six, [have] played drums for Reba McEntire for fourteen years, and have toured with Alabama and many other major artists. Also, you play guitar and several other instruments, and you sing. You record drum tracks for around four hundred sessions a year, and you are a songwriter, engineer, and a producer. You also perform in your group Lost Hollow with your wife. What is required for a musician to handle that type of schedule and pace?

TOMMY HARDEN: Well, it's pretty much insane.
When I walk in the house, it's like a hornet's nest—kids coming from all directions. But today's music scene is different from the

Chapter 23

1990's. If you were a session drummer and had worked your way to the upper echelon, you could work recording sessions at 10:00 a.m., 2:00 p.m., and 6:00 p.m., six days a week, if you wanted to. A lot of guys would be on their second marriages because they were never home.

But in this day and time, the entire—or should I say, traditional—music industry is shrinking. It's a period of refinement right now, and everyone is trying to figure it out. It's like the cat has fallen from the ceiling and is trying to figure out which way to turn to land with its feet on the ground. It feels like we're about halfway down, and we don't know how we're going to land.

A lot of the publishing companies have merged, and a lot of the record companies have bought each other out and merged as well, and people simply aren't buying CDs or any physical product like they used to. A giant selling CD today will sell five million copies, whereas fifteen years ago, Shania Twain sold twenty million copies of one CD. Today people are downloading their music, picking a single or two instead of buying the entire record. The one upside is that where there is change, there is also new opportunity.

I went for probably ten or twelve years doing a minimum of eight sessions a week [and] a maximum of around twelve or thirteen sessions per week, and it just went on and on and on. Then as the industry continued to reinvent itself, it started slowing down. But it started slowing down for everybody, including cartage companies. So right now, the thing that I tell people is "Don't be afraid to do more than one thing. Be a session player, be in a band, tour."

I remember the day I joined Reba's band in 2010. I was at [the] Malloy Boys studio. We were doing a Tim Rushlow record, and my buddy asked me, "Do you want to go out with Reba for six weeks?" I said no, because I was screaming with my schedule. I had more sessions than I knew what to do with. And back then, a very select few studio players could go out on the road and come back and not have it affect their ability to work. Going out with Dire Straits or Sting would add to your mystique, so you could come back, and it wouldn't affect you. But if you went out with a country artist and you [were] doing country records, back then, you were either a session player or a road player. If you went out on the road as a session player, it was almost like you were telling the town, "My work has slowed down, so I need additional work." Then if they figure that your work has slowed down, the next thing they think is "Oh, I wonder why. Maybe I shouldn't hire him." So I was very full of trepidation about going out on the road. But it was just for six weeks, one tour, and I thought I could justify my unavailability for that amount of time. So I took the gig.

I was very nervous about it, but it ended up working out well. Then Reba didn't tour for the next couple years because of her TV show. But around the time that we started doing more performances with her again, things in the studio had begun to slow down. So now what I say to anyone asking me for professional career advice is "Don't be afraid to do a road gig and to do sessions, to write, to produce, etc. Do it all!"

When you look at indie bands, you'll see the lead singer may be doing a solo project and then is also doing another project. They aren't afraid to get in there and mix things up. That really is the theme of what's going on now in the music business. So don't be afraid to wear a lot of hats.

MENZIE: Technology probably enables you to do some things on a slightly flexible schedule, as opposed to times when you must physically be there because the session is recorded live.

TOMMY HARDEN: Yeah, I do tons of tracks for people. I probably do three to five tracks every week in my home studio. I do the track, then email it, get in the car, drive to the studio, and then come home and have a writing appointment the next day. And then we have a Lost Hollow gig the following weekend. So it's busy, and it's good—crazy good.

MENZIE: Can you give an overview of what your job with Reba entailed?

TOMMY HARDEN: When the band first came together, we decided that our goal was to have as much fun with Reba as we could. We decided that we were going to rock out, have fun, and interact with her. Our job was to support her musically and to play the songs with authenticity and integrity. In her band you want to serve the song. There is no need to draw attention to yourself unless it's a featured moment.

The band had a good attitude. We supported her. We tried to play our butts off every night. The whole band was a fantastic group because it was made up of studio players. She decided at some point in her career that rather than having a road band, she wanted to hire studio players and take them out. The only difference to me between going into a studio like Ocean Way—or any great studio in Nashville—and going onstage with Reba was the people in front of you. With Reba we were playing with the exact same level of precision that we played with in the studio.

MENZIE: What special skill sets does it take to fill the drum position for an artist of Reba's status?

TOMMY HARDEN: You have to play great every night with Reba because she is phenomenal, and that's the standard she personally sets. She never sings out of tune. She is always energized and upbeat. I must say that I have learned a lot from watching her. I have never seen her disparage a single person. I've never seen her talk down to a single person. She treats the security guard the same way she treats a celebrity in the room. She's wonderful to everybody. I've watched her like a hawk for fourteen years, and I've just learned so much. So you have to play great. The level of precision in that band is impressive.

MENZIE: When you're on the road, do you follow a different health regimen? I'm sure you have to really watch your energy levels and physical health because a tour is so very physically demanding.

TOMMY HARDEN: I work out more when I'm on the road. I've got six kids at home, so I have more distractions, and my schedule in town varies from day to day. But when I'm out there on the road, we generally leave at the same time every day, so I've got until two or three o'clock every day to get up, work out, eat, [and] get some business done.

I get to work out almost every day on the road, and I really like that. At home, if I work out, I have to get up at seven o'clock in the morning or do it at ten o'clock at night. There seems to be no other time to do it. It is a very physically demanding show. We once played a show in Calgary, and we had a couple guys who had just joined the band, and that was their first show. They wanted to go out and get a drink afterwards, and I literally had nothing left. When I got back to the room, I just collapsed.

MENZIE: What is the average crowd size?

TOMMY HARDEN: I'd say the minimum crowd for Reba at a smaller casino would be around three thousand people. But larger shows like Calgary would average around 12,500, and the crowds are simply crazy with enthusiasm. They don't sit down the entire time. And Reba generally does arenas. The TV show really helped her popularity.

Let me say one more thing about the road, and this goes for any tour and is really important—the road hang is 50 percent of the battle. You've got to know that when you're crammed on a bus for ten days straight, . . . you're not going to be at each other's throats. You gotta know that the musicians being considered for the gig are going to be positive and they're going to be happy, and that's 50 percent of the battle.

And in the studio world in Nashville, it's remarkably similar. The people [who] are hard to get along with, [who] have an attitude or tend to be divas, rise and fall quickly. Because once people get a bad taste and realize you are hard to work with, well, word travels amazingly fast.

MENZIE: Will you speak a bit about why you've had success at such a rare level and other people just fall short? Do you think there is a secret to pass on to young players who are at universities or out gigging?

TOMMY HARDEN: Make sure that your chops are together. Learn everything that you can learn. In this day and time, it is easier not to know as much, because of technologies like Pro Tools. As a drummer or even as a singer, they can chop you up and fix you. But I say, "Don't do that. Don't be the person that they have to chop up and fix. Be the person that makes them say, 'Hey, I don't have to mess with this one.'"

Probably the biggest thing in my career was proactivity and persistence. When I moved here, I was told by several people, "Go get a job.

Chapter 23

It's going to take two years before anything happens." Nashville is a very slow town. It takes a long time. If you're moving here thinking it's going to happen in six months, don't even bother. I moved here in 1991, and I immediately got on the phone, and part of it was luck, I am sure. I had a songwriting buddy of mine who knew Eddie Bayers. He called him and said, "A friend of mine is a brand-new drummer in town. Can he tag along with you for a couple of days?" I shadowed him for two days. I went to a Mickey Gilley session, then I went to a demo session at Fireside Studio, and I gave him a little cassette tape, and it had a three-song demo on it. A lot of it was me doing the slick-chop thing, trying to be all Dave Weckl.

I found out at that time that Barbara Mandrell was looking for a drummer. I had a *Modern Drummer Magazine* where [I'd] read that Randy Wright was her musical director and drummer. I got out the phone book, found Randy Wright, and I called him. I didn't talk to Randy; I talked to his business partner, and they had already found a drummer for Barbara. But he said, "Oh, you're a drummer looking for work. Let's meet. Let's get together and talk." So I went and met him. I found out later that Steve Gatlin had called this guy an hour before and said, "I need a drummer ASAP, my drummer's quitting." I was literally the next guy to call Randy's business partner after that. When he asked what I'd been doing in town, I was able to get the gig with this one sentence: I said, "Eddie Bayers has been recommending me."

When I met Steve Gatlin, he pulled out a cassette, circled some songs, and said, "Learn these songs." So I went and lived with them for the next two weeks. My very first time playing for them was [a] sound check at the Minneapolis ice hockey arena, opening for Kenny Rogers. That was the first time they had heard me play. So I was able to get that gig with no audition.

Proactivity—I didn't wait for someone to call me. I'd still be waiting to this day. I went and made it happen. So go out and make it happen. Create something. Start a band. Anything that's forward motion is forward motion. You may not end up exactly in the direction that you want to be in, but you're going to be moving toward that direction, and later something's going to knock you in yet a different direction, and because that happens, you're going to meet another somebody, and on and on.

So [have] that and persistence. I'm telling you, when I started doing session work, I was on the road with Ricky Skaggs for three years, and it took me two and a half years of doing sessions before it kicked in. I'd have three sessions one week, then none, then two sessions, [and] then one. I'd get a little spurt of momentum and then another spurt of momentum, and then it would stop. I would start to think it was never going to happen, so I would do construction jobs. [I'd have] a job programming and mixing karaoke sing-a-long tracks, then later I'd be under a house, digging a ditch.

I didn't want to do something where people in the music industry would see me doing something else. I didn't want to work cartage. I didn't want to work at a music store, because when you do that, all of sudden, that's what they see you doing. So people saw me enough in the studio that they kept slowly seeing my face. And I remember the week it happened—two and a half years into doing studio work, I went from three sessions a week to ten sessions a week. And from that point on, it never stopped—literally, for twelve or thirteen years. It was busy, busy, busy all the time.

If I had to do it over again, I'm not sure I would have done what I did. I did what I did because it was a different time. Now you can do session work and start a band. Find the most talented two or three singers you can find, and create something that you own. Again, it's forward motion, even if you don't end up getting a record deal. It's going to open a door down the road; it's going to lead to something. But there's always that possibility that the thing you start, the thing that you create, could end up becoming the next The Fray or the next Mumford and Sons. And you're an owner. Man, all you need is five years of that, and then you're done. You can do what you want to do for the rest of your life.

MENZIE: What about major changes you see in the music business, good and bad?

TOMMY HARDEN: Well, the biggest one is that there are fewer sessions and more players, so you really have to go in and service the song. Play the song. I tell young players the best thing they can do for their craft as a player is become a songwriter. Play on your own stuff. Then you're going to hear your song five hundred times. Then you're listening as a songwriter and a song owner.

Chapter 23

Menzie: What's your take on streaming and "free" music? Because, as a musician, you got paid for sessions, but then if you sold a unit, you got paid for that too. All of that has changed.

Tommy Harden: Well, it's a catch-22. Music used to be free. Then sheet music came out in the late 1800s, and they would sell sheet music, and that's when the publishers came about.

And then with the advent of radio play, songwriters started to get paid per play. Now we have come full circle to where we used to be. There is more and more free music out there, yet now there are more and more opportunities to play. It is what it is. I don't necessarily agree with it, but it is the new norm.

When I moved here in 1991, my wife and I originally wanted to start a duet. But back then, it was the Garth years, and you had to be really country. Now, because of streaming and the internet, there are opportunities everywhere. We went to Europe. We went to England and did shows. Now all the rules are gone. There are no more rules. We started doing our own music, and we started getting twentysomethings tweeting, "I'm obsessed with your music." From an artist's point of view, that's great!

Menzie: What is the difference between being a working musician in Nashville versus [in] LA or New York?

Tommy Harden: Nashville is *the* most unique music city in the world. We still have full bands that get together every day. In ten to fifteen studios across Nashville, you will have a full band congregating and playing music. In LA and NY, for the most part, they build stuff one piece at a time. There will be a programmer who sits in a room. They will bring a guitar player in, or they'll send the track to a drummer who has their own studio.

We were doing a record in LA about six or seven years ago while we were out there, doing a road show. Dave Malloy found out we were there and booked a session. So we go to a 10:00 [a.m.] session. We booked a 10:00 a.m. and a 2:00 p.m. session. The 10:00 [a.m.] session actually started at 12:30 p.m. because they weren't ready to go at 10:00 [a.m.]. Sometime that afternoon, the engineer looked over at the producer and said, "This is awesome. I've never tracked a full band before." And I'm talking about a big studio engineer!

There are plenty of music cities. You can make a living in Austin. Chicago has a big jingle scene. Everyone knows about New York, but Toronto also has a big music scene. Portland, Vancouver, [and] Seattle all have big music scenes. It just depends on what you are looking to do. Some of those scenes are more band oriented, but you can do stuff in LA and NY, piecing stuff together and writing and producing. In Nashville you can do anything. You can be a pop artist here; you can be a country artist here. They're starting to do film scores here. You can do anything in Nashville.

Nashville is very proprietary. Nashville doesn't care what you've done outside of Nashville. It's funny, when Dave Hungate moved here, he was Dave Hungate. He'd played on all the Toto hits, he played on "Low Down," [and] he was on a gazillion records in LA. He moved to town and had to start doing demos again. That's because Nashville doesn't care what you've done outside of Nashville. Nashville does things so differently from anywhere else that it hardly translates.

MENZIE: Nashville seems to be impressed by genuinely great music and great playing. Hit records are one thing, but great playing is another.

TOMMY HARDEN: Nashville loves good music, and Nashville will open itself up to you if you are easygoing and persistent. It will definitely open itself up to you, but you won't be able to jump in line.

MENZIE: While you are a traditional musician, you are wise enough to embrace the continuing changes in technology. So what is your take on technology in today's music?

TOMMY HARDEN: You can't ever, ever stop keeping up. If you coast for two months, you're going to have to get back on the bandwagon. It changes so fast. There was an engineer [whom] I used to work for, a very busy engineer, who used to brag, "I don't like using Pro Tools." Well, pretty soon he was using Pro Tools. Then he'd brag, "I don't use this, I don't use computers." Pretty soon he was gone. He was never seen again.

Chapter 23

Many people [who] hire me know that I've got a rack, and I take it with me into sessions. The rack has a laptop and a machine, and a lot of people know that I can create loops. So that just gives you one more advantage.

MENZIE: What are the drawbacks of everyone now having the ability to record at home? Do you see that as something that is causing other problems?

TOMMY HARDEN: It's a phase that Nashville is going through right now, since the Florida Georgia Line record. They programmed the drums on that record and pretty much built it LA-style, one piece at a time. And since then, a lot of songwriters have figured out, "Oh, I can do this myself."

You could either spend time writing a song, or you could spend time programming a track that you've done. But there's no way you're going to be able to write the same number of songs if you're programming tracks, because that is very time intensive if you want to do it right.

But it has also allowed people like me to cut drum tracks at the house, so there's a give and take. There aren't as many sessions in town right now, but it's really just a phase that Nashville's going through. I've seen Nashville go through so many different phases, and they will last generally a year to eighteen months, and then it moves on to the next phase.

MENZIE: If something's got drum machines on it, who is programming them? Is it usually a keyboard player, or is it a drummer? Do you use them in your own tracking? Where do you run into that kind of technology?

TOMMY HARDEN: Oddly enough, I was just thinking about this yesterday. I am thinking about buying EZDrummer or something like that—only because I really like the feel of those tracks—and I want to be able to practice on them, and I want to be able to make what I'm doing feel like that.

They're making pretty good drum programs now, and they're making them so easy to program that anyone can basically do it. The thing is [that] you don't get the emotional lift. So it's very linear sounding. If you do the type of track where you slam it up against the wall and compress it and it's loud all the time, it works great, like the Florida Georgia Line stuff. But if it's something where you're going to lift the feel into the chorus, or you're going to lift and make the emotions go up and down like a roller coaster, that's very hard to do with a drum program.

MENZIE: Will you recount the discussion we had earlier about the pole, describing the relationship a musician has with a click track in the studio?

TOMMY HARDEN: I think I was talking about ways to visualize the relationship to the click. I tell folks to view it like a flagpole, or something along those lines. You can be right next to it. You can be five feet away from it. You can be five feet on one side or the other of it. You can stand behind it. You can stand in front of it. There are so many different ways to play on the click. You can even play on top of it. When I play with loops, I try to play a nanosecond on top because if I play behind, I hear flams with the loops. If you play right on top of it, it has a tendency to mask the flams. Hopefully, you don't have any.

Really, the goal for the drummer is to play on the click but [to] make it sound so relaxed that there's no question of where the time is. A lot of drummers can play on the click, but the question is [if] a lot of drummers [can] feel on the click. You've got to feel it and know exactly where that pocket is and know exactly where that backbeat is going to land. Being relaxed is the most important thing. Playing completely relaxed on the click is the goal.

There was one time I was at Ocean Way, and we were in the A room, and there was a band in the B room. So I stuck my head up to the door, and I listened to the other drummer. I was struck by how relaxed the track was. He wasn't beating the drums to death. He was playing at a very relaxed volume, and his pocket was very, very relaxed. He knew the secret—he allowed the pocket to breathe.

Steve Gadd said in an interview one time that when you get in the room, it really doesn't matter where the drummer plays on the click. What matters is what ends up on the track with the other people. So if you're in a room with people [who] are playing on top, and you play on the click,

Chapter 23

technically you are correct, but it's going to feel like crap. So what's the goal? Is the goal to prove that you are right, or is the goal to make good music? The goal with six people in a studio is to make good music together.

If the people are rushing, is it a problem? Hopefully not. Let's try to figure out a way—what I'll do is I'll try to play with them, and then I will slowly bring them back. A drummer moving on and off the click should move like the *Titanic*, not like a speed boat. It should move slow. And if you do that, then you'll kind of woo them back to where you are feeling the time, and that creates the opportunity for a good pocket to develop.

When there's a band playing to a click and you take the click away, all of a sudden, the drummer becomes the click, and the tracks become way tighter. I've seen it over and over and over again. When you listen to tracks from the seventies or eighties, especially the eighties, before they started using the click a lot, the tracks are so tight. And it's because the drummer was the click. When you take the click away, if you have a really good band in there, it just gets really tight. The time becomes the time feel, and that's magical.

MENZIE: I am sure you were elated to get your hands on Billy Cobham's kit for the Reba tour. I know from my research that you had a tremendous appreciation for Cobham and Gadd. So how do you incorporate those kinds of jazz influences into country and traditional recordings?

TOMMY HARDEN: You have to be picky with where you put them. I tell drummers not to be afraid to throw stuff like that in a song but [to not] throw it in at the beginning of the song. Establish the song; establish the groove of that song. Service that song, and then toward the end, once people have learned the song, then you've got a little more freedom to throw stuff around and keep it interesting.

One of my favorite bass players in town is Jimmy Lee Sloas. He plays a voracious groove, and he plays complete bass. He doesn't play for himself; he plays for the pocket. But about twice a song, it's like someone is coming out from behind a curtain and smacking you. He'll throw some little ditty or something tasty at you. By the time you realize he's smacked you, he's back to playing the bass pocket again. He always picks the right spot and a lick that is like a wink. It's artful! So, as a drummer, I'm probably going to put one or two things in that song, but I'm only going to do that once or twice a song. Any more than that and I'm going to end up getting a reputation for being too busy.

MENZIE: You play drums on "I Drive Your Truck." It was a Song of the Year [Grammy Award winner] by Lee Brice. Did you feel that song was special when you recorded it?

TOMMY HARDEN: Not really, but that's because I try to treat every song as if I wrote it. I just try to play the song to the best of my ability. Honestly, I play on so many songs that that approach is what constantly nets me the best results.

I have a sixth sense about songs. I have a songwriter I work for named Wade Kirby. He's had multiple number 1 hits; he's just a genius of a writer. He told me that usually there's about one or two songs a session where I'll walk in and go, "Wait, that's a big song." He said it happened six times in a row, and those were always the songs that got cut in the session. So at least I have one guy in town [who] listens to me.

MENZIE: When one of the guys [who] wrote "I Saw God Today" for George Strait says that, I think you can trust it!

What does a drummer need to know today about mic techniques and the production end of recording in order to be successful? Do you feel that the drummers who know more about it do better in sessions, or do you feel it's better that the engineers have their space?

TOMMY HARDEN: My whole thing is [that] if I move something, I always ask an engineer first. To me, it would be like an engineer coming in and repositioning my cymbal. If an engineer walked in and said my cymbal was too low and raised it up, I'd probably get pretty ticked off. I have had an engineer many times say, "I'm not getting the right floor tom sound," and I'll say, "Do you mind if I move the mic because I don't think it's in the right spot for this drum?" Nine times out of ten, they'll say, "Yeah, move it to where you think it should be," and then you get the right sound.

It's so important knowing how to do room mics. I've been

experimenting lately with a mic technique called the Glyn Johns. It's a four-mic technique for the drums. In indie music now, they don't close mic everything. When you do a close mic and . . . put it on an indie track, it sticks out like a sore thumb.

MENZIE: What is the secret to creating a unique drum track? Do you craft them just from the song's point of view, or do you track them knowing it will record well?

TOMMY HARDEN: I generally try not to go with the first. A lot of times you'll hear a song, and you'll want to immediately fall into what you normally do every day. I try to do something different, throw in some different beat so it doesn't sound like stock lick number thirty-two. I really try to create a groove that pays homage to the song but that [also] catches someone's ear. Maybe it will catch an A&R person's ear and get the song cut.

Sometimes it works when you throw something different in there. Don't be afraid to throw a tom in instead of a snare. I've got about fifteen different ways to create the idea of hitting a snare drum—without hitting a snare drum.

MENZIE: In the studio do you track with dynamics, or do you try to keep your pressure level consistent?

TOMMY HARDEN: In the studio, you don't play as hard. If I hit at a 50 percent level in the studio, then walk in the control room and listen back, it sounds like I'm playing at 100 percent. If I play at 100 percent level and go back in, then all of a sudden, you get to a point with the drums where you compress the mic and stuff starts sounding smaller and smaller. If you go back and listen to a lot of the heavy metal records in the 1990s, before they started sound replacing and laying samples over the tracks, the drums sound teeny-tiny because the players are beating the crap out of the drums, and the mic is like your ear. It just shuts down. If you look at YouTube videos of John Robinson playing drums, he looks like he is barely hitting the drums.

MENZIE: In the humble opinion of Tommy Harden, what is the best drum groove of all time?

TOMMY HARDEN: Oh my gosh. If I had to pick one, it would have to be Rosanna with Jeff Porcaro. I love playing that. To me, a drummer shows their ability by playing the shuffle.

We played [on the *Late Show with*] *David Letterman* when "Turn on the Radio" was on the radio—a huge hit for Reba. It ended up being a multiweek number 1. It's a deep, deep shuffle. The guys in the *Letterman* band, the old school sax players and trombone players, came up to us afterwards and said it was great to hear a band that can actually play a shuffle. Because, [with] these younger bands, there are so few of them that can actually play a shuffle. A shuffle, to me, shows what a drummer can do, and Jeff Porcaro's was brilliant.

I could also pick a dozen different Steve Gadd tracks, John Robinson tracks, and Eddie Bayers tracks. There are tracks that Eddie Bayers played that, to this day, blow my mind. I feel like if I live to be one thousand, I will never play on as many records as he has.

MENZIE: What is it like to compete for work in Nashville?

TOMMY HARDEN: You know, that's one of the maddening things. You've got to have really, really thick skin. There's no way you can look at a producer and say, "Please hire me." You can't do that. So you have to trust that what you're doing is great. You've got to make it better. You've got to always be striving to improve. Always be moving forward. And then, you've got to sit back and trust that your work is going to speak for itself.

But I've been on the other side of it as a songwriter, and as a songwriter, I don't want to always hire the same people. I feel like each person does something special in a certain area. So it's just a really good idea to keep your professional relationships fresh.

Nashville is a one-on-one networking town. When I get one-on-one with people and go have coffee and lunch, then my work picks up. When I'm hibernating at home, my work slows down. For me, being a father of six, I have to draw the line somewhere. I can't go out every night and press the flesh and go to songwriter things. I just can't. So I have to say, "This is the amount of work that I'm going to do, and my work is going to have to speak for itself," [and] "If you want me, here's my number. I hope I get to see you. I'm going to give you 1,000,000 percent and make your song sound like it's my own."

MENZIE: You have your own sound. Do you find it important to remain original when everybody wants you to do it like this person or that person? Obviously, there's pressure in this industry, but you have your own artistry. How do you approach that?

TOMMY HARDEN: You always have to be moving forward. I think of it akin to the East Nashville style of drumming, which is the vintage kit, fewer mics, and the snares all dumped out. It's very prevalent on the radio, so why wouldn't I be able to do that? But at the same time, I'm not going to sell out to that and not be who I am.

There's a balancing act. You've got to be who you are. You've got to be original; you can't go around being a copycat all the time. You know, there are certain fads that are going to go away in a couple of years, and if you've based your entire schtick on that, then you're going to go away too.

MENZIE: Talk to me a little bit about Pro Tools and how it has changed the way that recordings are done. You said you've been doing this since 1991, so I'm sure you've seen a few major changes.

TOMMY HARDEN: Back when I first started, I would drive the click myself, and I had a drum machine, and I had a rig set up where I could do the loops and drive the click at the same time. So I dedicated the click out, and then I mixed everything together. I'd hit the start button and play. Now, with Pro Tools, everybody wants to be gridded. Everybody wants their song to be already gridded. They don't want to have to go and figure that out afterwards. When we play, we play to the grid.

So now the engineers are feeding the click. And instead of me playing the loop all the way through the song, now I'll program it, and I'll give it to them. They'll chop it, and they'll grid it themselves, or I'll put it on a memory stick and take it to the control room. I know that's a lot of geek speak, but that's how it is.

With the advent of Pro Tools, people now are more interested in how well you play with Pro Tools. How precise can you be? Tom Bukovac is a great friend and one of the best guitar players and session musicians in town—he calls it target shooting. What we do now is see how close we can get to the target and still create something.

MENZIE: So now, on the opposite end of the spectrum, let's talk a little bit about Lost Hollow. Lost Hollow is your own personal project with your wife, Lorrie. Carole King and Reba recorded a song that you guys wrote on [the *Reba:*] *Duets* album. Can you describe the moment when you found out they were going to record "Everyday People" and why it was so special to you and Lorrie?

TOMMY HARDEN: It was one of the only times that we have target written, and it worked. We wanted it to be Reba's theme song for Habitat for Humanity because she's the spokesperson. I found out that she was going to LA to cut with an LA crew and she was going to do a duet with LeAnn Rimes. All of sudden, she put the song on hold, and we didn't hear anything for two or three months. And then, all of a sudden, one night I'm reading my email, sitting on the edge of the bed with my laptop, and Lorrie said I screamed like a girl scout on fire—Reba was thinking about doing "Everyday People" with Carole King. I later found out that Carole had sent her one hundred songs.

MENZIE: What do you look for in an artist that makes you accept the role of producer?

TOMMY HARDEN: I'm just looking for something that's different, something that stands out. I don't get too excited when an artist sounds like somebody else; I get excited when they have their own unique sound. What I really try to do is to create something that, when I take it into an A&R person's office, they're going to say it doesn't sound like anybody else. Because if it's really good, then they can't use that excuse, and we can move forward. If it sounds like Keith Urban, they already have Keith Urban. They don't need another Keith Urban.

Menzie: So when you go to produce somebody, where do you start?

Tommy Harden: Songs. The songs are so important. If I have any beef about indie music—and I love indie music—it is that there are hundreds, if not thousands, of artists who have the look, they've got the dress, they've got the vibe, they sing like the indie sound, [and] their production is grunged up the indie way, but there are so few of them [who] have a song that I'm going to walk out singing. The song is everything.

To make an artist happen, the stars have to line up. If the production's weak, that's a star that's out of line. It's not going to happen. If the songs are weak, it's not going to happen. If you can't sing and I've got to tune you to death, it's going to be pretty apparent that it's not going to happen. So everything has got to line up, and then after it lines up, it's got to be different. It has to be unique. That is so important. That is what Nashville is about. Nashville is all about the song being great.

Nashville is in a really weird spot right now. I feel that, more than ever, Nashville is kind of in a copycat phase. We're looking at the pop world and saying, "Let's pull from that and put it in Nashville." I feel like we've somewhat lost our identity, and I'm hoping that changes.

Menzie: Elaborate on what you believe is that something special.

Tommy Harden: Boy, if I could bottle that up, I'd be a multimillionaire. It's really just believability. Do I believe that this is contrived, or do I believe that this is real? You always want to try to write something that's real, and a lot of times you can't, but you can try to write something that's believable. To me, if it's got that genuine spark that makes me believe it, that's what I'm looking for.

Menzie: Do you have favorite songwriters like you have favorite drummers?

Tommy Harden: I am a huge Glen Hansard fan. He's the lead singer of the Frames, and they did a movie called *Once*. It was genuine music because this guy is a genuine musician instead of an actor being coached on music. They ended up winning an Oscar for a song called "Falling Slowly." I love his writing.

There's a guy named Jason Matthews—a big burly guy, real country. When it comes to being able to put pop radio melodies to a country format and meld them together believably, I've never seen anybody in town do it like he does. It's unbelievable.

We played at 3rd and Lindsley the other night. We were the first opening act, and we opened for two other acts, one of which just [had] signed a record deal. We were stopped by two students who are writers, and they were gushing. So, again, it gets back to the song. If the song is not great, you got nothin'.

Chapter 24

Procrastination

PROCRASTINATION IS THE ACHILLES' HEEL OF THE CREATIVE. For this book to be complete, it's imperative to address the topic of procrastination or, as many call it, "the frozen zone." Procrastination happens for more reasons than you can name, so let's look into a few. This will put you on the path to a better understanding of the time thief.

The first rule is to never postpone the excellent in search of the perfect.

A statement like that makes us wonder, Does this same thing happens to all creatives? Of course, the answer is an emphatic yes! Procrastination happens nearly every time we enter the creative zone because, in the creative zone, we are vulnerable. Just to get in the door, we have to completely let go of ego, allowing ourselves the grace and courage to invite the creative gods to join us.

The truth is we are afraid they won't. Thus, we partner with procrastination until we hear the creative gods pulling into the driveway. At that breakthrough moment, we tie ourselves to the chair and struggle to settle, and before we know it, the creative gods are bringing us coffee. Once again, we begin to breathe and create.

One challenge musicians and writers face in a creative business is that the words *creative* and *business* detest each other. Take a moment to reflect on the two very different natures of these beasts. Creativity is a state of flow, where everything potentially aligns. It's free thinking, reactionary, expressive, and fluid. Business, on the other hand, is disciplined, detailed, and based on a deadline. Business is a duty-driven discipline.

The humorous plot twist is that to succeed in today's music business, these two opposites need to marry.

Whether it's natural for us or not, it's a simple truth that to succeed in any creative undertaking, you must embrace discipline as king. When business enters the discussion, producing a product becomes our job. Therefore, deadlines become a true part of the discussion, which means procrastination has to die.

Although it's a behavior and not a substance, many successful people look at procrastination through the same lens as any other form of dependency. Therefore, to beat it, we must start by looking for the root cause, which always leads to the big reveal: the admission that you are honestly afraid of rejection!

So take your fears out to dinner, and have the ugly talk. Say out loud to your fears, "I don't think I'm worthy, and when nobody's looking, I will admit I'm scared shitless. I don't want to fail, much less face rejection and criticism, and because of that truth, I have allowed myself to live in 'the frozen zone.' I'm so frozen that I don't even know I'm procrastinating. I justify procrastination by calling it different names, such as business, overwhelm, exhaustion, or the ultimate creativity killer—tomorrow. I'm in complete denial!"

After you have the big admission talk, you face the truth, and pledge, "To kill procrastination, I am willing to face the fear of rejection!"

Then, you write out an inflexible strategy and hold yourself accountable, no matter what. You fight procrastination at every turn because the truth is, like any other distraction, you are never completely free from it or the struggle of feeling unworthy. The cure for this insidious little truth is to take it behind the barn and beat its ass while shouting out loud, "I am *worthy*!"

Procrastination is a natural by-product of being a creative. So, congratulations, you've passed the creative test if you find that procrastination is a natural part of your makeup. Those that have beaten the dragon say that it's better to admit the addiction of procrastination than to deny it—because denial is procrastination!

Another cause of procrastination is the feeling of being overwhelmed.

Chapter 24

In the beginning stages of a creative's career, there is so much to tackle that it often creates a state of inertia. In this case, organization is a good friend to partner with. One productive approach many business leaders embrace is to tackle only one task at a time. The most successful businesspeople I know believe multitasking is overrated. Exactly like a computer with too many windows open, it invites a crash. When that happens, nothing gets accomplished. These simple tips help us remember the old saying "Eyes on the prize." Myopic focus and consistent action are great strategies to help dismantle the challenge of procrastination.

Procrastination is often caused by the size and scope of a project or task.

The size and scope of a project deadline can be paralyzing. That is often the case when a strong new musical act breaks onto the scene with a hot debut record. Justifiably, their audiences and record labels expect the exact same quality—or better—on their second release. Generally, bands and artists have vetted their first material years in advance of signing with a label. The sophomore curse plagues the second works of many bands and writers because the material is put together with much less time dedicated to vetting it in front of audiences. The sheer size and scope of the task ends up coming back to haunt creatives, as it is such a monumental task to accomplish in a shorter time span. In the case of a sophomore project, expedience is now prioritized over quality, and because of intensified demand, the authenticity of the product often suffers.

There is no doubt that the demands on artists wreak havoc on their ability to create quality new material. Oftentimes, this pressure causes creative paralysis and procrastination. Historically, bands and artists end up dumping unvetted material at the last minute to meet deadlines. The truth is that it doesn't have to be this way, but the habit of being resolute must interrupt the addiction to procrastination.

Procrastination impedes us from pursuing our future selves. It is a coping mechanism that kicks in when we are mentally overloaded and lacking in creative energy. You can fight the procrastination "syndrome" by engaging in visualizations of the future you intend to have. Self-belief is your most potent tool for interrupting this condition. There is, however, one small catch. Your visualizations must be embraced as a future truth—heartfelt and genuine.

Visualizations offer us the best chance to bully procrastination because creative ideas have no time line tied to them. This enables us to let our imaginations soar. The bolder you see the details of your projected future, the greater the chances are of its manifestation. It's a personal ritual that invites creativity into the room, encouraging procrastination to leave.

To outsmart procrastination we must begin with a pledge to rid ourselves of the creativity killer, and we start by admitting that we have the habit in the first place. Then we prioritize purpose over procrastination. This means your words, actions, and intentions have to consistently align while you also allow yourself freedom from expectations!

The greatest secret that every successful artist knows is as follows: procrastination is a chess game you play with yourself. You want to make sure to be the better player.

Chapter 25

Sierra Hull

With multiple wins for International Bluegrass Music Association (IBMA) Mandolinist of the Year, Sierra Hull continues to push boundaries. In this interview Hull discusses heroes, musical boundaries, and standing strong when you know your direction must shift for you to remain an authentic artist. Sierra talks openly about the courage it took to fight for the Grammy-nominated album *Weighted Mind*.

After being signed to Rounder Records at the ripe age of thirteen, Sierra Hull has so far in her career accomplished what few artists, if any, have been able to accomplish in a lifetime.

Interview

Menzie: I thought I'd start with the story behind your work *Weighted Mind*. The album was a new direction for you and a true departure from your previous works. You had Béla Fleck produce the album, and certainly, Fleck is no stranger to pushing into new territory. How did you come to choose Béla?

Sierra Hull: When prepping for what I believed was material for the next record, I had recorded and produced six tracks by myself. It was a couple years before the *Weighted Mind* project came out. I wasn't really sure what I wanted to do regarding my musical direction, but I knew that it was not going to be like my other two albums. I had spent the years before that writing the new material, and I knew that the songs that I was writing would need to be presented a bit differently than the traditional bluegrass setting.

But I just couldn't think of exactly who I wanted to produce this project. As I got to thinking about everything it needed to be, I kind of went out on a limb and decided to produce it myself. And I thought, "I'll try to pick an engineer [who] will be an interesting choice." So I reached out to Vance Powell, who's a really great engineer here in Nashville. He's worked with a ton of folks [and is] mostly known for his work with Jack White. He has also worked with Chris Stapleton and a ton of other great artists.

MENZIE: Vance is a very respected gentleman.

SIERRA HULL: Vance has a very different kind of approach to recording. He does a lot of live to tape, so we went in a studio here in Nashville and cut six tracks live. We experimented with a live sound setting. I was playing a lot of guitar. I even played the electric guitar and a little banjo on one tune. We were doing a bunch of different kinds of things. I was getting a lot of input from different people around me at the time, including the record label and my management. I was sharing this new music that was different, but that felt really true to me somehow. But because the music was so different in style, it made folks on the business side nervous.

Finally, I had to get away from it for a while. During that time, I was frustrated, so I started talking to Alison Krauss, who has been a longtime hero and friend of mine. Alison was someone I trusted, and I was just trying to get some advice. I finally said, "You know, I feel like, at this point, what I really need is a producer. I'm tired of taking all the stress on by myself. I would love to just have somebody who truly knows what it's about." And I knew that it couldn't just be anybody.

So we were tossing around different ideas of what might make sense for this project, and she said, "You know who I think would be a good producer for you? There's nothing musically he doesn't understand, and I think he would be a great vocal producer—Béla." Truly, at that time, he wasn't the first person to come to mind—mostly because I knew that this was going to be very centered around the lyrics. But I started thinking about that. Béla hadn't produced a lot at that point, only a handful of albums, but he had focused on his own music and producing his own stuff. Oddly, I ran into him a few months later at IBMA. As fate would have it, he sat right behind me at the award show, and he tapped me on my shoulder and said, "Hey Sierra, it's Béla," and I thought, "Oh, you're the guy I need to see."

MENZIE: That might be divine intervention there, you know?

SIERRA HULL: No kidding. So we just kind of reconnected, and I told him my thoughts. Alison had suggested just talking to him about what I was doing, maybe playing him some of my stuff, to see if he could give any productive feedback. After we reconnected we ended up getting together a month or so later. Then, slowly, we started getting together and working and seeing where it could go, which ultimately led to him saying, "What happens if you just take everything away but mandolin and voice? Let's try that."

That moment kind of made me realize that I was, in some ways, adoring the musicians [who] were playing on my project so much that I was not leaving any room for myself on my own album. That idea was like the big thing that not only affected the album, but [it] ultimately affected me as a musician moving forward.

MENZIE: When I first listened to "Black River," what really jumped out at me was the quality of the fidelity in the production. There's a unique dimension that is created with space and subtle intricacies. A good example would be the airy sound of Ethan Jodziewicz's finger slides in the opening bass line. They just really breathe and seem to almost help with propulsion. Did Béla have a different approach to how this music was to be recorded than those you've recorded with in the past?

SIERRA HULL: There was one important difference—we made sure to try a lot of different things, and then we would have discussions about which setup sounded the best. I think it was more like we were willing to put in the work that it took and not just settle for the first setup we had. Something that works for one session doesn't always work for the particular music of another session.

Menzie: So there was a great deal of curiosity. Did Béla use different miking techniques than you had used prior?

Sierra Hull: When I recorded the things with amps, we used a bunch of different mics. We might have been recording with three or four different mics at a time, and then, depending on what songs needed what, we could sort of mix things in as needed. We used some room mics too.

Menzie: Will you walk us through the artistic considerations and personal feelings that led you to embrace the change in your musical direction?

Sierra Hull: Part of me thinks the change of direction musically was the result of my coming into a different period in my life personally and artistically. It had been a long time since I had released new music; there [were] almost five years in between albums. I was finding myself performing music but not feeling completely fulfilled, especially as a writer. I felt like I was starting to connect more with the newer songs I was writing. But in my current performance format, I felt that I wasn't able to showcase what I really wanted to express. So I think the direction change was the result of writing while reflecting on getting older. My music was just naturally becoming more introspective. It ultimately came out a bit differently, and I just decided to embrace that and go with it.

Menzie: So with the success you had already attained as a recording artist, what pushback did you get on the decision to adjust the direction of your musical expression?

Sierra Hull: I got more pushback during the time I tried to produce myself; I think [it was] before I even really had much of a chance to do anything. When you're working on a project, a lot of people want to know what you're doing, and they want to hear it and give feedback. It's kind of a natural part of the process when you're working with your team. Be it the label or management or even band people or whatever, people kind of want to be in on that. And I almost feel like, at this point, you have to be really careful with what you share with people too early.

Chapter 25

MENZIE: Amen.

SIERRA HULL: Other people's opinions can skew your own vision a little bit, and you can easily begin to doubt what you intuitively or truly believe, so when I started working with Béla, we didn't really play a note of anything for anybody. I pretty much didn't let anybody hear it until we were almost done.

I also think everybody was really excited that I was working with Béla and knew that whatever it would be, [it] would be great. There's that confidence that people around you get when you're working with somebody like Béla.

MENZIE: It must have been tough to sit on that stuff and not share it, because you were probably tremendously excited about it.

SIERRA HULL: I was definitely excited, but I also knew how much more exciting it was going to be for somebody to hear it when we really got the music where we wanted it. And having gone through that frustrating period of working on my other music and sharing stuff too early, I really wanted the people around me to hear it and like it. I was also [then] at a place where I knew it was right to wait because I trusted the quality enough.

MENZIE: There's a lot of freedom when you get to the point where you don't care—I mean, you obviously care tremendously—but when you get to the point where you're not so concerned about the judgment of others. It's riskier, but ultimately, it works out.

SIERRA HULL: And that was the good thing about working with somebody like Béla, who is one of my heroes. To have him go, "That's awesome," [and] "This is great." It's like, well, even if so-and-so doesn't like it, Béla likes it and I like it, so to me, that means enough to say I can trust it.

MENZIE: What, if anything, did your record label and your team suggest when you were in the first phases of your new direction, when it was just you, pre-Béla? Were they concerned about you embracing a different style? What was the feedback you were getting?

SIERRA HULL: You know, it's the little things. They were excited that I was doing the album—and one that wasn't just another bluegrass project. They were okay with that, and they felt like it was a natural evolution for me musically. Nobody was against that. But oddly, the toughest thing for me to hear were comments like, "You have too many ballads," or "It's too downtempo." And I was told that they thought that I should consider other songs by other songwriters.

MENZIE: Oh wow!

SIERRA HULL: That was the thing that frustrated me the most because I felt like . . . you guys don't understand this whole record. I have these songs that I feel sure about, and I'm needing to get them out there, and I couldn't truly explain that. I just knew that these songs were good.

MENZIE: Regarding the material, you were quoted in the *Huffington Post* [as] saying that you felt the proudest of the songwriting on the *Weighted Mind* record. "They just feel like they're coming from a truer deeper place." Can we talk about your songwriting—maybe put us in the room with you during the process?

SIERRA HULL: From the stuff that I recorded before, with Vance Powell, five of the six songs made their way onto the new project: "Weighted Mind," "I'll Be Fine," "Wings of the Dawn," "Compass," and what became "Stranded." "Lullaby" was around; "In Between" was around.

But then there was a period of writing other songs in between that first session, and [that included what] became the *Weighted Mind* tracking: "Choices and Changes," which was very much inspired by the frustration of everybody's feedback. "Fallen Man" was written after. "Queen of Hearts" was something that I was already kind of working on. A lot of these pieces had been around for a little while but then finally found their way and their form with some slight revisions.

MENZIE: When you're writing songs, is there an instrument that you prefer to compose on, or does that have to do with the song style and what you hear in your head?

Chapter 25

Sierra Hull: On the *Weighted Mind* songs, I had written a lot of that material on guitar. For example, "Wings of the Dawn," "Weighted Mind," "I'll Be Fine," [and] "Choices and Changes"—almost all of those songs started out with me playing and writing on guitar, sometimes with a riff or something on the guitar that kind of translated over to mandolin. If I'm writing now, it's sometimes on guitar, sometimes mandolin. It depends on what comes first, the melody or the lyrics.

Sometimes I might be writing a set of lyrics with no melody in mind whatsoever, and other times, when I discover a melody that I like, I'll go back through some of my lyrical ideas to see what I can build around the new melody. I don't really have any set formula.

Menzie: I know your tour has been tremendously grueling—you guys are playing every day. What toll does the demand of touring take on your writing?

Sierra Hull: I'd say it's really hard to get a lot of writing done while on tour. I've had the past week at home, and I've been spending some time every day working on ideas, but it's much easier to do when I have time off the road. [It's] mostly because, on the road, I don't have as much alone time. You're spending most of your day in tight quarters, either traveling or at a venue, and what little time you do have to yourself at a hotel, you're usually just going to sleep because you're tired from the travel. I find it a little bit more difficult to write in that situation because I tend to like alone time to really think and try ideas.

Menzie: I read recently that James Taylor will sometimes borrow a chateau from a friend and then go there for a month. He shared that it would sometimes take him a week just to center and clear himself before he could write. He has said, "You need to defend empty time." And when you think about how hectic the artist's professional responsibilities are and how sensitive the writing process is, there is little doubt that JT is right!

Sierra Hull: It's hard to argue with the truth.

MENZIE: Will you share a little bit about the process with Béla and bringing the songs and record to life?

SIERRA HULL: Once I started working with Béla and we started trying to review material, I would come in, and I would say, "Okay I have this song, and what do you think about this idea?" And I would play it. Finally, after the first time or two that we got together, we decided that it would be cool if I just took these songs and tried to work up solo mandolin and voice arrangements of them. It was through trying the stripped-down approach that I really started to feel like, "This is challenging but really fun and really freeing."

I wasn't having to worry about whether or not I was giving other instruments enough room to do this or that. And that was making me approach my playing in a different way. What better way to find yourself than to take everything else away? When you do that, there's really no choice except for you to become the music.

MENZIE: With the new album, you've put the creative emphasis on the totality of the music while, at the same time, keeping your virtuosity at the forefront. Was there concern about [the] reaction from ardent fans who may have wanted you to stay locked into the typical bluegrass band format that they'd come to know?

SIERRA HULL: I think I would have been more worried about that when I first was going in [and] producing my own stuff. Having gone through that frustrating period, I just thought to myself, "I can't help who doesn't like it. I gotta do what I gotta do and what I feel is right for me." So at that point, I wasn't worried about it anymore. I just had to say, "Well, if I like this and Béla likes this, then I gotta trust that there are plenty of other people that will like it too." Through touring, I have found that it's been really rewarding to see a lot of my bluegrass audiences respond even better than they used to. I feel like, in some way, the response is better because I think they know that I'm doing something that feels truly honest.

MENZIE: The music is very genuine, as are the performances. And they're very open—you're leaving a lot of room for the audiences to get to know you. The music is not overcrowded. But despite the format being less traditional, . . . the virtuosity remains as stellar as ever.

SIERRA HULL: I think people respond to that. Sometimes different audiences have different levels of musical understanding, but everybody is a genius when it comes to knowing if an artist is genuine or not.

MENZIE: There you go!

SIERRA HULL: It's like, as humans, we know that, and we pick up on it. I think the secret is it's important to play music you enjoy. It becomes natural to deliver a riveting performance because, after all, that's why fans support you. It's our job.

MENZIE: The record is mostly you and Ethan Jodziewicz, along with some very special guests. I've read that going with the bare bones format was a decision between Béla and you. What artistic curiosity led you to really accept that approach? Did you find that was a more natural format for the music you had written?

SIERRA HULL: At first, I was a little bit skeptical when Béla was saying, "What would happen if you just made a record with just you?" He was thinking [about] just mandolin and voice. We didn't know if anybody had really done that, and he thought it could be really cool.

And he said, "You know, I think your songs lend themselves to that type of treatment." Then with the arrangements, he was open to the idea of maybe adding an instrument here or there. But the more we talked about it, the more we just settled on the idea that if I did want another instrument, which I kind of felt like I did, then that's the direction we would go. I wanted to be able to go out and tour and have another musician to interact with at a show. I've done solo shows since, and there are occasions that I will do something like that intentionally, but for me to go out and play one hundred shows this year, I liked the idea of having musicians to be around and be inspired by. Because that interaction you have is pretty valuable. So we decided bass would be a good instrument. And then when I met Ethan and started working with him—he's just so talented, and he was really easy to work with, along with his being so into sound.

Then, of course, being able to have Justin [Moses] is sort of like connecting my previous world with this new world: to be able to have somebody like Justin, [who] can play so many different instruments and come up with such unique parts and also sing with me, which is something that I felt was a good addition to the live show. Then I would be able to do some things with the banjo and do some things with duo mandolins or whatever—you know, fresh ideas to make the live show fun.

MENZIE: Ethan was able to get all kinds of character out of his instrument, and Justin and Ethan complement you so well. Justin is definitely a diverse musician; he just plays so many instruments, and I didn't even realize he sang. His voice captures what you've done on the record with a lot of authenticity.

In the live show, you have a demanding role because you're carrying the melodic contributions vocally as well as instrumentally. Will you elaborate on that thought?

SIERRA HULL: Playing and singing simultaneously becomes natural if you do it long enough, just like with anything. The challenge, however, is that because you have three people, you're finding yourself trying to figure out how to make two or three people feel like you're not missing anything, that you're not missing the contribution from those other instruments or musicians. With more room, Ethan is able to get such a wide range of character out of his instrument. If we'd had more instruments, he probably would have a lot less room to do that.

MENZIE: Did it take a second to find a natural balance, playing live versus playing in the studio with the new formula?

SIERRA HULL: I think because we had spent time working on the arrangements and recording them, there was already a comfort that had started to develop within the band on the songs we had done. But the new format did mean that some of the mandolin stuff I was playing might be a little more complex than some of the stuff I had played in the past, and trying to sing and play certain things at the same time proved to be interesting, so there are certain pieces of this music that are a little harder to perform live. But Justin is more than capable when it comes to coming up with ideas that make the music work, and that's live and in the studio.

MENZIE: Switching gears a bit—what advice would you give a young player who comes to take on the town and wants to become known among the different circles? What are good practices that might give the new, younger musician a chance to meet some of the established players?

SIERRA HULL: I do think the more you can go out and be part of the live music scene and meet people—that's the thing. Like I said, I met Justin years ago at a festival, and I got to know Ethan through a recommendation from another great musician, Edgar Meyer, and the circle at some point kind of becomes small. But it is important to be out there and meet people and become part of the scene. I'm also confident that . . . a young musician [should] work hard on their music and become really skilled at whatever it is they want to do, whether it's as a singer or a player or a writer—or maybe all three. You gotta go out, and you gotta perform, and sometimes that can mean doing it at first for little to no money, but at least you are going out and you're getting yourself established and able to be heard and to meet people. I do feel like good talent speaks for itself eventually. And if you want it enough, if you are willing to work hard enough, I do believe that opportunities will come.

MENZIE: That's a great philosophy for success. On the album's title track, "Weighted Mind," it takes only seconds for the listener to realize you've headed down new and exciting musical roads. What really caught my ear was the independence of the mandolin lines against the vocal melodies. What practice rituals do you embrace for mastering the development of your skills?

Sierra Hull: It just takes doing it enough that it becomes second nature, and it depends on what comes most naturally to you. For some people, the playing would be harder; for others, the singing would be harder. So at some point, I had to become comfortable enough with the playing that I don't think about the playing anymore; I hate to say muscle memory, but it is kind of muscle memory. It's like training yourself to be able to do something without having to put a whole lot of thought into it. There are still times that I might have to think about the playing and try to just trust my singing or trust my playing. At some point you have to work on it enough to trust one of those two entities. Trust that your voice is going to do what you need it to do without full attention to it or that your playing is going to do what it needs to do without full attention to it. That takes working on those two things really slowly and with focus and tremendous intention. Sometimes if I'm playing something really hard on the mandolin, I might have to really slow it down and sing over it super slow so that I can become familiar with where a particular phrase falls on the vocal line. Then I can learn to connect those things. It just really takes doing a lot of slowing it down and then kind of trusting yourself to execute well what you spent time working on.

Menzie: When most mandolin players sing, they are usually strumming or chucking a rhythm pattern that supports the melody, which enables that artist to focus on the complexity of the moving vocal. However, your style is completely different. You play as if you are two entirely different people in the band. You have posted online a version of the song "Weighted Mind," and you make this feat appear truly effortless. What led you to develop a more linear and complex accompaniment style?

Sierra Hull: I was just looking for something to sound a certain way. I guess, in a sense, I loved the thought of the parts sounding like two different people. Because if you have other musicians around you, normally they can be there to play and add color in between the vocal lines. But when I realized that you don't always have that, I still wanted that sound to be there. I don't want to do a solo version of "Weighted Mind" where I only do the mandolin chop over it the whole time. Because then it would be a lot less exciting to listen to. I'm always trying to listen and consider, "What would I want to hear if it were two people playing?"

MENZIE: Other than practicing the parts slowly or having the parts down solidly, is there any particular practice technique that really helps develop that independence?

SIERRA HULL: This sounds obvious, but practice with the metronome. It's a good way to keep things in check and to ensure that what you're doing isn't affecting your timekeeping. When you're practicing both things at once, it's hard to think about your timing because you're already thinking, "Am I singing this vocal line in the right place or perfectly in tune, or am I playing this groove well?" Just hearing that constant pulse and having your internal clock sync with a metronome is very helpful.

It also helps if you record yourself. You can either video it or pull up a voice memo on your phone. That's something I do a lot. As a listener, I can tell when I'm lacking or when I'm doing a good job. This way, I know when I'm making improvements. I'll listen and go, "Oops, I'm really dragging there, and I need to work on that." I think the more you listen to yourself, the more you can critique your own playing, and I find that really helpful.

MENZIE: I'm a big Levon Helm fan, and I saw an interview with Levon where he was asked, "How do you coordinate singing lead vocals against your drum parts?" His answer was "It's one thing—I find it easier to play while singing because the vocal melody gives me the phrases, and where they breathe is where I embellish on drums to set up the next vocal phrase."

SIERRA HULL: Yes, absolutely!

MENZIE: Music journalist Peter Cooper wrote, "Hull's Bluegrass roots inform and inspire the soundscape, but bluegrass does not define or limit the album *Weighted Mind*. This is not bluegrass music or chamber music or pop music, this is original music from a virtuoso who tells the truth and speaks from herself." Do accolades of that caliber impose added pressure on you?

Sierra Hull: A little bit, but [it's] probably no more than I put on myself. Even when somebody says something so kind, it's really hard to ever think of myself that way. It's the kind of thing that makes you feel good to read, but at the same time, I don't necessarily linger on that too much.

Menzie: Probably a wise decision!

Sierra Hull: Those kinds of things are pretty fleeting. You get your moment of glory with putting out a new record, but then it's time to keep pushing onto whatever the next thing is.

Menzie: As an artist and a player, how do you see the role of mandolin changing in today's music?

Sierra Hull: Look at somebody like Chris Thile, who's really pushed things and paved a way for folks like me and so many others, [as well as] the folks before him, like David Grisman, [who] really took the mandolin and did things with it that people weren't used to hearing. I think it's only going to continue to evolve, and people will continue to try and find new ways of expression with that instrument, which is pretty exciting. I'm just a fan of the instrument. I'm a fan of seeing what people will continue to do with it.

Menzie: You play octave mandolin on several songs, and you seem extremely comfortable with the larger mandolin. It has a little bit of a hardier sound, and it seems to bring out a slightly different personality in your playing. Describe what the octave mandolin enables you to accomplish in your music.

Sierra Hull: The octave mandolin is good because we don't have the guitar in the live show, so we don't necessarily have that same mid-range kind of sound. The octave mandolin just gives me a different texture—you know, kind of like we were talking about Justin playing different instruments or Ethan being able to switch from bow to tips; it's a completely different texture. It has all the same type of things that a regular mandolin has but in a more guitar-like, sustained way. It's just a different sound for the listener and also fun for me to have a different outlet of expression.

MENZIE: Embracing a great tradition, you show huge respect and honor for your musical heroes. You've nurtured quality friendships with many of the old guard, as well as the new stars on the music scene. Will you run down a list of some of the artists [who] have influenced you the most?

SIERRA HULL: Oh man, there's so many. One of my earliest inspirations [was] Doyle Lawson and Quicksilver. That's some of the first music I remember hearing when I was young. Doyle was the mandolin player. Those harmonies! I can go back and listen to some of those old albums now and just almost cry. They're so nostalgic and beautiful. And then I got my first Alison Krauss album when I was nine years old. She was my biggest hero. So any of those albums are things that I always look back on and still consider some of my favorite pieces of music. I mentioned Chris Thile has been a huge influence on me, and Tony Rice is another favorite artist of mine.

Early on it was a lot of bluegrass influence because I spent the first ten years or so playing that music. Today there are so many different things I listen to, from Sara Bareilles to Dolly Parton, who is one of my biggest heroes, and Paul Simon, Joni Mitchell, Bonnie Raitt, and Michael Jackson. I tend to go on these different kicks of listening to different things at different times. That's what I'm really influenced by.

MENZIE: I think you've found the secret. [He laughs.]

SIERRA HULL: For me, there was also a beauty and benefit in growing up with ten years of being surrounded by almost nothing but bluegrass music because you really get an understanding of the genre, and you know the stylistic language of that particular type of music. Growing up, if I had exclusively listened to jazz artists like Wayne Shorter and Miles Davis and had really gotten into the jazz thing and immersed myself in that world, then I would more likely be at ease in that genre and eventually be able to speak that language. Right now, I really can't, although I enjoy listening to it. I do enjoy taking things from that music when I find something that strikes me, but bluegrass will always be the music that I really know the most about because that's my foundation.

MENZIE: You have very natural skills as a front person onstage, but not all musicians do. Who has been your biggest influence for that role?

SIERRA HULL: I think I've just been doing it for a really long time, and nowadays, I do watch artists from an entertainer's standpoint. Somebody like Dolly—she just blows my mind. She is just such a natural beauty all the way around.

MENZIE: Inside and out, she's amazing!

SIERRA HULL: I'll watch her do an interview, and I'm just like, "This woman is so beautiful and genuine in what she does!" It's really inspiring to see that. I was just watching a live show of the Punch Brothers yesterday and admiring how well their show was put together. There's some obvious thought that goes into what those guys do and the way they connect with their audience. Justin hosts a podcast called *The CosMoses Podcast*, and he just released an interview episode with Rhonda Vincent yesterday.

MENZIE: Rhonda—another gift!

SIERRA HULL: It's a great interview with her. I was listening to it yesterday at the park, and she talked about . . . how emceeing, for her, is still kind of an odd thing. She described seeing James Taylor play, and of course, when he first comes out, it's just James with his guitar, sitting on a stool, being James. But that format doesn't naturally work for her show, even though she loves it. I watch Michael Jackson perform and get all kinds of excited about putting on a show, but I know I'm never going to be flying across the arena on a lift.

Menzie: I don't know, maybe you got something there. [He laughs.]

Sierra Hull: But I do watch somebody like that and start thinking, "Dang, I just kind of stand there and play the mandolin. I hope the audience feels they're getting their money's worth."

Menzie: Speaking of Michael, I posted a video of Fred Astaire and Ginger Rogers the other day, and boy, it just blew up. It was interesting to see the spark that it evoked; people just love that quality of entertainment.

Sierra Hull: Oh yeah, Fred was obviously one of Michael's heroes, and I mean, it's pretty incredible the influence other artists have on you. Honestly, I'm a big Beyoncé fan. I think she's amazing. There's no denying what kind of crazy talent that woman has. If I could even start to do that, I'd probably be doing that too.

Menzie: In bluegrass, like all other music genres, there can be resistance to change. Certainly, there's no denying that today, technology continues to make its way into all musical styles, including bluegrass. Can you describe how technology has crept into the genre, which has traditionally been an acoustic style of music?

Sierra Hull: You mean technology in the sense of gear?

Menzie: Yeah, gear and how you use it on tour and what's different now in bluegrass performance [versus] back in [the] "porch pickin'" days, when bluegrass musicians used to stand with just a center mic and sing, and the harmonies were balanced by how close you were to the one mic in the center.

Sierra Hull: To be honest I kind of wish that those days were still a thing. I mean, if I could go out and stand in front of one microphone and perform my best and really feel like we could dominate doing that, that would be awesome. Even in that podcast, Rhonda Vincent talks about how she's got plenty of gear, and people sometimes will say, "Is that all you got?" They go out there with two or three microphones, and that's what they do. You don't see a lot of people that can really still do that. The Del McCoury Band are masters at that. When I was a kid and I saw them play, that was how they played. They all had on these cool suits, and they all had on some hats, and they're, like, all around this mic, and they're moving around in this certain way. I love and appreciate that, and there's an entertainment quality to that. I think some modern bluegrass bands might even benefit from learning how to do that.

MENZIE: That makes me think of Marty Stuart and His Fabulous Superlatives. You talk about Del, and both of those groups show reverence to the traditional. They balance the harmonies around one mic through their positioning, and it brings a special energy because it's a "group sing." The Beatles did it when they sang off one mic with two of the guys and one guy singing lead. It's also a great visual prop. The Temptations were masters at this visual, with the special tree mic stand they used. Technology is trying to have an argument with that. Bluegrass has, by historic measures, always been a performance of instrumentalists and vocalists [who] have kept formats simple and have let the music do the talking.

SIERRA HULL: Well, different people can pull it off, and some people can't. Even when I was doing the bluegrass band, I was five foot two, and the guy [who] was playing the guitar with me was six foot two. To gather and sing around one mic would've [made it] almost too hard to get the right balance of things just because of the height difference. We have quite a bit of gear in my current setup for a trio; we always like to say I have more gear now as a trio than we had with the bluegrass band. And in most cases, we do feel like it makes sense. We like having the in-ear monitors that we use because it's consistent and . . . allows us to have the same mix every night. You can go into a sound check and not have to spend two hours dialing things in. That makes things much easier on my sound engineer.

Chapter 25

MENZIE: Form follows function. I'm sure that makes the stage mix more consistent.

SIERRA HULL: At a festival, for example, where you have a short turnaround time and you need to get set up quickly, with [the] inner ears, you can already have sound levels set—or at least you are pretty close, which is nice. But take somebody like Del—those guys don't even use a monitor. I don't really know how they do it; they've just done it that way for years. They're old school. And some people can do that, some people can't. It's just like the stage presence we were talking about. You have to really know what works for you.

I've heard Ron Block say many times that he remembers being a teenager and going to a bluegrass festival and just putting a microphone on his D-18 [Martin], and he would hear it blasting across the festival grounds. And now I feel like even some sound engineers don't really know what to do with just a microphone. So often you hear people say they can't get anything out of it, or they complain about feedback in the monitors.

People see those old shows like *The Glen Campbell Good Time Hour* or *The Porter Wagoner Show*. On those old shows, they're getting insane amounts of sound out of a little microphone that's two feet away. Why can't we still do that? It's just a different time, and the quality of things and expectations are different as well. I just truly think that we don't have the same skill sets, because times have changed and new skill sets are necessary.

MENZIE: I agree 100 percent that the expectations are different, and in some ways, that's a good thing. Some acts do have the skill sets, but as you mentioned, when you watch something like the old shows *Hee Haw* or *The Smothers Brothers Show*, you're watching a lot of really natural adjustments, and though many new artists embrace those skills, it's most common among the outstanding musicians.

SIERRA HULL: One of the best examples of what we're talking about is The Punch Brothers. They've been doing this tour where they're only using one microphone. And they're all gathered around the mic that way.

It's available on YouTube, the whole thing. I watched it and I thought, "Man, that was so good." I stumbled across it again yesterday and started watching it again. Their show is put together really well. It's worth checking out just to see how awesome they sound around one microphone.

MENZIE: It's back to that word—authentic. I have seen that video; I believe it's listed as *Live at the Paramount Theater*. It's surreal how great the band's sensitivity is, and the interplay between members is otherworldly.

So what can up-and-coming bluegrass musicians expect as far as opportunities to work and make a respectable living?

SIERRA HULL: Well, it depends on what you're trying to do because there is definitely a feeling in this style of music, especially [on] the traditional side of things. I keep talking about Rhonda Vincent because I keep thinking about the podcast I heard with her yesterday. She's somebody who is super driven, very business oriented, really has her stuff together, and I can assure you she's made a good living from being a traditional bluegrass artist. Del McCoury is somebody [who's] really been able to make a good living because he's doing exactly the same thing that he's always been doing, but he's also taken on a really young audience, and he is able to go play a Bonnaroo-type . . . festival and all these other more jam-band type festivals, where he's kind of beloved. And that's in addition to traditional festivals.

You can make a good living doing this, for sure. It just takes a lot of hard work and dedication to getting to that place. It takes, as a lot of people say, paying your "dues," and you've got to be willing to go play for little pay for a while until you start getting the opportunities to actually make more money doing it. As Rhonda said in the podcast, there are a lot of really talented people out there, and they want to be on a record label, and they want to get signed, and they want to be able to have a career. And she was talking about a label like Rounder Records that basically helped establish her as an artist, but the reason a label like that was willing to sign her was because she was already able to have a tour schedule. And so it's like, What comes first? The chicken or the egg?

In order to get any attention from a record label, you need to show that you already have a bit of a following and fan base through touring. But how do you get those fans, and how do you get those gigs if you don't have an album out or something getting you the attention? It's a little bit hard to figure out how to get going. I was lucky to start so young because I didn't have to deal with some of it in that same kind of way. But the simple truth is you have to really want it and you have to be willing to work at it.

MENZIE: You have to make those sacrifices. You mentioned Rhonda. Man, the duets she does with Gene Watson—yikes! The combination of the two of them together is magic.

One of the last subjects that I wanted to cover is most often overlooked, but [it is] no less important to a rising musician—the business side of the music. There are so many details that need to be addressed before an artist [can] step onstage. Will you pull back the curtain and share what goes into the daily business responsibilities of Sierra Hull?

SIERRA HULL: I'm fortunate to have a good management team and a good booking agency. And because I have a record label, I'm not totally responsible for having to solely promote my music. But, of course, I am always working to promote myself as well.

At the end of the day, you're going to be the only one [who] can think about your needs twenty-four hours a day. It's ultimately your responsibility to make sure that the things that you're wanting to accomplish get done. It's important that you try and stay focused on making sure that everybody else is doing what they need to be doing to help get the important matters addressed.

For example, I don't necessarily book my own travel, but I'm always involved in the discussion of what hotel we're going to stay at or [in] booking flights. [I question,] Do we have the rental car we need? What's the merch situation like at this festival? I mean, there's so many things that go into it that are nonmusic related but that dramatically impact the musicians. And on top of all that, we need to have a good show prepared. Then, on top of that, doing something as simple as budgeting—keeping things organized for when taxes are due and making sure that quarterly payments are paid.

MENZIE: The mean old tax people.

SIERRA HULL: Yes, the mean old tax people! There's just a lot of things like that—responsibilities that you have to think about because, in a situation like mine, where I am the business owner and it's just me, it's not like I have a band where five people split the responsibility of taking care of these behind-the-scenes duties. You really have to make sure things are being taken care of.

Again, referring to a story Rhonda Vincent shared on the podcast, what she did was fascinating. Shortly after they got her bus, she was underneath the bus, in the bay at a festival, counting CDs, and Stonewall Jackson from the Grand Ole Opry comes by and scolds her and says, "What are you doing under there? An artist never gets underneath in the bay of the bus," implying she should have people for that. And she says, "Well, you know, the truth is I could have people for that." But she believes it's important to know what's going on in her business. As well-intentioned as people are, it's your career, and so you need to be aware.

I have learned a lot in the past few years about what that means, about relationships and dealing with people—how you deal with traveling in tight quarters with people for two months solid. It's not easy stuff. But when the details are handled properly, people are able to just see the show and think, "Oh, this is wonderful." And that's how it should be.

MENZIE: We were talking about Dolly Parton, and I've always felt that Dolly was a master of understanding business and the importance of branding. All major stars have to deal with the inconvenient truth that as success grows, branding becomes a more essential part of a sustained career. You don't reach success overnight, and although branding never outranks performance quality, it is nonetheless just as important. You balance both very well. How do you approach working with your brand?

Chapter 25

Sierra Hull: I'm starting to learn more and more what that even means. "What is the right way to brand yourself?" seems to be the big question. Who are you, and what do you really want to reflect to your audience? What is it about you that you want them to take home? It's the balance of understanding your values and putting yourself out there in a light that you can be proud of. It's important that you feel genuine about your work and that you communicate that message!

Menzie: I usually reference three examples when I discuss this topic with young musicians: the Beatles, Taylor Swift, and Dolly Parton. Willie Nelson would be another great example. A lifetime artist has to constantly be aware that they're in public all the time. You're human, you're in front of a camera, you're in front of a microphone, you're in front of a crowd—and with that comes a lot of responsibility. Dolly is just a genius, and she's always graceful. The Beatles went through many different phases with what they did, and yet their branding was always masterful, and Swift is completely unique with her ability to time things and design things.

I think, with the new phase that we're in, the artist is having to take on more of those responsibilities, and it's important to establish them early on. Because now that the big record companies are less in the discussion, the artists and musicians have inherited these responsibilities themselves.

Sierra Hull: It's such a different time. In today's world you have to be present almost every day to your fans, which is kind of exciting but also kind of sad because you lose some of the mystery. Obviously, Dolly is one of the most talented people in the world, and I'm a huge fan of hers all the way around, but I think a big part of her success (and she's very smart about this) is that when she is in public, she's very aware of presenting what she wants to present. And while being genuine, she's also aware that mystery goes a long way. When you are a celebrity of that magnitude, there are a lot of things people don't know about you, and they go crazy because they want to know. They want to know who her husband is and what he looks like and why he [doesn't] ever come out in public. Or [they're wondering], What is this about Dolly, what's that about Dolly?

You know, all the speculation. When I say I'm a Dolly fan, I really am.

Have you read her book? [It's] *Dolly: My Life and Other Unfinished Business*. It's super good. She talks about, at one point in her career, being one of the most photographed people in the world—right behind the pope and Madonna; they called her the queen of the tabloids because her face would be on covers everywhere; of course, people write stuff that isn't true and all sorts of other junk, but Dolly said she truly liked to be the queen of about anything. Because when she did have a project coming out, having her face all over the place, at every checkout counter all over the United States, was not necessarily a bad thing.

Now I'm not looking for that, but she is very smart in that she has kept enough mystery around herself that people can still sit around and wonder about her. There's a mystique that she created that's exciting. That mystique is almost lost on a lot of today's artists because everybody is so accessible.

MENZIE: I agree. It's a very delicate balance. So, in closing, this is a pretty simple question, but it's one that I think is really important. If there was one single piece of advice you would want to give tomorrow's musicians, one thing you would tell them [to] never leave home without knowing, what would that one piece of advice be?

SIERRA HULL: Never leave home without knowing? Hmm . . . the address to where you're going.

MENZIE: [He laughs.] There you go, it's that simple. Find out where you're going before you get there. Well, with musicians that might be tough.

SIERRA HULL: Yeah, you have to know where you're going. I know we're joking, but in all truth, I do think that if you're going to do this, you have to know that it's really important to be prepared, because there's no way you're going to perform your best if you're not prepared. I've been both prepared and not prepared, and I can tell you every time I'm prepared, it goes a lot better than when I'm not. I think it's important to love what

Chapter 25

you're doing enough to want to work on it long before you are out the door, going to your gig or going to do whatever kind of thing you might be doing. And that doesn't even just mean music—that could mean business, that could mean anything. Just [try] to stay focused on whatever you've got in front of you.

Menzie: That's beautiful advice and really important advice. Preparation equals sanity, and lack of preparation equals stress, and the by-product of that stress is stunted creativity. No app or plug-in or download in the world can help you when you're not truly prepared. Winging it with no prep is a fool's game.

Sierra Hull: Oh, yes, don't fall into that trap.

Menzie: I'd like to close with something Alison Krauss has said regarding you as an artist. I think it perfectly captures your essence, and I want to leave the reader with that thought: "You are endless and without boundaries."

CHAPTER 26

Tenacity

WHILE TENACITY ISN'T NECESSARILY THE FIRST WORD THAT COMES TO mind when we think of creativity, it is the secret ingredient in the creative stew. It is the driving force behind the scenes, which ensures that the creative work gets done. Tenacity's sibling is perseverance. The difference is subtle but important; to persevere is to stay the course and not quit, but to be tenacious is to be unyielding while considering different solutions and possibilities for achieving your desired outcome.

One not-so-secret secret among today's successful artists is that they are committed to pursuing additional disciplines in order to reinforce and support their personal growth, increasing their chances for success. These disciplines are in addition to the professional demands of their music careers. Tenacity is the necessary ingredient that empowers creatives to push into their best heights.

The idea behind this not-so-secret secret is embracing additional physical disciplines that enhance your creative nature. It could be yoga, running, strength training, a martial art, biking, hiking, long-distance walking, or numerous others. The one commonality within all of these particular disciplines, as with performance, is that they all have involve breath, movement, and concentration.

Why do musicians do this? It is because they are tenacious about achieving personal success. They understand that when a musician chooses the arts as their career, the rules change. It's no longer just a creative endeavor. Now livelihood is involved. Consistency becomes the standard and the new rule.

Chapter 26

By choosing music as a career, we go from a formula of fun to a formula of expectations and deadlines. There is still plenty of fun to be had—but only when our professional responsibilities have been met. This shift can often lead to a conflict with our creative nature. When that happens, tenacity is our best friend because it helps push us to get the job done.

One synonym of tenacity is single-mindedness. Some in the arts perceive this concept as dry or boring, so it should come as no surprise that many musical artists find tenacity their hardest row to hoe. That's because tenacity is not necessarily perceived as a creative trait, but successful musicians know it's the fire under the artistic pan that makes things cook.

Let's consider tenacity from a broader perspective. When we apply the word to a creative context, it means being completely unswayable in achieving success within our craft. Tenacity enables us to call up the energy to complete our vision and bring it to life even when we aren't inspired. It is the inner drive that stems from believing in something before it is created and developed. Tenacity adds horsepower to your vision, aiding you to be unrelenting until your goal is reached. Tenacity is the power of persistence when the creative has taken a hiatus and needs a moment to refresh.

Tenacity is the life blood of a creative. Think of any great writer, performer, or musician—tenacity is a core part of their way of life, enabling them with the strength to push through and make their dreams become a reality.

It's no secret that creatives work best "in the moment." But when the moment isn't naturally fluid, it's tenacity that comes to the rescue. When musicians enter the creative zone, they are truly inspired. In that moment musicians produce very quickly, and there is wonderfully mad genius being unleashed; time becomes an illusion. Tenacity is for those moments when your creativity is elusive.

Creativity is fickle and flirtatious; it takes immense pleasure in toying with our egos. Its visits do not guarantee it will stay, return, or deliver the special flow we so unashamedly seek.

At that point, tenacity plays a vital role in the creative process. It pushes us through when we just don't feel like we're up to the task, when we feel like details can wait. It's our best friend when we don't feel inspired.

Determination is another synonym for tenacity, indicating a sense of repeated commitment to a particular outcome. Most musicians agree that they are dedicated, but fewer can claim they are tenacious. When we are dedicated, we are consistent with our goals, working toward a committed plan. When we are tenacious, nothing is an acceptable deterrent.

We are best served by understanding all aspects of sustaining a career in the music business. Imagination, originality, and business all require tenacity. After we pledge to embrace music as our livelihood, we then have to embrace what that pledge really means. It means we show up first and push when we aren't inspired. We continually practice all necessary skills, including business skills, and we continue to learn new skills along the way. We intentionally leave distractions alone, and we take care of our health—physical, mental, and emotional.

To be a successful career musician, we must master all of the components of the music business, as well as our craft, and our personal well-being. All of that takes tenacity.

Chapter 27
Brent Mason

One thing everyone in the Nashville scene can agree on is guitarist Brent Mason. Brent is one of the most recorded session guitarists in history. Along with being a Grammy Award–winning artist, he is also a fourteen-time winner of the Academy of Country Music (ACM) Guitarist of the Year Award, and a two-time winner of the CMA Award for Musician of the Year; he has been nominated every year since 1991.

Brent has been named as one of the top ten session guitarists in the world, joining the ranks of Jimmy Page, Larry Carlton, Tommy Tedesco, and Steve Cropper. He has played on well over a thousand records and continues to add to this extensive resume. In October 2019 he was inducted into the Musicians Hall of Fame, and he has also been inducted into the Country Music Hall of Fame.

Interview

Menzie: Brent, what do you think the secret is to sustaining a career in today's music business?

Brent Mason: Well, the best advice I can offer a musician or an artist developing [his or her] career in today's business environment is just to stay plugged into what's going on. Listen like a detective, and be willing and able to adjust and change with the times. There are always going to be challenging business climates, so certain elements of reinvention are necessary. Also, always stay interesting.

Whether you're trying to stay commercial, stay working in Nashville, tour with an artist, be a studio musician, or even be an artist yourself, you have to develop your own style. Update yourself all the time, and listen to what's happening out there, and try to blend in. Of course, [do this] all the while maintaining originality.

MENZIE: With the continuing changes in the music industry and with the big companies no longer willing to take unsubstantiated risks, do you find the burden is more on the individual than it was at previous times in the music industry? How about as a studio musician?

BRENT MASON: Either as a studio musician or someone trying to get a record deal as an artist—both situations are a little harder now, with social media everywhere and how the music business's infrastructure has changed due to digital and things like file sharing coming onto the scene. Today the labels are interested in what size fan base you've developed through social media. They are looking for somebody [who] has a large, established fan base. That's a big part of the attraction now. The budgets aren't as luxurious as they used to be due to digital music and streaming. Digital music is easily accessible but not as lucrative for anyone.

The studio musicians really don't deal with the record label bureaucracy as much; we're contracted and hired by the producers, and we work through the AFM [American Federation of Musicians] union. We don't have to deal with as many of the administration parts of the record labels as the artist would.

MENZIE: Do you find that more people are asking you to do demo work because of digital? Or do you feel that more people are trying to do their own demos because of this technology shift?

BRENT MASON: Because of the technology shift, there is less demo work for pro studio musicians. It's just easier for somebody with a home studio and the convenience of having [his or her] own equipment to make home demos now. There's so much software that you can have drums and bass [and so on], so people all over are in their cubby holes, making their demos now, and there is not as much professional demo work going on.

Chapter 27

Back when I started, you had to book a big studio or you weren't going to get a big sound. You had to have a lot of the "human element" involved to make the records, and the budgets were better. So this whole in-home technology approach has taken away the widespread work for demos that used to be done here in Nashville.

MENZIE: I'm sure the quality of innovation is reflected in that truth as well. I recently watched an interview with Vinnie Colaiuta where he talked about the creative magic that happens when you have a group of four or five excellent session musicians playing live in a room. He also reflected on the extraordinary value of their collective contributions.

BRENT MASON: What songwriters do now is a group of songwriters will have a demo day for all of them. It's kind of a compilation of songwriters [who] come in and track their songs.

But here's the other side of that—today some of the demos with pro players sound so good that they just turn them into records. So you never know if that demo that you're playing on will be turned into a record or not, until you turn around a month later, and your pay has been updated. That's one benefit of the energy of a live session and the sound of a great studio. You never know what the next big thing is going to be or who it's going to be.

MENZIE: What are the important things that most younger players overlook while preparing to be a working pro? Is there an area that you feel they underestimate?

BRENT MASON: Some people will say to me, "I'm thinking about coming to Nashville, and I'd love to establish myself as a studio musician." And I say, "Well, the hardest thing to do is just to head right to the studio. You've got to establish yourself first within the music community here, and it's all about being at the right place at the right time." That whole cliché rings true.

I tell them it's a culture, and you're not going to have much luck getting to know anybody if you just stay a short while. You've got to settle down here [and] get yourself a place and live here at least for a while.

You'll probably have to get a job somewhere, waiting tables or whatever, but in the meantime, you can hit the writer's hot spots at night and just be at the right place at the right time. You've got to be a phenomenal, magnificent player because they all come here from all over. You might think you're the best player from your hometown, but then you come here, and that's everybody. I see the competition as a good thing; it keeps you on your toes and makes you a better player. It inspires you to continue working on your craft.

MENZIE: What you just described is an old-school philosophy, which is something I truly appreciate about Nashville.

BRENT MASON: Yeah, it's definitely old-school, and it's good to have an understanding of the inner workings of cliques. There will always be cliques. I'm older now and established and, luckily, I'm at the point where I don't have to spend late nights out until two in the morning and schmooze and politic. It's always fun to play live with great players, but it's about the hang. You have to do that. You've got to have that encouragement and interaction with fellow players and that whole yearning to make it. The network is about camaraderie with other folks; you meet people, and you get out there.

There are musicians who go out and hit certain clubs like the Basement or 3rd and Lindsley, where all the in crowd goes to hang out and see the next new wave of something. You keep yourself on your toes, and that keeps you plugged into things and abreast of changes.

Another topic for rising players is the need for dealing with rejection. You've got to be resilient and ready for rejection because you're going to encounter lots of it. It's in your best interest to understand that that's just part of the reality, so don't be discouraged by it. Rejection never goes out of style. You just got to hang in here and give it some time. Of course, you have to keep working to be a phenomenal musician.

MENZIE: Some people say the changes in the music business have brought lots of new opportunities. Others say that, because of these changes, there are a lot of challenges. Can you reflect on both?

CHAPTER 27

BRENT MASON: One definite change is that there is a lot more competition here now, and that may be due to the fact that everyone who is trying to succeed in music understands that it's all happening here. Or maybe it's because of social media or video sites like YouTube. Now people can connect much faster with people across the ocean or anywhere in any state.

Back before social media, a musician or singer might feel a little more isolated from Nashville, so it might take a while for them to build their confidence enough to finally make their way here. But now, with shows like *American Idol*, *Nashville*, and *The Voice*, people kind of see what the producers of shows like that [they] want them to see. It's all about the glamour and excitement. The downfall to the romanticization of Nashville is the recording business is still about talent. There's more competition out there, and the gates are flooded just a little bit more than it seems like they used to be.

MENZIE: How important a role do you think history plays for new musicians, especially musicians interested in studio work?

BRENT MASON: History plays a huge role in everything [and] certainly for me personally. Some young people may look at me as somebody they listen to, but there are many pioneers and so many greats that had [an] influence on me. Young players should go further back and listen to James Burton or Albert Lee or Reggie Young.

To be a successful studio musician, you've got to do a lot of studying, like where the song originates from and who developed the style and who was influenced by it. Study your history; go as far back as possible, and know your sources. I am a student of all music. There's never a time where I don't try to look something up or explore a style that I want to apply or research something that inspires me.

MENZIE: One thing that surprises drummers is when I suggest to them that they should listen to great singers and songwriters and not just other drummers. I have no doubt that there are artists other than guitarists [who] have influenced you.

BRENT MASON: I enjoy listening to artists like Stevie Wonder and Ray Charles, as well as any and all of the greats. Because I'm a session player, I have to be a chameleon. I'll run into a session and be playing on an Alan Jackson tune one day and playing behind Natalie Cole on a different day. It goes from one extreme to the next, so you need to really listen to all styles of music.

MENZIE: There's a lot of jazz influence in your playing as well.

BRENT MASON: Yes, along with a lot of different types of guitar players [who] have influenced me. Way back, I listened to Chet Atkins and Jerry Reed for the country style, and because my mom and dad played country music, I knew all about Merle Haggard, Buck Owens, [and] even Texas swing. They were playing big band music—but with string instruments. My dad liked that, and that's where I got some of my jazz influences. Then that turned into me buying a Pat Martino album, and then I went from that to Jeff Back and Jimi Hendrix. A lot of guitarists today love Stevie Ray Vaughan, who you know was inspired by Jimi Hendrix, and Hendrix was inspired by a lot of old blues players. It's a big pool to dip out of.

MENZIE: Were you influenced at all by Danny Gatton?

BRENT MASON: Yeah, but not as much as you might think. Gatton was truly a monster guitarist, but initially, he wasn't somebody [whom] I followed when I was a kid. I was following more the guys I just mentioned—Jerry Reed and Roy Nichols (the guitarist for the Merle Haggard band) for the country stuff and Don Rich for the Bakersfield sound, along with Albert Lee and James Burton. On the rock side, I was definitely into Jimi Hendrix and Jeff Beck quite a bit. And the jazz guys I listened to were Pat Martino, George Benson, and then Wes Montgomery and Lenny Breau from Canada.

MENZIE: After a player embraces the importance of studying music history, how can they come into their original voice on guitar? Will you address the importance of being an individual and getting your own sound?

BRENT MASON: I listened to a lot of different players like the ones I mentioned, and together, they influenced and kind of made up my style by my meshing all those players together. I can hear all those players in my playing. Plus, when I was mainly playing a Fender Telecaster, I was lucky to be one of the guys to start a trend in Nashville by going back to the roadhouse country music idea and embracing the importance of amplifiers in the studio. Back then, before I was getting into sessions, they were pretty much playing in the direct mode—playing direct, no amp, [and] not even drums were being miked.

MENZIE: You're talking about the mind-sets of the recording studios.

BRENT MASON: Yeah. When we came in, we were dragging in old, smoky amplifiers that we used out in the clubs, and they asked, "Can't you run direct? We don't need amplifiers." And I go, "What? That's crazy!"

I understood that approach if you were playing R&B music, where you could run direct like Paul Jackson Jr. [had done] on a Luther Vandross record and such. But country music, to me, was all about smoky Fender amps, and so I was kind of lucky to get in early on the wave of that in the 1990s, when we went back to amplifiers. Stuff like that all helps a player develop their style and sound.

MENZIE: Recently, I saw a video clip of Dweezil Zappa recording the David Bowie classic "I'm Afraid of Americans" in Sunset Studio. It's something that he did as a tribute to Bowie. He talks about going into the studio and trying to achieve a particular sound with an all-analog approach, using equipment akin to [how it] was used originally in the time period that Bowie recorded [in]. Great guitar players understand that there's a lot of physicality to creating the sound they want.

BRENT MASON: Oh, there definitely is. They have a lot of different preamps now that emulate amplifiers better than ever, but there's nothing, to me, like a microphone in front of a speaker cabinet. It records the room with it.

The air around it also plays a part in the sound. And I know they can sample that, but it's not the same. It doesn't have the dynamic space around it.

I love the way an amplifier sounds. One winter day, you take an amp into a studio, and it acts completely different than on a warm summer day in the same room. Maybe the air is a bit different that day, or something else is a little different that day. It's strange—it's all about the science and the physicality, like you said, and I still think that's the cooler way, so I think that's what Dweezil's talking about with certain gear.

I find that, in Nashville, they're really of the same mind-set that I am. Nashville is the melting pot of all kinds of music, but everybody just loves and welcomes amplifiers. You no longer have to fight an engineer on that.

MENZIE: It's not unusual for you to have three sessions in a day. How do you prepare for that kind of workload? Will you talk about three-a-days for a bit?

BRENT MASON: Well, first of all, the three-a-days you're talking about certainly happen less often now than they used to. I don't work as hard as I did back in the 1990s or early 2000s—nowhere near it. But there are more peripheral things going on now to keep me busy.

Now I don't do as many sessions, and I don't think there are as many sessions done by anybody anymore. Like I said, everybody cuts stuff in their own little home studios now. They can work on it and manipulate the tracks to where they feel it's right, doing this and that to get the parts to sound the way they want. You lose the spontaneity of playing with other musicians and lose honest expression, but the sonic product usually comes out clean.

The three-a-days—those session days still happen but just with less frequency. But here's something rising players need to understand: you have to have other things going. You must diversify. Guys like Leland Sklar and other big-name studio musicians have always landed real high-paying road gigs. I've never had to do too many of them, luckily, but I've gotten into doing things like Skype lessons.

Here's another thing, too, that would interest you: there is a good market in remote recording sessions, where people send tracks now to us. I'm not seeing another person. All they want is the way I play 1970s stuff. People send me files to play on, and then I send the work back, and they drop it into the tracks. That's more of my work now than physically getting into the car and driving to Music Row and doing three sessions. It used to be that I was just a session dog. It's a little different these days.

MENZIE: Do you have [an] interest in producing?

BRENT MASON: I haven't done a lot of producing. I don't really have the passion for that right now, and I honestly don't have time for it either. It takes a lot of nurturing, and it's something you have to put a lot of time into, with managing details like finding the right artist. There are a lot of talented people out there, but to work with them and develop them takes a lot of time. I really don't have the time to do it. It's never been a successful or fulfilling thing for me.

But I've gotten more into doing my own stuff, like shows and clinics and developing pedals, and such—my own signature brands. For me, that fits better and goes farther than getting into the production society.

MENZIE: Nashville, more than anywhere else, still favors live bands in the studio. Discuss the contribution that the chemistry of a live band made up of world-class musicians makes to a session.

BRENT MASON: I love the human element when recording, but nowadays, you see less of that. There's not nearly as much as there was a few years back. It goes back to everybody sending you tracks, and that approach can have its own unique challenges. The request might be "Somebody from London has played drums on this, will you put the guitar on it?" "Well, is there a bass on it?" "We're going to put the bass on after you put the guitar on," and I say, "No, no—put a bass on it first because I want to hear music."

But then when I go into the studio in Nashville and I see a drum set up, I say to myself, "A drummer! Ah, now we can play!" There's a lot of interaction that goes on that you can't get the other way, and we're still doing that in Nashville more than anybody. I guess the best word for it is spontaneity, because you are playing off each other in real time, with real emotion. It makes you more creative.

The rhythm tracks are best done live, and then you can spice it up or do some lead work later. There were times, before file sharing, we'd spend all day on a song, then have fifteen minutes to do a solo before we had to move on to the next song. So that's the beauty of digital sharing. Now you can just say, "Hey, could you send that to me? I'll put a couple of options in for the solo, and you can let me know which you like." So there are some advantages to that approach.

MENZIE: So both ways have some unique merit.

BRENT MASON: Yeah, but that interplay when you're sitting in the same room with others and doing a song—there's nothing like it. Everybody plays off [of] each other. There's a certain ebb and flow that goes on that you can't match. It's not even close.

MENZIE: I caught a show that you played with Vince Gill, Paul Franklin, and Michael Rhodes. The way you and Paul Franklin played off of each other was special; there was such a natural chemistry between you. It was almost like you would finish each other's lines, and it was amazing to watch. Chemistry obviously plays a big part in the quality of what somebody hears.

BRENT MASON: Oh, [it's] definitely a big part—huge!

MENZIE: You also [played] a lot with bassist Michael Rhodes. I love the way he [interpreted] the time feel and the groove. Will you talk a little about that unique Nashville feel?

BRENT MASON: Well, the Nashville feel is kind of derived from Muscle Shoals, being that it is so close to Nashville. I think there was always such a great respect for Muscle Shoals and the Memphis players [who] came out of there. It naturally drifted into Nashville.

In the studio, when the producers would explain what type of groove they wanted on a song, they would say they want "this feel," and they would always refer to the style of Muscle Shoals. They would also refer to Motown—specifically, those records that came out of the Detroit period, with the Funk Brothers. Or producers would also say, "This is the Philadelphia sound" when referring to Gamble and Huff songs, or [they'd say,] "This is the LA sound" and refer to songs with the Wrecking Crew.

Everybody and every region has their own feel. There's all kinds of different styles, and then you just respect all of that and understand what makes that music sound good. But again, Muscle Shoals always had that laid-back groove—in the pocket, just like early Motown, and we always make reference to that because it really feels good, especially if you're playing something R&B or a style like that.

Nashville just kind of brought that in because [of how] a lot of players came from Muscle Shoals or Memphis, like Reggie Young and even some of the people that came from LA. You had Larry Londin, who played drums on the later Motown records after Benny Benjamin from the Funk Brothers. Chet Atkins was smart—he brought a lot of those people into the Nashville sound early on because he knew they had that ability to bring that feel to Nashville. It was sort of all delegated from Chet and Owen Bradley and all those guys.

MENZIE: Earlier, we were talking about amps in the studio. What are your must-have, go-to tools when you go into a recording session? Your Telecaster, obviously—Fender now makes a signature Brent Mason model, and PRS [Guitars] also made you a guitar.

BRENT MASON: I love Paul Reed Smith, and Paul . . . when we had that big flood in Nashville a while back, we lost a lot of instruments. A lot of people had equipment at the Sound Check facility, which is by the river, and everything got flooded. A lot of my guitars were brought back to life by Joe Glaser, who is a respected guitar luthier here in Nashville. I've known Joe a long time. He really saved a lot of my guitars.

But I also lost a lot, and because I did, Paul helped me. He told me that he had a baritone from PRS that he wanted me to see, and when I went to the factory in Maryland, I was really impressed with the integrity that went into building PRS guitars—not just the aesthetics of the product but all the love they put into their instruments and the attention they give to the pickups as well. So he brought some guitars for me to play, and that's when I kind of fell in love with some PRS guitars. They also built one of my guitars.

But I'm glad you mentioned my working relationship with Fender. They have done an extraordinary job in producing the Brent Mason Model Tele. They have truly captured the spirit of the instrument. The only thing that doesn't come with it is the Don Kelley backstory on how it ended up in my hands, but you can find that online.

I am asked to do a lot of different things when I'm hired to do a recording session, so I have to be prepared for anything, and I have to have the proper arsenal to be ready. When cartage is budgeted, I'll have two trunks of guitars brought in, and they're going to consist of a few different Les Pauls and probably a twelve-string guitar, maybe a Rickenbacker—a PRS or whatever it may be, perhaps a baritone guitar. I take some Fenders, definitely a Strat, and, of course, my Tele.

When you're coming in to do a Nashville session, you always have a Les Paul or a 335, a couple of Fenders, a Strat, and a Tele. It helps to have a Gretsch, something with a Bixby on it, because they might want to do something back in that retro style, and Gretsch is a great guitar for that style. It has a sound that's well loved here in Nashville.

Then I have amplifiers that I bring in; there are a lot of different Fenders, like a Deluxe, blackface Deluxe, Twins, and Super Reverbs. I bring several to pick from so I have an idea of what they might want that day.

Then I have an amp rack. I have Marshall heads and something like a Matchless, and I bring a Fender Bassman 50 watt in there. That particular amp is a 1967. And [I bring] my new signature amp, the Vintage Sound 45. So I have that and then some foot pedals, some boutique pedals that would have delays. And I bring various distortion pedals and wah pedals, tremolo pedals, . . . analog delays, and some different kinds of crazy effects. We might throw a pedal in there that has a Leslie effect or some kind of a tempo-generated tremolo or a vibrato pedal.

MENZIE: So you basically bring an array of tools to cover every possibility, and you'll paint when you get there.

Chapter 27

Brent Mason: Exactly, but you've got to have it there, although sometimes budgets are smaller, so I may run up there and say, "Hey, I'm going to grab a Deluxe and throw it into the back of the truck, and I'm going to bring a little stomp box pedal board, and I'm going to bring these three guitars—a Tele, a gold top Les Paul, and a Strat. That should do well for today."

Now [with] all the equipment I mentioned, cartage would bring that in if a session had a budget for it so the gear is all there if you need it.

Menzie: So that the reader understands, Sound Check is a great example of a cartage company that provides several services, such as outside transportation for gear, labor, storage, and backline rentals. And [do] you rent a personal storage bay as well?

Brent Mason: Yeah, we all work with cartage companies. They load up a big trailer of our stuff, and the guys roll it in the night before or a few hours before. Then they come back and pick it up and roll it back to storage.

Menzie: Can we talk about some boutique amps that you're fond of, along with the old Fenders you described?

Brent Mason: I have always gravitated toward the old Fenders. I love them, but there are some great new amps as well. I have a signature model amp with Vintage Sound, Rick Hayes's company. It's the Brent Mason Signature 45, and there's also the Vintage Sound 22, a great amp for the studio. They kind of left their design reminiscent of the old Fenders a little bit, as far as the look and style of those amps. I love those amps, and of course, I will always love the sound of the old Fenders. You just have to find them in good shape, which can be tricky to do. Also, [I like] Little Walter amps. Phil Bradbury's company makes a great amp. Vince Gill uses one, and they have a great sound too.

I'm a fan of old vintage guitars, instruments, and amps and stuff. You just can't beat them, because they have so much character. Of course, there's a lot of upkeep on them; they're a little more rickety for traveling, but if you just keep them freshly tubed and tuned up, they're the best.

Menzie: Let's talk about your relationship with Wampler Pedals.

Brent Mason: Yeah, I've known Brian a long time. I kind of helped Brian get started, in a way. He got started through customizing pedals. I'd give him my pedals, and he'd make them sweeter and better. Finally, he came up with his own brand, and we've made a pedal or two together that we collaborated on, and those have been successful.

Menzie: I've noticed there are scads of guitar players [who] are always breaking down your stuff to drive traffic to their personal YouTube channels. They will take something you've played and attempt to dissect it, but the problem is—they take it apart logically, as opposed to musically. Another problem is that they never discuss your right-hand style or your attack on the guitar, which is really physical, or why your feel is your feel. Will you address those topics?

Brent Mason: I find that a lot of times, if you type in my name, it goes to somebody who's playing my licks or somebody who's trying to explain the work I've done, and in truth, it kind of irks me a little bit because I'm saying, "Hey, that's not quite right." Or they'll break something down, and that's not quite right either. I found that topic really surfaced when I started doing Skype lessons. The information isn't always accurate; for example, maybe I actually started that lick in "this position" on the guitar. At least with [lessons with] me, they are getting the real information, and now they can learn why I chose to do what I did and what influenced me to make the decision instead of just breaking down licks. This way, there is musical logic injected back into the conversation.

Menzie: Even if the YouTuber has the notes right, there's a special physicality when you play that is undeniable.

Brent Mason: I always say that whenever someone originates something, they're always going to play it the best because they originated it. Anything else is a duplicate. I'll try to play somebody else's style or feel, and that'll be the story with me too. I might be playing a Wes Montgomery lick, but only Wes played it with his feel.

Chapter 27

There's a rumor that floats around that Wes played with that thumb style and octave approach because neighbors complained, and he had to stay quiet inside of his apartment.

MENZIE: Wes—one of a kind. Will you talk a little bit about the acrylic fingernails you use? You and James Taylor have that approach in common.

BRENT MASON: Mine are acrylic nails, and it's not a very elegant way of doing things. [It's] certainly not very attractive, but when you superglue acrylic fingernails on, it's purely for practical purposes. I wouldn't necessarily advise anybody do it that way, because your real nails get very thinned out. You have to pop the fake nails off occasionally because your real fingernails need to breathe. I only put those fingernails on two of my fingers on the right hand because it's definitely thinned out the actual nail. It would take a long time to rehabilitate the nail to the point where I could use the real one and get it thick again.

I think it's a company called Nailine that makes those fingernails, but suddenly, the product got really thin. As time went on, Nailine started making them thinner, and they weren't as good for playing guitar anymore. It was causing me a problem. So my wife went on eBay and bought every fingernail that Nailine made that were the old, thick style. Now there's no more left in the world. I think they're all in my closet! Because of her, I've got a life supply of fake fingernails.

MENZIE: You also use a thumb pick. I understand you got that technique from your dad, who played the Merle Travis style.

BRENT MASON: Yeah, my dad played [with his] thumb and first finger, which was Merle Travis's style. He'd listen to him, so he played that way. Later, I remember, he also played with a pick and a strum, but he liked to get the thumb pick out and play Chet Atkins and Merle Travis kind of stuff, and when he was out playing with his band, he would strum.

MENZIE: To get to the level of mastery you have achieved, you must have certain rituals or routines that you believe work.

BRENT MASON: My regiments have kind of changed now because I've been at it so long. I no longer have a set or methodical way I practice. Now it's more about [how], when I hear something in my head, I grab a guitar and see if I can play it fluidly right away. Or it's about developing a musical or melodic idea or another way to voice something on the guitar or express an idea that I like on guitar. Or I'll hear something that's playing on TV, and I grab a guitar and figure it out, or [I play] just a chord progression or a composition that may come to mind. But as far as staying limbered up, I may just run over arpeggio scales or some pentatonic or some chromatic licks just to stay smooth. But I don't think there's anything too rudimental or any certain thing that I do consistently. My life centers around guitar all the time, so at this point, my routine has morphed into a spontaneous approach because I play guitar every day. When I was younger and developing my techniques, I had a more specific regiment.

MENZIE: So when you were coming up, the approach to learning was putting on a record, picking up the needle, and putting it back over and over until you figured out the song or the part you were working on?

BRENT MASON: Yeah, that's the era I come from, exactly. I would repeat returning the needle until there was a big old groove dug into the album where my favorite part of that song would be. We lifted the arm of the record player over and over to learn the licks because, back in the vinyl record days, we really didn't have many choices for metronomes other than the swinging-arm, piano-style metronomes. Today I would advise somebody to play to—or just grab—some drum program like Drumgenius, where you can practice your songs at a certain speed and make sure you're playing tight with it.

The first time I came to Nashville, I was about sixteen, and I noticed everybody played time a lot tighter, and my tempos varied a little bit. So when you're learning your trade and you're learning the guitar, the main thing is playing real tight. Because when you play with professional players, they're going to hold your feet to the fire with that.

Chapter 27

MENZIE: Pros know where the time is and respect it. You learn about that the hard way.

BRENT MASON: Even singers need to learn how to sing in the pocket if they want to make the pro level. A lot of the younger singers find that out later in their careers. It's about laying it back. Again, it's doing that Muscle Shoals thing.

MENZIE: Singers have really gotten into runs. It's like the love of a great whole note with tone and color no longer holds any value.

BRENT MASON: We can manipulate music so much now that it's become the norm to just tune it up and put it in a perceived pocket where they might think it feels good. If you took Ray Charles's records and started tuning them up and quantizing them, it would be a travesty. Just terrible. Music is not about perfection, it's about expression.

MENZIE: Are you a Beatles fan?

BRENT MASON: Oh yeah, but I was a little bit younger than some of the Beatles fans I grew up around. [As] I got older, I really loved and respected their music—still do. We were doing some kind of guitar clinic in Big Fort, Montana, and one of the questions asked was, "Rolling Stones or the Beatles?" I said, "Beatles," just because of the compositions and the originality.

MENZIE: Speaking of originality, I love your quote "Never do what they think you will do, or your career will be cut short." Will you expound on that a bit?

BRENT MASON: By that I was clarifying the importance of originality in your playing and reinvention in your approach to studio session work. And there are two sides to that—on some sessions, you are hired because of a previous musical contribution or a style that the artist or contractor has heard you play on another record, and they want that vibe recreated.

For example, if you come into a session, and they need this certain thing that they've heard you do, that's what you try to create for them. But if you're playing on a session, and the artist hasn't really specified or clarified what they need or want, and maybe they think you're going to play a certain lick or in a particular way, and they're thinking, "We know what he's going to play, but let's see what he does," you may take a different angle on it, and before you leave the studio, they'll go, "Wow! That was so cool. I didn't think you were going to do that. We thought it was going to be good, but we didn't think you were going to do that."

So you always have to have that reinvention and element of surprise. That's what sustainability as a session player is all about—you've got to stay interesting. You have to do that anyway because music changes. It evolves into something else, so you can't keep playing your same things because they will run their course. Reinvention is very important.

MENZIE: Are you inspired by some of the music and players you're seeing nowadays?

BRENT MASON: Oh yeah, there's some great music out there, but not so much in the mainstream. Earlier, you mentioned James Taylor and that he always had those abilities musically, lyrically, and compositionally. And you do see those levels and that kind of stuff—like when Sting or John Mayer came onto the scene. You say to yourself, "There's an old soul there," and I see a lot of that with people like Ed Sheeran. There's always that organic thing. Like if you go out to good festivals, you see all kinds of great original things, but you have to dig down in there a little bit to find them. It's definitely out there, and it finds its way through social media. But if I listen to the top 40 radio, it's always been [the] cookie-cutter kinds of things that are not as inspiring to me.

MENZIE: Your work is nothing short of phenomenal; there's a sense of spirit there that's truly important. I really appreciate you taking the time to let people in on your thoughts.

BRENT MASON: Thanks for asking me to contribute.

MENZIE: The reader and I won on the deal, trust me.

Chapter 28

Self-Mastery

Mastery takes many forms, and if you are in the arts, you bump into disciplines as soon as you seek any level of advancement. However, self-mastery is altogether different because it is not about any one particular success or accomplishment. Self-mastery is the understanding that your life is your canvas.

The challenge of writing about self-mastery is sobering because, in truth, it is an indefinable goal. The journey toward self-mastery, however, is an honorable pursuit, and the good news is it only takes a lifetime. So let's begin!

Self-mastery is an ever-changing idea based on an ideal of heart.

Many confuse self-mastery with perfection or success, but perfection and success are goal-driven concepts, whereas self-mastery is a philosophy of life. The attempt of self-mastery is a continual human endeavor and, as with music, is ever changing and always elusive. Akin to our relationship with craft, we attempt to earn its grace. Self-mastery is intangible, mysterious, and beautifully imperfect.

As you embark on your musical journey, you will encounter every type of situation and every personality imaginable. However, the one person you will always have with you is yourself. Though you will reinvent yourself many times along your path, you are the only person who takes your entire journey, the only one who knows the absolute truth about your dreams, fears, habits, goals, and work ethic. People outside of the arts use words such as "lucky" or "gifted" when describing a successful artist's career. While those descriptors may be true, most everyone with talent would agree that success is a reflection of continued hard work. And yet success is just a passing tone compared to the difficult undertaking of self-mastery.

By definition, self-mastery is seeking your most purposeful life and holding yourself to your highest standard throughout ever-changing circumstances. It is not about perfection. It is about honesty, intent, and conviction. When you decide to walk the path of self-mastery, it will take a while to gain perspective on what that philosophy entails. There are no overnight sensations here—we are talking about embracing a unique long view of an expressive, creative, and purposeful life.

Try to imagine your future as if you were a music producer directing an artist, but in this case, you play both roles. Zoom out. Be objective, playful, and creative, and set ridiculously high standards. It is your life, so you can rewrite the game plan any time you feel inspired to do so. You make the rules. That is self-mastery.

Look at the big picture of your intended life's work, and visualize your entire contribution to the arts. Look at your personal idea of family. Look at all aspects of your life, and then decide what is important and what is not. As heady as it sounds, that is the position you want to be in. Self-mastery is not just about the music—we already know that is the end zone. It's bigger than that: self-mastery is about embracing the entire purpose of your life.

Think of yourself in the same light as you would a great song. Great songs are timeless, but even great songs vary with every rendition, and they are never expressed exactly the same way twice. A performer's responsibility is to serve the song, and you can look at the responsibility of self-mastery through the same lens. You are unique, soulfully searching for opportunities to express your individual creativity. As you progress on your personal journey, you awaken and begin to prioritize purpose over achievement. At that moment, your artistry is born. Embracing self-mastery is taking on your life as the editor, knowing when the story is good and heartfelt and when it is heartbreaking and counterproductive. It takes a master to admit when a course correction is imminent. Artists who embrace this understanding have long, healthy careers. Artists who do not pay a heavy price.

Chapter 28

Let's look at Sting as an artist who is a stellar example of self-mastery and as someone who can play any and all styles of music from original rock to avant-garde and back again.

Sting has demonstrated incredible longevity and prowess throughout his career, both with the Police and even more so as a solo artist. He is an incredible writer, a great musician, and a magnetic stage personality. He is known to be very health conscious and disciplined in yoga. I would go so far as to say he is widely known for the example he sets in self-mastery.

In an interview available on YouTube that I highly recommend, Rick Beato asks Sting about his songwriting process and how he came up with the unusual format for the song "Fortress around Your Heart."

Sting replies, "It starts with the three chords, and then I just go on an adventure with it! You know, find it. The song writes itself; you just have to be open to it, and you have to be in a state of grace where the music tells you where it wants to go. I just trust that the harmony of the moment will lead me in the right direction."

In regards to self-mastery, we must also take note of Sting's attention to health consciousness as a lifestyle choice. The demands of touring are grueling, recording sessions are grueling, public appearances are grueling, creating can be grueling, and always having to be everything to everybody is grueling. Those kinds of demands take their toll—emotionally, physically, and mentally. You can fake your way through it for a while, but to play the long game, all aspects of your physical, mental, and emotional health need to be well cared for and a priority.

For every action, there is a consequence, and with every consequence, there are new opportunities. Self-mastery is embracing the wind as a factor when setting and resetting our personal sails, knowing that storms are part of the equation, as is the calm.

Self-mastery is the unconditional pursuit of personal growth—we either move toward it or move away from it, one thought and one action at a time.

Chapter 29

Jamie Tate

A GRAMMY AND EMMY AWARD-WINNING RECORDING ENGINEER, mixer, and producer, Jamie Tate began his career working at several different iconic studios and, in 2004, opened the Rukkus Room, a multi room recording and mixing facility in Nashville. He has worked on a number of popular recordings, including dozens of hit records and chart-topping songs, making him a highly sought-after mixing engineer and producer. His credits include work with artists such as Taylor Swift, Alan Jackson, Justin Moore, Marty Stuart, Billy Bob Thornton, Brooks & Dunn, Phil Keaggy, as well as labels including Big Machine Records, Universal Records, and Sony Records.

INTERVIEW

MENZIE: At a time when the music industry seems to be contracting and redefining itself, it appears that you see these changes as new opportunities, and you're recording a lot of young artists.

JAMIE TATE: Well, the purpose is to help these artists who don't have access to major record labels. Everybody comes to town wanting to be either a musician or an artist, and they don't know anybody. I try to help them establish some sort of recorded history that doesn't sound like crap. When possible, I help them record an album that is actually like major label quality and help them get heard by whomever they want. That seems to be the big thing now—record labels don't really seem to be a priority to a lot of people anymore. You can make a really good living just from going on the road and playing. I think a lot of people are recognizing that they can become internet stars without the help of record labels. Pomplamoose and other bands like that are doing really well on their own. They're refusing record contracts because they make more money by themselves.

MENZIE: A great example of what you are saying is the band Walk off the Earth. I am fascinated by their work, and with bands like that, it almost seems like we're kind of back in the time of the sixties, when you put together road shows.

JAMIE TATE: Very much so. I was talking the other day about how nobody does full shows anymore. They do half-hour bits, half-hour sets. And that's what a show is nowadays—five or six different people doing half-hour sets or twenty-minute sets. It's also like the sixties because it's a singles market now. You don't do albums anymore, you do EPs [extended plays] and single pieces of work.

MENZIE: I think that's where the digital industry has now played a big role. You used to have to buy a complete work, but now you can pick the seeds you want. If you download something two minutes long, maybe that's the tune you like the best, but you're not getting the artist's conceptual end of it anymore.

JAMIE TATE: First of all, I'm not sure how many artists nowadays think like that. They think that every song is a potential single. Studios put the same amount of work into every song.

Some become singles, and some don't. I really miss the concept of having one overarching idea and making an album surrounding that idea. I did this awesome record with Marty Stuart back in 1999. We were nominated for a couple of Grammys for it, but it was a concept record. It told a story of this guy who caught his wife cheating, and it told the story by taking you through the history of country music. We had Ralph Stanley on there, [and] we had Johnny Cash on there, along with Emmylou Harris and George Jones. They were all narrating different pieces of this puzzle and taking us through the different decades of country music. Not one song was picked as a single, and it tanked hard because the label didn't know what to do with it. But it was awesome. I just wish we could get back to those days, you know? *Abbey Road* side two and *Dark Side of the Moon*—that kind of stuff.

MENZIE: Artists are great with creativity. They're great with concepts. They write a tune, they have an idea, but they're not necessarily great with the details of organization or putting together the business side.

JAMIE TATE: Definitely. Artists are not business minded. They're creative. Artists know how to create stuff, engineers know how to create stuff, [and] musicians know how to create stuff, but they don't always know how to sell it. The most important thing is the sales pitch. We all know people who had big hit records—maybe they're not the best singer, but they're either good at selling themselves or they have a team around them that [is] good at selling them. That's so important.

MENZIE: What kind of artist gets Jamie Tate's attention?

JAMIE TATE: Somebody with good songs. Honestly, that's most important. If the songs aren't there, there's no reason for any of this. There's no reason for microphones or recording gear or great musicians if the songs aren't good. That's basically it. That's what gets me excited.

MENZIE: Nashville is a songwriter's town, but there seems to be a slight divide between great songs like "Whiskey Lullaby"-type . . . material versus tailgates and beer songs. Do you think that ever changes back?

JAMIE TATE: We've been thinking that for ten years. It hasn't happened yet. Every song is still about tailgates and beer and tattoos and bonfires and daisy dukes. How many songs can you write about that? I thought the bro-country thing was going to go away, but it hasn't.

MENZIE: I think money is the deciding factor, but the town is still crawling with amazing songwriters.

Chapter 29

Jamie Tate: We record so many amazing songs in demo sessions. The songwriters know it, [and] we know it. We record them just to keep our sanity. These songwriters in town are true professionals; they do it every day of the week. They're amazing. But I don't fault them at all for trying to stay relevant and make money, so if they want to write a song about beer cans, that's fine with me.

Menzie: How does the Rukkus Room get on a singer-songwriter's radar?

Jamie Tate: The reputation of the studio's quality is our best tool for getting on someone's radar.

Menzie: When you record a developing artist, do you offer input on what you believe works?

Jamie Tate: A label will put you in media school and tell you how to do everything, as well as how to dress. They'll straighten your hair, or they'll put curls in it. They will tell you what to wear, what kind of hat to put on. When I work with someone, I watch and see what their personalities are, and then I just give suggestions. I see artists as characters. Lady Gaga is a character. Tom Petty was a character. It's who they are, and you know exactly what you're getting. I think that branding needs to be there. I simply offer another point of view based on my experience. I try to contrast what's happening now to historic models while, at the same time, sharing my thoughts on where I believe the market is now.

The reason the Beatles were so awesome was because every album was something different, and they blew your mind all the time. And I love that. I'm not sure that would work now. I'm not powerful enough to test the waters.

We've got to play with the rules we have now, and the rules are completely different than they were even when I started. It's just crazy, and you have to keep up. Part of the problem now is nobody knows exactly what to do. Everybody's scared. Everybody's doing everything out of fear. There are only a few real, true artists because [everyone else is] mimicking and recording what's popular and on the radio. That's not how you make progress in music.

Menzie: And it's not the way you become an iconic artist either.

Jamie Tate: Oh no, exactly. That's not the way you become an iconic artist. A while back, I cut an album for a guy who already had seven number 1s. He is the only guy on the radio who sounds like him, but now the new album is going to sound like everybody else. I just think that's a really bad move.

Menzie: Everyone has their idea of why a recording is special. For you, what stands out as a unique recording or a special moment in the world of modern music?

Jamie Tate: I guess I can just tell you which records influence my ear the most. When I was in sixth grade, I heard a live Billy Joel record, *Songs in the Attic*. I was fascinated by the drum sounds. The liner notes said it was recorded and mixed by Brian Ruggles and Jim Boyer. So the next time Billy came to town, I went to the front-of-the-house engineer, Brian Ruggles. I called him by name. I said, "Hi Mr. Ruggles. Would you please sign my CD?" He was so impressed. He let me meet the band and Billy, and they all signed my CD. He suggested I read *Mix Magazine*, as well as some other books. I was in sixth grade, and he kind of set me on my way.

Then there's Jellyfish's *Spilt Milk* album. It's just beyond brilliant—the recording and mixing. The kick drum has such power to it, which you didn't hear in the eighties. It had bottom end. It sounded like Queen, [and] it sounded like Henry Mancini. It sounded like everybody I love.

Then an album came out called *Extreme Three*, and the drum tones were so punchy and loud that I listened to it for like eight straight hours.

Oh, and the Beatles' *Revolver*. Those four albums are pretty much everything I ever want to accomplish. So that's my palette basically.

Menzie: You play drums, right?

Jamie Tate: I hit drums. While Tommy Harden is living in this world, I am not a drummer. He is one of the best all-around musicians I have ever had the pleasure of working with.

Chapter 29

Menzie: Tommy has absolutely no ego, yet his tonality on the kit is insane. It's so deep.

Jamie Tate: Our house kit is his old "A kit." I just loved the sound of it, so I bought it when he got a Yamaha endorsement and had to get rid of his [other] pro drums. That's the same kit that's been on all these hit records I've been a part of. He makes the kit sound so good. Other drummers come in, and it sounds completely different when they play.

Menzie: Absolutely. There's an art to creating tone, especially drum tones. The sound is in the player's hands as much as it is in the instrument.

Jamie Tate: Very few drummers understand tone. A lot of young guitarists know tone, but drummers—they just hit, and they expect it to sound good. There are only a handful of drummers in town who understand how to hit a drum to make the tones sound great, but Tommy Harden does.

Menzie: One thing that I've learned to really appreciate is people, like Steve Gadd, who understand and respect what a long note is. Gadd feels the true length of the note value, and Tommy plays very similarly. That feel lets a song breathe.

Jamie Tate: Yeah, absolutely. Tommy talks about Steve Gadd a lot. He respects the hell out of him.

Menzie: When we go back and study any of the amazing moments in contemporary music, a magical element or some special characteristic seems to exist, especially with renowned studios and engineers. What characteristics of the Rukkus Room make it special for you?

Jamie Tate: The Rukkus Room has a really great drum room. It has thirty-foot ceilings. The big room is nice and large. It's not too live. Like, for example, Ocean Way Studio here in Nashville is an old church, and it's hard to get anything useful out of there. Drummers love playing in there, but the room is too damn big. You can't capture anything usable for recordings. Here the room is just the right size.

MENZIE: Drums can really get lost in that kind of setting. So you feel that just the vibe and design that you have constructed have a sound that you're able to consistently work with?

JAMIE TATE: Yeah. It's really versatile here. It's not too big, but it's not small. Plus, the design is really good. It was designed by Gene Lawson of Lawson Microphones. Lawson is located in Nashville, and Gene designed this place from the ground up in 1981 to be his studio. It has three feet of poured concrete on the ground, and there's three feet of poured concrete on the ceiling. It's a noncombustible building, so my insurance rates are really low. It has floating rooms. It was designed as a studio, not a converted house, like every other studio in Nashville. The control room sounds pretty great. The rooms themselves are just perfectly sized, and there's no outside interference. They sound great—nice and even.

MENZIE: Do you have any favorite studios that have influenced what you're looking for in sound?

JAMIE TATE: Not really. It's more engineers. It's more music—because any good engineer can make any studio sound good. If you were to give three engineers a Pro Tools session, you're going to get three completely different sound mixes.

I think people put too much emphasis on which studio you record the music in. You need to pick your engineer and see where they want to work. That's the most important thing. I've struggled mixing tracks from big-money studios because they weren't recorded properly.

MENZIE: Nashville is one of the last great music towns to use live bands when recording.

JAMIE TATE: Oh, there's nothing else like it. We usually track with five to eight players, and they're all playing off each other. There's something about having these guys all in a room as it's all going down in the headphones—having it sound like a record already as you're going down the first pass—that makes you feel like you're king of the world. There's just something to that.

MENZIE: There's something about chemistry that's completely unique to music when there's that energy and vibe. You can't see that on a record, but you can feel it and certainly hear it!

JAMIE TATE: Right. And if the guitarist, who overdubs third, comes up with a great lick, and the keyboard player missed it because they overdubbed second—you know, you can't join in on that lick.

Or if they come up with a great lick and say, "Man, that sounds like an organ part. Maybe we should have the organist play." Well, they're already gone. They've already been paid. You'll have to pay them again.

And when you do create something great, it's not necessarily the version that the label wants to do anything with. In Nashville there's a lot of instances where they'll find an artist, and they'll stick that artist with three, four, five, six, [or] even eight producers, then they'll all cut sides on them. Then they'll all turn them in, and the label picks what they think the direction of the artist should be.

Sometimes you just hit it out of the park. You know you got it right, but that's not the version the label picks up. When you hear the final version, it's a generic, whatever song. Production is flat, almost mono. It has no fidelity, but that's what the label picked up. So we don't always know what they need to fill their niche. They have a grand scheme of things, and we're just not privy to that information.

MENZIE: Maybe they need to be privy to your information.

JAMIE TATE: That's how it used to be, but it's not that way anymore. They used to just record a song; turn it into the label; say, "Here's our record"; and the label says, "Thank you" and prints it. That's not how it works anymore.

I love the old way. Those are the records that everybody loves. When somebody is allowed to break through with something that's different, those are the records we love. Personally, I've worked on several projects that anticipated a new trend [but] then never got the light of day or got any notice. Then somebody comes out with the same thing, and they're on *Billboard*, and they're millionaires. It's luck of the draw.

MENZIE: So what other great artists and engineers have influenced you most?

JAMIE TATE: I love to listen to *Revolver*, *Pet Sounds*, [and] *Sgt. Pepper*. Those are an endless source of inspiration for me. As far as other influences, two names that come to mind are Chris Lord-Alge (Eric Clapton, Phil Collins, Sheryl Crow) and Bob Clearmountain (David Bowie, Hall & Oates, the Rolling Stones, Bruce Springsteen). Those are my two favorites of all time. Those two guys have been at it [for] thirty, forty years now. They're just amazing. Production-wise, there's also Jeff Lynne. There's just something about what he does that I love. I mean, he does his thing, but he's the best at it. One thing that really bothers me is how people get labeled as dated. It frustrates me.

MENZIE: Interestingly, some artists with decades-spanning careers, like Willie Nelson, have dodged that bullet.

JAMIE TATE: Yeah. He's iconic. He's cool. Somehow he got labeled [as] cool. I recorded him. He's awesome. But why him, and not Don Williams?

MENZIE: I agree with that 100 percent, but for some unique reason, some make it through.

JAMIE TATE: Like Merle Haggard. Everybody sings about Merle Haggard in their songs, even though they don't know who the hell he is. Every once in a while, when they're in there singing, I'll ask, "Do you know who Hag is?" And they say, "I think it's Merle Haggard, right?" And I'll say, "Yeah, name a song of his." And they usually can't do it.

MENZIE: I had a young guitarist ask me to suggest a unique guitarist to study for a school project, someone who had a big impact on music. I asked him if he knew who Chet Atkins was. He looked at me and said no. So I said, "It helps when you go back a bit in time. You've got to catch up on the icons." He was smart enough to heed the advice.

JAMIE TATE: Here's how I explain it: you've got to go back to the original source. The Beatles, the Stones, and the people that influenced them, and so on—those people built the ground floor for us. Other people have done offshoots of that, but still the source is what was done fifty years ago. That's where everybody learned it. Why use the imitation as your inspiration? Go to the original source. For example, most folks know the Beatles were heavily influenced by Little Richard.

MENZIE: You're sought out specifically to mix a great deal of material for radio. What's your approach to getting a great radio mix, and what are the challenges of creating quality dimension in a small-speaker setting?

JAMIE TATE: I mix on an old pair of Apple computer speakers. I mix really, really quietly. When I'm working, someone chewing gum will distract me because it's so quiet in there. Also, I mix with the speakers off to my side. I know it's weird, but they're off to my left side because that's the way most people listen. Nobody listens sitting right there between two speakers. And I find that when I mix with the speakers off to my side, the center sounds louder than the stuff [that's] panned left to right, so I try to make the stuff that I pan left to right a little louder than the center, and that gives me a wider image. I don't know why I started doing it that way, but I've been doing it for fifteen years now.

I was in the studio where Bob Clearmountain was mixing way back in the mid-1990s, and he had the speakers so quiet that somebody sneezed and it scared us. The challenge is to get it to sound great when it's quiet, and so I forced myself to learn how to mix quietly, and it worked.

Now I've done it for so long that I know what it's going to sound like. I know where the bass is going to land because I'm used to hearing it so quietly. It was a challenge when I first started, but now I don't think I could do it any other way.

MENZIE: Will you address the changes in how recorded music is done today as opposed to, say, ten years ago?

JAMIE TATE: Well, yeah. We don't need to play in time or sing now, which is unfortunate. We have people with Pro Tools [who] can make anyone sound like a star. [The] engineers nowadays . . . there are very few of us who started in the analog world. When I entered the business, the first five years were strictly analog tape. I still have an analog console. I still use vintage gear. But nowadays, everyone just uses plug-ins, and my problem is—when I get these files to mix, I can tell that they were recorded by a Pro Tools technician and not an engineer. There are no cross fades. They'll do punches without a cross fade, and every time there's an edit, it ticks. It's frustrating because it takes me two to three hours per song to clean up all these things and fix all the edits.

MENZIE: What, if anything, have we lost or gained in the transition to today's current music trends and methods?

JAMIE TATE: Oh, it's great. Any sort of DAW system—you can do whatever you want. You have total flexibility, total freedom. If you want something to sound like Motown, you can do it because you've got Motown plug-ins. If you want this song to sound sleek and modern, you can do that too. You can do it on the fly between songs. You can do it without spending tens of thousands of dollars on new gear that you need. It's great. I love that.

But because of that, there is not as much desire to really learn how to use the stuff—you know, the "first" tools. They don't know how to put a mic on a drum set, they just put a mic up there and watch it flicker and say, "Oh, I'll inflate stuff later."

Last Friday I inherited a group to produce. They've become quite successful on satellite radio. I'm producing their next couple of songs for them, and I pulled up the drum tracks and they were unusable. The engineer, who is a well-known popular mix engineer in town, recorded them. They said he didn't care what they sounded like, because he was going to replace them anyway. Then I realized [that] he doesn't know how to record drums because he started as just a Pro Tools technician.

CHAPTER 29

And the drummer was so heartbroken because he has this custom-made drum set, and he took all this time picking out the cymbals and all the snare drums. He tuned them to perfection, and then you hear his song on the radio, and it's some guy's sample that the tech has been using for five years. [It] sounds like everybody else. It's really a shame.

I had them in here last Friday, and I told the band, "We're going to strip everything down except the click track," and we recorded the song all new, which they'd never done before with this other producer. At the end of the first take, they asked, "How many of those little tracks did you have in the headphones? That sounded like a finished record." And I said, "None. That was all you guys." They couldn't believe it.

MENZIE: Any artist who creates needs a medium. Yours is obviously the mixing console. Today I see so many younger sound engineers [who] mix with their eyes by looking at VU [volume unit] meters. What's your advice to engineers who are just getting started?

JAMIE TATE: I'm really big into a listening test—playing their mix and then playing my mix. Just compare your stuff to others because there are amazing examples of perfect recordings out there. Pick a Tom Petty record, and see how close you are to actually being competitive with a record like that. I make it competitive on purpose because that's really what it is. Nobody knows who you are, so you have to stand out just as much as somebody like Tom Petty does.

MENZIE: What is your opinion of engineers [who] seem to need to have a big signature on a recording? They almost play the role of a creator.

JAMIE TATE: There's two trains of thought. I'm a big movie buff, and my favorite directors are the ones who are very stylized. You know, Terry Gilliam is a perfect example. Edgar Wright is another perfect example. He did *Shaun of the Dead* and *Hot Fuzz*. He's very stylized, and I love his movies.

There are some people in music who are very stylized, like Phil Spector. Then there are some people who are more transparent, like Phil Ramone. He just did exactly what was perfect for the music. It depends on what you're going for. If you're trying to record for Steely Dan, then you want it as characterless as possible. Whereas if you're recording the Beatles, you want the person who is really, really stylized, like Jeff Emerick.

When I first heard *Revolver*, it floored me because I'd never heard anything like that. You know, that compression and making the drums pop—that got me excited. I think I kind of tend to go toward engineers and producers who are very stylized.

MENZIE: Right. Engineers [who] have a good signature. I always hear people talk about Elvis and the fact that Sam Phillips captured such a unique sound. RCA [Records] had a different sound. Of course, it was great because it was still Elvis, but there was something about Sam and Sun Studios that was magic.

JAMIE TATE: Right. Exactly. Those are great records. You can't beat them. Whoever recorded Elvis at RCA here in Nashville was also amazing. [They are] beautiful recordings. I forgot his name.

MENZIE: They were better technical recordings.

JAMIE TATE: I agree, [they were] technically better. But if you look at the Beatles after *Rubber Soul*, those are technically better recordings, but I personally prefer the Geoff Emerick and Ken Scott version of the Beatles because they had more personality to them.

MENZIE: On your webpage is a flowchart called "Modern Recording" that has garnered a lot of attention. You illustrate how half a million dollars' worth of processing gear is squished into a ninety-nine-cent MP3 and listened to on twelve-dollar headphones.

JAMIE TATE: You know, I really wish I would have put nine-dollar headphones—because that's how much they are now. I'm so out of touch.

MENZIE: You overpaid. It's okay. You got the point across. [He laughs.] Can we have some fun and have you name some consistent absurdities you frequently encounter in the recording business?

JAMIE TATE: [He laughs.] One artist, she wanted to keep recording her scratch vocals so the musicians would have something better to play with. We were already done with the track and had already moved on to punching. I was punching the bass guitar, and she was getting upset because I wasn't also punching her scratch vocal at the same time. That's absurd. She would have liked us to have wasted two hours to get her scratch vocals better so the musicians could be inspired by it to play better.

It's also just the perception of things. It's about production and mix. I can take crappy sounding tracks and make a really great-sounding mix out of it. So it's not really about the recording quality. It's about the song and the mix and arrangement of the song. That's all that really matters.

MENZIE: I believe you're the perfect example of what I call the new-musician model. You pay homage to tradition and authenticity, but you embrace new technology and ideas. You have no loyalty to either. You challenge all traditions, both old and new, musical and technical. In response to somebody asking you about auto-tune, you said, "It's easier to know when something is perfect than to know when it's cool."

What's your take on the current state of the industry, and will you take the gloves off a little bit so that we can see what a successful music-industry pro like yourself is exposed to?

JAMIE TATE: Like [the] day-to-day stuff?

MENZIE: Yeah, what illusions you can help them pierce by saying, "I'm an industry pro, and here's what I think is important."

JAMIE TATE: I'm about to face my third round of recalls on an album, and I swear I can't hear the difference between my original mix and the second round of recalls, even though I'm the one who made the changes. That's just the control factor. The producer had to have his changes. The artist brought in his changes. Then the label just heard them Monday, and now they have another list of changes they want. It's completely a control thing. If you have a cool idea, that's great, but on one of these songs, I completely muted the drums for the bridge and put in an 808 kit and some other loopy kind of stuff, and nobody has noticed it yet. They're so caught up in making sure that the vocal is too loud at all points in the song. Every time I recall a mix, it gets worse and worse and worse, but they think it gets better because they have more control. And as a counter point to that, of the last three, four, five, or six songs I've mixed that went number 1, one was a rough mix. One was a demo mix. There was absolutely no input from the producer, the artist, or the label, and they still went number 1. That kind of shows you the dichotomy of reality here.

What really matters is the song. Do people like the artist? Do people like the song? That's all that matters. I did great mixes of them, and obviously, the best mixes I do are the ones with the least amount of input from other people. They take what's cool and make me mute it.

MENZIE: You said something else that's interesting to me: something that has really changed is the balance between harmonies and lead vocals. It used to be that the lead vocal was up during the verses, and then during any kind of harmony parts, it was balanced to what would make the chord correct. Nowadays, they are way in the back, and so the chord sounds really funny to my ear because you've got the middle part a time and a half louder than it should be. That seems to be a trend.

JAMIE TATE: Here's what that's all about—music these days is not recorded for music's sake. It's recorded to perpetuate the career of the singer. And because of that, the most important thing is the vocal. If the lead vocal and background vocal are musically balanced, then the lead vocal is sharing the spotlight with the background singer, and that's not acceptable. It's incredibly cynical, but it's absolutely true.

It actually puts a lot of things in perspective. We argue about which is the best mic for this and which is the best compressor for that. [We ask,] What sample rate? What sample frequency should we record at? It doesn't matter—it's all about the lead vocal, and that's just how music is nowadays. It wasn't like that back in Zeppelin's day or the Beatles' day.

I love harmonies. Harmonies are why I listen to music. They're just really important to me, and it kills me to raise the lead vocal so much that it buries the background vocal, but that's just how it is currently in the industry.

MENZIE: As an engineer, how do you feel about streaming services like Spotify and Apple Music?

JAMIE TATE: [I] hate it. The only thing I like about it is that people have access to all the music they want. Every other aspect of it I hate because people are digesting single songs. They aren't digesting albums. There's no loyalty to certain artists like we used to have. We used to be able to identify a person's personality by the kind of music they listened to. That's gone. You knew the person who listened to Zeppelin was that type usually. You knew the person who liked Elvis over the Beatles was another type. It was cool. It was awesome. It was how you identified yourself, and now that's gone, not to mention all of the economic downfalls of it. There's just not enough money coming in to support this huge monstrosity.

MENZIE: Without CD and record sales, how do you see the recording or touring artist generating income?

JAMIE TATE: [With] the ticket sales, the T-shirt sales. I think that's what's keeping us alive now—that and radio royalties. I think we all just know that regular royalties are going to diminish as time goes on, so what else is going to be there to support the whole industry? You know, right now, publishing is the big cash cow. It's going to be streaming somehow, [as well as] merch sales. I'm pretty sure that's how the record labels are keeping their lights on right now. Everything hinges on those live performances.

It's so scary at times that I choose not to think of it, but somehow it will right itself. People always have to have their tunes. People will still want to be music stars. So somehow it will figure its way out. It has to.

MENZIE: Diminishing all the sources of income can't be good for the artist or the industry.

JAMIE TATE: It's reliant on bands connecting with their audience. My first piece of advice to artists is to get a mailing list. Do a show, and get a mailing list. That email address is more valuable than selling a CD to that person because then you can have direct contact with them [and can] keep them updated on what you're doing. Connecting directly with your fan base is how independent artists keep going.

MENZIE: Right. Which is easier than it used to be because there didn't used to be some of the tools that we have now.

JAMIE TATE: Yeah, it's much easier. You can reach someone twenty different ways now.

MENZIE: I also hear people saying, "I don't have to watch it live. I can watch it on a streaming service, Netflix or YouTube or whatever."

JAMIE TATE: Yeah, and then they never get around to it.

MENZIE: It used to be about the experience. It was about being there. It was unique.

JAMIE TATE: And when you talk about experience, what about the experience of going to the record store? On Friday or Saturday nights, we used to go to Tower Records with other like-minded people and search for something we hadn't heard before or make friends in the store because we were all similar personalities. As a record collector, that's what I'm really sad about.

MENZIE: But it's nice to see a resurgence of that experience, like Grimey's in Nashville. What do you think somebody coming up as a tech has to do to find success?

JAMIE TATE: They have to make friends with someone who's working. You have to get in the environment; you have to be in the studio and be around musicians. That's the only way to do it. I was speaking at a local college in front of several classes, and one day, I gave an invitation to everyone. I said, "Somebody did this for me, and I am just kind of paying it forward. If anybody wants to come to the studio and watch a tracking session or a mix session or whatever, this is an open invite to everyone." I talked to several hundred kids that day, but only one person approached me. And that one person is still with me two years later. I helped her understand that she was a good candidate for a career in songwriting. She's getting amazing cowrites, we just recorded an EP for her, and we're about to do a video. She is getting ready to be pitched to record labels right now. So you've got to get in the environment. If someone gives you an opportunity, don't ignore it, and when you do come in, don't stare at your phone the whole time, like many do. I had a kid from a local high school shadow me today, and he stared at his phone the whole day.

MENZIE: What is it like to pick up a Grammy or an Emmy? How did that change things for you?

JAMIE TATE: It doesn't change things as much as you would think. It's a great marketing tool, so you mention it no matter what, but you would think it would have this huge impact on your career, and it's somewhat marginal. It looks good on the mantel though—if you remember to put it out.

MENZIE: Speaking of awards, and because you've worked in the past with some of the production on things like Taylor Swift, what's your take on hugely successful, platinum albums?

JAMIE TATE: It would be really, really important for somebody to get a platinum record now. Everybody was getting them for a while. There were so many people getting them that they were just white noise. There were only three last year, I think. They're all in the country market except for Pink. That's pretty big news. I don't know. Maybe they'll lower the numbers that you need—one million is platinum and five hundred thousand is gold. Who knows? I think they'll just become more cherished.

I don't know anybody who has theirs on display without prompting. Seriously, it's weird. Nowadays it's more important to be able to post on social media that you have some kind of success. That's perceived as the cool thing.

MENZIE: So what do you see on the horizon for recording and for the music business?

JAMIE TATE: Hmm. I think now is a time of redefining for the music business. Things may get a little worse before they get a lot better, as far as the singer-songwriter stuff goes. I think things are going to go even further into the electronic dance music world before we finally rebel and see good songs and real artists reemerge. I don't know anybody in town who's not in therapy over this. It's a tad scary right now, but isn't that always the case?

We always seem to find a way. That's what gives me hope. Somewhere there is a young artist writing a song or shedding [his or her] instrument or maybe even developing a new technology—who [it is] we don't know yet. At the drop of a hat, [he or she] could be the next big thing.

CHAPTER 30

WILDEYES

IN A TIME IN MUSIC WHERE FORMULA REIGNS SUPREME, WILDEYES stands out as a truly unique and original band. Emily Kohavi, Daniel Kohavi, and Max Hoffman blend their talents, voices, and vision to create hauntingly original music. In the same breath, they add the perfect complement of mesmerizing visuals to their shows. WILDEYES is a harmonious blend of yesterday, today, and tomorrow.

INTERVIEW

MENZIE: I think one of the hardest questions for musicians today is "How do you turn music into a means of gainful employment?"

EMILY: There is no nice little road. You have to hack down all these trees—climb over this one and scale over that one.

MENZIE: Creating a market in music is very subjective and takes an entrepreneurial spirit. It's not like sports.

DANIEL: It's much more subjective than sports, which brings in a whole other dynamic. It's not about [asking,] "Are you good enough to beat the person you're playing against?" It's about whether or not there is a market for you. Is there a group of people who are going to pay your salary?

MENZIE: As the band has developed, you, as musicians, have sought to learn different instruments, whether [you're] doing it for the band or a particular song. And it's once you've identified a need that you develop the skill set. That's actually inverted from what many people traditionally do.

MAX: It's like—this song calls for a banjo, so let's learn the banjo. Instead of [saying], "Hey, I know the banjo, so let's put the banjo in this new song."

DANIEL: I think everything in the band comes from that philosophy. Whatever we do, it's to serve the song.

MENZIE: You work backward from the song's point of view—that's a demanding master to serve. That takes a lot of courage, a lot of vision, and a lot of work.

MAX: I think there's something exciting about doing something you haven't done before. It gives you a new perspective.

MENZIE: If you look at groups like the Beatles or the Band or even the Beach Boys, there [were] all kinds of sound experimentations going on in the studio. They were also experimenting with different miking techniques and sound textures in an attempt to bring unique qualities to the songs.

One of the things that really jumps out at me about WILDEYES is that I see that same respect for authenticity and appreciation for unique qualities, both sonically and visually. How have you arrived at your approach? It's not mainstream, and a lot of people wouldn't take that risk. I should also mention that I know of very few groups that work as diligently as WILDEYES does on their visual presentation.

MAX: When we were first looking for producers, a bigger producer . . . we played for said something interesting about our sound: "You guys are like the new rock 'n' roll. You're moving past the fine-tuned, cleanly produced formula. You let your music speak for itself."

Chapter 30

MENZIE: I believe that is an issue for the music industry to address. We've got this clean machine that makes money, but the industry has amazing artists [who] have a lot more they want to say with their music.

MAX: People want to hear humanity in songs. You want to hear struggle, and you want to hear that grit. If it's too perfect, then no one can relate to it. Our approach came together naturally somehow between us. We aren't big fans of the disingenuous formulas that permeate so much of the airwaves in the music scene today.

MENZIE: We've gotten to a point where technology fixes so many things that used to require actual technique. Mechanics are often removed from the process. As you said, humanity has been reduced, so the product now has become homogenized.

MAX: Recently, when we played the Firefly Festival, almost every artist there was playing to a track. When we were talking to some of the sound people, they were struck by the fact that we didn't use tracks, that we actually played our instruments. It's the world we're living in. It's pop music: people want it, and people are getting it.

MENZIE: I think we can all agree that the mainstream listener today is fed a musical diet that's low in nutritional value, but there is still great material available. There is a new movement gaining momentum with unique artists, like Brandi Carlile or Chris Stapleton, and the listeners are realizing that they do actually want it.

DANIEL: I think that Chris Stapleton's music has answered that question of "Do [listeners] want that?" You put out a real, live record with real players playing good music with good songs, and people love it. So people definitely want that.

But about authenticity, I think that part was easy for us because we weren't catering to anything when we started this band. Max has been in Nashville longer, so he has more bluegrass influences. I grew up around all the R&B and pop influences. That's what captured me. The three of us agreed that although we come from very different places, we were just captivated with this Nashville, true, old, Willie Nelson, Texas feel.

However, we quickly fell out of that and into what we are today as we realized that we can maintain who we are as writers and our influences within this organic sound. It was authentic because it couldn't really be anything else. We just thought it was cool and, more importantly, honest.

Max: When we first moved to Nashville, I just didn't connect to the current idea of country music. But just a few years down the line, I got this urge to understand the original, true simplicity of honest country music, and I wanted to just play it and be a part of it—the front-porch thing and being a part of that culture. There's something truly special there. It's just about playing music; it's literally about nothing else but playing music and having a good time, and I feel like that doesn't happen with other genres.

Menzie: How would you describe WILDEYES' style of music? Daniel, you had mentioned that there's a dash of traditional in there, and what really jumps out to me are your lyrics. Emily, do you write most of the lyrics?

Emily: I feel like it's very equal. Sometimes Max writes a song all by himself, then we instrumentalize it and bring it to life. Sometimes, I write a song all by myself, then we bring that to life. And then sometimes Max brings a verse and a chorus, and we finish the rest of it together. "Crazy in the Blood" was a Frankenstein because we pieced it together. So it all makes sense when it's finished, but you would be surprised at where the finished product comes from.

Menzie: When I listen to your music, I hear songwriting that's unique and that has a true respect for great vocal harmonies. All the great artists are artists first—Dylan didn't come out and say, "I gotta get on a roll, let me write a pop song and have success follow." That's the same quality I see in this band—authenticity. It's truly a high-risk proposition. And when I look at you guys, I think, "That's all risk for the right reasons."

Jason Isbell hits me that way, [and] so does someone like Sturgill Simpson. It's because the music is so completely genuine. You can't fake that.

DANIEL: You're absolutely right.

MENZIE: Visually, you guys have developed this great presentation that is completely captivating. It's really old-school and unique.

I spoke with Sierra Hull in her interview for this book about the Del McCoury band and how, when someone sees Del live, they witness what traditional bluegrass bands do extremely well. They all sing around one mic, bobbing and weaving in and out. I'm also a big Marty Stuart fan, and when you see how these groups perform live, there's great respect for that porch tradition you refer to. There's great respect for history and high-quality live performance.

When you work in a band, agreeing on style and presentation can be hard. You've got to be bold enough to admit when something's not working when you are developing your sound and your show. How does WILDEYES work through that?

DANIEL: I think there are three leaders in this band [who] are all meeting in the middle and who are all extremely opinionated about what we think is good and what we think is compelling.

MAX: We're always arguing with each other—but in a productive way. I think it's a healthy sign that we're arguing and grappling with ideas.

DANIEL: We care about what we do and we're unwilling to settle for less than our best. When stuff is 90 percent good, we're going to fight over that last 10 percent.

MENZIE: How does the argument get settled?

MAX: I feel like if it's not inspiring us, the song gets tossed. Because everyone must be completely engaged in a song and fully excited about it. If we're not and we have not accomplished bringing our own thing to the table, there's no point.

Emily: If it's not working, the song doesn't even make it that far. We don't stop at 90 percent. If a song only gets to 90 percent, we figure out a way to fix it.

Max: We're always bringing new songs to the table, and if there's a song that's good, then we all get behind it. But if it's just okay, we usually toss it before it even sees the light of day.

Emily: The Bluebird Cafe does open mics, and you're allowed to sing a verse and a chorus of a song. Amy Kurland, the Bluebird Cafe founder, is a songwriter, and she feels she can tell in the first ten seconds if it's going to be a good song or not. With us, it's kind of the same thing. We can tell in the first thirty minutes of working on a song whether it's worth it or not. I know with some writers, their philosophy is to always finish no matter what, but we usually can tell right away if what we are working on has the makings of a great song or not.

Max: If you have something that really grabs you, a verse/chorus or even just the first verse—for me, it can be just a first line that motivates [me] to write the rest of the song.

Emily: All our songs have extremely good first lines. At times we've switched verse one and verse two around so that every one of them opens the way we think it should.

Max: We want people engaged within the first few seconds of the song.

Menzie: What's the saying? [Is it] "You've got six seconds to do something that's going to get somebody's attention"?

Daniel: How long is the scan button on your radio? Three seconds? Probably the closest we've come to that is our latest song we've been working on. Max wrote the bulk of it, and we're all refining it. But there are some moments when we're so sick of it. Thankfully, we've hung in there with it. We also brought a producer into the mix, which provides another voice. It's a great song. I'm glad we fought through it.

Chapter 30

Menzie: Do you ever write something and say, "Let me get away from that for a day or so"?

Max: Yes, you want a fresh mind. I'll write a song, then come back to it a couple days later to make sure it's good.

Menzie: The last time we hung out, you guys were talking about the idea of finding the right producer. After interviewing different candidates, who did you settle on, and how was that process?

Emily: We got some names from different people. Some of them were bigger producers with major labels, and some of them were with smaller labels. The choices were all across the board. Then we went and talked to all of them. All the producers pretty much said the same thing: that we're great, they wouldn't change a thing—just put a mic in front of us and let us do our thing. But we were kind of looking for that fourth band member. We wanted someone to come in with something creative.

The guy that we settled on is Eddie Spear from England. He's worked with Dave Cobb for several years, and he's been on multiple huge projects. He's about our age, and he's been working under the great producers the whole time he's been in America. We are excited to be working with him.

Max: We met with multiple producers, but with Eddie, we just sat down and talked with him, and the connection was genuine for all of us.

Daniel: Anyone who knows what's happening in Nashville knows that Eddie Spear is a superstar, and he has the steadfast goal of getting the very best from you.

Max: He's also the first guy [who] really had a vision for our album. At our very first meeting, he had great ideas.

Emily: We played Eddie a set of around twenty songs. He took notes and then chose the exact same seven songs that we believed to be our best material.

MENZIE: Nashville has a lot of writing room setups for cowriting teams, [which are] akin to the old Brill Building approach, whereas when you guys are writing, you are creating your sound. It sounds like that's what Eddie sees in you guys—true originality.

EMILY: We will be in the studio for four days. We will also have live drums (Chris Powell) and bass (Brian Allen) with us.

MENZIE: How did you pick the studio?

EMILY: Eddie picked Sound Emporium; he said it was one of his favorite studios. Kacey Musgraves, Willie Nelson, and Alison Krauss have all recorded there. We wanted to track live, and we wanted bass and drums on some songs, so with the way they built this studio, everyone can be in the same room, but there's not a lot of bleed from mic to mic.

DANIEL: Even before we met with producers, we all agreed that we wanted a producer who had a vision, not someone who was going to just press record. As a band, when we write, we write so that it's complete with the three of us, but Eddie's concept was to add some bass and drums. We all agreed that some songs don't need it, but there were a number of songs where we wanted to make a record that's going to stand the test of time, and everyone felt a rhythm section was a requirement to achieve that record feel.

EMILY: A heartbeat.

MAX: I think it's important for all musicians and bands to understand that when they arrive at the point of needing to seek a producer, being able to find the right producer, one [whom] you can trust, is huge. Because their job is to know what will work in the marketplace. We bring the art because we love the art. A great producer signs on because they help bring the final touches to the vision. The authenticity is why a great producer signs on in the first place.

Chapter 30

Daniel: Everything that Chris Powell and Brian Allen do is going to completely serve the song, and that's the whole point of it. That's why Eddie picked them. Chris has played drums with several artists, including Brandi Carlile and Anderson East. Brian has recorded and played with artists as diverse as Jason Isbell and Robben Ford, and they both do a lot of work with Dave Cobb. Chris is known for his sensitivity; you can feel the groove, and he has complete command. In fact, we had to switch around our schedule at the last minute because Chris got called to play at the White House. We completely changed the schedule because Eddie believed it was that important that Chris and Brian play together. They are part of Dave Cobb's A-team at RCA studio A.

Menzie: Because they're a rhythm section, that makes a big difference. They're going to be intuitive, and you guys are intuitive, so the lock on the feels will come together nicely.

Daniel: And I think that because our songs are so well rehearsed and we have such a vision for everything with this band, it will come together easily.

There are so many aspects about making this record that are scary. First, we're recording it live, and we only have four days. They seem to strongly believe that that's part of the recipe for making a great record: not knowing exactly how it's going to go down. It'll be the first time Chris and Brian have heard the songs, so they'll bring a fresh new life to the music.

Menzie: Is it your intent to get a finished product in four days?

Max: Yes.

Emily: Ten songs. He only wanted to do ten songs because we're going to do vinyl.

Menzie: Tell me how you guys feel about the market for your band.

Emily: Thank you, Chris Stapleton, thank you, Sturgill Simpson. These people have proven that there's a market for us. That's why we know this is okay.

Daniel: They've provided space in the market that we can live in.

Menzie: One fascinating thing I love about the Beatles' story is that they forged their own new market. They came from the idea that "This is what we do, we're not doing it just for the market." Although I do think Lennon had a pretty good idea of what would work.

Max: I think they controlled the market.

Menzie: They certainly ended up controlling it. In the oddest of ways, I think they still do.

Daniel: I think that's how we approach it; you could freak out all day, asking yourself, "Is this going to work?" But no one truly knows.

Menzie: Agreed, I believe when the quality is there, the audience can be developed organically because you have something that's unique and special.

Daniel: And that's how we feel about it. If a label opportunity comes up that we think is favorable, great. Our job is to keep developing our sound and keep moving forward while finding whatever avenue it takes to get people to hear our music.

Menzie: As artists, when you commit to a special original project that you truly believe in, it takes time to develop that project, as well as a following, but you still need to eat. So do you all do freelance and side gigs? Emily, I know you've done tours with several major artists. Rising musicians need to hear about that work ethic. There is no magic bullet other than hard work.

Chapter 30

Max: If this band hadn't formed and it wasn't magic and it wasn't the right timing and there wasn't the response we were getting, I wouldn't have quit my job. But that's just me. Some people are major risk takers, and they'll live out of their car, or they'll tour with a band that isn't ever going to be uniquely successful. They'll tour just because they want to go on tour.

Menzie: Yeah, a lot of people think the bus matters.

Max: Yeah, and that's cool if you have the right product and you're playing the right gigs.

Emily: They say there's three things—there's the hang, the money, and the music. You have the perfect gig if you have the trifecta. It's usually good money and good people, but not great songs. It's very rare that you have all three. We've got the good songs and the good people.

Menzie: With this band, the rest is just a matter of time. I think we can all agree that the entire music business is turbulent and risky. I don't think it's ever entirely comfortable for any artist or businessperson.

Emily: And once you have success and you get there, there's no guarantee you're going to stay there. Sure, you can land a good gig, but then in a year, you could be back to driving for Uber.

Menzie: Getting comfortable with an income in the arts is a mistake, and it can also be a creative trap. Lots of industry professionals and bands of name fall into that trap. You see it all the time. In many cases nobody wants to mess with the formula because it's working, and so the writing quality becomes mundane or even trite.

Emily, will you shed some light on your career steps? I want the readers to know that you've played for some major artists.

Emily: I moved to Nashville, and I was going to grad school because I thought I wanted to be a session player. When I got here, I got lucky because I met someone who needed a sub. The CMAs were happening, and this girl was supposed to play in the string section, but she got a job with Cirque du Soleil. So I filled in for her at the CMA Awards. Then someone else canceled on the Martina McBride tour, and there was a strings contractor I knew in town who actually worked for Martina. I owe a lot of my opportunities to that friend because she was the one who put me on the CMAs. She suggested that I do the Martina tour. Then the next year, the Trace Adkins tour came out, and she said, "I'll let you audition for this because I think you can do it." In between all this, I'm playing the CMA Award shows and the CMA Christmases and those sorts of things. When you do the CMAs, you are a part of the string section, and you play for whatever artist goes on, so I got to play for Chris Stapleton, George Strait, Keith Urban, Carrie Underwood, Rascal Flatts, and Martina—lots of great artists.

MENZIE: Tours and shows?

EMILY: The tours I've done have been with Martina McBride, Trace Adkins, Kacey Musgraves, Phoebe Bridgers, Hozier, and Niall Horan. But when I was gone from Nashville, I wasn't getting session work. I stopped going to grad school, and I turned down a lot of things.

MENZIE: You bring up an important point around the idea of networking—the importance of not only having to be in the network but also the necessity of being available.

EMILY: If you're going to tour, then you tour, and you hope that you will always be with an artist. And you hope that this artist keeps you around or, if they don't, that you've networked enough to the point where you can hop on somebody else's bus. Some of the players were nervous because they would be gone for an entire month, and they were session players. I was gone for a year and a half, which doesn't seem like a long time, but it is a long time to say no. You say no to someone once, and they may not call you back. You say no twice, they're probably not going to call you back. And if you say no three times, sayonara.

MENZIE: That's an imperative understanding.

CHAPTER 30

EMILY: And never be late for something! There was a girl who was late for the CMA Awards, and she's never done anything since.

MENZIE: That's another important point that I think rising musicians need to understand. The music business is competitive and sometimes unkind. Success is not always based purely on musical skills. Determination is a huge factor in success, and that's a different kind of skill set. The ability to recover from a major setback is also a vital tool, and so is building relationships.

EMILY: I got called for the CMA 50th Anniversary Awards and got to play with Chris Stapleton and Dwight Yoakam when they performed "Seven Spanish Angels." Moments like that quickly remind us how blessed we are to play music and do what we love to do. Then I got the opportunity to do the Christmas tour with Kacey Musgraves. After the Kacey tour, we started hitting WILDEYES hard.

We're at the point now where we're trying to book more and more shows, and the venues want to see numbers. They want to see views on YouTube.

MAX: We've got some good people on our team who are helping us out a lot.

EMILY: We know we are very close.

MENZIE: As much work as you have put into this project, you have to be excited about the fan base you have built. You've signed on to work with Eddie Spear, you've gone in with an engineer, and you are always working on your material. Now that all of that work is done, what would you like to see happen for you?

MAX: We've been asked that question so many times, especially when we were interviewing producers, and I think what we all want—the number one thing that we said—was longevity. [We want] that and being able to create the art that we want to create.

MENZIE: That's the hardest trick—longevity.

MAX: Oh yeah, just to be a trusted, accomplished artist is not an easy thing to do.

EMILY: We don't want to retire. I wanna play music until I die.

MAX: Yeah, we still want to be writing the same quality of songs that we're writing today—or better—in twenty years. I think that's the most important goal. We also have a lot of business goals, but the music—that's number one.

DANIEL: I think that there's this thing that happens when you decide you want to do music for a living. You see the perceived gatekeepers out there—labels, booking and marketing, all that stuff. And there's this group of people who are just like anyone else, but for some reason, they have the key, and the tendency is to think that the moment those gatekeepers say yes to whatever you're doing, you'll achieve some sort of arrival, and that's what success is. But success is all about creating something that's true and good and artistic.

And if you're convinced that what you do is really special, you have to take on the responsibility of making it work for the long term, which means making harder decisions and finding ways to stay true to your vision.

MENZIE: In my opinion, the long play is the hardest part. Winning a contract is one thing; sustaining a career in music is a very different matter.

DANIEL: For a lot of people, it's about being rich and famous. Records one and two are successful, then record three comes out, and it's like, "Who are we now?" So the trick to sustaining a career is to create truly good stuff that is also compelling to you.

It gets harder and harder as more voices are involved in the decisions.

Chapter 30

So you must be completely committed to doing what you want and intend to do. Everyone on our team is aware of that, which is important!

Max: I second that!

Emily: You know I'm in!

Chapter 31
Emily Kohavi

Emily Kohavi of the previously interviewed WILDEYES is an extraordinary musician and is talented enough to say, "Sure, no problem" to any unique opportunities that come her way. She doesn't know resistance. Along with performing in her original band WILDEYES, Emily has performed with noted artists: Kacey Musgraves, Carrie Underwood, Martina McBride, Phoebe Bridgers, Hozier, and Niall Horan.

During this interview we laughed as Emily recounted the mad experience of auditioning for Hozier's touring band. This is a perfect example of how successful musicians think: no matter the challenge, even when it's a crazy one, they go for it anyway. This interview also reflects beautifully on the bond between Emily and her husband, Daniel ("Babe"), who helped coach her through the eye of the hurricane-like preparation for this unique world tour.

Interview

MENZIE: You've been in Nashville for a while, and you have played on several major tours and worked with multiple major artists. How did you come to be considered for the Hozier tour in particular?

EMILY KOHAVI: Out of the blue, I received an email from Hozier's musical director, Alex Ryan.

MENZIE: How did Alex become aware of your resume?

Chapter 31

Emily Kohavi: I got on his radar because one of the background singers in Hozier's band was close friends with Eddie Spear, and Eddie produced the WILDEYES record *Beauty and Sadness*. Though I had never actually met her [the background singer] in person or hung out with her, she messaged us when the record came out and said she loved the songs.

Hozier had a female guitarist who also played fiddle and sang background vocals in his band, and I think they had been on tour for about a year when she decided that she wanted to return to doing her own music. But Hozier had already planned on doing another year of touring, so that's when the announcement came out that they were going to replace her. Right after that is when I got the email from Alex Ryan, the musical director.

It came at a particularly good time for me because WILDEYES was in between a lot of things, and we were in the process of redefining our direction. WILDEYES had succeeded in getting on the *Billboard* charts, and now we were working to figure out how to break out to the next level. There's still a little bit of mystery to that, as I'm sure most bands can relate to. WILDEYES was also dabbling with the idea of building our own studio. A lot of different ideas were floating around. It's the ongoing discussion—do we do everything ourselves or take a cue from other artists who have cracked the code?

In my personal career, I've been lucky to observe the inside track of top-level music industry teams. I've been able to witness some of the approaches the teams of the marquee artists incorporate. So I've seen firsthand the overall marketing strategies, and I've witnessed the behind-[the]-scenes phone calls and watched the way these teams execute their agendas.

As a musician, I believe you can do everything up to a point, but then someone has to take the reins to get you to that next level. You know the old adage: "It's not only what you know but who," and sometimes that is how they look at things. There are many times when a fresh perspective is exactly what you need. It can really give you new insights into ways to accomplish your own goals.

So the Hozier email came at the right time. They were looking to replace violin, voice, and guitar. While I am well versed on my main instruments of voice and strings, as well as several other instruments, guitar is not my main instrument. I love playing guitar, but I would not call myself a "shred master."

As I read the email, I thought, "This is amazing!" The producer contacted me and said "Kristen [the singer] is vouching for you, and I'm vouching for you, so it looks like the job is yours as long as they think you are the right fit." So we set up a time to meet.

MENZIE: Were they in Nashville?

EMILY KOHAVI: Yes, they were. Alex explained that they were going to be in Nashville doing a show the following week, so we set up a time to get together. Hozier was doing a show at the Grand Ole Opry with his Wasteland, Baby! tour.

I attended the show because I wanted to be prepared for when we met. I wanted to honestly say, "I loved this song or that song." I wanted to show them I was invested, and I wanted to see what the show looked like. I didn't know too much about Hozier's music at the time except for "Take Me to Church." I had heard he was unique in concert and put on a great show.

MENZIE: I remember how incredibly popular "Take Me to Church" was—a huge song.

EMILY KOHAVI: I learned quickly that a lot of people around the world are really into Hozier and, of course, "Take Me to Church," but I didn't know how completely connected and dedicated his fan base was.

I took a bunch of videos during the show because I had my eye on the girl I would be replacing, and I watched what she was playing on the guitar. She played guitar extremely well, which really hit me because there are several female guitar players [who] play well and who also sing, but there are fewer truly excellent female guitarists who also play violin and who can also sing effortlessly as they play guitar. She was a uniquely gifted musician.

MENZIE: Hozier really understands staging as well.

EMILY KOHAVI: Oh, I came to find that out. He definitely does, and it's not by chance. Raine Hozier Byrne is his mom, and she is a phenomenal

Chapter 31

visual artist. And his father is a drummer. So his exposure to the arts has very deep roots.

MENZIE: Operation and balance. These are words that come across very clearly when you look at any video footage of the band in concert.

EMILY KOHAVI: Oh yeah, but here's what you don't see—he has a female up on the lighting rig, and there are a lot of girls on the crew. In my experience it's rare to see girls working in those positions because the opportunities generally don't exist. And I will share gladly that I was excited to be on a tour with talented women in so many different roles.

MENZIE: Someone has to go first and break the old mold. It takes courage and conviction, and it says a lot about Hozier's character.

EMILY KOHAVI: Yes, totally! Then I come to find out later [that] he just picks the best of the best. He looks for the best sound engineer, and if it happens to be a girl, then great. He does want balance if possible. And most of his crew was not from America. There were only three Americans in the entire operation. The lady rigger was Canadian, and his production manager is from Ireland.

MENZIE: So you went to the concert and watched the girl whose role you would fill.

EMILY KOHAVI: Yes, and maybe two days later, the musical director said, "We're going to meet at this particular address. Bring your guitar. Here are two tunes for you to work up." Then I listened to them, and I'm thinking, "Yikes." The first one was "Dinner & Diatribes," so I started with that. My husband Daniel really helped me a lot. He just kept pushing. He was a great coach.

MENZIE: Each instrument comes with its own language and its own private hell. That's what makes this story so compelling. With enough time and with your capabilities, this undertaking still would have been an insane challenge, but in this case, you had very little time to prepare.

Emily Kohavi: Yeah, and with guitar, as you said, there's a whole different language and more techniques you have to learn. Even though you're "speaking music," there are the subtle differences between instruments that can really frustrate a person no matter how much they know about music and even if [they] do learn things quickly. You don't automatically sound comfortable.

So I got the first song down. I learned it and felt pretty comfortable with it. I worked it up to speed with good feel, but of course, my fingers felt like little monsters were eating the tips down. It was terrible; as everyone reading this already knows, guitar strings are a lot bigger than violin strings. They dig into your fingertips, eating them like little gremlins. So I went to Walgreens, and I got some liquid Band-Aids and covered the top of my fingers, which gave me a little relief. Eventually, it wore off, so I dumped superglue all over my fingers because it was so painful. But I had to keep going.

You know how this works—you prepare for a bazillion hours, then go right to sleep because then it marinates into your brain. When you wake up, it's a little bit more cooked into your memory.

Menzie: First, you comprehend that truth, and then you also have to do the work, but it's worth it.

Emily Kohavi: Yes, it is. But the truth is [that] it does. It does get into your "under brain." You have this intuition that develops because it's now baked in your subconscious. And I had every intention of using every trick in the book in executing these parts on guitar as well as I would have on strings, even though there was a short runway, so it was slightly crazy making. If they had asked me to play anything else, I would be screwed because I didn't have a huge repertoire to fall back on.

So I got the song "Dinner & Diatribes" down, and I got the song "No Plan" down, and I was on my way. I used this app called *The Amazing Slow Downer*. It's a great tool for if you're big into transcribing solos but maybe, at first, the solo is a bit fast. Or if there's a tricky lick, you can stick the file in the app and slow it down so that you can hear more clearly.

But here's the cool part: it keeps it in the correct key. For example,

Chapter 31

say there's a fast run, and you can't precisely make out all the notes, with the app, you can hear them all in half speed. It's amazing, so that's what I used. On my main instruments, I have a long history of picking off parts, so I am more used to the mechanics. With *The Amazing Slow Downer*, I could close the gap quickly.

MENZIE: I know what level of musician you are, so you being inconvenienced by having to learn to play yet another instrument at performance level is hysterical—because you already play something like a hundred instruments, right?

EMILY KOHAVI: [She laughs.] Unfortunately, while I dabbled on guitar, it was the instrument I needed to play proficiently for the job that I really wanted. I knew I could do it given enough time, so I was determined.

Here's when the story gets some comic relief. I'm driving in for the audition, and [I'd] been so focused on guitar gear that, of course, on the way there, I realized I'd forgotten my violin. So I had to go back and get that. It's a good thing I left early!

It's probably important to mention as well that most violinists don't usually have a guitar pedal board just lying around their house, and most of the guitar work I do in our band is performed on an acoustic. I had to call up my dear friend Danny from church and ask to borrow his pedal board for the audition because, as I'm listening to the songs, I'm hearing all these effects. I realized I would need distortion, delay and reverb, [and so on].

So, of course, there was that additional learning curve to deal with. Thank God for Danny and for my husband, Daniel, because the pressure was starting to make me slightly crazy, and I began kind of freaking out, thinking, "I'm never going to get this all done in time."

But Daniel talked me off the ceiling. We got everything working, and I realized that the real takeaway here was when you are a working musician, you are never really 100 percent in control or 100 percent comfortable. Learning to work through your discomforts is the key to sanity and success.

Oh, I also made blueberry muffins—that's very important. Any time I've brought food to an event, it's always helped me make friends. So I got the basket of blueberry muffins, my violin, [and my] guitar, and I'm walking to the house. I knocked on the door. I was greeted by Alex, the musical director. We're unloading the car, and then Hozier shows up.

Interestingly, I have done several tours with major artists, but this was the first time the artist was personally at my initial audition. I didn't know he was going to be [there], but the more I thought about Hozier and his music, the more it made total sense: "Of course he's here!" Before, it's always been the musical director and maybe the artist's manager. So I was impressed but also a little nervous. Sometimes you can use that nervous energy in your favor.

MENZIE: Hozier being there really speaks to his character.

EMILY KOHAVI: He is in every nook and cranny of his business. Alex is also his bass player, and he had a little synth, so he just played the chords on the synth. Hozier, whose first name is Andrew, got his guitar and said, "Let's do 'Dinner & Diatribes,'" so we played it together. They seemed to appreciate what they heard and took into consideration that I'd only had the music for two days. There were a few variations in the chorus changes that Hozier wanted voiced a particular way, so he took the time to show me what those voicings were. I made the adjustments, so immediately, he could tell we would work well together.

They played the tune much slower than the recording, which was nice. Then we went to the second song, and that went well too. They asked how long I had played guitar, and I was honest and said it had only been a couple months with the electric. I got an amusing look, so I added, "But I always work really hard!"

Then Hozier showed me this funk rhythm, and it was a style that was really different for me, so that moment wasn't my favorite. I just didn't feel like I played my best or as naturally as I normally do or as I wanted to. The audition concluded, and they shared that they were also considering a few other people. I said, "It's really nice to meet you, and make sure you get a muffin." The energy lifted just a bit. They said, "Wow, these muffins are great! You'd really love our tour because we're all really big foodies." It's funny how simple civilities can positively affect how someone perceives you.

Chapter 31

MENZIE: Had they ever heard you sing?

EMILY KOHAVI: Yes, I did sing a little bit at that audition. They had me sing some harmony parts while I was playing a few of the riffs. They were trying to see what my range was and how it would match up with their other singers. They knew what they needed.

As I was getting ready to leave, heading toward the door, [I met] my worst enemy: a guy with a guitar and a violin, and he's got muscles, the cool haircut with the smile, and he's probably done tours with the likes of Carrie Underwood and Miranda Lambert since he was sixteen, playing electric guitar and violin. In my mind he can totally whoop my ass. That little doubt devil starts creeping in. I hate that doubt guy. I've worked my whole life to rid myself of doubt. But you always have to work at it. I always strive to be as flawless as possible when I audition, but in this case, I was annoyingly human. I felt this experience was a healthy opportunity for me, and in the back of my mind, I just knew I was a good fit for the band.

So when I got home, I showed Daniel the funk riff from the third song, and he reviewed the techniques with me that would bring it to life. I decided I had to own it.

Fast forward to a week later. Though I hadn't heard anything, a few folks I knew suggested to me that I was still in the running. And in the meantime, I had played that funky little riff thingy a zillion times. I started taking videos of myself playing it so I could send them a video of me playing that style. I wanted to show them that I now owned the riff and the style that I'd previously had trouble with. I wanted them to see my work ethic because whether it's blueberry muffins, singing, violin, or a funky little guitar riff, my work ethic is always the same. I felt it was important that they know that.

MENZIE: That's really smart.

EMILY KOHAVI: Well, oddly, I think it worked. I sent it to Alex and said I wanted them to know that I'd been working on this technique, that I think it's really fun, and that I work harder than anyone. Alex emailed back and said they appreciated it. Then I didn't hear anything for a month. I was thinking I didn't get the position, but later, I came to understand that they were just really that busy with the demands of touring and with continuing to audition musicians for the job. During festival season, most of the time, they are doing at least four or five shows in a row, and there are even times that it's ten shows in a row before they have a day in between.

Another month goes by and, again, nothing. Then I got this email from Alex saying, "Emily, if you would like to join us, we would be happy to have you. The job is yours! We would like to fly you out to the next couple of shows—I think they were in Minneapolis and Cincinnati—so you can hang with us and get to know everyone."

MENZIE: Wow, how quickly things can shift and change! Also, what a classy way to have you meet everybody.

EMILY KOHAVI: It was really good because I got to watch the guitar player I was replacing and sit down with her. During sound check they even ran every song for me that involved her playing guitar so I could get a video of her hands. That was really helpful. They had a little sign on the bus that said, "Welcome Emily" and a little bunk ready for me.

Then I had two weeks to learn the catalog of songs and have them memorized in show order, along with the other songs that Hozier might choose to throw in as substitutions.

The show was not on a click track, and they used absolutely no prerecorded tracks. The show was completely live. That was so refreshing and also very cool. I love that because that simply does not happen anymore with big shows. Imagine that—you actually get to genuinely play with the bass player and the drummer, and you get to create the pocket and groove.

MENZIE: That's awesome.

EMILY KOHAVI: Keep in mind that [it] creates some new realities because, although there are some violinists that groove, not all do. They're normally playing as a section under a conductor. You don't ever learn "groove" as a string player in a section.

Chapter 31

Menzie: I don't think everyone understands just how different that reality really is or how crucially important that understanding is. Because now we're embracing the concept of feel, and that is a universe in and of itself.

Emily Kohavi: I'm still dialing that in. It's so different from section playing. It's ears and gut, and it's where trust and instinct take precedent. Sometimes I'll ask the guys in WILDEYES to play something for me so I can work on it and "find it." Some days I have it automatically, and other days, it's elusive.

Menzie: To me, the difference is allowing breath and understanding the space between the notes—the human factor. Humorously, Nashville's concept of the pocket and a European concept of the pocket aren't exactly the same.

Emily Kohavi: You are very right, and that truth can make you slightly crazy. In the two weeks that followed, I had to learn all the songs in the show. Daniel was helping me every day, and we decided to cancel every gig WILDEYES had, every session. We completely cleared the calendar for me to have extra time to learn the Hozier show.

To begin my madness routine, I started with practicing four hours a day. I specifically focused on my guitar technique, and I moved to a six-hour routine, then eight hours. As I began working on the catalog, I quickly ended up working twelve hours a day. The circumstances demanded that level of commitment.

The show was ninety minutes long. Then Hozier had another ten to twelve songs he could possibly pull into any set. Hozier is a big fan of polyrhythms, and he has a couple songs that have a lot of polyrhythms going on, like "Sweet Music," where the rhythm is created like a braided rope. One part overlays another, but all the parts work as one to create the feel. The drummer plays a pattern that repeats but is independent from the hand-clap rhythm, and the hand-clap rhythms are based on a clave phrasing. While this is all going on, there is a backup vocal line sung over the rhythms while Hozier is playing a different rhythm on his guitar that is independent from his vocal, and this is where I play the Jackson 5–funk thing on top of all that. And then, of course, also sing! So getting it to feel relaxed and natural and in the pocket—that was madness.

MENZIE: They say that repetition is the mother of skill!

EMILY KOHAVI: "Sweet Music" was definitely something that was going to have to simmer, but that way of thinking about music and performing was now an exciting new reality and, although it was demanding, I was loving it. I looked at all the prep like a mission, understanding the time frame in which I had to do it. It was a survival mind-set, and that mind-set kept me focused and sane. But it really was emotionally draining, so I even upped my protein intake by forty grams a day. I did an extra two protein shakes each day. I don't know if it helped, but I was centered—kind of like training for the Olympics.

MENZIE: You were definitely in training mode. It was a complete immersion.

EMILY KOHAVI: I took every little edge of advantage that I could.
    I eventually learned all the songs, and I was comfortably running the show. I was given a recording of the show without the girl I was replacing performing and one show with her performing. That way I could learn everything and then practice running it.
    I was playing to a recording of a show they did in Glastonbury, which is this big festival they do every year, and it was helpful and fun because I could hear what Hozier was saying in between songs.
    So day one of rehearsal comes, and by this time, I have collected a bunch of guitars—there are guitars everywhere. Because of all the musical demands of the show, I think I ended up with six guitars that I needed to play, as well as two different violins. I showed up to rehearsal with an absolute army in my trunk, all my axes and my amp, and I'm now the proud owner of two pedal boards. One cool perk of getting the gig was that I could honestly justify buying a bunch of very cool gear. Carter Vintage Guitars had this awesome Rickenbacker that I bought, and Vintage

Chapter 31

King Audio helped with my pedal board needs. The Rickenbacker is really nice. It not only plays well and sounds great, but it also has this unique vintage look, very Beatlesque. And onstage, in front of thousands of people, that matters.

MENZIE: It sure worked for John and George.

EMILY KOHAVI: Yes, and you can't argue with that. We show up to rehearsal and, presto, I have a guitar tech. So, a shout out to Cody! He was a true gift on the tour. As I settled into my new reality, he was always right there to assist me until he knew I was comfortable. Cody was a pro's pro—a true lifesaver. He always called me Miss Emily, and he knew Hozier's music inside and out, so he knew what effect my different settings and the sounds [would make] things work. Cody definitely made my life easier, allowing me the ability to focus on the music.

At rehearsal it took me a minute to settle my nerves. It seems true that the higher the stakes and the more important the gig, the harder we are on ourselves. Any mistakes or oversights we make tend to get exaggerated in our own minds.

But everyone was very happy. The musical director said that we were making really great time. I had everything memorized, so he didn't have to teach me anything. There was nothing to teach; we were just going through the show and making small adjustments.

MENZIE: You have a mesmerizing stage presence, one that's completely infectious. That, too, is an art form. Some people get that, and some people don't.

EMILY KOHAVI: Well, regarding the show visuals, Hozier wanted the general blocking to be consistent because he had learned when to step this way or that way, and the audience always reacted positively when there was interaction between band members.

MENZIE: So you went through the rehearsals and survived.

Emily Kohavi: Yes, and we actually got through every song smoothly by the second day. Hozier was very impressed with how well everything clicked. He was excited [and] happy, and most of all, I think he was relieved.

We did two days of rehearsals with just the band, without the big sound system. Then we did three more days with everything, the sound guys, crew, [and so on], checking all aspects of the show. Then we took [off] the last two days of rehearsal from playing music and went golfing because the chemistry was coming together nicely. Hozier could have just said [that] we were done with rehearsals, so everyone can take the next two days off. But instead, he planned an activity, and we all went to Topgolf in Nashville, which was hilarious. And then we left for the tour.

Just to put all the crazy prep work in perspective—my first show with them was Lollapalooza, where there were eighty thousand people in the crowd. I think [that] over the four days of Lollapalooza, the attendance is around four hundred thousand fans.

Menzie: Eighty thousand people! Fortunately for you, you've played a lot of high-pressure shows.

Emily Kohavi: Thankfully, I had. I've played several awards shows like the CMAs, and I think your typical arena show is somewhere between twenty thousand to thirty thousand people. I've done a lot of those types of shows, but this was my first huge festival.

Menzie: Was there a big difference in the arena experience versus playing for eighty thousand at a festival?

Emily Kohavi: No, not really, because you really can't see the people. You hear that they're there, and you see some people in the front sections, but then you just see colors that look like mountains and waves. It looks like nature, only a little pixelated. You're not sure what is what, but you know there are a ton of humans out there. Oddly, I wasn't nervous onstage with Hozier.

Chapter 31

MENZIE: How did playing guitar in a large stage, [as opposed to] playing violin in more intimate settings, alter your approach to your visual performance?

EMILY KOHAVI: Funny you should ask that—I worked on being comfortable with the guitar postures and big staging exactly like I worked on the music. The movements and the body positions on guitar are so different from the violin, and visuals in this band were extremely important.

At my hubby's suggestion, I actually worked with a full-length mirror the last couple of days. I also watched videos of my favorite concert musicians, and then I just jumped in.

It was certainly a different mind-set. The role I was filling in the band was as the second guitar player. Sometimes I doubled riffs, sometimes I kept a riff going while Hozier would be singing, and sometimes the guitar parts were an integral part of the ensemble. No matter what I was playing, my number one job was to bring additional energy and excitement to the music and the performance. But you can't really rehearse energy, so it's not until you are onstage, performing with the other musicians around you, that you are able to create and feed off of the band's energy. That's what makes live performance so special.

We did this one song, "Angel of Small Death and the Codeine Scene," that has a violin solo. I don't think we played it at Lollapalooza, because I think the first time I did this backbend style move was at the Newport Folk Festival. I remember thinking it was showy, but it was appropriate because it was a flashy, kind-of-dramatic solo with a very energetic ending. The crowd went nuts. The band loved it, so that became a thing in the show. I kind of got myself into trouble because it's actually quite difficult to do a backbend at the end of your violin solo and walk backwards to your place in heels.

MENZIE: What effect did playing a high-energy tour and major festivals have on your ideas for WILDEYES? As your fans can attest, WILDEYES is also a very visual band, but the style is different.

EMILY KOHAVI: Historically, most of our songs for WILDEYES had been written in a singer-songwriter style, but after experiencing this tour, the band and I realized and agreed that there is a productive place, as well as a necessity, for more energetic material in our WILDEYES show, especially as we intend to do more festivals. The new material has a lot more rock 'n' roll energy. This transition took patience in developing because we didn't want to abandon our initial vision, and making a stylistic transition is a tricky undertaking [that is] never without a little bit of discourse. WILDEYES enjoys doing festivals because we crave the energy of a good outdoor show, and we're not going to ever get to the next level if we don't have a great, energetic festival set.

MENZIE: The visual reinforcement brings the music to life because the audience may not hear the subtle nuances that musicians hear. Visual reinforcement connects the dots for the audience.

EMILY KOHAVI: And without them, you don't have a career. We were talking about this just yesterday while discussing marketing and branding—our favorite established artists, like Fleetwood Mac or Queen, knew how to package their mystique both onstage and off. Visually, nothing was left to chance.

MENZIE: You've got to think like a complete industry, and what you just went through is a good example of it being done right.

EMILY KOHAVI: You're basically an entrepreneur, a small business, and just think—if a label gets involved, they're going to see if your business model is working, if you have fans, how much money you're generating, and if there is an opportunity for them to make the project more successful. If so, they'll get on board.

MENZIE: The music must always be protected, but to do so, there is also the responsibility of managing the details of business. Both are necessary, and if you get either one wrong, you lose. You must protect your art, and you must understand how business works.

Chapter 31

Emily Kohavi: The longer I am in the music business and the harder we work as a band, the more I appreciate the success of major artists. Some people are quick to put down high-visibility artists like John Mayer, but I feel that John Mayer has the entire package. He's good-looking, he's a good performer, he's a good songwriter, he's a good player, he's a good singer, and he also puts on a great show. Being successful and sustaining that success is the most difficult thing in the world, so who are we to say anything about any major artist in that position? You really have no idea of the difficulty and the pressures a major touring artist experiences.

Menzie: Many musicians feel guilty about their success because of the foolish belief that success diminishes the authenticity of their art, but without success, no one knows about their art.

Emily Kohavi: There might be great bands out there making amazing music, but how is anyone ever going to know about them if they don't want to think about making money? No one will ever know about the great music that they've made, because they didn't want to take on the responsibility of learning the business side of making music.

Menzie: What were some of your big takeaways and favorite moments from the Hozier tour? Do you have any final thoughts you could share?

Emily Kohavi: The biggest takeaway for me, outside of performing the music, was how well Hozier ran his organization and how considerate he was of others. He always considered the impact of every decision he made and reviewed the impact of every detail. He showed amazing grace to everyone around him, whether that was providing extremely nice hotel accommodations for the band and crew or not charging his fans an extra fee for his meet and greets. He always scrutinized how his decisions affected those around him.

As far as my favorite moments go, it has to include the camaraderie between the musicians and the consistent effort we put into the show every night. Everyone brought 100 percent to the music and to the show.

The performances were always fresh, genuine, and packed with energy. We never left anything on the table. The audiences were great, and every night, we witnessed packed arenas with thunderous applause and thousands of cell phone fireflies when Hozier performed a special ballad. It was really something to witness and be a part of. My other big takeaway was learning to embrace and enjoy the art of business, [as well as] focusing on remembering that it is also an art form that needs to be developed, just like the craft of music making.

Chapter 32

The Outro

"There is a constant and compelling urge within man to find the magnificent life."

—Anthony Norvell

Creatives are driven to express.

Professionally sharing your artistic gifts with the world is a hard-earned opportunity. Therefore, the amount of competition for top positions is rightfully fierce. So follow your drive, trust it, adjust your plan as needed, and be unwilling to compromise your principles, your vision, your work ethic, or your integrity.

For the record, that's nonnegotiable!

When the arts choose you as their medium for expression, it's a calling, and those who are committed enough to participate in the arts as a profession must understand what that entails completely. When you choose music as a profession, you play for keeps, and the stakes are high.

Our true responsibility as musicians is to make the listeners feel something.

That is the rule, and it will always be the rule.

Our challenge as artists is to awaken and stir emotions in the listener. Our job is to change their state. How you accomplish this is up to you. The greats figured it out, and that's what makes the greats elite.

According to myth, the door to the greats is left unlocked intentionally, but the bouncer at the door is tough to get past. Rumor has it that the bouncer goes by the nickname of Artistic Scrutiny, and I've heard he never takes a day off. The word on the street is that sometimes he will let in Clever, and many times, he has let in Unique, but he always lets in Brilliance and Authenticity. I have also heard he's thrown out Trendy and Mindless on several occasions. As they say in the biz, it's a tough crowd!

As we continue to pursue our professional careers, though we believe we are clear about our intentions, the music industry quickly introduces us to any deficiencies we may have overlooked. The industry gleefully exposes us to any and all of our naivety and flawed business strategies.

We are tested quickly with both successes and setbacks. At that point, we are provided the opportunity to adjust our game plan, and with luck, we gain a little confidence or humility as our resolve is tested. The good news is that through the challenges and achievements we encounter, our resolve strengthens and our vision gains clarity.

When we arrive at the intersection of success and failure, we are presented with the opportunity to realign our priorities. These moments of realignment often define our success.

It's no secret that success is not always based solely on talent. The truth is that success is always a combination of talent, vision, timing, professionalism, and a large dose of hard work and tenacity—topped off with a serving of humility and a dollop of luck.

When musicians pursue their professional careers, it's understood right from the start that the pursuit is a marathon, not a sprint. Just as the best practice is to serve the song, it is also a best practice to pace ourselves to the finish line when running a marathon-style career.

On your artistic journey, you will morph through many incarnations of your artistic persona, and you will sport many hats. You may start as a solo artist only to intersect later with a band that enhances your ability to express. You may have the opportunity to produce or cowrite. Perhaps professional circumstances will offer you better career opportunities or a better chance for career longevity. If, by chance, you decide to leave one situation for another, there are a few simple rules you should always honor.

Never sacrifice your reputation by poorly handling a business matter, and never burn bridges.

Chapter 32

There is a right way to handle business affairs. The secret is to conduct your business as if you were the other party. Always consider how you would want to be treated if you were on the receiving end of your decisions, and always treat others with the same respect you seek. Most of us have heard the saying "Be nice to people on your way up because you will meet them again on your way down." In the music business, that is a fundamental truth.

If money defined success, all wealthy people would be blissfully happy. I think we can all agree that's not the case. What many people don't grasp is that money is an energy. And like anything else, it is an exchange of value—nothing more, nothing less. If you get the art of money right, that's one less problem you'll have, but simply having money doesn't mean your life will be without challenges.

Money is a medium, and you need it to enable financial freedom and the accomplishment of your goals. But it's just one of many necessary parts of the success formula.

Does fame define success? Let's recall what Andy Warhol said in 1968: "In the future, everyone will be world-famous for 15 minutes."

Fame is like blue jeans in that it has a natural tendency to fade. That being said, as long as you don't define yourself by your fame, fame is no different than a roller coaster ride. Hopefully, your admission ticket isn't too expensive.

Career longevity and industry respect are two metrics of success I truly admire. They are the natural by-products of vision, craft, talent, imagination, and hard work. In today's music business, longevity is usually accomplished by embracing those attributes and adding a twist of diversification and humility.

A stellar example of this approach is Bleachers' front man and producer Jack Antonoff. There is a reason he is considered a top producer in music today. Here are a few boxes Antonoff has checked:

Multiple instrumentalist: check

Vocalist: check

Successful songwriter and lyricist: check

The Outro

Diversification of musical genres: check

Imagination: check

Creation of new and unique sounds and textures: check

The ability to blend those sounds together and create great sound pairings: check

The gift of listening to other artists' ideas and working as a strong cowriter: check

Grammy-winning Producer of the Year (Nonclassical): check

Multiple Grammy Awards for Production and Songwriting: check

Antonoff's music industry success speaks volumes and influences many. Today's music industry favors this type of independent entrepreneurial model because the "big box" model is wounded, which means two irrefutable truths for musicians.

The first is that control and responsibility have shifted back to the artists. That's the good news.

The second is that when you have this control, it puts all decision making—both artistic and entrepreneurial—squarely on you. This means you inherit the opportunities both for success and failure with creativity and business. That will remain the model until you have gained enough success to decide if you will choose to partner with others or not. That is why I push into the topics of personal success as hard as the artistic factions.

Again, I quote Steve Gadd: "They call it the music business for a reason."

Here are my final thoughts:

Study multiple genres of music, study communication, and, most of all, study the greats!

If you choose to be part of music history, you only have to do one simple thing: write yourself into the story!

Chapter 32

How would you like to be remembered? Write that script.

Do you wish to be a philanthropist and work to lift others up? If so, write that script.

Are you multitalented—an amazing singer, a quiet songwriter, a flashy instrumentalist? Write the script.

If you don't clearly visualize your role in music, then your chances of success are slim, and music history will be written without your voice.

You are the only one who defines your role in music history!

You don't choose music; music chooses you.

You have gifts that make the world a better place.

And that's why you're here.

Chapter 33
Bernard Purdie

There are few drummers who have left their mark as indelibly as Bernard Purdie. The man even has a beat named after him: the *Purdie Shuffle*. He will be mimicked for decades to come, and drummers are forever grateful for his contributions. His wisdom is pithy, with a wink of humor. We can all learn a lot from Mr. "Rock Steady."

Interview
Menzie: Bernard, whenever I see you, I always genuflect for the simple reason that your iconic drumming has influenced so many players in the music business over the years—and not just drummers but bass players and plenty of other studio musicians. You've used inventive techniques to create your stable and incredible pocket in your drumming on songs such as "Rock Steady" by Aretha Franklin, "Babylon Sisters," and "Home at Last" by Steely Dan; these are just three examples of your propulsion, and [it's] timekeeping at its musical finest. Will you start by telling us a little bit about your book *Let the Drums Speak!* [*The Life Story of the World's Most Recorded Drummer*]?

Bernard Purdie: Yes. Well, it has taken only fifteen years to get it together, and I am tickled pink. It's my autobiography, and a third of the book covers my upbringing as a youngster. So I am really happy about that because it really does work. I am extremely pleased because we touched on a lot of good things. And it is a very, very positive book.

It's really about my journey, and it covers just about every facet of

Chapter 33

the music business. I need people to know and understand that it takes a lot just to be a drummer. You've got to learn your craft—that is number one. Then you've got to learn about the music business in order to make your craft work and to survive in the music world. You only have a few good years, as they call it. Everybody wants you when you're young. Nobody wants you when you're older, and then, of course, when you're old, forget about it. Now there is a trend that's benefiting the super young and the super old, so it's the guys in the middle who are catching the devil right now. You have to know both craft and business.

MENZIE: One consistent truth about the music business is that trends change on a dime, but you are not only an old-school legend, you're still an active drummer doing sessions, gigs, and other projects. What are the significant changes you've witnessed in the music business over the course of your career?

BERNARD PURDIE: Years ago, analog was the only way to do things. Well, analog has come and gone, and although it's still used, it's expensive. Now we are into digital. It is cheaper, and it is faster, but all the warmth from the analog world is lost. So now they're trying to find the warmth from the analog world and see if they can bring that to the digital world. Somebody is going to invent it and really make it happen.

I can take you back to the man who invented multitracking. I was working with Les Paul for several years, and he is the one who actually taught me how to "fix" records—actually, [to] fix drum parts and all those little things. This was in the early part of the sixties. Personally, I didn't know that what Les was doing was innovative. I didn't know that other people weren't doing it. All I knew was that I was able to fix records because of what he was doing and how he was doing it in the control room. As things went on, I started to learn what it meant to overdub, to actually help fix records. I got very, very good at it because he told me I was a natural.

During that time 50 percent of my work in music was fixing other people's records. Overdubbing—that's what it was called. Consequently, you had a lot of people in the industry who thought they knew everything about the business, and, of course, they found out that they really didn't. That's how things transformed over the years. That's how session players came into prominence.

I feel lucky, and I feel very honored to have spent a lot of time with Les Paul. I learned my craft, and I learned it well. He let me know how important things were, but he also let me know what I was contributing to it because I had something to offer. I had a "feel" that generated some excitement and complemented the sound. I really couldn't tell you exactly how all of these things were happening; all I knew was that I was good at it. I pulled things together. I feel like I went right down the middle. This was in the pre–click track days, and sometimes you had to track to fix a slower part or a faster part. But I felt like what I played, with my overdubs and my fixing of the records, was able to pull the musicians and the music together. That was what Les Paul was telling me. This was my gift. I had something that most people just didn't have. I learned to create and to make things work and happen, but it took a while.

MENZIE: This process of overdubbing was very revolutionary at the time, and you were coming into prominence at that same time as well. You were one of a handful of musicians who could step into overdubbing, or "punching," which was very awkward for most drummers. You have amazing timing. Not every drummer is blessed with that gift. You also have a signature sound, and you understood how to work within the realm of restrictions and needs that the studios had. We've now gotten to a point in the industry where everything is recorded with a rigid click or on a grid with prerecorded drum sounds, and in that process, a lot of personality is sacrificed. What advice would you give to a young drummer about the changes in the way studios are currently recording drum tracks?

BERNARD PURDIE: Well, you can make a click track work, but it has to work from you because the quarter note doesn't change. You can be right on it, right behind it, or on top of it. A click track can be thought of as an instrument, and if you look at it that way, you won't have a problem. You can create a feel around it. Most folks don't know how to incorporate dynamics with a click, so that was my incentive. You have an inner clock. That click track can work for you if you know your inner clock. Let the music breathe. Don't pressure yourself. Don't think of the click track as something to restrict you. Let the music flow out of you. Even if it means playing behind the beat some, playing right on the beat, or [playing] on top. You can do that with any song, but you've got to feel it. It has to be a positive attitude. Otherwise, you are going to be in serious trouble because you're going to sound like a machine.

MENZIE: Changing gears a bit, what business advice do you think would serve young musicians who are coming up in the music field today? What do you think has changed about the ways we do business as freelance artists, studio musicians, and performers?

BERNARD PURDIE: You must understand your craft. There is no limitation to what you can do when you really know your craft. I don't care whether it's guitar, piano, bass, or drums. You must learn how to make that instrument breathe, talk, sing, play, and perform before you can start getting into the business of the music itself. Today the businesspeople want you to be self-contained because if you're self-contained, then they don't have to worry about four or five different people in the band. They only have to worry about one: the one who is a reader, writer, composer, performer—an artist. They get all that in one. And that's the business side.

That means that one person gets the money, and they can do what they want with it. And the record label is not responsible.

MENZIE: How do you think that affects a drummer in today's industry? You probably agree that having more skills protects musicians?

BERNARD PURDIE: It affects the drummer even more because the drummers are not usually the band leaders. They work for the artist, so diversification in skill sets helps. It helps if you sing, and it helps if you play additional instruments.

MENZIE: Speaking of vocals, you were the musical director for the legendary Aretha Franklin.

Bernard Purdie: Yes, I was for about five years, but I was a drummer first.

Menzie: As both a drummer and a director, what did your job with her entail?

Bernard Purdie: I know, it's hard to believe, but [I was the] drummer, yes. Band leader, yes. Conductor, yes. Front man, yes. Sound man, yes. Lighting, yes. All of this was part of the job. And I still had to deal with everybody else in the band as well. It became my responsibility. I ended up being the travel agent. I oversaw everything. It was a way of life. It was something that needed to be done. I didn't have other people working for me except band members.

Menzie: Did you run the rehearsals? I'm going to guess that putting the songs together might have fallen on your shoulders as well.

Bernard Purdie: A lot of it, yes. When it came down to the records, it started out with Aretha and usually with me, and then we'd bring in the other folks. Then we'd move on to the next step, which would be the arranger and then the writer. We had all these different facets going on. My job was to be in the middle and to make sure everything went smoothly. I had to do it from both sides of the fence, and I loved it because I was good at it. I learned that when you have to deal with a diva, you deal with a diva. This lady would always be awarded that courtesy because that's who she was. She was a legend!

Menzie: You've had the honor of working with so many greats. Will you share with us what it was like working with a legendary musician like Chuck Rainey or a group like Steely Dan?

Bernard Purdie: Yes. It is always about learning to compromise. And I'm going to say that again—sometimes you just need to shut up and let others speak. You've got to leave it alone until it comes down to a point where what you say is going to enhance what they're saying. You hired these people because they are so good at what they do. Don't interfere with it. You hired them because they are creative; you hired them because they can do the job.

It was always a treat to be in the studio with Chuck Rainey, Cornell Dupree, [and] Richard Tee. But it's the complete opposite sometimes, when you're working live. You've got to learn how to retreat. You're not going to get the same thing that you did in the studio because they want to create something else when it's a live show. They want to feel that energy and share what they have. They can move the music a little bit more. They can change and don't necessarily have to play what they played on the record.

MENZIE: I use an expression called antenna, meaning that you just have to put the music ahead of you and take your own sense of ego out of it.

Would you tell us a little about the Steely Dan sessions? "Babylon Sisters"—I think everyone should be tied to a chair and made to listen to that because that pocket is so infectious.

BERNARD PURDIE: [He laughs.] Steely Dan, they were perfectionists. Well, I am a perfectionist. Chuck Rainey was a perfectionist. Paul Griffin was a perfectionist. Everybody [who] played was. When you put these people together, you've got to give them some leeway. It was a feel, it was the notes themselves, [and] it was how it was played and when it was played. So you have to take all those things into consideration. You have to make everybody happy, but don't be afraid to speak your mind if you know that what you are doing is right or wrong. If it's wrong, it's not going to work. It's not going to fit.

I just know what I want. I also know what I need to hear. But I also realize that when they hire you, they want to hear what they want to hear. So you've got to be diplomatic. You've got to give them what they ask for. But then you take them to the next step—you know, put my own little thing in to make me feel good, to enhance what is already there.

I'll give you an example: "Home at Last." The first time that they asked me about doing "Home at Last," they had already pre-recorded it three or four times with the whole band. They said they didn't want a shuffle. They wanted straight eighth notes. I said okay, and I listened. And as I was listening, I started smiling. Halfway through the song, they stopped the music and asked, "Why are you smiling? Do you have your idea?" And I said, "Oh yeah. I know exactly what I want to play. I want to play the Purdie shuffle."

"No, no, no, *no*! We don't want a shuffle! We don't want that!"

I said, "You've never heard it! Once you've heard it, you will know exactly what the Purdie shuffle is, and it's gonna work with the song!"

And I was very calm and very quiet. I didn't raise my voice. I got my line from what Chuck Rainey was playing. Chuck started his thing. I did my half-time and started with the Purdie shuffle, then things progressed. And you had to see the expressions on their faces in the control room. They all just stood up because, yes, that was exactly what they were looking for, and they didn't know it. Now that's magical. Thirty-five or forty years later, every drummer in the world has to learn the Purdie shuffle.

MENZIE: You influenced Led Zeppelin with that, and you also influenced Jeff Porcaro. They asked him where he got the feel for "Rosanna," and he came right out and said he stole it from Bernard Purdie. Someone who also stole from Bernard Purdie—John Bonham. Those musicians understood what a magical creation you had come up with. And it pulses!

You have such an incredibly identifiable sound. Do you think we have lost the appreciation for a signature sound in today's recording industry?

BERNARD PURDIE: No, we haven't. We just have to understand that there are other people out there who have the ability to create but maybe just haven't had the chance to do it. Because everybody [who] plays can do something of their own that they feel is natural, something natural for that person. We can all learn and be technical, but now you've got to take that technique, and you've got to learn how to bend the notes a little bit. You've got to slide into some things, not smack it so hard other times. But you've got to put it together as a whole unit. That's what it's about. We all have something to offer, but we only have it after we learn our craft—then we start being creative.

Chapter 33

MENZIE: One of the ideas you hit on early in this conversation is that nowadays musicians not only have to learn the craft and the art form of their instrument, they also have to understand how business works. There's craft and then there's artistry, and then the business side of it is a craft they need to learn as well.

BERNARD PURDIE: You have to. Because this is called the music business. It's only 10 percent music and then 90 percent business. We don't want to be bogged down, but you've got to understand that this is the money. How you are going to survive, and how you are going to be good at what you do.

MENZIE: I've tried not to focus too much on techniques in these interviews, but I've had the fortune of seeing you up close, and you do this wicked ghost note finger-tap thing when you cross stick. Will you talk a little bit about that technique and how you came up with that? You also sing a lot of parts, so you are verbally connected to the pocket as well.

BERNARD PURDIE: The finger taps . . . well, they basically came from the rebound and from the control of the stick. When you play it straight, you've got rebound in your stick. But the idea is you've got to allow the stick to work for you. What I had to do was learn to control that. So I did that first with my fingers.

When I was growing up, I used to hear the trains going by the house at night—chuck-a-da, chuck-a-da, chuck-a-da—and [they] would get faster and faster. But with the Purdie shuffle, you don't have to get fast. The worst thing that you can do (and something that interrupts the flow of the groove) is to be fast. You let it lay—chuck-a-da, chuck-a-da, whack-a-da, chuck-a-da / chuck-a-da, chuck-a-da, whack-a-da, chuck-a-da, [and so on]—and you let your fingers do the walking; you let your fingers do the talking! And to add better connection, you do the grunting and singing of the sounds. The short answer is . . . that's called feel.

The rebound is the same thing [as] when you're doing cross stick with it, letting it flow. After, it gets recorded and it gets played back and you say, "Oh man, they're gonna love this." All you're doing is helping yourself keep time without it being super loud. The loud part is going to be where you're going to put the back beat, and the back beat can be put on any notes that you want.

MENZIE: Would you expand on the concept of singing the rhythm sounds a little bit? It's an old-school technique, one that I think absolutely needs to be kept at the forefront of the discussion because it's such a cool thing.

BERNARD PURDIE: Basically, it's using your voice as a fifth limb. I like to think of it as humanizing the feel. It connects you more to the groove and to your feel. If you can't sing your parts, it means there may be a gap in how you are connecting to the music.

MENZIE: Humanizing—love it!

BERNARD PURDIE: The music comes from us first. I also practice at slower tempos. By slowing the tempo down, you get a chance to breathe and dig into the groove.

MENZIE: I think the takeaway for the reader is [that] by singing your parts, you are more connected to the feel.

BERNARD PURDIE: It's all about connection, and I absolutely do feel it by singing it. I also always know internally where my 1 is. That's the pulse that matters. Knowing where 1 is will do it for you every time. You relax your hands and feet and lock in your time instinctively. You don't worry about it being loud or worry about where the accents are going to be, you just feel it—you are the time.

MENZIE: Donald Fagen said in an interview that you put signs up by your drums that said, "You've gone and done it—you've hired the hitmaker." What is your secret to making so many hit record grooves?

BERNARD PURDIE: The first thing that you need to do is stop thinking with a predetermined mind-set, because you don't know what you are going to come across until you get into the studio. You gotta wait and find out. Now, for me, the easiest part is if I have the music score or the lead parts. With the music, I can sing the phrases, [and] I can sing the rhythms. The notes tell me exactly what is going on. It makes things so much easier because you don't have to think about what you are going to do. There it is in front of you. That is the mistake that too many drummers have made—don't go in there with anything preconceived. Go and look at the music, and see what you have: see what the rhythms are and what the melody is. Being able to sing the melody, being able to sing the rhythms—you have to put it in perspective.

MENZIE: That is what so many of the greats do. They take it and sing their parts first and get a total conceptual understanding before they take it to their instrument.

BERNARD PURDIE: I didn't know that in the beginning. I learned it as I went along, but that is exactly the right way to do it.

MENZIE: It's obvious to anyone who sees you play that you are completely immersed in the music and you are completely connected to the moment. When you play, you let the music take you on a journey. What advice would you give to young drummers in order for them to grasp the importance of that concept?

BERNARD PURDIE: It's all about the music. It's all about the understanding. It's all about allowing it to flow. We get caught up with some of the wrong things, like speed or playing ten thousand notes. If you understand musically what it is that makes things work, it's always less is more. The less that you have to play, the better you're going to sound, but you have to make it work because that is your job: keep the time always. You're the timekeeper, and now learn where the flow of the music is going. Then you can follow.

At the same time, you learn how to lead once you follow. But you have to learn the rhythms, the melody, and the playing first, before you can start running out there and being a super leader. It's also necessary to understand the importance of a positive attitude. If you have a positive attitude, you can do anything. You can take the music to any place you want. But at the same time, you realize that less being more also works. Now you're back in control.

MENZIE: Something that I see in many of the touring drummers these days is that everything has to be forte, everything has to be extremely loud, almost knock-you-over loud. But when you play, you have a lot of inside volumes, and you have a lot of midrange volumes and loud volumes as well. You can also explode in a New York second when it's time to make that intense dynamic range happen. How do you create that kind of pocket?

BERNARD PURDIE: Well, I learned to create that because dynamics are everything to me. It's always been that way and always will be. When you are able to do any song dynamically, from the bottom all the way up to the top and back down, then you've captured what you're supposed to capture. You are now being the singer. You're now being the player. You're now being the instrument of choice for what's going on. You've got to allow yourself to feel the rhythm. You must dynamically learn that. Then you're listening to what everyone else is listening to. Then you can go ahead and play your part. Dynamics are the key to everything that a drummer does.

MENZIE: Drummers sometimes have a tendency to think *dynamic* means "turned down," but it means to play musically.
One of the most iconic drum moments ever recorded—and one of my personal favorites—is your break in Aretha Franklin's "Rock Steady." I use that as an example all the time to let people hear a really fun, intricate, musical drum break. Would you tell the story about how that came to be?

BERNARD PURDIE: We were all in the studio together, and Aretha was sitting at the piano with the music. As we were running things down, she got happy. We were so into the groove and the feel of the song that the music fell off the piano. So she called for somebody to come in and pick up the music because she didn't want to stop. Somebody picked it up—Reeve Martin. We continued, and she continued, too, because she was singing. She kept singing, and in reality, it was like sixteen bars. So we just never stopped. And then as we were going along, I hopped in a little bit of a solo there. It was awesome. It was absolutely awesome to play that solo and keep things going. But it was all part of the dynamics. That whole thing was an accident. We tried to do it again, twenty or thirty more takes, but they didn't work, and we ended up going back to when the music fell off the stand, and they used the demo.

MENZIE: That really underlines the fact that the artistry can be spontaneous; it can be natural. You have to know your craft well so that technique doesn't get in the way and you can just respond to whatever the magic moments are. You'll never get that moment if you try programming it in advance.

In closing, what are some of your favorite moments you've had with artists? And what are some of your favorite songs?

BERNARD PURDIE: The thing is, I've had so many favorite times with so many different artists. They were great for me, and each one of them was exceptional, like "Rock Steady"—because what happened there is that the drums and the vocals were equal throughout. And then, of course, there's Steely Dan—so many different songs with them. But then I turn around, and I love Hall and Oates' "She's Gone." There have been so many wonderful moments in my life with records that have become multi million sellers and that are now standards. There are hundreds, literally hundreds, that are standards of the world.

MENZIE: That's the fun part of your story. I want to make sure that tomorrow's musicians understand that important work has been done and it's work that needs to be reviewed, recognized, and understood.

I want to thank you for all the unique contributions you've given us in your musical career. We must never forget to honor the legends, like you, [who] brought us here. And I just want to say thanks for the interview and taking your time. You're a gracious man, and I appreciate it more than I can say.

BERNARD PURDIE: It's my pleasure, sir. Definitely my pleasure. I enjoyed it immensely.

Chapter 34

The Idea

THE *IDEA*.

It often starts small. It's usually something that just randomly pops into your head. At first blush, you may dismiss it, until the idea begins to nag you, and it won't leave you alone. A few days pass, and the idea revisits you. This time the tone is different—it's slightly more urgent, slightly more serious. The idea has no intention of leaving you alone, because it wants to be expressed, and it has picked *you* as the vehicle.

Maestro, pen, please . . .

Index

3rd and Lindsley, 279
360 deal, 94
The $150,000 Music Degree (Barker), 92–94

absolute pitch, 61
Accents and Rebounds (Stone), 177–78
access, 297–98
accolades, 261
accompaniment, 259–60
accountability, 169. *See also* responsibility
acrylic nails, 290
Adkins, Trace, 327
Advanced Techniques for the Modern Drummer (Chapin), 178
advertisements, 94
AFM. *See* American Federation of Musicians
Against All Odds (Ray), 194
Aja: drummers on, 62; Rainey on, 62–63
Allan, Davie, 193
Allen, Brian, 324
Allen, James, 220

"All for the Love of Sunshine," 195
Alvin, Craig: on creativity, 142; on Fitchuk, 132–33; on *Golden Hour*, 132–45; on Grammys, 145; on Hall, 151–52; on Kunkel, 137; on mixing, 148–49; on Muscle Shoals, 150–51; on Musgraves, 132–45; on Phillips, 152; on practicing, 147–48; on RCA Studio A, 153; on Renn, 133; on style, 133; on voice, 134
"Always Remember Us This Way," 23
Amazing Slow Downer, 335–36
American Federation of Musicians (AFM), 277
amplifiers: Cobb on, 17–18; emulating, 282–83; Mason, B., on, 282–83, 287–88
amp rack, 287
analog technology: Purdie on, 354. *See also* vinyl; Specific analog technologies
Anderson East, 20

"Angel of Small Death and the Codeine Scene," 344
antenna, 358
Antonoff, Jack: influence of, 351; success and, 350–51
anxiety, 77
Arnold, Eddy, 202
Arrows, 193
Art of the Start (Kawasaki), 113
art-only perspective, 85. *See also* creativity
As a Man Thinketh (Allen, J.), 220
assumptions, 1
Atkins, Chet, 305–6; Cobb on, 24–25; Curb on, 186; influence of, 158
Atkins, Rodney, 203
attorney types, 86
audiobooks, 210
auditions: Gonzalez on, 34–35; Kohavi, E., on, 335–39
authenticity: Cobb on, 16; Kohavi, D., on, 318–19. *See also* honesty; original content
Autobiography of a Yogi (Yogananda), 53, 76
automation, 209

"Babylon Sisters," 172, 353
baggage, 70–71
balance, 105
"Ballad of a Teenage Queen," 201
Bareilles, Sara, 262
Barker, Rick: on advertisements, 94; background of, 81–83; on Borchetta, 83; on conversations, 95; on education, 91–92; on expectations, 80–81; on fan base, 84–85, 87–88, 96; on power transfer, 94; on publishing rights, 95–96; on record deals, 89–90; on registration, 95–96; on resource models, 95; services offered by, 95–99; on streaming, 85; on success, 85, 89–90, 95–96; on Swift, 91–94; on terminology, 98; on work ethic, 84
Barresi, Joe, 31
Bartholomew, Dave, 200
Basement, 279
Bass Bootcamp, 75
Baxter, Skunk, 112
Bayers, Eddie, 230
Baylor University, 188
Beatles, 130, 301, 309; branding and, 270; Cobb on, 8–9, 11, 15; Mason, B., on, 292; Rainey on, 67–68; rejection of, 222; Tate, J., on, 300; tour 1965, 67–68
Beato, Rick, 296
Beauty and Sadness, 332
Becker, Walter, 54
Begin Again, 28
Bellamy Brothers, 195, 196
Belmont University, 102, 188; alumni relationships, 106–7; balance and, 105; Fisher on, 104–5; internships, 107; music therapy at, 107–8; Performing

Arts Center, 109; responsibility and, 105; skill sets learned at, 103, 105–6; songwriting program at, 108; success and, 105–6
Benioff, Mark, 76
Benton, Brook, 195, 199
Beverly, Frankie, 207
big band, 178–79
"Big in Vegas," 195
Big Machine Records, 80, 116–17
Billy Jack, 195
Blackmun, Harry, 218
"Black River," 250
Bleachers, 350–51
Block, Ron, 266
"Blueberry Hill," 200
Bluebird Cafe, 321
"Blues Theme," 193
Bonham, John, 359
Boone, Debby, 196, 197
bop jazz, 179
Borchetta, Scott, 80; Barker on, 83
Bowie, David, 282
Boyer, Jim, 301
Bradbury, Phil, 288
Bradly, Owen, 200
branding: Beatles and, 270; examples, 270; Fisher on, 104; Hull on, 270; Kohavi, E., on, 345; Parton and, 269–71; Swift and, 270; Tate, J., on, 300
Brice, Lee, 203, 237
bridges, 55–56
Brill Building, 204

Brock, Napoleon Murphy, 42–43
bro-country, 299
Brooks, Garth, 201–2
Brown, James, 114
Brown, Ray, 57
Brown, Sawyer, 195, 197
Buddhism, 53
budgeting, 268–69
Bukovac, Tom, 241
Burdon, Eric, 195
Burke, Solomon, 195
"Burning Bridges," 195
Burns, Ken, 200; Curb on, 201–2
business skills, 4
Byrne, Raine Hozier, 333

CAA. *See* Creative Artists Agency
Caesar, Shirley, 66
Cal State, 188
Campbell, Ashley: advice from, 126; on genres, 117–18; on honesty, 118; on Jackson, C., 124–25; on McCartney, 121; on Nashville, 127–28; on networking, 126–27; on success, 126; on touring, 119–20; on writing, 123–24
"Candy Man," 195
Carlile, Brandi: Cobb on, 17; Grammys and, 22
cartage companies, 288
Carter, June, 201
Carter, Mel, 195
Cash, Johnny, 200, 202; Curb on, 201

Cassidy, Shaun, 196
Castro, Rod, 95
Chaka Kahn, 59
Chantels, 199
"Chapel of Love," 199
Chapin, Jim, 177–78
character, 16
Charles, Ray, 9, 16
Chester, Gary, 178
Chiccarelli, Joe, 148
chorus, 55–56
"Chuck E's in Love," 59, 65
Churchill, Winston, 219
Clapton, Eric, 18–19
Claremont, Bob, 306
clarity, 77–78
Clearmountain, Bob, 305
Clement, Jack, 201
click tracks: Harden on, 235–36; Purdie on, 355–56; Rainey on, 57
Clinton, Bill, 217–18
CMA. *See* Country Music Association
Cobb, Dave: on amplifiers, 17–18; on Anderson East, 20; on Atkins, C., 24–25; on authenticity, 16; on Beatles, 8–9, 11, 15; on Carlile, 17; on character, 16; on Charles, 16; on community, 6–7; on competition, 6–7; on concept albums, 18–19; Curb on, 190–91, 204; on Eagles, 11; on Emerick, 9; on guitar tones, 17–18; on Holly, 11; on honesty, 16; influence on, 9–11; on Isbell, 17; on Jennings, 16–17; on Johns, 9; on Kramer, 9; on Little Richard, 10–11; on Low Country Sound, 19–20; on Nashville, 24; on O'Brien, 9; on optimism, 7; on Phillips, 15; on Presley, 11; on producers, 8–9; on RCA Studio A, 12; on Redding, 10, 16; on Rogers, 16; on *Southern Family*, 18–19; on Stapleton, 16; on Starr, 7–8; on Stewart, R., 16; on success, 22; on technology, 13; on vinyl, 14; on voice, 16–17
Cobham, Billy, 236
Colaiuta, Vinnie, 278
Colter, Jessi, 18–19
Columbia Studio A, 190
communication: Famularo on, 160. *See also* conversations; listening
community: Cobb on, 6–7; hip-hop and, 6. *See also* networking
comparisons, 1
compassion, 214
competition: Cobb on, 6–7; Harden on, 239–40; Mason, B., on, 280
compromising, 357–58
concept albums, 18–19
Conley, Savannah, 20
consistency, 273
conversations, 95
Cooper, Bradley, 23

Cooper, Peter, 260–61
Country Music Association (CMA): Awards 2015, 20–21; formation of, 200–201
Creative Artists Agency (CAA), 23–24
creativity: Alvin on, 142; discipline and, 244–45; DIY business model and, 210–11; entrepreneurship and, 111–12; Mason, B., on, 285; organization compared with, 46; procrastination and, 245; spontaneity and, 46; tenacity and, 273–75. *See also* imagination
Crocker, Frankie, 66
Crow, Sheryl, 199
Curb, Mike: on Arnold, 202; on Atkins, C., 186; on Bartholomew, 200; on Brooks, 201–2; on Burns, 201–2; on Cash, 201; on Clement, 201; on Cobb, 190–91, 204; on Curb Records, 193–98; on five year plan, 194; on Flamingos, 199, 203–4; on Goldner, 199; historical preservation of, 189–90, 206–7; on homeless, 206–7; on James, S., 202; on McGraw, 201; on Mike Curb Foundation, 206–7; on Nashville, 195–97; on normal distribution, 205; on Ram, 200; on RCA Studio A, 190–92; on streaming, 205–6; on teaching, 187–88; university involvement of, 188–89; on *Wild* Angels, 193; on writing, 203–4
Curb Records, 185, 190; Curb on, 193–98
The Cycle of Self-Empowerment (Famularo), 159, 165, 167–68

dancing, 170
Davis, Sammy, Jr., 195
Daytona State, 188
demo work: Mason, B., on, 277–78; Tate, J., on, 300; technology and, 277
Derrick, Butler, 219
Desert Rose Band, 195
destructive lifestyles, 100–101
determination, 275
Devil's Angels, 195
DeVitto, Liberty, 174
Digital Harmonic, 111–12
digital technology: Fisher on, 103; Purdie on, 354. *See also Specific digital technologies*
dignity, giving away, 77–78
"Dinner & Diatribes," 334–35, 337
disagreements, 59–60
discipline: creativity and, 244–45; success and, 113
distractions, 70–71, 184; defining, 181; ego and, 182; fear and, 183; relationships and, 181–82; substance abuse and, 182–83. *See also* destructive lifestyles

DIVA Jazz Orchestra, 30
Dixie Cups, 199
DIY business model, 212; creativity and, 210–11; mindset and, 211; motivation and, 209; problems with, 210; success and, 209–10; technology and, 208
Dolly (Parton), 271
Domino, Fats, 200
doo-wop, 56
Dorn, Joel, 59
"Do Wah Diddy Diddy," 105
"Drink You Away," 20–21
Drumgenius, 291
drum groove, best, 239
Drumm, Rick, 174
drum machines, 291; Harden on, 234–35
drummers: on *Aja*, 62; Famularo on, 170–72, 175–76; Rainey on, 56–58, 63–66. *See also Specific drummers*
drum tone, 302
Dupree, Cornell, 358
Dyer, Wayne, 164
dynamics, 363

Eagles, 11
Edmondson, Jeff, 203
education: alternatives, 91; Barker on, 91–92; costs of, 91; Famularo on, 175; specializations, 91–92. *See also* learning; skill sets; teaching; *Specific education institutions*

Edwards, Gordon, 65
ego, 358; distractions and, 182; Rainey on, 51, 54–55
Eilish, Billie, 199
Elliott, James, 108
Emerick, Geoff: Cobb on, 9; Gonzalez on, 31
empathy, 214
empowerment, 165
emulation, 40–41
"The End," 8
engagement, 321
engineers: Cobb on, 8–9. *See also* producers; *Specific engineers*
entertainment attorney, 86
enthusiasm, 170
entrepreneurship, 113, 115; creativity and, 111–12; responsibility and, 114; success and, 110
Everett, Shawn, 136
"Everyday," 11
"Everyday People," 241
"Everything Must Change," 75
Exile, 196, 197
expectations, 3–4; Barker on, 80–81; success and, 85
experience, 55
Extreme Three, 301
"Eye to Eye," 59

Fagan, Donald, 361; Rainey on, 54
failure: studying, 100–101. *See also* rejection
"Falling Slowly," 243

fame: Hull on, 271; Kohavi, D., on, 329; success and, 350
FAME, 150–51
family, 166–68
Famularo, Dom, 73; on accountability, 169; background of, 159–61; on big band, 178–79; book recommendations from, 177–78; books by, 159, 164–68; on bop jazz, 179; on communication, 160; on dancing, 170; on drummers, 170–72, 175–76; on education, 175; on empowerment, 165; on enthusiasm, 170; on family, 166–68; on Firth, 168; on Follet, 173; on Gadd, 172; on Gladstone, 177; on human mind, 160; on influences, 178–79; on jazz fusion, 179; lessons from, 161–62, 170; on Moeller technique, 177; on motivation, 160; on negativity, 164; on networking, 176–77; on opportunity, 165; on passion, 168; on perseverance, 169; on piano, 170–71; on Purdie, 172; on responsibility, 169; on skill sets, 160, 166; on Stone, 177; on teaching, 161–62; travels of, 175–76; on visualization, 164; on world rhythms, 176; on Zildjian, 168
fan base, 163–64, 328; Barker on, 84–85, 87–88, 96; of Hozier, 333; Hull on, 255; identifying, 96; Mason, B., on, 277; of Swift, 92
fear: distraction and, 183; of rejection, 245; Tate, J., on, 300
Fender: Mason, B., on, 287. *See also* guitars
festivals: Kohavi, E., on, 343–44. *See also Specific festivals*
finger taps, 360
Finneas, 199
"Fire and Rain," 137
Firefly Festival, 318
Firth, Vic, 168
Fisher, Robert, 189; on Belmont University, 104–9; on branding, 104; on digital technology, 103; on internships, 107; on power transfer, 103; on responsibility, 105; on skill sets, 103; on social change, 104
Fisk Jubilee Singers program, 188
Fitchuk, Ian, 132–33
five year plan, 194
Flack, Roberta, 68–69
Flamingos, 199, 203–4
Fleck, Béla, 248–55
Florida Georgia Line, 234, 235
Follet, Jules, 173
For King and Country, 197
"Fortress around Your Heart," 296
Four Seasons, 195, 197
Fourteen Modern Contest Solos (Pratt), 178
Frames, 243

Franklin, Aretha, 353; Purdie on, 357, 363–64; Rainey on, 66–67
Friedman, Alan, 212

Gadd, Steve, 351; Famularo on, 172; Harden on, 235–36; Rainey on, 57–58, 65–66
Gadson, James, 57
Gallimore, Byron, 201
gatekeeping, 329
Gatlin, Larry, 122
Gatlin, Steve, 230
Gatton, Danny, 281
genres: Campbell on, 117–18. *See also Specific genres*
Ghenea, Serban, 136
Ginsberg, Ruth, 218
Girard, Chuck, 187
Gladstone, Billy, 177
Glaser, Joe, 286
Golden Hour, 132–33; Alvin on, 134–45
Goldner, George, 199
"Gone Away," 69
Gonzalez, Scheila: on auditions, 34–35; on Emerick, 31; on emulation, 40–41; on practicing, 40–41; on Santiago, 41–42; on streaming, 39; on teaching, 38; on vinyl, 38; on women, 43; on Zappa, D., 31–33; on Zappa Plays Zappa, 42–43
Gordon, Jon, 219–20
Gordy, Berry, 70
gospel, 197

Grammys: Alvin on, 145; Campbell on, 120–21; Carlile and, 22; categories, 50; Stapleton and, 22; Zappa Plays Zappa, 42–43
Grant, Natalie, 197
"The Great Pretender," 200
"Green Power," 10
Griffin, Paul, 358
Grisman, David, 261
"Guess Things Happen That Way," 201
guilt, 346
guitars: Cobb on, 17–18; Led Zeppelin sound, 17; Lynyrd Skynyrd sound, 17; Mason, B., on, 286–87; tone, 17–18; Zappa, D., and, 32

Haggard, Merle, 202; Tate, J., on, 305
Hall, Rick, 151–52
Hall and Oates, 364
Hansard, Glen, 243
"Happiness Is a Warm Gun," 8
Harden, Tommy: background of, 225; on best drum groove, 239; on click tracks, 235–36; on competition, 239–40; on drum machines, 234–35; on Gadd, 235–36; on home recording, 234; on honesty, 242; on indie music, 242; on loops, 235; on Nashville, 232–34, 239–40, 242; on networking, 239–40; on

original content, 240; on perseverance, 229–31; on Pro Tools, 240–41; on Reba, 227–29; on room mics, 237–38; on Sloas, 236–37; on streaming, 232; on studio levels, 238; on success, 229–30; Tate, J., on, 301–2; on technology, 227, 229, 233–35, 240–41; on touring, 228–29
harmonies, 311–12
Harrison, George, 8
Hatcher, Harley, 195
Hathaway, Donny: perfect pitch of, 61; Rainey on, 60–61, 68–69
Hay, Colin, 30
Hayes, Rick, 288
health consciousness, 296
Healy, Matty, 130; rejection of, 222
Heartache and a Song, 133
Hebb, Bobby, 199
Helm, Levon, 260
"Helter Skelter," 8
Hendrix, Jimi, 281
Here, There, and Everywhere (Emerick), 31
"Highwayman," 121–22
Hill, Napoleon, 113
Hinduism, 53
hip-hop community, 6
historical preservation, 189–90
history: Mason, B., on, 280; studying, 100–101; success and, 280; Tate, J., on, 305–6

Hoffman, Max, 316; on longevity, 328
Holly, Buddy, 11
"Home at Last," 353, 358–59
homeless, 206–7
home recording, 234
honesty: Campbell on, 118; Cobb on, 16; Harden on, 242; Riley on, 214; self-mastery and, 295
Honolulu Community College, 189
Howard, Ron, 112–13
Hozier, 331–32; crew, 334; fan base of, 333; Kohavi, E., on, 337–43, 346–47; staging and, 333; on voice, 337
Hull, Sierra: on accolades, 261; on accompaniment, 259–60; on bluegrass, 262–63; on branding, 270; on budgeting, 268–69; Cooper, P., on, 260–61; on fame, 271; on fan base, 255; on Grisman, 261; on influences, 261–64; on mandolin, 261–62; on McCoury, 267; on metronome, 260; on networking, 258; on Parton, 263, 270–71; on Powell, 249; on practicing, 259–60; on preparation, 271–72; on Punch Brothers, 266–67; on pushback, 251; on reinvention, 250–52; on responsibility, 268–69; on technology, 264–66; on Thile, 261; on touring, 254; on traveling, 268; on Vincent,

263–64, 267, 269; on *Weighted Mind*, 248–55
Hungate, Dave, 233

"I Ain't Never Loved a Man the Way I Loved You," 66
IBMA. *See* International Bluegrass Music Association
"I Can't Stand the Rain," 199
ideas, 366
"I Don't Know What You've Got, But It's Got Me," 10–11
"I Drive Your Truck," 237
Ienner, Jimmy, 222
Ighner, Bernard, 75
"I'm Afraid of Americans," 282
imagination, 131; examples of pushing, 130; expanding, 129
income, 44–45; basic principles of, 89; Tate, J., on, 312–13; traps, 326. *See also* money; side hustle
influence, 155, 157; of Antonoff, 351; of Atkins, C., 158; on Cobb, 9–11; defining, 156; Famularo on, 178–79; Hull on, 261–64; Mason, B., on, 281–82; of Purdie, 353, 359; Tate, J., and, 301, 305–6
Ingram, Jack, 83
inner voice: clues, 28–29; finding, 27–29
innovation, 278. *See also* creativity
inspiration, 293
intention, 159

International Bluegrass Music Association (IBMA), 248
internet radio, 86
internships, 92; Belmont University, 107; Fisher on, 107
"I Only Have Eyes for You," 199
Isbell, Jason, 23; Cobb on, 17; voice of, 17
Isley Brothers, 68
isolation, 58
"I Walk the Line," 201

Jackson, Carl, 122; Campbell on, 124–25
Jackson, Mahalia, 67
Jackson, Michael, 264
Jackson, Stonewall, 269
Jamerson, James, 69–71
James, Sonny, 200, 202
Japan, 71–72
jazz fusion, 179
Jellyfish, 301
Jennings, Waylon, 18–19; Cobb on, 16–17; voice of, 16–17
Jobs, Steve, 76
Jodziewicz, Ethan, 250, 256; voice of, 257
Joel, Billy, 301
Joe Porcaro's Drum Set Method (Porcaro), 63
Johns, Glyn, 18–19; Cobb on, 9
Jones, Quincy, 58, 60
Jones, Rickie Lee, 59, 64–65; Rainey on, 63
Judds, 195, 197

Katz, Gary, 58–59, 61–62
Kawasaki, Guy, 113
"Keep on Knocking," 10
Kelly's Heroes, 195
Kennerley, Paul, 18–19
Kilgore, Merle, 201
King, Carole, 241
King Curtis, 66–68
Kirby, Wade, 237
KISS FM, 81
"Kiss You All Over," 196
Knightly, Keira, 28
Kohavi, Daniel, 316; on Allen, B., 324; on authenticity, 318–19; on engagement, 321; on fame, 329; on gatekeeping, 329; on Powell, C., 324; on Spear, 323; on Stapleton, 318
Kohavi, Emily, 316; on *Amazing Slow Downer*, 335–36; on auditioning, 335–39; on branding, 345; on engagement, 321; on festivals, 343, 344; on Hozier, 337–43, 346–47; on learning, 335–36; on Mayer, 345–46; on McBride, 327; on practicing, 334–41, 344; on Spear, 322–23; on success, 345–46; on touring, 327, 331–32; on work ethic, 338; on writing, 319
Kramer, Eddie, 9
Krauss, Alison, 249
Kunkel, Russ, 137
Kurland, Amy, 321

Lady Gaga, 23
Lamond, Joe, 189
Lawson, Doyle, 262
"The Leader of the Pack," 199
leadership, ix; Purdie on, 362–63; Riley on, 214–16
learning: Famularo on, 161–62, 170; Kohavi, E., on, 335–36; Mason, B., on, 291; Purdie on, 353–54; skill sets at Belmont University, 103, 105–6
Led Zeppelin, 359; guitar sound of, 17
Lee, Will, 10
Lennon, John, 8
Les Paul, 355
Let the Drums Speak! (Purdie), 172, 353–54
"Let Your Love Flow," 196
Lewis, Jerry Lee, 201
listening: Rainey on, 52, 54; Riley on, 214; to yourself, 260
Little Anthony and the Imperials, 199
"Little Honda," 186–87
Little Richard, 10–11
Live at the Apollo, 114
live tracking, 15
LLC, setting up, 86
Lombardo, Tom, 132–33
The Lonely One, 116–17
longevity: Hoffman on, 328; Mason, B., on, 276–77; of Sting, 296; success and, 350
loops, 235

Lord-Alge, Chris, 305
Lost Hollow, 241
Love, Mike, 187
"Love Me Tender," 11
Lovett, Lyle, 195
Low Country Sound, 19–20
Lynne, Jeff, 305
Lynyrd Skynyrd, 17

MacLarty, Mack, 218
Madonna, 222
mailings lists, 312
Malloy, Dave, 232
mandolin, 261–62
Mandrell, Barbara, 230
Mann, Manfred, 105
Manring, Michael, 50
Martin, Dean, 12
Martin, George, 8
Martin, Reeve, 364
Martinez, John Anthony, 48–49, 73–74
Mason, Brent: on acrylic nails, 290; on amplifiers, 282–83, 287–88; on amp rack, 287; background of, 276; on Beatles, 292; on competition, 280; on creativity, 285; on demo work, 277–78; on Drumgenius, 291; on fan base, 277; on Fender, 287; on guitars, 286–87; on Hendrix, 281; on history, 280; influences on, 281–82; on inspiration, 293; on learning, 291; on longevity, 276–77; on Montgomery, 289–90; on Muscle Shoals, 285–86; on Nashville, 278–80, 284–86; on original content, 292–93; on practicing, 291; on preparation, 283–84; on regional styles, 285–86; on reinvention, 276–77, 293; on remote recording, 283–84; on Sheeran, 293; on Smith, P. R., 286; on Taylor, 293; on thumb picks, 290; on Travis, 290; on voice, 282; on Wampler Pedals, 289; on YouTube, 289
Mason, Harvey, 57
Master Studies (Morello), 178
Matthews, Jason, 243
"Maybe, It's Time," 23
Mayer, John, 115; Kohavi, E., on, 345–46
McBride, Martina, 327
McCartney, Paul, 8; Campbell on, 121
McCoury, Del, 265; Hull on, 267
McGraw, Tim, 196; Curb on, 201
meditation, 52–53
Men at Work, 30
Messina, Jo Dee, 197
metronome, 260
Meyer, Edgar, 258
Mike Curb College of Entertainment and Music Business, 105, 188
Mike Curb Congregation, 195, 197

Mike Curb Foundation, 185; Curb on, 206–7
Miller, Roger, 123
mindset, 46–47; DIY business model and, 211
mixing: Alvin on, 148–49; Claremont and, 306; with eyes, 75; Tate, J., on, 303, 306–12
Moeller technique, 177
money: Rainey on, 51; success and, 350
Montgomery, Wes, 289–90
Morello, Joe, 178
Morgan, Kurt, 33
motivation: DIY business model and, 209; Famularo on, 160
Motown, 69–71
multitracking, 354–55
Muscle Shoals, 14; Alvin on, 150–52; Mason, B., on, 285–86
Musgraves, Kacey, Alvin on, 132–45
Music Industry Blueprint Podcast, 80, 87; Castro on, 95
music therapy, 107–8
"My Sharona," 122

Nailine, 290
Nashville: Campbell on, 127–28; cliques, 279; Cobb on, 24; Curb on, 195–97; Harden on, 232–34, 239–40, 242; isolation from, 280; Mason, B., on, 278–80, 284–86; networking in, 239–40; sound, 12

Nashville Rescue Mission and Safe Haven, 206
National View Radio Tour, 92–93
"The Natural Man," 195
negativity, 164
Nelson, Willie, 305
networking: Campbell on, 126–27; Famularo on, 176–77; Harden on, 239–40; Hull on, 258; in Nashville, 239–40
The New Breed (Chester), 178
"New Kid in Town," 11
"No Plan," 335
normal distribution, 205
Norvell, Anthony, 348
Nussbaum, Bernard W., 217
Nyro, Laura, 65

O'Brien, Brendan, 9
"Oh, What a Night," 195
Once, 243
opportunity, 165
optimism, 6; Cobb on, 7
Orbison, Roy, 200
organization: creativity compared with, 46; procrastination and, 246; tools, 210
original content, 47; Harden on, 240; Mason, B., on, 292–93
overdubbing, 355
Owens, Buck, 195
Owning Now (Famularo), 168
Ozark, Steve, 128

Parton, Dolly, 123, 262; branding and, 269–71; Hull on, 263, 270–71
passion: Famularo on, 168; Riley on, 220–21
patience, 169
"Peaches en Regalia," 42–43
Peebles, Ann, 199
"Peg," 64
perfect pitch, 61
performance rights organizations (PROs), 86, 96
Perkins, Carl, 201
perseverance: Famularo on, 169; Harden on, 229–31; tenacity differentiated from, 273
Phillips, Sam: Alvin on, 152; Cobb on, 15; no plan approach of, 14
piano, 170–71
Pilgrimage Music Festival, 75
Pink Floyd, 194
Pirates, 64–65
platinum records, 314
Platters, 200
Pomplamoose, 298
pop music, 200
Porcaro, Jeff, 239, 359; Rainey on, 63–65
The Positive Dog (Gordon), 219–20
Powell, Chris, 324
Powell, Vance, 253; Hull on, 249
The Power of Intention (Dyer), 164

power transfer: Barker on, 94; Fisher on, 103
practicing: Alvin on, 147–48; Gonzalez on, 40–41; Hull on, 259–60; Kohavi, E., on, 334–41, 344; Mason, B., on, 291; Purdie on, 361; visualization, 78
Pratt, John, 178
preparation, 74; Hull on, 271–72; Mason, B., on, 283–84; Rainey on, 54–55
Presley, Elvis, 200; Cobb on, 11; rejection of, 223; vision and, 77
pressure, 183
Preston, Aubrey, 190–91
procrastination, 244; causes of, 245–46; creativity and, 245; organization and, 246; visualization and, 246–47
producers: Cobb on, 8–9; Rainey on, 58–61. *See also Specific producers*
promotion tools, 210
PROs. *See* performance rights organizations
Pro Tools, 307; Harden on, 240–41
publishing rights: Barker on, 95–96. *See also* registration
Punch Brothers, 266–67
Purdie, Bernard: on analog technology, 354; on click tracks, 355–56; on compromising, 357–58; on digital technology, 354; on Dupree, 358; on

dynamics, 363; Famularo on, 172; on finger taps, 360; on Franklin, 357, 363–64; on gifts, 355; on Griffin, 358; influence of, 353, 359; on leadership, 362–63; on learning, 353–54; on Les Paul, 355; on multi-tracking, 354–55; on practicing, 361; on Purdie shuffle, 360–61; on Rainey, 358; Rainey on, 57, 65–66; on self-containment, 356; on Steely Dan, 358–59; on Tee, 358; on timing, 355–56; on voice, 361; on volume, 363
Purdie shuffle, 353, 359; Purdie on, 360–61
purpose, 220–21
pushback, 251

Quicksilver, 262
Quin, Paul, 174
Quonset Hut, 190, 202

Rainey, Chuck: on *Aja*, 62–63; on Beatles 1965 tour, 67–68; on Becker, 54; on bridges, 55–56; on Brown, R., 57; on Caesar, 66; on chorus, 55–56; on click tracks, 57; on disagreements, 59–60; on doo-wop, 56; on Dorn, 59; on drummers, 56–58, 63–66; on ego, 51, 54–55; on experience, 55; on Fagan, 54; on Flack, 68–69; on Franklin, 66–67; on Gadd, 57–58, 65–66; on Hathaway, 60–61, 68–69; on isolation, 58; on Jamerson, 69–71; on Japan, 71–72; on Jones, Q., 58, 60; on Jones, R. L., 63–65; on Katz, 58–59, 61–62; on King Curtis, 66–68; on listening, 52, 54; on Manring, 50; on meditation, 52–53; on money, 51; on Motown, 69–71; on perfect pitch, 61; on Porcaro, 63–65; on preparation, 54–55; on producers, 58–61; on Purdie, 57, 65–66; Purdie on, 358; on *The Sessions* panels, 73–74; on skill sets, 54–55; on Steely Dan, 62–64; on success, 51–52; on Tate, 57; on Taylor, 61; on technology, 49–50; on timekeeping, 57–58; on Toto, 64; on tuning, 61; work of, 48; on yoga, 52–53
"Rainy Night in Georgia," 199
Ram, Buck, 200
Ramone, Phil, 308–9
Rawls, Lou, 195
Ray, Eddie, 194
RCA Studio A, 6, 11, 13; Alvin on, 153; Cobb on, 12; Curb on, 190–92; original layout of, 191
RCA Studio B, 189–90
Reba, 226, 239, 241; Harden on, 227–29
record deal, how to get, 89–90
Record Label Ready, 86

Redding, Otis: Cobb on, 10, 16; Rock and Roll Hall of Fame induction of, 10
references, 1
registration, 95–96
reinvention: Hull on, 250–52; Mason, B., on, 276–77, 293; success and, 349; of WILDEYES, 332
rejection: of Beatles, 222; dealing with, 223; famous, 222–23; fear of, 245; of Healy, 222; of Madonna, 222; Mason, B., on, 279; perspective and, 223; of Presley, 223; responding to, 223–24; of Rowling, 223; of Sheeran, 222; success and, 223; of U2, 222
relationships, distractions and, 181–82
relative pitch, 61
remote recording, 283–84
Renn, 133
reputation, 349
resource models, 95
respect, 350
responsibility: Belmont University and, 105; entrepreneurship and, 114; Famularo on, 169; for feeling, 348; Fisher on, 105; Hull on, 268–69; success and, 86, 95
retro products, 209
"Revolution," 8
Revolver, 301; Tate, J., on, 309
"Rhinestone Cowboy," 121

Rhodes, Michael, 285
Rice, Tony, 262
Richard Tee Committee and the Gadd Gang, 61
Righteous Brothers, 197
Riley, Richard: on compassion, 214; on Derrick, 219; on empathy, 214; on honesty, 214; on leadership, 214–16; on listening, 214; on passion, 220–21; on *Positive Dog*, 219–20; on purpose, 220–21; on style, 215; on success, 219, 220–21; on Supreme Court, 217–18; on technology, 216; on values, 217
Rimes, LeAnn, 196, 197
"Ring of Fire," 201
Ritter, Tex, 200
Robbins, Marty, 200
Rock and Roll Hall of Fame, 10
"Rock Steady," 353, 363–64
Rogers, Paul, 16
Ronstadt, Linda, 193
Room at the Inn, 206
room mics, 237–38
"Rosanna," 359
Roulette Records, 199
Rowling, J. K., 223
royalties, 312
Ruffalo, Mark, 28
Ruggles, Brian, 301
Rukkus Room, 297, 300; design of, 302–3; Tate, J., on, 302–3
"Rumor," 203
Russell, Leon, 151

Index

Ryan, Alex, 331–32, 337

salary structure, 93–94
Santa Barbara Unsigned Heroes, 81
Santiago, James, 30; Gonzalez on, 41–42
Scarborough, Claude, 218
Second Harvest, 207
self-containment, 356
self-mastery: defining, 295; honesty and, 295; of Sting, 296; success differentiated from, 294
The Sessions panels, 173–74; Rainey on, 73–74
Sheeran, Ed: Mason, B., on, 293; rejection of, 222
"She's Gone," 364
side hustle, 45
Sidewalk Records, 194
Sinatra, Frank, 12
Sinclair, Alexander, 222
single-mindedness, 274
singles, 298–99
Singleton, Shelby, 201
Skaggs, Ricky, 231
skill sets: Belmont University, 103, 105–6; Famularo on, 160, 166; Fisher on, 103; Rainey on, 54–55. *See also Specific skill sets*
Sloas, Jimmy Lee, 236–37
Smith, Joe, 196
Smith, Paul Reed, 111–12; Mason, B., on, 286
"Smoke Gets in Your Eyes," 200
social change, 104

Social Media for Music, 89
Songtrust.com, 95–96
songwriting: at Belmont University, 108; Campbell on, 123–24; Curb on, 203–4; Kohavi, E., on, 319; Sting on, 296; Taylor and, 254
Sound Check, 288
Sound Emporium, 323
Southern Family, 18–19
Spear, Eddie: Kohavi, D., on, 323; Kohavi, E., on, 322–23
Spilt Milk, 301
spontaneity, 364; creativity and, 46
staging, 333
standards, 46
Stapleton, Chris, 7, 12, 18, 20–21; Cobb on, 16; Grammys and, 22; Kohavi, D., on, 318
A Star Is Born, 22–24
Starr, Ringo, 7–8
Stax, 19
Steely Dan, 54, 59, 353, 364; Purdie on, 358–59; Rainey on, 62–64
Stewart, Brian, 203
Stewart, Marty, 298–99
Stewart, Rod, 16
Stick Control (Stone), 177
Sticks 'n' Skins (Follet), 173
Sting, 296
Stone, George Lawrence, 178; Famularo on, 177
Stone Poneys, 193

streaming: Barker on, 85; Curb on, 205–6; Gonzalez on, 39; Harden on, 232; Tate, J., on, 312. *See also* internet radio; YouTube

style: Alvin on, 133; Mason, B., on regional, 285–86; Riley on, 215; Tate, J., on, 308–9

substance abuse: distractions and, 182–83; pressure and, 183. *See also* destructive lifestyles

success: Antonoff and, 350–51; Barker on, 85, 89–90, 95–96; basis for, 349; Belmont University and, 105–6; Campbell on, 126; Cobb on, 22; defining, ix, 4, 350; describing, 294–95; discipline and, 113; DIY business model and, 209–10; entrepreneurship and, 110; expectations and, 85; fame and, 350; guilt and, 346; Harden on, 229–30; history and, 280; longevity and, 350; managing, 3; money and, 350; Rainey on, 51–52; reinvention and, 349; rejection and, 223; respect and, 350; responsibilities with, 86, 95; Riley on, 219–21; self-mastery differentiated from, 294; tenacity and, 275; understanding, ix–x

"Sunny," 199

Sun Records, 14; culture around, 19

Supreme Court, 217–18

"Sweet Music," 340–41

Swift, Taylor, 80, 83, 88; Barker on, 91–94; branding and, 270; development of, 92–93; fan base of, 92

"Take Me to Church," 333

targeted advertisements, 94

Tashian, Daniel, 132–33

Tate, Grady, 57

Tate, Jamie: on access, 297–98; background of, 297; on Beatles, 300; on branding, 300; on bro-country, 299; on Claremont, 306; on demo work, 300; on drum tone, 302; on fear, 300; on Haggard, 305; on Harden, 301–2; on harmonies, 311–12; on history, 305–6; on income, 312–13; influences on, 301, 305–6; on Lord-Alge, 305; on Lynne, 305; on mailing lists, 312; on mixing, 303, 306–12; "Modern Recording" flowchart by, 309; on platinum records, 314; on Ramone, 308–9; on *Revolver*, 309; on royalties, 312; on Rukkus Room, 302–3; on singles, 298–99; on streaming, 312; on style, 308–9; on technology, 307

Taylor, James, 263–64; Mason, B., on, 293; Rainey on, 61; tuning and, 61; writing and, 254

teaching: Curb on, 187–88; Famularo on, 161–62; Gonzalez on, 38. *See also* learning
technology: analog, 354; Cobb on, 13; demo work and, 277; digital, 103, 354; DIY business model and, 208; Fisher on, 103; Harden on, 227, 229, 233–35, 240–41; Hull on, 264–66; overuse of, 209; Purdie on, 354; Rainey on, 49–50; Riley on, 216; Tate, J., on, 307. *See also Specific technologies*
Tee, Richard: perfect pitch of, 61; Purdie on, 358
Temptations, 265
tenacity: creativity and, 273–75; perseverance differentiated from, 273; success and, 275; vision and, 274
"Tennessee Whiskey," 20–21
terminology, 98
Thile, Chris, 262; Hull on, 261
Think and Grow Rich (Hill), 113
thumb picks, 290
Timberlake, Justin, 20–21
timekeeping: Purdie on, 355–56; Rainey on, 57–58. *See also* click tracks; metronome
Titelman, Russ, 59
"Tomorrow Never Knows," 130
tone: drum, 302; guitar, 17–18
Toto, 64
touring: Beatles, 67–68; Campbell on, 119–20; Harden on, 228–29; Hull on, 254; Kohavi, E., on, 327, 331–32
traveling: Famularo of, 175–76; Hull on, 268. *See also* touring
Traveller, 12
Travers, Joe, 33
Travis, Merle, 290
Troutt, Bill, 189
Tubb, Ernest, 200
The Tune of Success (Rainey & Martinez), 48–49, 73
tuning, 61
"Turn on the Radio," 239
"Twilight Time," 200
Twitty, Conway, 200

U2, 222
University of Hawaii, 189
Urban, Keith, 242

Vai, Steve, 33, 42–43
values, 217
Vanderbilt, 188
Veasley, Gerald, 75
Venet, Nick, 187
Victory Hall, 206
Vincent, Rhonda, 265; Hull on, 263–64, 267, 269
vinyl: Cobb on, 14; Gonzalez on, 38
vision, 79; Presley and, 77; setting, 78; tenacity and, 274; visualization differentiated from, 77
visualization: Famularo on, 164; as practice, 78; procrastination

and, 246–47; vision differentiated from, 77
voice: Alvin on, 134; Cobb on, 16–17; doo-wop era and, 56; Hozier on, 337; of Isbell, 17; of Jennings, 16–17; of Jodziewicz, 257; Mason, B., on, 282; Purdie on, 361. *See also* inner voice
Volkman, John, 12
volume, 363
Voodoo Labs, 30, 41

Walk off the Earth, 298
Walsh, Joe, 7–8
Wampler Pedals, 289
War, 195
Warhol, Andy, 350
"The Ways of a Woman in Love," 201
Webb, Jimmy, 122
Weighted Mind, Hull on, 248–55
Wexler, Jerry, 67
what factor, 155, 156; quality of, 158
Whitehouse, Dick, 195
White Mansions, 18–19
who factor, 155, 157
why factor, 155–57
Wild Angels, 193
WILDEYES, 316–47; reinvention, 332
Williams, Don, 305
Williams, Hank, Jr., 195, 197

Wilson, Brian, 187
Wilson, Jackie, 67
women, 43
"Won't Be Long," 66
Word Records, 190
work ethic, 46; Barker on, 84; Kohavi, E., on, 338. *See also* determination; discipline
world rhythms, 176
Wrecking Crew, 14
Wright, Randy, 230
Wynonna, 197

yoga, 52–53
Yogananda, Paramahansa, 53, 76
"You Are My Sunshine," 18
"You Light Up My Life," 196–97
"Young Love," 202
YouTube, 289

Zappa, Dweezil, 30; on Bowie, 282; Gonzalez on, 31–33; guitar of, 32
Zappa, Frank, 32; commitment to, 33
Zappa, Gail, 33
Zappa Plays Zappa (ZPZ), 30; Gonzalez on, 42–43; Grammy award for, 42–43; initial incarnation of, 35–36
Zeppelin 1, 17
Zildjian, Bob, 168
ZPZ. *See* Zappa Plays Zappa

About the Author

Menzie Pittman. Source: Craig Hunter Ross

Menzie Pittman has worked in the music industry as a drummer, music educator, clinician, music business owner, entrepreneur, writer, speaker, board member, and music advocate for more than thirty-five years.

He hails from a small hamlet west of Washington DC, and his passions are his daughter, music and the performing arts, writing, and golden retrievers.

About the Author

The founder of the Contemporary Music Center in Haymarket Virginia, Menzie won the National Association of Music Merchants (NAMM) Dealer of the Year award in 2016. He also served on the NAMM board of directors from 2012 to 2015.

Menzie writes the Small Business Matters column for *MMR Magazine* and has been a frequent speaker at NAMM's Idea Center and the College Music Society. He has also spoken at multiple universities, inspiring, educating, and listening to the young musicians who are the primary audience for this book.

Menzie has been featured on the covers of *Music Inc. Magazine*, *MMR Magazine*, *Music Educators Journal*, and *Playback Magazine*. He has also been featured in *Washingtonian Magazine* and *Canadian Music Trades Magazine*.

www.ingramcontent.com/pod-product-compliance
Lightning Source LLC
Chambersburg PA
CBHW022007300426
44117CB00005B/72